THE
SOLAR DECISION BOOK
OF HOMES

A Guide to
Designing and Remodeling
for Solar Heating

THE SOLAR DECISION BOOK OF HOMES

A Guide to Designing and Remodeling for Solar Heating

Richard H. Montgomery
with
Walter F. Miles

175 YEARS OF PUBLISHING

1807 1982

JOHN WILEY & SONS

New York   Chichester   Brisbane   Toronto   Singapore

Copyright © 1982, by John Wiley & Sons, Inc.

All rights reserved. Published simultaneously in Canada.

Reproduction or translation of any part of
this work beyond that permitted by Sections
107 and 108 of the 1976 United States Copyright
Act without the permission of the copyright
owner is unlawful. Requests for permission
or further information should be addressed to
the Permissions Department, John Wiley & Sons.

Library of Congress Cataloging in Publication Data:

Montgomery, Richard H.
The solar decision book of homes.

  Includes indexes.
  1. Solar heating.   I. Miles, Walter F.
II. Title.
TH7413.M66   697'.78   81-16397
ISBN 0-471-08280-5 (cloth)   AACR2
ISBN 0-471-87523-6 (paper)

Printed in the United States of America

10 9 8 7 6 5 4 3 2 1

To Donna with love

PREFACE

In 1977, when Jim Budnick and I collaborated on *The Solar Decision Book*, (Wiley, 1978) which taught the design and utilization of active solar systems, I said: "This book is opinionated. The opinions are mine. Some may not agree with them, while others will recognize a restatement of their own work."

I would like to repeat those words here because a controversy is raging in the solar industry relating to passive solar design versus active solar heating systems.

The active solar system advocates see little value in passive solar design. The passive solar designers see little value in active solar systems.

However, I believe that active and passive solar techniques should be blended together to produce the most practical and economical results. An existing home in an established neighborhood usually has limited potential for passive remodeling. Here, active heating designs will most likely yield the best results.

On the other hand, a new home that is properly sited and oriented has excellent potential for passive solar construction. Passive solar design will generally yield high value in this situation.

Some will disagree with this hybrid solar approach. Others will embrace it. Few will ignore it. I recommend it.

This book has been written to aid American home owners in modifying their present homes to make better use of solar energy, put good conservation into practice, and design and build new, energy-efficient, solar-utilizing residences.

As you plan for the use of solar energy in your home, take the principles outlined in this book and the advice and counsel of others with opposing opinions. None of us has all the answers yet. Invest with care. Be certain that the advice you are getting comes from a knowledgeable source. Do not rush into a major investment until you have all the facts that you can gather.

Most solar is common sense. If you do not understand what is being suggested, restudy your plans before you move ahead.

It has been six years since I started learning about and working with solar energy. In these six years the solar industry has come of age. Its equipment is reliable and performs well. Performance standards have been set. And the market has grown from nothing to about $500 million annually. But the use of solar energy has spread slowly. Only slight market penetration has been accomplished. Much remains to be done to complete the "solarization" of America. I hope that *The Solar Decision Book of Homes* will help.

Richard H. Montgomery

ACKNOWLEDGMENTS

I would like to acknowledge the contributions of Robert Pirtle, acquiring editor at Wiley, who urged me to write this book and who provided strong support and encouragement throughout the preparation of the final manuscript.

I found myself reaching back to the late 1950s for experience when I undertook this writing. At that time, I was engaged in building large, custom residences in partnership with my father. A number of fine craftsmen in home building helped teach me much of what I have passed on in this book. Special mention should go to Joe Gaudette, Stanley Jezak, Harry Johnson, Eddie Gaudette, and Bernard Wilder, whom I have not seen for more than 20 years. The houses that they helped build will outlast both them and myself.

The American Society of Heating, Cooling and Refrigeration Engineers (ASHRAE) is a tower of strength to any author writing in this field. I have drawn extensively on this association's publications. I highly recommend them to anyone working in the solar field. *Architectural Graphic Standards* (Wiley, 1980), the standard reference text of most builders and architects, was also used constantly during the writing of this work.

The work in solar heat transfer of John Duffie, William Beckman, and Sanford Klien at the University of Wisconsin led to the publication of F-Chart, a computerized solar design tool that is universally used throughout the solar industry. F-Chart was used to plot the solar information in this book. Not only I, but an entire industry owe thanks to this group for their work, which may be found in two other Wiley publications: *Solar Thermal Processes* (1974) and *Solar Heating Design, by the F-Chart Method* (1977).

I also thank the following reviewers for their useful critiques and suggestions: Edward Kelley, A.I.A., Sun Structures, Inc.; Anna Fay Friedlander, Friedlander Associates; Robert Stewart, P.E., Vermont Technical College; Warren Hedstrom, University of Maine; Robert Werner, Jr., P.E., A.T.A. Corporation; Jim Van Valkenburg, Merrimack Valley College; and Douglas Taff, PARALLAX.

R.H.M.

CONTENTS

DECISION 1   Achieve Energy Independence with Solar Heating

We have lost our energy independence and must gain it back. Solar-heated homes can help us do that. Although solar technology is uncomplicated, we do need to understand the principles involved in order to use the sun's energy economically.

DECISION 2   Understand Solar Radiation

The sun's energy strikes the earth at different angles depending on the season, the hour, and the geographic area. The amount of radiation available is a function of a number of different factors. Once you understand these factors, you will be able to use solar energy effectively.

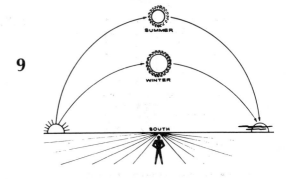

DECISION 3   Calculate Your Available Solar Energy

The United States has been split into 24 solar zones. The solar data have been tabulated for each of these 24 zones. Once you have determined your zone, you can then calculate your available solar energy with simple mathematics.

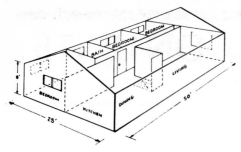

You must study heat losses in order to determine your building's energy needs. The materials of construction, the layout of the rooms, and the tightness of the doors and windows determine what your heat losses will be.

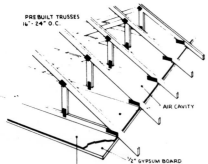

It is important for you to own an energy-efficient home if you are to make good use of the sun's energy. This means that you must convert your home to a high energy efficiency home before proceeding to install solar.

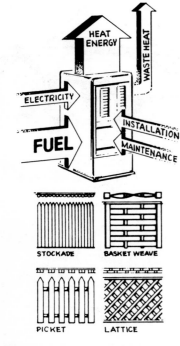

Much of the decision to install solar is an economic decision. You must be able to determine what your future costs of conventional fuels will be in order to determine if solar will provide good economics for you.

Unless your building faces in the proper direction, it will be hard for you to make good use of the sun's energy. You can make changes in your present home to improve its solar orientation at reasonable cost.

Some rooms need more heat than others. Some rooms need morning heat whereas others need afternoon heat. The proper planning of your building's interior is important if you are to make maximum use of solar radiation.

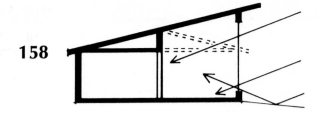
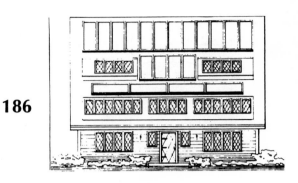
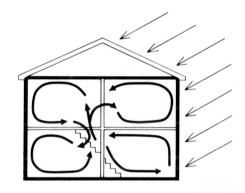

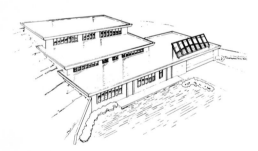
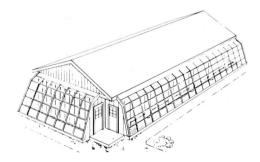

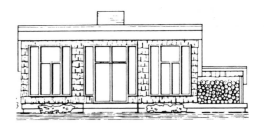
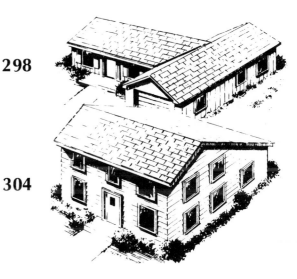

TABLES

WORKSHEETS

DECISION
1

Achieve Energy Independence with Solar Heating

Americans prize independence above all else. During the last 200 years, they have fought and won the battle for political independence from England and the battle for economic independence from the unreasonable demands of employers during the industrial revolution.

Now all Americans are engaged in a battle to win energy independence. The winning of this battle is just as important to the health and well-being of every American family as were the battles for political independence and economic independence.

This book will not review how Americans descended into foreign fossil fuel slavery. That story is now well known by all and does not need repeating. Instead, the book will concentrate on winning independence with solar heat.

This chapter is an overview of what you need to learn in order to put the sun to work for you in an economical and efficient manner. You are not expected to learn any details in this chapter. All the details will be explained as you go through the remaining 19 chapters in the book.

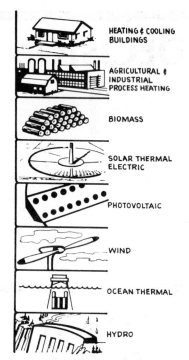

Figure 1.1. Solar energy is many diverse technologies.

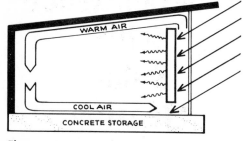

Figure 1.2. A simple passive solar system.

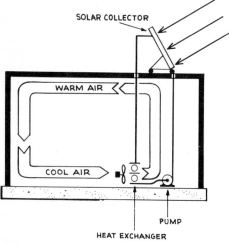

Figure 1.3. A simple active solar system.

What is Solar Energy?

The Department of Energy has divided solar energy into eight individual technologies: the heating and cooling of buildings, agricultural and industrial process heating, fuels from biomass, solar thermal electric, photovoltaic, wind, ocean thermal electric, and hydropower (see Figure 1.1). These eight technologies form three major groups of end uses: thermal heating and cooling, fuels from biomass, and solar electric. In this book you will study the heating and cooling of residential buildings.

Solar Heating and Cooling of Buildings: The Technologies

Two separate technologies provide the solar heating and cooling of buildings. One technology is *passive solar design*. The other technology is *active solar design*.

Passive solar design is as old as the human race. Up until about 100 years ago, buildings made extensive use of solar energy. They were oriented and sited to make maximum use of the sun. They were built of materials that soaked up the sun's energy and retained it. And they took advantage of the sun's position in the sky to gain winter heat and summer cooling.

Such systems are called *passive solar systems*. Passive solar system designers:

- Use the building as the solar collector.
- Build the structure into an efficient heat trap.
- Give the building elements the ability to store the collected heat.
- Provide natural means to circulate the energy throughout the structure.

But not all houses are oriented, sited, and constructed in a manner that allows passive solar systems to provide the maximum solar heat. Many existing and new houses will need active solar systems to augment their passive design elements (see Figure 1.2)

Active solar systems are systems that add solar collectors to the building, retrofit the structure into an efficient heat trap, add solar storage, and use external energy to move the stored solar energy to the point of use (see Figure 1.3).

When active and passive solar systems are combined in a structure, they are called *hybrid solar structures*. In these structures, passive solar design is used as much as possible, then active solar system equipment is added to complete the heating or cooling job.

The Economics of Solar Technology

Homes are expensive. Designing them to heat and cool with the sun's energy adds to the building's initial cost, although total costs are lowered over the life of the structure.

There is an order of addition with solar technology that should be followed so as to get the highest return for your dollar of investment:

- First, build an energy-efficient structure. Insulation and other energy conserving measures provide very high return.
- Second, make your design as passive as possible. If the building element can act as a structural element as well as a solar element, you get two functions for the price of one.
- Third, install active solar systems where needed to maximize your use of the sun's energy. Because you generally only need heat for part of the year, the return on your investment is generally lower.

Today, both active and passive heating systems are an immediate economic alternative to oil and electricity. Once natural gas is completely deregulated, both passive and active solar equipment will be good economic alternatives to it.

Keep in mind that although the initial cost of the system is higher than monthly purchases of fossil fuel, solar heating devices are energy producers, not energy consumers. There will be little or no fuel to pay for. But you must pay for the device itself.

You Must Do Your Homework

In order to remodel your present home into a hybrid solar home or to supervise the building of a passive solar home, you must do some homework so that you understand how solar heating works (see Figure 1.4). You will start this homework in Decision 2. The balance of Decision 1 will be devoted to reviewing what your homework will consist of.

First, you need to study solar radiation. You need to know how to pinpoint your location on earth, how to understand the details of the earth's annual orbit around the sun, and how to tell solar time.

Second, you must learn how to plot solar angles using sun-path diagrams and how to draw a projection of the solar window.

Third, you must understand the nature and type of radiation that comes from the sun. This will allow you to determine the amount of energy that your home will see.

And fourth, you must learn about the three types of radiation that you can collect and how to maximize their collection.

Calculating Your Available Solar Energy

Solar energy varies by geographic location, so you must study solar radiation variability and available data for your area. The country has been broken down into 24 solar radiation geographic blocks to allow you to do this (see Figure 1.5). Tables of solar radiation data have been established for each area.

The calculation of the amount of radiation data that strikes your home is done by using the solar radiation tables and some trigonometric functions. You will learn how to use these functions to tabulate the amount of energy available for your use. When you are finished with Decision 3, you will know just how much solar energy you have to work with.

Determining Your Building's Energy Needs

What is heat? What is temperature? How is heat energy gained and lost? You must know the answers to these three questions in detail if you are to determine the energy needs of your building (see Figure 1.6).

In Decision 4 you will study how heat is transmitted through building structures. You will learn how to calculate the heat losses during the winter months. You will study how to calculate the heat gains in a residential structure during the summer months. When you have finished Decision 4, you will be able to quickly calculate heating and cooling loads for your home.

Building an Energy-efficient Home

At today's prices, homes must be energy efficient (see Figure 1.7). Energy is no longer cheap in cost nor plentiful in supply.

Figure 1.4. You must do your homework.

Figure 1.5. Learn how to calculate your available solar energy.

Figure 1.6. Learn how to determine your building's energy needs.

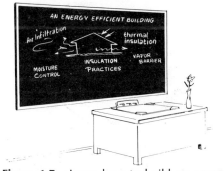

Figure 1.7. Learn how to build an energy-efficient building.

Your study of energy efficiency will start in Decision 5 with a study of fuels and their combustion so that you can make an intelligent choice of fuels for your home. You should be aware of the vast differences between fuel oil, natural gas, electricity, and other fuels.

You will study air infiltration and ventilation of buildings. These two items must be properly controlled if you are to be comfortable without extra cost. The control of moisture and its role in maintaining comfort and structure life must be learned. You need to know all about thermal insulation and vapor barriers so that you can make some intelligent choices of materials for both new structures and remodeling. And you need to be thoroughly grounded in thermal insulation practices so that you can use your money wisely.

You will finish your study of Decision 5 by doing a heat load analysis of a home constructed with three different levels of insulation. This will prepare you to audit your own home and make the required improvements.

Estimating Your Future Fuel Costs

Fuel is purchased by the gallon, by the kilowatt-hour, and by the hundred cubic feet. Your first task in Decision 6 is to learn how to convert these costs into a common measurement of dollars per million Btu (see Figure 1.8). Then you must learn at what efficiencies common fuels burn. You must understand the cost of installing, operating, and maintaining furnaces and other heat-producing devices. Such devices have finite lives over which they produce specified amounts of heat. Replacements are needed as they age. Maintenance is required during their lifetime, and energy is required to operate them.

The cost of fossil fuels is rising rapidly. So is the cost of new and replacement equipment. You must learn a way to estimate what these costs will be over the next 10 years. Then you will know how much to spend on solar heating.

You will finish your study of Decision 6 by doing a 10-year fuel cost analysis for the three heat loads established in Decision 5. This will again help you audit your own home in terms of future fuel costs.

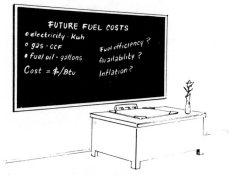

Figure 1.8. Learn how to calculate your future fuel costs.

Planning Your Home's "Solarization"

There are five major steps to a solar plan for a building structure. The building's orientation must be studied. The building's interior layout must be planned. The maximum amount of solar energy must be collected. The collected energy must be stored until it is needed. And the stored energy must be distributed throughout the structure when it is needed.

Orienting Your Building

Building orientation has to satisfy many aesthetic, political, and social needs as well as provide for solar energy collection (see Figure 1.9). You must have privacy but be able to communicate with the outside world. You must have pleasing views of the local scenery in order to be satisfied with your orientation. If your building already exists, chances are that it was oriented more for aesthetics than for solar utilization.

In northern latitudes buildings must be oriented to receive maximum winter sun and minimum wind. In southern latitudes, the opposite may be true. In Decision 7 you will study building orientation and learn how best to orient your building. Or if it already is built, how best to utilize its present orientation. Chances are that you will want to do some remodel-

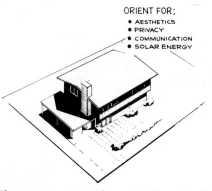

Figure 1.9. Learn the principles of building exterior orientation.

ing after the orientation of the existing building has been studied. Decision 7 will lay the groundwork for making those remodeling decisions.

Planning Your Building's Interior

A home is normally used for daily living, sleeping, storage, and transportation-equipment storage. So a home consists of four basic parts (see Figure 1.10).

Each part of the home has its own energy requirements that are related closely to the activity carried out within that part of the home. For daily living, natural lighting and good outdoor visual communication must be coupled with a demand for thermal energy to maintain comfort without excessive clothing. For sleeping, privacy, room for toilet activities, and storage of clothing must be coupled with enough thermal energy to remain comfortable under the bedcovers and while bathing and dressing. Storage areas need artificial lighting and small amounts of thermal energy. The transportation-equipment area needs can vary according to the activities undertaken there, but generally they are related to a minimum of thermal energy.

In Decision 8 you will study the requirements of the four basic residential modules, learn how to fit them into different home designs, and see how they can be arranged to make maximum use of solar energy.

Using Your Full Solar Potential

When the outside air temperature is below 65°F, your building will most likely require heat. When the outside air is above 80°F, the building will most likely require cooling.

Solar energy is usually used to add heat to a building. Proper solar construction can contribute to cooling by preventing solar energy from entering the building during hot weather.

There are two ways to bring solar energy into a building. The energy can be collected outside the insulated envelope of the house's exterior and pumped or blown inside. Or the energy can be transmitted through the insulated envelope with a light-transmitting opening such as a window.

Solar energy is kept out of the building by erecting a barrier between the sun and the building's interior. The insulation in the walls and the ceiling acts in this manner. Shading devices may also be employed to keep the sun from entering the building.

Structural Elements In Decision 9 you will study the five basic structural elements in a house—the walls, the floors, the foundation, the roof, and the ceilings—in order to determine the role that each can play in either admitting or denying the entrance of solar energy (see Figure 1.11). You will learn how each can be altered to increase or decrease the flow of energy, what treatments hold the highest priorities, and how the seasons of the year affect the way in which you treat each structural element.

Windows are highly effective transmitters of heat energy, but they have low insulation values. So energy gained during the sunlight hours will rapidly flow back outdoors at night unless the windows are protected with shutters or other devices.

Almost any wall can be made into a solar collector. You will study the details of how to deal with wall collectors. And you will learn the advantages and disadvantages of using the different types.

You will learn that the final solarization of any building is unique to that structure, its orientation, and its geographic location and that the use of windows and solar collectors requires careful consideration of many dif-

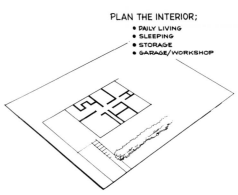

Figure 1.10. Learn the principles of interior design.

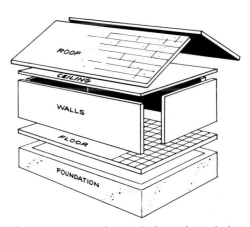

Figure 1.11. Understand the roles of the building's structural elements.

ferent technical and aesthetic factors that must all be placed in harmony if the maximum benefit is to be derived from the sun's energy.

When you have finished Decision 9, you will know how to plan and build the windows and collectors that are needed to use your full solar potential.

Storing the Collected Energy

Solar energy is only available from sunrise to sunset. Most of it is available from 10:00 A.M. to 2:00 P.M. The amount varies according to the time of year. In Decision 10 you will study the daily availability of solar energy, the building's thermal energy requirements, thermal mass, and thermal heat storage unit theory.

You will study specific heat and thermal conductivity so that you understand the effects of materials on thermal mass and temperature change. Then you will design storage units using masonry, water, and phase-change salts (see Figure 1.12).

When you have finished Decision 10, you will know how to design and build solar storage units for residential buildings.

Distributing the Stored Energy

Energy from storage must be distributed throughout the house when it is needed. In Decision 11 you will learn about heat distribution through radiation, conduction, and convection augmented by mechanical means such as pumps, fans, and blowers (see Figure 1.13).

You will learn how the interior partitions within the house affect air travel during the day and night and in the winter versus the summer. You will study furnace distribution systems for hot air and hydronic heating. You will study solar heat distribution systems. And you will learn how to integrate these systems into your present heat distribution system.

When you have finished your study of Decision 11, you will know how to design and build solar heat distribution systems and how to integrate them into the fossil-fueled furnace system.

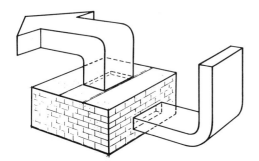

Figure 1.12. Learn the principles of solar energy storage.

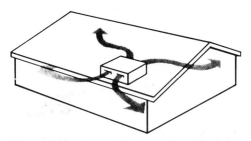

Figure 1.13. Learn the principles of heat energy distribution.

Figure 1.14. Study earth-insulated houses.

The Earth-insulated Solar House

Over most of humanity's existence, earth-insulated houses have played a major role in providing shelter. It is only during the last few hundred years that humankind has moved away from the use of the earth to provide warmth and shelter.

The Underground Space Center at the University of Minnesota has studied earth-sheltered housing design in detail. The results of their work is published in *Earth Sheltered Housing Design* (Van Nostrand Reinhold, New York, 1979).

Decision 12 offers homeowners a comfortable and economical approach to earth-sheltered designs with modern building materials (see Figure 1.14). You will learn about the principles of earth-sheltered designs and the advantages and disadvantages of such houses.

The Air-envelope Insulated House

A structure with double walls and openings between floors allows the circulation of air around the structure by natural convection currents (see Figure 1.15). As the temperature on the north side of a building tends to be lower than that on the south side during the sunlight hours, the natural convection currents are strong during the day. Such a structure appears to offer a number of advantages in using solar energy despite its increased construction costs. You will learn about air-envelope houses and examine their advantages and disadvantages in Decision 13.

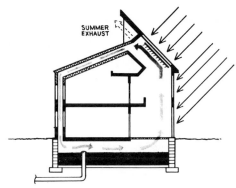

Figure 1.15. Study air-envelope houses.

The Traditional House, Solarized

America's traditional homes are typically ranches, split-levels, and two-story houses (see Figure 1.16). They contain three to four bedrooms, two baths, living and dining rooms, family room, kitchen, garage, and, usually, a basement.

These types of houses were not originally designed with the use of solar heating in mind. But they all can be readily adapted to the effective use of solar energy by using the principles outlined in this book.

Decisions 14 through 16 cover traditional house designs. Here you will find elevations and floor plans for a number of traditional houses. The houses are designed at about 1600 sq. ft., but the size can readily be increased or decreased if desired.

Figure 1.16. Study how America's existing homes can be "solarized."

The Contemporary Solar House

Decision 17 contains plans for two contemporary solar houses (see Figure 1.17 for one example). The depart from the traditional concepts in order to maximize the use of solar energy. But they do not go as far as the earth-insulated or the air-envelope houses. They are designs for gracious, modern living in the manner to which Americans are accustomed. They are designed to be constructed by any knowledgeable contractor using readily available materials and skills.

The Solar Greenhouse

The authors have chosen to present one greenhouse design in Decision 18 that can be used freestanding or against a building. The design lends itself to construction by a home carpenter.

Figure 1.17. Study two new contemporary solar designs.

The Solar Vacation Home

The authors chose a "chicken coop" design for their vacation cottage presented in Decision 19. Then they peeled back half the roof to open the south side of the cottage to the sun. It is a worker's design planned for simplicity and low cost do-it-yourself construction.

Making a Decision

In this introductory chapter you learned that solar heating offers a way to eliminate fossil fuel slavery in America. You saw how you could help America regain its energy independence.

You were introduced to solar energy. You saw that it embraced a number of technologies—one of which is the heating and cooling of buildings. You learned that the solar heating and cooling of buildings called for two basic technologies: active and passive solar systems. Then you learned that the intelligent use of solar energy requires some homework. Finally, you reviewed what this homework consisted of.

By now you should be ready to move into learning how you can cut your fossil fuel costs by using the sun. Solar energy is readily available for all people in all geographic locations. Solar energy can be used in all styles of housing including some new styles designed specifically for taking maximum advantage of the sun.

Best of all . . . your present home . . . the one that you own now . . . can most likely make good use of solar energy. Your decision at this point should be to study exactly how you can accomplish this.

DECISION
2

Understand Solar Radiation

Our sun is a thermonuclear furnace that transforms hydrogen into helium through nuclear fusion, a process that releases huge amounts of energy. This energy radiates out from the sun. A small part of it is intercepted by the earth. On the average, the outer edges of the earth's atmosphere receive about 429.5 Btu/hr/sq ft of area.

However, all this energy does not reach the earth's surface. The ozone in the air absorbs much of the ultraviolet radiation. The air's molecules filter out much of the red light, causing a blue sky. Dust particles and water vapor diffuse and scatter energy throughout the atmosphere.

The earth's rotational axis is tilted from the plane of the earth's orbit around the sun. This causes longer days in the summer and shorter days in the winter. It also changes the altitude of the sun in the sky from season to season so that the sun is higher in the sky in the summertime. As the earth rotates, the sun moves across the sky from east to west. This changes the angle at which the sun's rays strike the earth. As a result of these changes, the amount of solar radiation that strikes any spot on the earth varies from hour to hour, from day to day, and from season to season.

In this chapter you will study the earth and its movement through the solar system. You will learn:

- A system that has been devised to allow you to pinpoint your location on the earth.
- The details of the earth's annual orbit and how to tell solar time.
- How to plot solar angles from sun-path diagrams and how to draw a projection of the solar window.
- The details of solar radiation and how to determine the amount of radiation that your structure will see.
- The three different types of solar radiation that you can collect and how to maximize their collection.

What Is Energy?

Energy is the capacity to do work. You cannot see it. You cannot taste it. It has no sound, feel, or smell. Yet without energy, life could not exist.

There are many forms of energy and many ways in which to produce energy. Some of the major forms of energy are mechanical energy, electrical energy, and heat energy. Solar energy is heat energy.

Heat is a familiar and useful form of energy. It can, for example, cook food, warm a house, heat water, and dry clothes. Heat energy, or thermal energy as it is also known, can be produced by burning a fossil fuel such as gas, fuel oil, or coal. It can be produced by electricity, chemical reaction, or nuclear fission. Or it can be produced by the sun's rays.

Measuring Energy   In the English system of measurement, energy is measured in *British thermal units* or *Btu*. A Btu is the amount of energy that is needed to raise the temperature of 1 lb of water by 1°F. You would need 10 Btu to raise 1 lb of water 10°F or 10 Btu to raise 10 lb of water by 1°F.

A Btu is a very small amount of energy. A gallon of fuel oil will produce about 130,000 Btu. So will 10 lb of coal. One-hundred feet of natural gas will produce about 100,000 Btu. A barrel of crude oil contains about 5.8 million Btu.

Throughout this book you will see the notation *MMBtu*. MMBtu stands for 1 million British thermal units. You will also see the word *quad*. Quad is an abbreviation for 1 quadrillion British thermal units, which would be written as 1,000,000,000,000,000 Btu.

Electrical energy is usually measured differently. It is measured in *watts*. For convenience, the notation *kilowatts* (kw) is generally used. A kilowatt is 1000 watts. Large amounts of electrical energy may be stated as *megawatts*. A megawatt is 1 million watts.

Watts can be converted to Btu with the use of a simple formula: watts × 3.413 = Btu/hr. And Btu can be converted to watts by this formula: Btu/hr × 0.293 = watts.

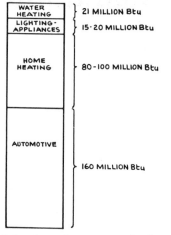

Figure 2.1.   Annual energy needs of a typical family of four.

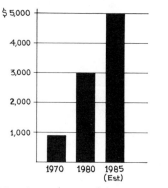

Figure 2.2.   Annual cost of the energy needs of a typical family of four over the period 1970 through 1985.

Typical Energy Needs and Costs

A family of four might need about 21 MMBtu/yr to heat its domestic water. If it lived in the Midwest, it might take about 80 to 100 MMBtu/yr to heat its home. Lighting and appliances might use about 15 to 20 MMBtu/yr. A standard-sized 1974 automobile might take about 160 MMBtu to drive it 15,000 miles. So a typical annual energy need for this family would be about 300 MMBtu. Figure 2.1 illustrates these needs.

In 1970 a typical annual energy bill for that family would have been about $900. In 1980, if the same family burned the same fuels, the bill would have been about $3000. By 1985 that bill will most likely rise to around $5000. Figure 2.2 illustrates this huge cost increase.

A Map of the Earth

You must be able to pinpoint your location on the earth if you are to make the maximum use of the sun. A system of coordinates called *latitude* and *longitude* has been developed with which to do this.

The earth rotates one revolution eastward per day around an *axis of rotation* extending through the North and South poles. In Figure 2.3 this axis of rotation is shown as a dashed line.

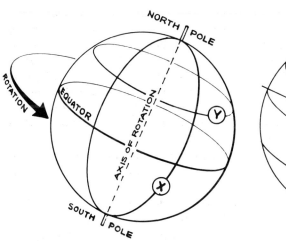

Figure 2.3. Earth's basic coordinates.

Figure 2.4. Major parallels of latitude.

Around the outside circumference of the earth, situated midway between the poles and at right angles to the polar axis lies an imaginary line known as the *equator*. The equator cuts the earth into two hemispheres: the Northern Hemisphere and the Southern Hemisphere.

The equator is known as a *great circle*. A great circle is any circle whose plane passes through the center of the earth. Other smaller circles, with all points equidistant from the poles and at right angles to the polar axis can also be drawn. These are called *parallel circles*, or *parallels of latitude*. The circle labeled Ⓨ in Figure 2.3 is a typical parallel of latitude.

A circle around the earth's circumference that passes through the North and South poles, and whose plane passes through the axis of rotation, is known as a *meridian circle*. All meridian circles are great circles. The circle labeled Ⓧ in Figure 2.3 is a meridian. Any number of these meridians, known as *meridians of longitude*, can be drawn.

Latitude

The major *parallels of latitude* for the earth are shown in Figure 2.4. A parallel of latitude is any small circle drawn parallel to the equator, at right angles to the polar axis, and equidistant from the poles. Note that each circle is labeled by degrees and direction. The number of degrees that it is labeled is determined by measuring the angle that is formed between a line projected from a point on the circle to the center of the earth and a line projected from the equator and the center of the earth. The direction is designated by determining whether the circle lies north or south of the equator.

Thus circle Ⓧ in Figure 2.4, which is labeled 50°N latitude, lies between the North Pole and the equator at an angle of 50°. The circle labeled Ⓩ lies south of the equator at an angle of 30°. It is called the 30°S parallel of latitude.

If you were told that New York City lies at 42°N latitude, you would know that it lies somewhere on a circle that lies north of the equator at an angle of 42° with the equator. You would not know where on that circle it lies. For that you must determine the longitude.

Longitude

Meridians of longitude are great circles that pass through the North and South poles and whose plane passes through the axis of rotation. Some meridians of longitude are shown in Figure 2.5. Meridians of longitude are also designated by degrees and direction.

Figure 2.5. Major meridians of longitude.

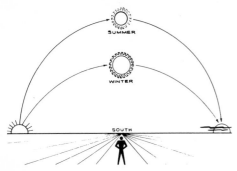

Figure 2.6. What you see daily.

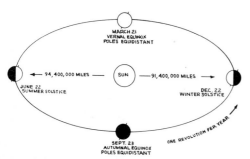

Figure 2.7. The earth's orbit around the sun.

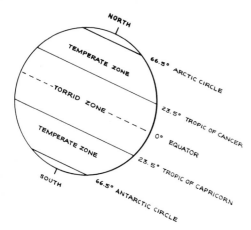

Figure 2.8. The earth's three climatic zones.

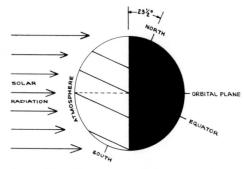

Figure 2.9. The winter solstice.

Many hundreds of years ago when Great Britain ruled the seas and a navigational system was needed, a meridian of longitude that split the earth in half from north to south and passed through the town of Greenwich, England, was established. This is known as the *Greenwich meridian* and is designated as 0° longitude. All other meridians are described by measuring the angle created by projecting a line from the meridian to the center of the earth and a line from the center of the earth to the Greenwich meridian. The direction is described by stating whether the meridian lies east or west of the Greenwich meridian.

Now if you were told that New York City lies at 42°N latitude and 72°W longitude, you would know exactly where New York City was on the surface of the earth.

The position of any point on earth may be described by stating its latitude and longitude. These terms will be used throughout this book to describe geographic position. You can relate your position on the earth to them by using maps containing these coordinates.

The Earth's Orbit

Primitive people saw the sun rising in the east, traveling across the southern sky, and setting in the west. They deduced that the sun circled a flat earth daily. We know today that the earth is round, that it rotates once on its axis daily, and that it travels around the sun annually. But we see the same phenonoma that early people saw, and we tend to forget about the earth's orbit. Figure 2.6 shows what human beings view daily.

The earth circles the sun in an elliptical path at an average annual distance of 93,000,000 miles. This is called the *orbital plane*. Figure 2.7 shows the details. The earth makes one rotation about the sun per year.

The earth also spins on its own axis. The axis of rotation passes through the North and South poles. The rate of rotation is one revolution per day.

The axis of rotation of the earth is not at right angles to the orbital plane. Instead, it is tilted about an average of 23.5° from that plane. As a result, the calculations of the angle at which the sun strikes a point on the earth's surface become somewhat complex. This tilt of the axis of rotation from the oribital plane is what causes the different seasons and the varying hours of sunlight on the earth.

The Earth's Climatic Zones

Because of the tilt of the axis of rotation, the earth has three climatic zones: the torrid zone, the temperate zone, and the frigid zone. Figure 2.8 shows these zones. The *torrid zone* is the region between the parallels of latitude where the sun is directly overhead at solar noon at least once during the year. The *temperate zones* are the regions where the sun is never directly overhead, but always appears above the horizon every day of the year. The *frigid zones* are the zones where the sun is below the horizon for at least one full day during the year.

The frigid zones lie between a parallel of latitude at 66.5° north and south of the equator and the earth's poles. The temperate zones lie between the 23.5 and 66.5° parallels of latitude on either side of the equator. And the torrid zone lies between the 23.5° parallels of latitude.

The Winter Solstice The word *solstice* means "sun standing still." On December 22, the winter solstice, the sun would appear to be standing still to a person standing on the Arctic Circle. It would always appear at the same point on the horizon. And it would be above the horizon for a full 24 hr. Figure 2.9 shows the winter solstice.

At the winter solstice, the earth is the closest to the sun, but its axis of rotation is tilted away from the orbital plane. As a result, the daylight hours in the Northern Hemisphere are the shortest. The sun's energy has to pass through more of the earth's atmosphere to reach its surface. These two effects combine to give the Northern Hemisphere its coldest weather. The opposite is true in the Southern Hemisphere.

The Summer Solstice On June 22, the summer solstice, the sun would appear to be standing still to a person standing on the Antarctic Circle. It would always appear at the same point on the horizon. And it would be above the horizon for a full 24 hr. Figure 2.10 shows the details.

At the summer solstice, the earth is farthest away from the sun, but its axis of rotation is tilted toward the orbital plane. As a result, the daylight hours in the Northern Hemisphere are the longest. The sun's energy has to pass through less atmosphere to reach the earth's surface. As a result, the Northern Hemisphere has its longest days and its hottest weather. Again, just the opposite occurs in the Southern Hemisphere.

The Equinox The word *equinox* means "equal nights." During its rotation around the sun, the earth reaches a point twice where the poles are equidistant from the sun. These are known as the *vernal equinox*, which occurs on March 21, and the *autumnal equinox*, which occurs on September 23. Because the two poles are equidistant from the sun, all points on the earth, except the poles, have exactly 12 hr of daylight and 12 hr of darkness. The vernal equinox is illustrated in Figure 2.11.

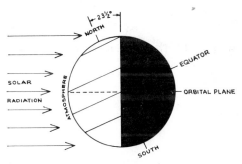

Figure 2.10. The summer solstice.

Solar Time

To understand solar time, pretend that you are out in space looking down on the earth at the time of the vernal equinox. Directly below you is the North Pole. Drawn for you to observe are meridians of longitude every 15° around the earth. The details are shown in Figure 2.12. To your left is the sun. One point on the earth points directly at the sun. This point is labeled noon. The earth is rotating at a rate of one revolution per day. This means

$$\begin{array}{r} 360° \\ \div\ 24 \quad \text{hr} \\ \hline = 15° \quad \text{hr} \end{array}$$

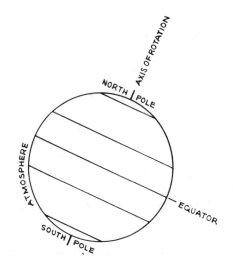

Figure 2.11. The vernal equinox.

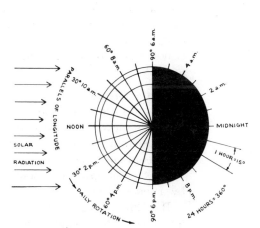

Figure 2.12. Understanding solar time.

$$\frac{60\ \text{min}}{\div\ 15°}$$
$$=\ 4\ \text{min/°}$$

Figure 2.13. The four time zones in the contiguous United States.

Figure 2.14. How to convert from civil time to solar time. (Reprinted by permission from R. H. Montgomery and J. Budnick, *The Solar Decision Book,* John Wiley & Sons, Inc., 1978.)

that each hour it is turning 15 angular degrees. So at 1:00 P.M. the point that you were watching would have moved to the meridian of longitude that is labeled 1:00 P.M. Each succeeding hour the point will move another 15° of latitude throughout the day and night. When 24 hr have passed, the point will have returned to noon. Fifteen degrees of longitude equals 1 hr of earth time. So when it is solar noon at the Greenwich meridian, it is 5:00 P.M. solar time at the 75° West meridian and 7:00 A.M. at 75° East meridian.

For convenience, time on earth is not calculated in solar time but in *civil time*. Civil time is arbitrarily set by having all the clocks within a zone covering approximately 15° of longitude set the same. The local civil time for a selected meridian near the center of the zone is called the *standard time*. In the United States (not including Alaska and Hawaii), there are four time zones. These time zones and their standard meridians are shown in Figure 2.13.

Standard time and solar time do not always agree because the earth's orbit and speed vary and a solar day is slightly longer than 24 hr. It is necessary to convert if you wish to determine solar time from your local standard time. Figure 2.14 shows how this is done.

TO CORRECT LOCAL STANDARD TIME TO LOCAL SOLAR TIME

1. Determine the longitude meridian for your location.
2. Select the standard time longitude meridian for your location:

Standard Time Zone	Standard Time Longitude
Eastern Standard	75° longtitude
Central Standard	90° longitude
Mountain Standard	105° longitude
Pacific Standard	120° longitude

3. Multiply the difference between your longitude and the standard time longitude by four minutes per degree.
4. If you are EAST of the standard time longitude, ADD the minutes to the standard time.
5. If you are WEST of the standard time longitude, SUBTRACT the minutes from the standard time.

6. Correct for the time of year, by adding or subtracting the number of minutes shown:

Time Of Year	Number of Minutes
January 1	-5
February 1	-13
March 1	-13
April 1	-5
May 1	+2
June 1	+2
July 1	-3
August 1	-6
September 1	0
October 1	+10
November 1	+15
December 1	+12

Example:
1. Location: 72°
2. Standard time longitude: 75°
3. 4 minutes/degree × (75°-72°) = 12 minutes

4/5. Uncorrected solar noon = 12:00 + :12 = 12:12 PM
6. For November 1: 12 + :15 = 12:27

On November 1 for a location at 72° longitude, Solar Noon occurs at 12:27 EST.

Solar Angles

Precise solar angles can be calculated for any point on the earth at any time by using geometry and trigonometry, provided that the latitude, the time, and the sun's declination are known. However, for your purpose, it is not necessary to go to these lengths. Sun-path diagrams can be used instead.

Sun-path Diagrams A *sun-path diagram* is a graphic projection of the path of the sun across the sky as projected onto a horizontal surface. Figure 2.15 shows such a sun-path diagram for 40°N latitude. On the sun-path diagram the altitude of the sun above the horizon is described by a number of concentric circles labeled from 10 to 80°. The geographic bearing of the sun from solar south, which is called the *azimuth*, is described by a series of radial lines at 10° intervals around the circular diagram.

The elliptical curves on the diagram represent horizontal projections of the sun's path throughout the year on the 21st day of each month. The months are designated by Roman numerals where I = January and XII =

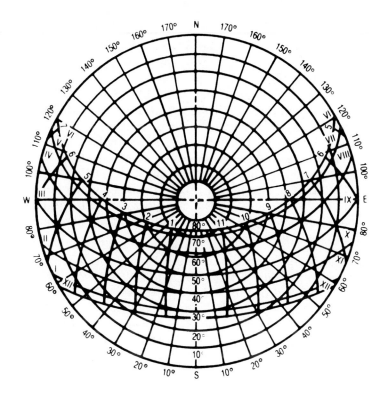

Figure 2.15. Sun-path diagram for 40°N latitude.

December. The time of day is indicated by the Arabic numerals located at the uppermost ellipse.

To find the sun's position on February 21 at 3:00 P.M. in any geographic location at 40°N latitude, you proceed as follows:

- Select the February path of the sun. This is the elliptical curve labeled II.
- Locate the curved line labeled 3. This represents 3:00 P.M.
- Note where the two lines intersect. This is the location of the sun. It will be 50°W of solar south at an altitude of 24° above the horizon.

Appendix A contains sun-path diagrams for 24, 28, 32, 36, 40, 44, 48, 52°N latitude. Most of the sun's energy that is used in heating or cooling a building comes between the hours of 9:00 A.M. and 3:00 P.M. So the curved lines representing these hours would be about the useful limits of collection.

The Solar Window

Imagine that the sky is a transparent dome with its center at the solar collector of the house where the solar energy is to be used as shown in Figure 2.16. The sun-path diagram can be used to draw a solar window on this dome. The bottom of the window would be described by the path of the sun on December 21. The top of the window would be described by the path of the sun on June 21. The west side of the window would be described by the location of the sun at 3 P.M. The east side of the window would be described by the location of the sun at 9:00 A.M. On March 21 and September 21, the sun would pass through the center of the window. This is shown in the side view of the skydome shown in Figure 2.17.

A Mercator Projection of the Solar Window The solar window can also be plotted on a flat surface. This is called a *Mercator projection*. Figure 2.18 shows how a Mercator projection of a solar window is drawn. The

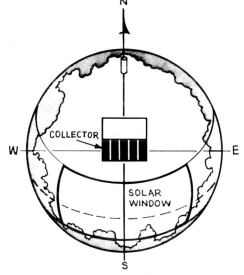

Figure 2.16. The solar window.

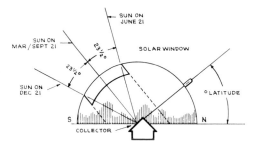

Figure 2.17. Side view of the solar window.

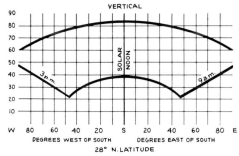

Figure 2.18. Mercator projection of the solar window.

Understand Radiation **15**

baseline of the graph represents the horizon. It is divided into vertical lines that represent meridians of longitude. The top line of the graph represents vertical, or directly overhead (a 90° angle from the horizon). Horizontal lines are drawn across the graph for each 10° of altitude.

This particular solar window is for 28°N latitude. It was drawn by transferring the data from the 28°N latitude sun-path diagram to this flat surface. As can be seen from the graph, on December 21 at 9:00 A.M. in the morning, the sun is 22° above the horizon and is located 45°E of solar south. At solar noon, the sun is due south at an altitude of 38°. At 3:00 P.M. in the afternoon, the sun is 45°W of south at an altitude of 22° above the horizon. The summer solstice can also be described in the same manner, as can the sun at the equinox, or at any other time of the year, by using the sun-path diagram to plot the sun's path. However, all points at other times of the year will fall inside the solar window.

Plotting Solar Shade The Mercator projection is ideal for plotting solar shade, as shown in Figure 2.19. Solar south is determined. The outline of the shade of the yard or building plot is determined using a sextant, a transit, a sun scope, or a home-built instrument such as the one shown in Appendix D of *The Solar Decision Book* (Wiley, New York, 1978). This outline is transferred to the projection. Shade that sticks up into the solar window will shade the sun from the building. Because its exact location is shown, the gross effect on daily solar collection can be calculated.

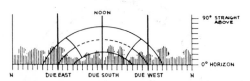

Figure 2.19. Plotting shade on a mercator projection.

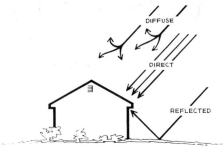

Figure 2.20. The three types of solar radiation.

Solar Radiation

Three types of solar radiation reach a building: direct radiation, diffuse radiation, and reflected radiation. Figure 2.20 shows these three types.

Direct radiation consists of parallel rays coming directly from the sun. These are the types of rays that cast a shadow on a clear day.

Diffuse radiation is scattered rays that have been deflected by the earth's atmosphere before they strike the structure. These rays can come from any direction. This is the type of radiation that is seen on cloudy days.

Reflected radiation is solar radiation that hit some other object before striking the building. It depends on the type and shape of the building's surroundings.

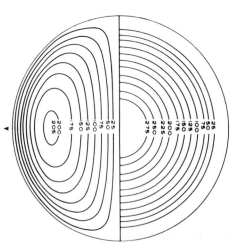

Figure 2.21. A graphic solar radiation calculator.

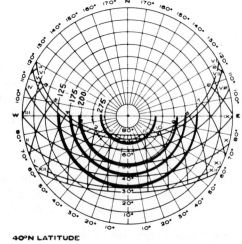

Figure 2.22. Horizontal radiation calculation.

Direct Radiation

On the first of January, 444.1 Btu/hr strike the outer edge of each square foot of the earth's atmosphere. On the first of July, the figure has dropped to 415.6 Btu/hr/sq ft because the earth is slightly farther from the sun. On the average over the entire year, 429.5 Btu/hr/sq ft strike the atmosphere. This is known as the *solar constant*.

As the radiation passes through the earth's atmosphere, some of it is scattered by collision with gas molecules, water droplets, dust, and other particles. So at most, only about 250 to 300 Btu/hr/sq ft of solar radiation strikes the earth's surface.

The radiation that reaches any given spot is dependent on the latitude, the azimuth, and the angle of the incident surface from the horizontal. The precise amount can be calculated. But for your purposes, this is not necessary. Instead, a graphic radiation calculator can be used. Figure 2.21 shows this calculator.

The radiation calculator is drawn to the same scale as the sun-path diagrams. The upper half of the radiation calculator shows the amount of radiation falling on 1 sq ft of horizontal surface; the bottom half of the calculator shows the amount of radiation falling on 1 sq ft of vertical surface.

The calculator assumes that it is a clear day. It only shows direct radiation, not diffuse and reflected. To use the radiation calculator, superimpose either the horizontal or the vertical half over the proper sun-path diagram and read the direct radiation directly from the curves.

Horizontal Surfaces In Figure 2.22, solid, heavy lines representing radiation levels of 125, 175, 200, and 275 Btu/hr/sq ft on a horizontal surface have been drawn on a 40°N latitude sun-path diagram. A study of this illustration will show that the clear-sky direct radiation between the hours of 11:00 A.M. and 1:00 P.M. is about the levels in the following table:

MONTH	RADIATION LEVEL	NOON SUN ALTITUDE
January	125	30°
February	175	41°
March	210	50°
April	250	62°
May	275+	70°
June	275+	74°
July	275+	70°
August	250	62°
September	210	50°
October	175	41°
November	125	30°
December	100	26°

The major reason for this difference in radiation per hour reaching a square foot of the earth's horizontal surface is the change in the sun's altitude. As shown earlier, on December 21 the sun's altitude at solar noon is about 26° above the horizon. So a square foot of solar radiation, which is measured at right angles to the sun's rays, strikes the earth at a low angle. This spreads the sunlight over a much larger area than 1 sq ft, as is shown in Figure 2.23.

On June 21, the sun is at an altitude of about 74° at solar noon. So a square foot of solar radiation strikes a much smaller area of the earth's surface and its energy is more concentrated. This can be seen in Figure 2.24.

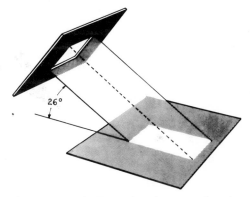

Figure 2.23. In December the sun strikes the earth at a very low angle and its energy is spread over a wide area.

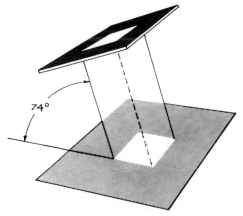

Figure 2.24. In June the sun strikes the earth at almost a right angle and its energy is concentrated in a small area.

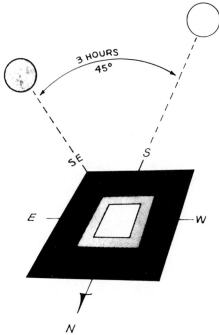

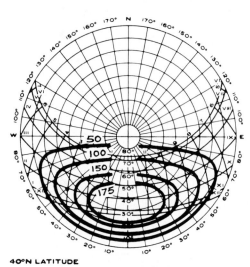

40°N LATITUDE

Figure 2.26. Vertical radiation calculation.

Figure 2.25. At 9:00 A.M. or 3:00 P.M. the sun is lower in the sky and the radiation is scattered over a large area.

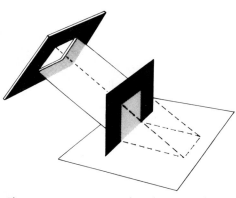

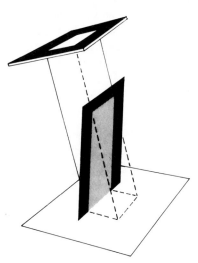

Figure 2.27. In December the sun is low in the sky and its energy is concentrated onto a small vertical surface.

Figure 2.28. In June the sun is high in the sky and its energy strikes a very large vertical surface.

On March 21, the radiation striking a square foot of the earth's surface at solar noon is about 210 Btu/hr and the sun is at an altitude of 50° above the horizon. But at 9:00 A.M. or 3:00 P.M., the sun is at an altitude of only 32° above the horizon. Additionally, the sun is about 58° east or west of south. So the sun's radiation is spread over an even wider area, as shown in Figure 2.25. This lowers the radiation striking the earth's surface to about 130 to 140 Btu/hr/sq ft at that time of day. Horizontal surfaces see more energy per unit of area in the summer than in the winter.

Vertical Surfaces In Figure 2.26 solid, heavy lines representing 50, 100, 150, and 175 Btu/hr/sq ft on a vertical surface are superimposed on a 40°N sun-path diagram.

On December 21 at solar noon the radiation level on a square foot of vertical surface is about 200 Btu/hr/sq ft. This is about twice the radiation that falls on a square foot of horizontal surface at that time.

On June 21 at solar noon, the radiation level is about 75 Btu/hr/sq ft. This is about one-quarter of the radiation striking a horizontal surface at this time.

The reason for this difference can be seen by looking at Figures 2.27 and 2.28. On December 21, the sun is low in the sky and its energy strikes a small vertical surface. On June 21, the sun is high in the sky and the sun strikes a very large vertical surface. The energy striking the surface at 9:00 A.M. and 3:00 P.M. still drops off, just as it does on horizontal surfaces due to the sun's movement from east to west in the sky. South-facing vertical surfaces see more energy in the winter months than in the summer months.

Tilted Surfaces The maximum amount of direct radiation can be collected when the surface of the collector is tilted so that it is perpendicular to the sun's radiation. Then the radiation falls on the smallest possible surface. Figure 2.29 shows how this angle, called the *right-angle collector-tilt angle,* is determined.

Figure 2.30 shows the proper tilt angle at 40°N latitude for each month of the year to have the collector at right angles to the sun's direct radiation. The right-angle collector-tilt angle at the equinox is equal to the latitude at which it is installed. Or in this case, an angle of 40°.

During the year, the sun increases and decreases from its altitude at the equinox by equal amounts, rising higher in the summer and sinking lower in the winter. At all latitudes in the United States, this annual change runs 23.5°. To collect the maximum amount of direct radiation during the winter months for heating purposes, the collector should be tilted about latitude plus 11 to 12°; or at 40°N latitude, about 51 to 52°. However, as you will see later, a somewhat greater angle is often suggested so that large amounts of reflected energy can also be collected.

To collect direct radiation best on an annual basis, the collecting surface should be tilted equal to the latitude. To collect the maximum direct radiation in the summer half of the year, the collecting surface should be tilted at latitude minus 11 to 12°. Figure 2.31 shows the details. Figure 2.32 illustrates the changing angle of the sun. At the time of the equinox, the altitude at any point on earth is equal to 90° minus that latitude. At the summer solstice, the sun has increased in altitude by 23.5°. At the winter solstice, the sun has dropped in altitude by 23.5° from its altitude at the equinox.

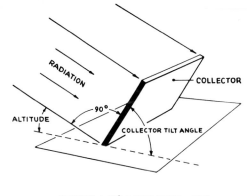

ALTITUDE + 90° + TILT ANGLE = 180°
TILT ANGLE = 180° - 90° - ALTITUDE
OR, TILT ANGLE = 90° - ALTITUDE

Figure 2.29. The right-angle collector-tilt angle for any month is at 90° minus the altitude of the sun.

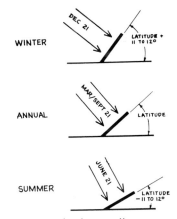

Figure 2.31. The best collection angles for collecting solar radiation.

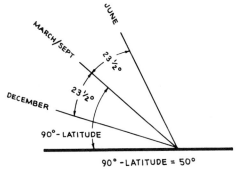

90° - LATITUDE = 50°

Figure 2.32. The changing altitude of the sun throughout the year.

MONTH	SUN'S NOON ALTITUDE	TILT ANGLE
January/November	30°	60°
February/October	41°	49°
March/September	50°	40°
April/August	62°	28°
May/July	70°	20°
June	74°	16°
December	26°	64°

Figure 2.30. The sun's altitude and the right-angle collector-tilt angle at 40°N latitude for each month of the year.

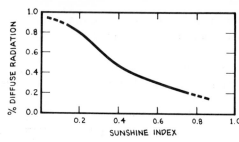

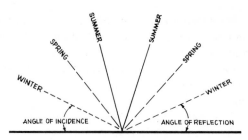

Figure 2.33. Relationship of diffuse and direct radiation: the sunshine index. (As developed by B. Y. H. Liu and R. C. Jordan in *Sol. Energy,* Vol. 4, pp. 1-19, 1960.)

Figure 2.34. The angle of incidence equals the angle of reflection.

Diffuse Radiation

The amount of solar radiation striking the outer edge of the earth's atmosphere—the solar constant—was described earlier as 429.5 Btu/hr/sq ft. It was also stated earlier that only 250 to 300 Btu/hr/sq ft of direct radiation strikes the earth's surface on a clear day. What has happened to the balance of the radiation?

As the sun's radiation passes through the earth's atmosphere, it is both scattered and absorbed by the gases, the water vapor, and the dust that make up the atmosphere. This scattering and absorption are complex phenonoma that have received careful study. The results are best understood by studying an empirical relationship called the *sunshine index.* The sunshine index is the ratio of the measured total radiation falling on a horizontal plane to the solar constant.

Sunshine Index

In the 1960s, B. Y. H. Liu and R. C. Jordan made extended studies of the amount of solar radiation that hit the earth's surface. From their studies, they performed a statistical analysis that showed that a firm relationship exists between the sunshine index and the amount of diffuse radiation.

When the sunshine index is 100%, that is, under clear sky conditions, they showed that about 15% of the sun's radiation is lost to the atmosphere. So when the sun is directly overhead and shining on a properly tilted surface, the direct solar radiation striking the earth's surface calculates to be a maximum of about 365 Btu/hr/sq ft.

When a dense cloud cover, about 4 to 5 miles thick, covers the sky, almost no direct radiation hits the earth's surface. All the radiation received is diffuse. Only about 5% of the solar constant is received, or about 21 Btu/hr/sq ft.

Obviously, the average condition that normally exists lies between the two extremes. As a result, both direct and diffuse radiation are very important to solar collection. The graph in Figure 2.33 shows the relationship developed by Liu and Jordan.

It is not necessary for you to calculate the percentage diffuse radiation. In Decision 4, the sunshine index is used in a computer program to calculate the total radiation for different geographic areas. You should, however, understand that diffuse sunlight can come from any direction in the sky, that it is additive to the direct radiation, and that it is a function of the amount of cloud cover.

$$
\begin{array}{r}
429 \text{ Btu/hr/sq ft} \\
\times\ 0.85 \\
\hline
= 364.7 \text{ Btu/hr/sq ft}
\end{array}
$$

$$
\begin{array}{r}
429 \text{ Btu/hr/sq ft} \\
\times\ 0.05 \\
\hline
= 21.45 \text{ Btu/hr/sq ft}
\end{array}
$$

Reflected Radiation

Reflected radiation is the radiation that is reflected to the collection surface by the ground or by other adjacent surfaces. Under the right conditions, large amounts of reflected energy can be collected.

Two angles are important when working with direct solar radiation reflection. These are the *angle of incidence* and the *angle of reflection*. The angle of incidence is the angle that the sun's rays make with the reflecting surface. The angle of reflection is the angle at which the radiation is reflected from the reflector's surface. In solar radiation, *the angle of incidence always equals the angle of reflection*. This is shown graphically in Figure 2.34.

The Laws of Triangles   In order to work with reflected radiation, you will need to know some basic laws about triangles. These mathematical laws come from geometry and trigonometry.

Look at Figure 2.35. The first triangle is called an *oblique triangle*. In an oblique triangle, the sum of the angles equals 180°. An exterior angle equals the sum of the opposite two interior angles.

Next look at triangle 2. This triangle is called an *equilateral triangle*. All the angles are equal. Each angle is 60°. The lengths of the sides are equal, but they can be any length.

Now look at triangle 3. This is called a *right triangle*. In a right triangle, one angle equals 90°. The sum of the other two angles also equals 90°. The sum of the squares of the two shorter sides equals the square of the longest side.

Triangle 4 is an oblique triangle that has been broken into two right triangles by drawing a line from the largest angle to the longest side that is at right angles (perpendicular) to the longest side. This is known as the triangle's *altitude*.

Working with Right Triangles   When a triangle is a right triangle, *trigonometric functions* may be used to determine the size of angles and the lengths of sides. There are six major trigonometric functions of a triangle: the *sine*, the *cosine*, the *tangent*, the *cotangent*, the *secant*, and the *cosecant*. To understand these functions, refer to Figure 2.36.

In a right triangle, the side opposite the right angle is called the *hypotenuse*. The side opposite the angle being discussed is called the *opposite* side. The side that makes up one of the sides of the angle under discussion is called the *adjacent* side. The other side is the hypotenuse.

The trigonometric functions are the ratios between the lengths of the various sides. As the angles change in size, the ratios change. But the ratios are always the same for the same size angles no matter what the length of the sides. These ratios are all shown in Figure 2.36. Note that in writing formulas the name of the trigonometric function is shortened for convenience.

These ratios have been calculated to a high degree of accuracy by mathematicians and placed in tables. Figure 2.37 gives tables of sines, cosines, tangents, and cotangents to work with. Only whole degrees have been shown on these tables. A complete table would contain more detail. In Figure 2.38 some examples have been worked out. The answers are given to the nearest whole degree.

If you know two angles and the length of one side, or the lengths of three sides, or one angle and the length of two sides, you can find the size of the other parts of the triangle with the use of the tables.

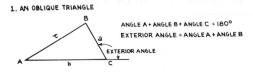

1. AN OBLIQUE TRIANGLE

ANGLE A + ANGLE B + ANGLE C = 180°
EXTERIOR ANGLE = ANGLE A + ANGLE B

2. AN EQUILATERAL TRIANGLE

ANGLE A = ANGLE B = ANGLE C = $\frac{180°}{3}$ = 60°
LENGTH OF A = LENGTH OF B = LENGTH OF C

3. A RIGHT TRIANGLE

WHEN ONE ANGLE = 90°
$a^2 + b^2 = c^2$
ANGLE A + ANGLE B = 90°

4. A TRIANGLE'S ALTITUDE

OBLIQUE TRIANGLES CAN BE SPLIT INTO TWO RIGHT TRIANGLES BY DRAWING A LINE FROM THE LARGEST ANGLE PERPENDICULAR TO THE LONGEST SIDE.

Figure 2.35.   Oblique, equilateral, and right triangles.

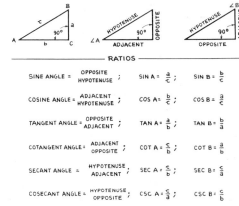

RATIOS

SINE ANGLE = $\frac{OPPOSITE}{HYPOTENUSE}$;	SIN A = $\frac{a}{c}$; SIN B = $\frac{b}{c}$
COSINE ANGLE = $\frac{ADJACENT}{HYPOTENUSE}$;	COS A = $\frac{b}{c}$; COS B = $\frac{a}{c}$
TANGENT ANGLE = $\frac{OPPOSITE}{ADJACENT}$;	TAN A = $\frac{a}{b}$; TAN B = $\frac{b}{a}$
COTANGENT ANGLE = $\frac{ADJACENT}{OPPOSITE}$;	COT A = $\frac{c}{a}$; COT B = $\frac{a}{b}$
SECANT ANGLE = $\frac{HYPOTENUSE}{ADJACENT}$;	SEC A = $\frac{c}{b}$; SEC B = $\frac{c}{a}$
COSECANT ANGLE = $\frac{HYPOTENUSE}{OPPOSITE}$;	CSC A = $\frac{c}{a}$; CSC B = $\frac{c}{b}$

Figure 2.36.   Names of the sides of a right triangle.

RIGHT TRIANGLE

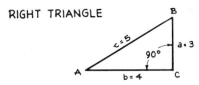

EXAMPLES

1. $a^2 + b^2 = c^2$; $(3)^2 + (4)^2 = (5)^2$; $9 + 16 = 25$

2. SIN A = $\frac{3}{5}$ = .6000
    FROM THE TABLES; ANGLE A = 37° *

3. SIN B = $\frac{4}{5}$ = .8000
    FROM THE TABLES; ANGLE B = 53° *

4. TAN A = $\frac{3}{4}$ = .7500
    FROM THE TABLES; ANGLE A = 37° *

5. TAN B = $\frac{4}{3}$ = 1.333
    FROM THE TABLES; ANGLE B = 53° *

* ANSWERS GIVEN TO THE NEAREST WHOLE DEGREE

Figure 2.38.   Some examples of solving a right triangle.

ANGLE	SINE	COSINE	TANGENT	COTAN-GENT	ANGLE	SINE	COSINE	TANGENT	COTAN-GENT
1	0.0175	0.9998	0.0175	57.29	46	0.7193	0.6947	1.0355	0.9657
2	0.0349	0.9994	0.0349	28.64	47	0.7314	0.6820	1.0724	0.9325
3	0.0523	0.9986	0.0524	19.08	48	0.7431	0.6691	1.1106	0.9004
4	0.0698	0.9976	0.0699	14.30	49	0.7547	0.6561	1.1504	0.8693
5	0.0872	0.9962	0.0875	11.43	50	0.7660	0.6428	1.1918	0.8391
6	0.1045	0.9945	0.1051	9.514	51	0.7771	0.6293	1.2349	0.8098
7	0.1219	0.9925	0.1228	8.144	52	0.7880	0.6157	1.2799	0.7813
8	0.1392	0.9903	0.1405	7.115	53	0.7986	0.6018	1.3270	0.7536
9	0.1564	0.9877	0.1584	6.314	54	0.8090	0.5878	1.3764	0.7265
10	0.1736	0.9848	0.1763	5.671	55	0.8192	0.5736	1.4281	0.7002
11	0.1908	0.9816	0.1944	5.145	56	0.8290	0.5592	1.4826	0.6745
12	0.2079	0.9781	0.2126	4.705	57	0.8387	0.5446	1.5399	0.6494
13	0.2250	0.9744	0.2309	4.331	58	0.8480	0.5299	1.6003	0.6249
14	0.2419	0.9703	0.2493	4.011	59	0.8572	0.5150	1.6643	0.6009
15	0.2588	0.9659	0.2679	3.732	60	0.8660	0.5000	1.732	0.5774
16	0.2756	0.9613	0.2867	3.487	61	0.8746	0.4848	1.804	0.5543
17	0.2924	0.9563	0.3057	3.271	62	0.8829	0.4695	1.881	0.5317
18	0.3090	0.9511	0.3249	3.078	63	0.8910	0.4540	1.963	0.5095
19	0.3256	0.9455	0.3443	2.904	64	0.8988	0.4384	2.050	0.4877
20	0.3420	0.9397	0.3640	2.747	65	0.9063	0.4226	2.145	0.4663
21	0.3584	0.9336	0.3839	2.605	66	0.9135	0.4067	2.246	0.4452
22	0.3746	0.9272	0.4040	2.475	67	0.9205	0.3907	2.356	0.4245
23	0.3907	0.9205	0.4245	2.356	68	0.9272	0.3746	2.475	0.4040
24	0.4067	0.9135	0.4452	2.246	69	0.9336	0.3584	2.605	0.3839
25	0.4226	0.9063	0.4663	2.145	70	0.9397	0.3420	2.747	0.3640
26	0.4384	0.8988	0.4877	2.050	71	0.9455	0.3256	2.904	0.3443
27	0.4540	0.8910	0.5095	1.963	72	0.9511	0.3090	3.078	0.3249
28	0.4695	0.8829	0.5317	1.881	73	0.9563	0.2924	3.271	0.3057
29	0.4848	0.8746	0.5543	1.804	74	0.9613	0.2756	3.487	0.2867
30	0.5000	0.8660	0.5774	1.7321	75	0.9659	0.2588	3.732	0.2679
31	0.5150	0.8572	0.6009	1.6643	76	0.9703	0.2419	4.011	0.2493
32	0.5299	0.8480	0.6249	1.6003	77	0.9744	0.2250	4.331	0.2309
33	0.5446	0.8387	0.6494	1.5399	78	0.9781	0.2079	4.705	0.2126
34	0.5592	0.8290	0.6745	1.4826	79	0.9816	0.1908	5.145	0.1944
35	0.5736	0.8192	0.7002	1.4281	80	0.9848	0.1736	5.671	0.1763
36	0.5878	0.8090	0.7265	1.3764	81	0.9877	0.1564	6.314	0.1584
37	0.6018	0.7986	0.7536	1.3270	82	0.9903	0.1392	7.115	0.1405
38	0.6157	0.7880	0.7813	1.2799	83	0.9925	0.1219	8.144	0.1228
39	0.6293	0.7771	0.8098	1.2349	84	0.9945	0.1045	9.514	0.1051
40	0.6428	0.7660	0.8391	1.1918	85	0.9962	0.0872	11.43	0.0875
41	0.6561	0.7547	0.8693	1.1504	86	0.9976	0.0698	14.30	0.0699
42	0.6691	0.7431	0.9004	1.1106	87	0.9986	0.0523	19.08	0.0524
43	0.6820	0.7314	0.9325	1.0724	88	0.9994	0.0349	28.64	0.0349
44	0.6947	0.7193	0.9657	1.0355	89	0.9998	0.0175	57.29	0.0175
45	0.7071	0.7071	1.0000	1.0000	90	1.000	0.000	—	0.0000

Figure 2.37. Table of trigonometric functions for right triangles.

$$\text{Secant} = \frac{1}{\text{cosine}} \qquad \text{Cosecant} = \frac{1}{\text{sine}}$$

If the triangle is an oblique triangle, the altitude can be drawn and the parts of the triangle may be determined with more complex relationships as shown in Figure 2.39.

TO FIND	WHEN KNOWING	USE THIS FORMULA
a	A B b	b sin A ÷ sin B
a	A B c	c sin A ÷ sin (A + B)
a	A C b	b sin A ÷ sin (A + C)
a	A C c	c sin A ÷ sin C
a	B C b	b sin (B + C) ÷ sin B
a	B C c	c sin (B + C) ÷ sin C
a	A b c	$\sqrt{b^2 + c^2 - 2bc(\cos A)}$
b	A B a	a sin B ÷ sin A
b	A B c	c sin B ÷ sin (A + B)
b	A C a	a sin (A + C) ÷ sin A
b	A C c	c sin (A + C) ÷ sin C
b	B C a	a sin B ÷ sin (B + C)
b	B C c	c sin B ÷ sin C
b	B a c	$\sqrt{a^2 + c^2 - 2ac(\cos B)}$
c	A B a	a sin (A + B) ÷ sin A
c	A B b	b sin (A + B) ÷ sin B
c	A C a	a sin C ÷ sin A
c	A C b	b sin C ÷ sin (A + C)
c	B C a	a sin C ÷ sin (B + C)
c	B C b	b sin C ÷ sin B
c	C a b	$\sqrt{a^2 + b^2 - 2ab(\cos C)}$
A	B a b	sin A = a sin B ÷ b
A	B a c	½(A + C) + ½(A − C)
A	C a b	½(A + B) + ½(A − B)
A	C a c	sin A = a sin C ÷ c
B	A a b	sin B = b sin A ÷ a
B	A b c	½(B + C) + ½(B − C)
B	C a b	½(A + B) − ½(A − B)
B	C a c	sin B = b sin C ÷ c
C	A a c	sin C = C sin A ÷ a
C	A b c	½(B + C) − ½(B − C)
C	B a c	½(A + C) − ¼(A − C)
C	B b c	sin C = c sin B ÷ b
d	a b c	(b² + c² − a²) ÷ 2b
e	a b c	(a² + b² − c²) ÷ 2b
Area	C a b	½ab ÷ sin C

Figure 2.39. Formulas for solving an oblique triangle.

Determining Reflected Radiation Effects

The laws of right triangles are used on the next few pages to describe the effects of reflected radiation. In passive house construction, reflected radiation can add much solar energy to the house, so it is important to understand how reflection can be used.

Vertical Surfaces In the winter when the sun is low in the sky, large amounts of solar energy can be reflected from the ground to the surface of a vertical collector. At 40°N latitude, the sun's rays strike the ground at about a 26° angle at solar noon in December. So the energy striking on a

Tan 26° = 7 ÷ x
Tan 26° = 0.4877
$\qquad$ x = 7 ÷ 0.4877 = 14.35 ft

Tan 50° = 7 ÷ x
Tan 50° = 1.1918
$\qquad$ x = 7 ÷ 1.1918 = 5.87 ft

Tan 74° = 7 ÷ x
Tan 74° = 3.487
$\qquad$ x = 7 ÷ 3.487 = 2.01 ft

horizontal surface for about 14 ft in front of the wall is reflected onto the collector. This is shown in Figure 2.40.

Figure 2.41 shows the same surface with the sun's rays coming from an angle of 50°, as would be seen at the equinox. The energy from about 6 ft in front of the wall is reflected onto the collector.

Figure 2.42 shows the same surface on June 21, the summer solstice. Now the energy from about 2 ft in front of the collector strikes it.

However, in all three cases the same amount of energy is reflected. The amount of solar radiation per square foot is much higher in June than it is in December.

If the ground is sloped away from the vertical sidewall as is shown in Figure 2.43, where the ground is sloped away at a 15° angle, then large amounts of energy can be collected in December, reasonable amounts at the equinox, and no energy in June. The most favorable angle can be calculated using the sun-path diagrams.

If the system demands high rates of solar energy during the summer months, then the ground should be sloped upward as shown in Figure 2.44, where the ground is sloped upward at a 15° angle.

Horizontal Surfaces Reflection from the ground to horizontal collector surfaces is not as apt to happen. Nor is it as easy to contour the landscape to reflect the solar energy deliberately.

Tilted Surfaces The best tilt for direct solar radiation collection during the winter half of the year was shown in Figure 2.31 to be about latitude plus 11 to 12°. Let us now examine that tilt angle for its effect on reflected radiation.

Figure 2.45 shows the reflection angle at the winter solstice. When the collector is tilted at an angle of 52°, the reflected energy from about 2¾ ft in front of the collector strikes it. If the collector is tilted to 90° so that it is vertical, a small loss in direct radiation is seen, but the energy from about

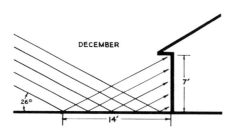

Figure 2.40. The solar reflection angle at 40°N latitude at the winter solstice.

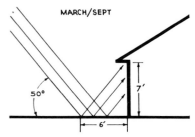

Figure 2.41. The solar reflection angle at 40°N latitude at the equinox.

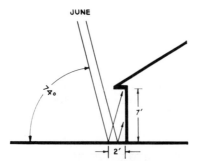

Figure 2.42. The solar reflection angle at 40°N latitude at the summer solstice.

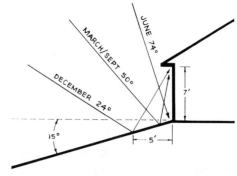

Figure 2.43. Effect of sloping the ground away from a vertical collector.

6 ft of surface in front of the collector is reflected to its surface. That is a large net gain in total energy if the surface has even fair reflectivity.

Figure 2.46 shows the reflection at the equinox. No reflected energy is collected when the collector is tilted at 52°. When the collector is tilted at 90°, there is more loss of direct radiation than there was at the winter solstice, but the reflection from about 2½ ft of surface area is gained. Again, with even fair reflectivity, there should be a net gain in energy collected. So when placing tilted collectors on horizontal surfaces for wintertime collection, a tilt angle of up to 90° may be indicated for maximum total energy collection.

However, when the same situation is examined for a pitched roof, a completely different picture may emerge. In Figure 2.47 a collector is mounted 52° from the horizontal plane on a 30° pitched roof. Now the solar radiation at the winter solstice strikes the roof at an angle of 56°. The reflection angle is 86° from the horizontal plane. Little reflected energy can be collected even when the collector is mounted in a vertical position. So on pitched roofs, care should be taken to examine the angles of incidence and reflection carefully before deciding on a final tilt angle.

Reflectance The amount of the energy that reflects from a given surface is a function of the composition, the smoothness, and the color of the surface. Reflectance is usually stated in percentage of energy reflected. Figure 2.48 gives some reflectance values for common surfaces. Other materials that are not in the table due to lack of data but that have high reflectance are marble chips, beach sand, white painted surfaces, and highly polished metal surfaces. You can be guided by the amount of light reflectance. Energy reflectance will be similar.

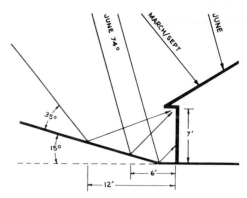

Figure 2.44. Effect of sloping the ground toward a vertical collector.

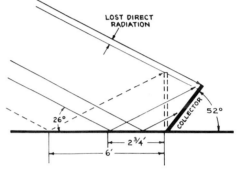

Figure 2.45. The collector angle at the winter solstice must be increased to gain the maximum energy collection.

SURFACE TYPE	TYPICAL REFLECTANCE IN %
Aluminum foil	92-97
Aluminum sheet	80-95
Aluminum paper, polished	75-84
Aluminum paint	30-70
Bituminous driveway	10-12
Concrete, new	30-35
Concrete, old	20-25
Green grass	20-30
Snow, clean	65-75
Tar and gravel roof	13-15

Figure 2.48. Table of typical solar reflectances.

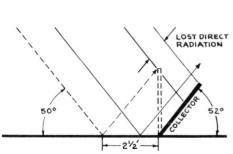

Figure 2.46. An increase of collector angle at the equinox contributes to an increased total energy collection.

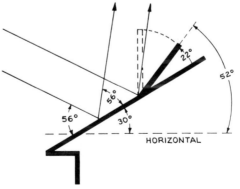

Figure 2.47. An increased collector angle on a pitched roof will most likely not increase energy collection.

Making a Decision

In this chapter you learned the basics about solar radiation. First you studied latitude and longitude so that you could determine your location on the earth. Then you studied the earth's orbit around the sun, where you learned about the changing seasons and the changing intensity of solar radiation with location and time.

You also learned that the amount of solar radiation at any given point on the earth could be quickly estimated using sun-path diagrams and radiation calculators, but also that the direct radiation shown on these diagrams only told part of the total radiation picture and that the sunshine index had to be used to calculate the effects of cloud cover. Last you learned that solar radiation could be reflected and you studied reflection principles and effects.

The basic information that you learned in this chapter will make it possible for you to make many informed decisions as you design and build your solar system.

DECISION 3

Calculate Your Available Solar Energy

If you can look across the street and see your neighbor's home, then you are receiving some measurable solar energy. For much of solar energy is light. Even on the cloudiest of days, you can usually see across the street quite clearly. But as you learned in Decision 2, that energy can vary from as much as 365 Btu/hr/sq ft to as little as 21 Btu/hr/sq ft, depending on the clearness and the cloud cover.

You can take the daily reports of your weather bureau and calculate day-by-day how much solar energy is available in your area. But this is a long, time-consuming task that will take many days to complete. And it involves hundreds of individual calculations.

A number of special computer programs are available to accomplish these calculations. These programs contain the weather and the sun data for hundreds of different locations. Twenty-four of these locations have been chosen for use in this book to give you representative data that you can rely on.

In this chapter you will:

- Study solar radiation variability and data.
- Break the country down into 24 solar radiation blocks and solar radiation tables.
- Learn how to calculate the amount of solar radiation striking your building.
- Tabulate the available solar energy by month and by season.

When you have finished, you will know just how much solar energy you have to work with.

Solar Radiation Variability

There is no way to predict accurately how much solar radiation will be available tomorrow, or next Thursday, or a week from Sunday. It is possible to predict fairly accurately how much solar radiation will be available during the month of December or March or any other month. But again, considerable variation will exist. The solar radiation during a year can be predicted more accurately. The average radiation over a number of years can be predicted very accurately.

Solar Radiation Data

Solar radiation data exist for the entire United States. The most useful data are in *The Climatic Atlas of the United States,* which is available from the U.S. Government Printing Office. Check your local library for a copy. This publication gives maps of annual and monthly values of percentage of possible sunshine, total hours of sunshine, mean solar radiation, mean sky cover, wind speed, and wind direction.

On a local level, the best source of information is the local records of the weather bureau, now known as NOAA, the National Oceanographic and Atmospheric Administration.

This solar radiation data base, which is constantly being updated and improved, has been studied extensively by a number of researchers. From these studies, researchers have developed computer programs that can be used to predict the amount of radiation that will occur over a number of years in almost any given location.

A computer program developed by researchers at the University of Wisconsin, known as *F-Chart,* will be used in this book to give you reliable solar data that can be used in your location. You will not need to research the solar data for yourself.

The Needed Solar Radiation Data

Figure 3.1 shows the basic solar design data that you will need. You will need monthly design data for horizontal, vertical, and tilted surfaces. As your structure may not face directly south, you will need this data for a number of directions, as shown in Figure 3.2. Design data will be provided for structures that face east, southeast, south, southwest, and west. The data will be presented as monthly averages for 100 sq ft of surface area.

Radiation Data Blocks

Figure 3.3 shows the United States divided into 24 geographic blocks. First the country was divided into six north-south strips using the 75th, 85th, 95th, 105th, 115th, and 125th meridians of longitude. Then it was further subdivided east to west using the 30th, 35th, 40th, 45th, and 50th parallels of latitude. Then a major weather data station for each block was chosen.

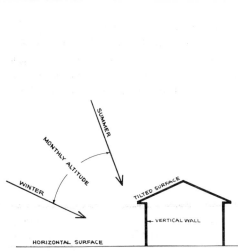

Figure 3.1. The solar design data that you will need.

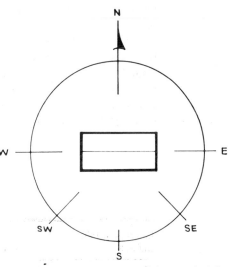

Figure 3.2. Design data will be needed for five orientations. This building faces south.

Solar Radiation Tables

More than 250 weather stations in the United States are collecting solar data under NOAA's *SOLMET* (*solar meteorological*) project. SOLMET is a national program to assess the amount of solar radiation available throughout the United States more accurately. This data has been collected and placed in the F-Chart program by the University of Wisconsin. Complete details on F-Chart are available in a report titled *EES Report 49-3, Chart Users Manual* from the Systems Analysis branch of the Solar Energy Research Institute, Golden, Colorado 80401. F-Chart is presently considered the best available program for analyzing solar system performance.

John Wiley & Sons, Inc., has published two major textbooks covering F-Chart design in depth: *Solar Energy Thermal Processes* (J. A. Duffie and W. A. Beckman, 1974) and *Solar Heating Design by the F-Chart Method* (J. A. Duffie, W. A. Beckman, and S. A. Klein, 1977). Readers desiring more information on the methodology are referred to these texts.

Figure 3.3. The United States divided into 24 geographic blocks.

Estimating Solar Radiation Data

Estimating solar radiation data is complex and requires the use of higher mathematics. Many authors of passive solar books have chosen to use the direct and diffuse radiation data and to perform trigonometric analysis. Such analysis gives a relatively poor result as compared to the sophisticated analysis of F-Chart, which integrates all the known factors relating to the amount of energy falling on a unit area of collecting surface monthly. The reader is urged to make maximum use of the F-Chart data in order to obtain the best solar radiation data available at this time.

The Selected Weather Stations

Obviously to include all the design data for 250 plus weather stations in this book would be impractical. And unnecessary, as the stations chosen are quite representative of the geographic blocks unless you live at a different elevation or near a large body of water. If better design data is desired for a large commercial installation, the Solar Energy Research

Institute in Golden, Colorado, should be consulted for additional F-Chart data.

One weather station has been chosen for each of the 24 geographic blocks shown in Figure 3.3. These stations are listed in Figure 3.4. Each station has been given a number that corresponds to the number assigned to the geographic block in which it is located. Once you have determined which block you are located in, you can proceed to use that number in reading the solar radiation tables.

GEOGRAPHIC BLOCK	CITY	STATE	APPROX. LATITUDE
1.	Spokane	Washington	47°N
2.	Great Falls	Montana	47°N
3.	Fargo	North Dakota	47°N
4.	Duluth	Minnesota	47°N
5.	Sault Sainte Marie	Michigan	46°N
6.	Caribou	Maine	47°N
7.	Medford	Oregon	42°N
8.	Pocatello	Idaho	43°N
9.	Lincoln	Nebraska	41°N
10.	Chicago	Illinois	42°N
11.	Rochester	New York	43°N
12.	Blue Hills	Massachusetts	42°N
13.	Fresno	California	36°N
14.	Grand Junction	Colorado	39°N
15.	Wichita	Kansas	37°N
16.	St. Louis	Missouri	38°N
17.	Greensboro	North Carolina	36°N
18.	Atlantic City	New Jersey	39°N
19.	San Diego	California	32°N
20.	Phoenix	Arizona	33°N
21.	Fort Worth	Texas	33°N
22.	Jackson	Mississippi	32°N
23.	Charleston	South Carolina	33°N
24.	Tampa	Florida	28°N

Figure 3.4. The weather stations representing each geographic block.

The Solar Radiation Tables

Four solar radiation tables have been tabulated by running F-Chart for the 24 listed weather stations and determining the amount of solar radiation falling monthly on 100 sq ft of collecting surface. These tables are:

Figure 3.5. Monthly Solar Radiation on a Horizontal Surface.
Figure 3.6. Monthly Solar Radiation on a South-facing Vertical Surface.
Figure 3.7. Monthly Solar Radiation on a Southeast- or Southwest-facing Vertical Surface.
Figure 3.8. Monthly Solar Radiation on an East- or West-facing Vertical Surface.

GEOGRAPHIC BLOCK	JAN	FEB	MAR	APRIL	MAY	JUNE	JULY	AUG	SEPT	OCT	NOV	DEC	TOTAL
1.	1.35	2.20	3.62	5.16	6.35	6.69	7.58	6.33	4.50	2.35	1.45	0.87	48.46
2.	1.58	2.36	4.14	4.74	5.99	6.54	7.26	6.05	4.47	2.99	1.70	1.28	49.10
3.	1.45	2.20	3.52	4.63	5.76	5.82	6.33	5.43	3.85	2.77	1.45	1.35	44.55
4.	1.52	2.18	3.67	4.41	5.52	6.11	6.33	5.34	3.68	2.65	1.40	1.19	44.00
5.	1.52	2.33	4.07	4.63	6.01	6.08	6.55	5.45	3.56	2.47	1.16	1.09	44.93
6.	1.57	2.37	4.19	4.42	5.42	5.31	5.82	5.14	3.68	2.40	1.22	1.21	42.76
7.	1.35	2.19	3.79	5.35	6.73	7.22	7.99	6.88	4.97	3.18	1.68	1.05	52.38
8.	1.89	2.58	4.17	5.75	6.63	7.24	7.71	6.74	5.25	3.77	2.27	1.77	55.78
9.	2.17	2.63	3.97	4.69	5.67	6.03	6.14	5.81	4.56	3.71	2.29	1.97	49.62
10.	1.95	2.39	3.73	4.31	5.68	6.12	6.02	5.55	4.25	3.03	1.74	1.50	46.27
11.	1.54	2.07	3.45	4.40	5.87	6.33	6.56	5.60	4.10	2.88	1.59	1.30	45.71
12.	1.78	2.22	3.47	4.19	5.38	5.72	5.71	4.96	3.89	2.85	1.75	1.47	43.40
13.	2.13	3.06	5.01	6.03	7.28	7.71	7.63	6.93	5.56	4.29	2.67	1.83	60.11
14.	2.65	3.35	4.91	5.90	6.91	7.83	7.67	6.64	5.54	4.32	2.91	2.47	61.11
15.	2.54	2.95	4.37	5.22	6.22	6.66	6.66	6.16	4.94	3.93	2.71	2.26	54.62
16.	2.01	2.54	3.95	4.76	6.05	6.33	6.49	5.71	4.62	3.52	2.30	1.76	50.04
17.	2.35	2.81	4.05	5.19	6.09	6.22	6.18	5.43	4.56	3.76	2.69	2.13	51.44
18.	2.02	2.63	4.40	4.78	5.63	6.34	6.49	5.45	4.34	3.45	2.33	1.82	49.69
19.	3.03	3.54	4.89	5.13	5.63	5.64	6.25	5.70	4.93	4.13	3.14	2.80	54.82
20.	3.39	4.21	5.95	7.11	8.27	8.18	7.45	6.99	6.28	5.17	3.75	3.20	69.97
21.	2.88	3.31	4.86	5.45	6.41	7.10	6.99	6.72	5.53	4.50	3.30	2.79	59.85
22.	2.42	2.89	4.32	5.33	6.26	6.22	6.22	5.84	4.74	4.13	2.75	2.31	53.43
23.	2.89	3.13	4.48	5.70	6.29	6.19	5.98	5.67	4.51	3.92	3.15	2.47	54.37
24.	3.74	4.04	5.45	6.03	6.80	6.34	6.09	5.66	5.02	4.63	3.95	3.45	61.19

Figure 3.5. Monthly solar radiation on a horizontal surface in MM/Btu/100 sq ft/mo.

GEOGRAPHIC BLOCK	JAN	FEB	MAR	APRIL	MAY	JUNE	JULY	AUG	SEPT	OCT	NOV	DEC	TOTAL
1.	3.06	3.72	3.99	3.64	3.22	2.93	3.44	3.85	4.23	3.25	2.97	1.85	40.15
2.	3.84	4.10	4.72	3.31	3.04	2.87	3.32	3.67	4.18	4.51	3.74	3.39	44.67
3.	3.21	3.57	3.74	3.17	2.89	2.58	2.92	3.24	3.41	3.91	2.80	3.44	38.89
4.	3.43	3.51	3.93	3.00	2.79	2.68	2.92	3.18	3.23	3.69	2.67	2.83	37.87
5.	3.38	3.83	4.46	3.15	2.99	2.66	2.99	3.23	3.09	3.31	1.95	2.42	37.44
6.	3.59	3.97	4.68	3.01	2.74	2.40	2.73	3.07	3.24	3.22	2.71	1.68	37.70
7.	2.16	2.93	3.60	3.33	2.99	2.71	3.09	3.66	4.10	3.98	2.71	1.68	36.94
8.	3.65	3.72	4.09	3.61	2.97	2.74	3.06	3.62	4.43	5.07	4.25	3.86	45.07
9.	3.98	3.52	3.62	2.80	2.51	2.32	2.49	3.00	3.54	4.60	3.88	3.95	40.21
10.	3.63	3.23	3.46	2.63	2.57	2.40	2.52	2.96	3.36	3.65	2.75	2.83	36.00
11.	2.80	2.81	3.28	2.78	2.73	2.54	2.78	3.08	3.35	3.60	2.62	2.52	34.91
12.	3.28	2.97	3.22	2.59	2.49	2.32	2.45	2.70	3.08	3.43	2.86	2.86	34.25
13.	3.16	3.69	4.27	3.23	2.70	2.35	2.54	3.14	3.98	4.82	3.98	2.86	40.72
14.	4.90	4.62	4.51	3.39	2.81	2.57	2.76	3.26	4.26	5.35	5.07	5.06	48.54
15.	4.24	3.65	3.72	2.89	2.50	2.28	2.43	2.93	3.58	4.44	4.24	4.07	40.97
16.	3.21	3.10	3.41	2.71	2.51	2.28	2.46	2.82	3.41	3.99	3.54	3.00	36.44
17.	3.59	3.26	3.29	2.79	2.39	2.12	2.25	2.55	3.16	4.02	3.95	3.48	36.84
18.	3.37	3.35	3.96	2.77	2.43	2.32	2.51	2.76	3.24	4.00	3.75	3:29	37.76
19.	4.36	3.91	3.72	2.53	2.08	1.85	2.06	2.44	3.14	4.04	4.23	4.34	38.72
20.	5.28	5.06	4.79	3.40	2.55	2.10	2.27	2.88	4.15	5.54	5.59	5.44	49.06
21.	4.08	3.60	3.70	2.67	2.25	2.02	2.17	2.75	3.55	4.52	4.53	4.33	40.16
22.	3.18	2.99	3.22	2.60	2.20	1.92	2.05	2.46	3.00	4.01	3.51	3.28	34.43
23.	4.11	3.35	3.38	2.78	2.22	1.93	2.02	2.43	2.87	3.81	4.27	3.66	36.83
24.	4.82	3.98	3.70	2.54	2.00	1.71	1.80	2.14	2.84	4.05	4.82	4.75	39.14

Figure 3.6. Monthly solar radiation on a south-facing vertical surface in MMBtu/100 sq ft/mo.

GEOGRAPHIC BLOCK	JAN	FEB	MAR	APRIL	MAY	JUNE	JULY	AUG	SEPT	OCT	NOV	DEC	TOTAL
1.	2.34	3.02	3.70	4.05	4.01	3.82	4.53	4.57	4.22	2.76	2.30	1.42	40.74
2.	2.90	3.32	4.36	3.66	3.77	3.73	4.33	4.33	4.17	3.79	2.87	2.53	43.78
3.	2.45	2.91	3.48	3.52	3.59	3.30	3.74	3.80	3.42	3.32	2.19	2.58	38.32
4.	2.61	2.87	3.67	3.33	3.43	3.46	3.74	3.73	3.24	3.13	2.09	2.14	37.45
5.	2.58	3.12	4.15	3.50	3.74	3.44	3.86	3.81	3.10	2.83	1.55	1.84	37.51
6.	2.73	3.23	4.34	3.34	3.37	3.02	3.44	3.58	3.24	2.75	1.69	2.20	36.94
7.	1.72	2.46	3.44	3.84	3.96	3.84	4.42	4.58	4.22	3.44	2.17	1.33	39.44
8.	2.83	3.09	3.89	4.18	3.92	3.87	4.30	4.51	4.56	4.35	3.32	2.94	45.75
9.	3.10	2.96	3.49	3.24	3.27	3.19	3.37	3.73	3.68	3.99	3.07	3.03	40.13
10.	2.83	2.71	3.31	3.00	3.32	3.27	3.36	3.62	3.47	3.18	2.21	2.19	36.47
11.	2.19	2.36	3.12	3.14	3.50	3.44	3.71	3.73	3.43	3.11	2.09	1.95	35.77
12.	2.56	2.50	3.08	2.93	3.17	3.09	3.21	3.24	3.17	2.98	2.28	2.21	34.42
13.	2.54	3.16	4.22	3.98	3.95	3.76	3.91	4.21	4.29	4.27	3.21	2.27	43.76
14.	3.82	3.87	4.37	4.05	3.90	3.96	4.07	4.20	4.50	4.65	4.00	3.86	49.24
15.	3.34	3.11	3.66	3.47	3.44	3.36	3.50	3.79	3.81	3.93	3.39	3.16	41.97
16.	2.55	2.65	3.33	3.19	3.40	3.25	3.47	3.56	3.60	3.52	2.84	2.35	37.71
17.	2.87	2.81	3.26	3.38	3.32	3.11	3.22	3.28	3.39	3.59	3.20	2.74	38.17
18.	2.66	2.84	3.84	3.24	3.21	3.29	3.50	3.43	3.40	3.51	2.99	2.55	38.48
19.	3.51	3.41	3.79	3.18	2.97	2.75	3.12	3.29	3.49	3.69	3.47	4.43	40.10
20.	4.20	4.36	4.85	4.50	4.22	3.77	3.67	4.05	4.64	4.98	4.51	4.24	51.99
21.	3.29	3.15	3.77	3.38	3.34	3.34	3.44	3.86	3.96	4.10	3.70	3.42	42.76
22.	2.60	2.64	3.28	3.29	3.26	2.98	3.10	3.35	3.33	3.67	2.91	2.64	37.04
23.	3.32	2.94	3.44	3.54	3.28	2.98	3.00	3.27	3.17	3.47	3.50	2.92	38.83
24.	3.95	3.57	3.93	3.50	3.31	2.87	2.89	3.08	3.31	3.81	4.03	3.82	42.06

Figure 3.7. Monthly solar radiation on a southeast- or southwest-facing vertical surface in MMBtu/100 sq ft/mo.

GEOGRAPHIC BLOCKS	JAN	FEB	MAR	APRIL	MAY	JUNE	JULY	AUG	SEPT	OCT	NOV	DEC	TOTAL
1.	1.21	1.86	2.81	3.73	4.32	4.44	5.13	4.50	3.43	1.88	1.26	0.74	35.32
2.	1.46	2.02	3.27	3.39	4.05	4.33	4.90	4.27	3.40	2.49	1.53	1.20	36.30
3.	1.28	1.83	2.68	3.28	3.86	3.80	4.21	3.77	2.84	2.23	1.23	1.25	32.27
4.	1.36	1.80	2.81	3.11	3.69	4.00	4.20	3.70	2.71	2.12	1.18	1.07	31.75
5.	1.35	1.95	3.15	3.27	4.04	3.98	4.35	3.78	2.60	1.94	0.93	0.94	32.27
6.	1.41	2.00	3.27	3.11	3.62	3.46	3.84	3.55	2.71	1.89	0.99	1.09	30.95
7.	1.04	1.67	2.75	3.68	4.41	4.64	5.21	4.68	3.58	2.42	1.32	0.80	36.21
8.	1.57	2.03	3.07	3.99	4.35	4.66	5.04	4.59	3.83	2.96	1.89	1.52	39.49
9.	1.76	2.00	2.83	3.14	3.65	3.81	3.91	3.85	3.19	2.81	1.82	1.63	34.40
10.	1.60	1.83	2.67	2.90	3.68	3.89	3.86	3.70	2.99	2.27	1.35	1.21	31.95
11.	1.25	1.59	2.50	3.00	3.85	4.06	4.26	3.78	2.93	2.19	1.26	1.07	31.74
12.	1.45	1.69	2.49	2.82	3.49	3.64	3.67	3.30	2.74	2.13	1.38	1.21	30.00
13.	1.58	2.22	3.49	3.98	4.62	4.80	4.80	4.51	3.81	3.11	2.01	1.37	40.32
14.	2.15	2.57	3.52	3.97	4.45	3.95	4.89	4.39	3.90	3.27	2.34	2.05	42.45
15.	1.97	2.17	3.04	3.44	3.94	4.15	4.19	4.01	3.39	2.86	2.08	1.78	37.03
16.	1.54	1.86	2.76	3.14	3.85	3.96	4.10	3.73	3.18	2.57	1.76	1.36	33.82
17.	1.77	2.01	2.76	3.39	3.83	3.85	3.85	3.48	3.07	2.68	2.02	1.62	34.33
18.	1.58	1.96	3.13	3.18	3.60	3.98	4.12	3.57	2.99	2.54	1.82	1.44	33.90
19.	2.21	2.49	3.28	3.28	3.48	3.44	3.84	3.60	3.25	2.85	2.27	2.07	36.07
20.	2.55	3.05	4.09	4.64	5.19	5.03	4.61	4.46	4.23	3.69	2.81	2.44	46.78
21.	2.09	2.32	3.26	3.49	3.98	4.34	4.31	4.26	3.67	3.14	2.40	2.06	39.32
22.	1.72	1.99	2.87	3.41	3.88	3.79	3.82	3.68	3.11	2.84	1.96	1.66	34.73
23.	2.10	2.18	2.99	3.66	3.90	3.78	3.67	3.58	2.96	2.70	2.28	1.80	35.60
24.	2.61	2.73	3.55	3.78	4.14	3.81	3.68	3.50	3.21	3.08	2.75	2.43	39.28

Figure 3.8. Monthly solar radiation on an east- or west-facing vertical surface in MMBtu/100 sq ft/mo.

These four tables provide enough data so that trigonometric *interpolation* of the results can be performed with a fair degree of accuracy for other tilt angles and directions. Interpolation is the process of estimating an unknown value from two known values.

Look at Figure 3.5 and note the data for geographic area number 9, which is Lincoln, Nebraska. In the column headed Total, you will see that 100 sq ft of horizontal collector surface will collect 49.62 MMBtu/yr on the average over a number of years. Go to Figure 3.6 and read the same line and column. You will see that a south-facing vertical surface of 100 sq ft in the same location will collect 40.21 MMBtu in an average year. However, if you examine the data for each month, you will see that the collection on a horizontal surface is better in the summer months whereas the collection on a vertical surface is better during the winter months.

The data from the four radiation tables for geographic area 9 have been tabulated in Figure 3.9 for discussion and comparison. Below the 12-month data, the radiation for the heating season has been tabulated. This is the five months of November through March that represent 83% of the annual heating needs.

An analysis of the data will show that the vertical collector facing from south to within 45° of south will give the most energy at the time it is needed for heating. Further analysis would also show that if the choice of collecting surface were limited to vertical or horizontal surfaces, the horizontal surface would give the most radiation if the collecting surface were to be used to power air conditioning in the summer months. Of course, the installlation of a surface tilted at the best angle for the latitude would outperform either the vertical or horizontal surface.

MONTH	HORIZONTAL INCIDENT SOLAR	SOUTH VERTICAL INCIDENT SOLAR	SE/SW VERTICAL INCIDENT SOLAR	E/W VERTICAL INCIDENT SOLAR
January	2.17	3.98	3.10	1.76
February	2.63	3.52	2.96	2.00
March	3.97	3.62	3.49	2.83
April	4.69	2.80	3.24	3.14
May	5.67	2.51	3.27	3.65
June	6.03	2.32	3.19	3.81
July	6.14	2.49	3.37	3.91
August	5.81	3.00	3.73	3.85
September	4.56	3.54	3.68	3.19
October	3.71	4.60	3.99	2.81
November	2.29	3.88	3.07	1.82
December	1.97	3.95	3.03	1.63
Total	49.62	40.21	40.13	34.40
November	2.29	3.88	3.07	1.82
December	1.97	3.95	3.03	1.63
January	2.17	3.98	3.10	1.76
February	2.63	3.52	2.96	2.00
March	3.97	3.62	3.49	2.83
Total	13.03	18.95	15.65	10.04
% Total	26%	47%	39%	29%

Figure 3.9. Radiation data for Lincoln, Nebraska, at different collector angles and directions.

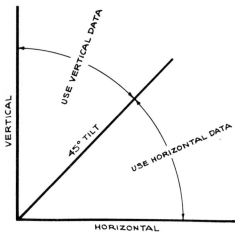

Figure 3.10. Proper data to use in interpolation of odd angles.

Figure 3.11. Tilt angle factors for vertical radiation data.

Interpolating from the Radiation Tables

Solar radiation data for tilted surfaces are found by multiplying the horizontal or the vertical data by a tilt angle factor. For tilt angles from 0 to 45°, use the horizontal data. For tilt angles from 45 to 90°, use the vertical data. This will give you the most accuracy. Figure 3.10 shows the details.

A table of tilt angle factors has been calculated for you in Figures 3.11 and 3.12. The relationships are essentially linear, so that angles falling between the ones shown can be interpolated with good accuracy.

SUN'S ALTITUDE	COLLECTOR TILT ANGLES			
	80°	70°	60°	50°
20	1.05	1.06	1.05	1.00
30	1.09	1.14	1.15	1.14
40	1.13	1.23	1.29	1.31
50	1.19	1.35	1.46	1.53
60	1.29	1.53	1.73	1.88
70	1.46	1.88	2.24	2.53

SUN'S ALTITUDE	COLLECTOR TILT ANGLES			
	40°	30°	20°	10°
20	2.53	2.24	1.88	1.46
30	1.88	1.73	1.53	1.29
40	1.53	1.46	1.35	1.19
50	1.31	1.29	1.23	1.13
60	1.14	1.15	1.14	1.90
70	1.00	1.05	1.06	1.05

Figure 3.12. Tilt angle factors for horizontal radiation data.

How the Tables Were Calculated The tables in Figures 3.11 and 3.12 were calculated using trigonometric functions of the sun's altitude ($\angle a$) and the collector tilt angle ($\angle t$). Figure 3.13 shows the formula used for the factors in Figure 3.12, while Figure 3.14 shows the formula used for the factors in Figure 3.11.

In Figure 3.13 the same amount of energy falls on the horizontal surface (by) and the tilted surface (cy). The relative area of the horizontal surface to the area of the tilted surface is dependent on the length of line c versus the length of line b, since y is the same on both surfaces.

The tilt angle factor is determined by comparing the size of area by to area cy. For example, when

b = 1 ft
y = 1 ft
$\angle a$ = 30°
$\angle t$ = 40°

then

$$c = \frac{\sin a}{\sin (a + t)} = \frac{0.5000}{0.9397} = 0.532$$

and when

c = 0.532 ft
b = 1 ft

then

cy = 0.532 sq ft
by = 1 sq ft

By inspection, the energy falling on surface by equals the energy falling on on surface cy, so

$$\frac{cy}{by} = \frac{0.532}{1}$$

and when,
cy = 1 sq ft
then

$$\frac{1}{0.532} = 1.88 \text{ units of energy/sq ft}$$

and surface cy receives 1.88 units of energy per square foot.

The tilt angle factor describes the amount of energy falling on 1 sq ft of tilted surface when 1 unit of energy is falling on 1 sq ft of horizontal surface. For example, when,

by = 50 Btu/hr/sq ft
tilt angle factor = 1.88
then
cy = (by)(tilt angle factor)
cy = (50)(1.88) = 94 Btu/hr/sq ft

The tilt angle factor multiplied by 100 gives the percent energy falling on 1 sq ft of tilted surface compared to the energy falling on 1 sq ft of horizontal surface. For the preceding example, the tilted surface receives 188% of the energy falling on the horizontal surface or 88% more energy per square foot.

Figure 3.14 shows the formula that was used to calculate the tilt angle factors used in the table in Figure 3.11. The same mathematical procedures are followed.

Calculating Odd Angles In many cases, you will be using angles that fall between the angles shown on the tables. Determining the factors that you should use is done by *interpolation*.

The data shown are essentially linear or straight-line, so interpolation can be carried out using *ratio analysis*. Ratio analysis is best described by showing you an example.

Let us assume that you wish to calculate a tilt angle factor for a 23° sun altitude using the data in Figure 3.11. As shown in Figure 3.15, the difference in sun altitudes between 20 and 30° is equal to 10° whereas the difference in tilt angle factors at a 40° tilt angle is 0.65. So the ratio of 3 to 10 is equivalent to the ratio between ? and 0.65 or ? = 0.195. Subtracting 0.195 from 2.53, the tilt angle factor for 23° sun altitude at a 40° tilt angle is 2.34 (rounded).

SUN'S ALTITUDE	TILT ANGLE FACTOR
20°	2.53
23°	?
30°	1.88
10° difference	0.65 difference

$$\frac{3}{10} = \frac{?}{0.65}$$

? = 0.195

23° tilt angle factor = 2.53 − 0.195 or 2.335 (2.34 rounded)

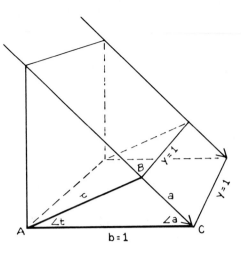

c = b Sine C ÷ Sine (A+C)

$$\frac{1}{c} = \frac{\text{Sine}(\angle t + \angle a)}{\text{Sine}\angle a}$$

$$c = \frac{\text{Sine}\angle a}{\text{Sine}(\angle t + \angle a)}$$

Figure 3.13. Determining the amount of energy that falls on a tilted surface when using horizontal data.

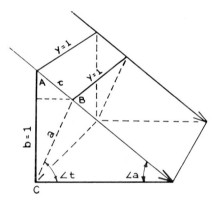

a = b Sine A ÷ Sine (A+C)

$$a = \frac{1 \times \text{Sine}(90° - \angle a)}{\text{Sine}[(90° - \angle a) + (90° - \angle t)]}$$

$$\frac{1}{a} = \frac{\text{Sine}[(90° - \angle a) + (90° - \angle t)]}{\text{Sine}(90° - \angle a)}$$

Figure 3.14. Determining the amount of energy that falls on a tilted surface using vertical radiation data.

Figure 3.15. Interpolating the tilt angle factor for an odd altitude.

Calculate the Energy **35**

Figure 3.16 shows how to perform an interpolation for an odd tilt angle. The same procedure is followed. This gives a tilt angle factor of 2.39 (rounded) for a tilt angle of 35° at 20° altitude.

SUN'S ALTITUDE	TILT ANGLE FACTOR		
	40°	35°	30°
20	2.53	?	2.24

40° − 30° = 10° tilt angle difference

2.53 − 2.24 = 0.29 tilt angle factor difference

$$\frac{5}{10} = \frac{?}{0.29}$$

? = 0.145

35° tilt angle factor equals 2.53 − 0.145 = 2.385 (2.39 rounded)

Figure 3.16. Interpolating the tilt angle factor for an odd tilt angle.

If the tilt angle factor for a 45° tilt angle and a 23° altitude were needed, a double interpolation would be required. This is shown in Figure 3.17. First, interpolate for the tilt angle factor at 30° tilt angle and 23° altitude. This is 2.08. Then interpolate for the tilt angle factor at 35° tilt angle and 23° altitude. This is 2.24.

SUN'S ALTITUDE	TILT ANGLE FACTOR			
	40°	35°	30°	
20	2.53		2.24	
23	2.39	?	(2.08)	0.31 difference
30	1.88		1.73	

$$\frac{3}{10} = \frac{?}{0.51} \qquad ? = 0.153$$

2.24 − 0.153 = 2.08

$$\frac{5}{10} = \frac{?}{0.31} \qquad ? = 0.155$$

2.39 − 0.155 = 2.24 (rounded)

Figure 3.17. A double interpolation.

Your Solar Radiation Availability

To determine the availability of solar radiation at your building, you must know the building's orientation; its size; the tilt angles of the walls, roof, and ground; and the extent of any shading that will interfere with the sun's rays.

Building Orientation

Building orientation is a determination of the direction that the structure faces. In Figure 3.18, side *a* faces south, side *b* faces west, side *c* faces north, and side *d* faces east.

You can determine a building's orientation in three common ways: by using a compass and correcting for magnetic deviation, by observing the sun's location at solar noon when it is due south, or by observing the location of the North Star on a clear night.

If the structure shown were located in Lincoln, Nebraska, and had a flat roof, then side *a* would see 402,100 Btu/sq ft/yr, sides *b* and *d* would each see 344,000 Btu/sq ft/yr, and the roof would see 496,200 Btu/sq ft/yr.

Building Size

If the structure were 25 ft wide, 50 ft long, and if the sidewalls were 8 ft high, then the structure would see 278.9 MMBtu over the heating season. The details are shown in Figure 3.19.

The Ground Reflection

Additional radiation will strike the ground around the building. If the ground is composed of reflective materials and if it is pitched at the proper tilt angle, additional energy would be reflected onto the walls of the structure and would add to the structure's radiation collection. This reflected energy can be very substantial.

The Shading

The building may be shaded by trees, other structures, or other obstacles. If the shading protrudes into the solar window, then the amount of energy that is blocked must be deducted from the total energy received. This blocked energy, just like reflected energy, can also be very substantial.

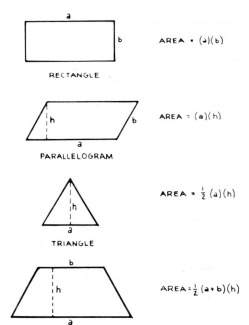

Figure 3.21. Formulas for calculating roof areas.

Determine the Square Feet of Surface Area

Most building structures are more complex in shape than the simple flat-roof structure shown in Figure 3.19. A method of determining the size of the various wall and roof areas must be established in order to work with accuracy.

You need to be concerned with nine basic building roof styles: gable, hip, gambrel, flat, mansard, salt box, cape cod, contemporary gable, and split gable. These nine basic building roof styles can be combined into many complex shapes. Figure 3.20 shows these nine basic building roof styles. These roof shapes consist of rectangles, triangles, parallelograms, and trapezoids. Their area can be calculated using the simple formulas shown in Figure 3.21.

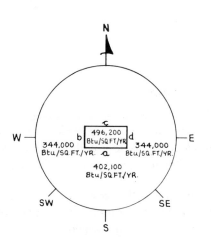

Figure 3.18. Building orientation and solar radiation per direction of orientation for Lincoln, Nebraska.

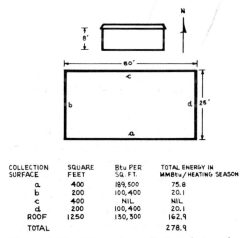

COLLECTION SURFACE	SQUARE FEET	Btu PER SQ. FT.	TOTAL ENERGY IN MMBtu/HEATING SEASON
a	400	189,500	75.8
b	200	100,400	20.1
c	400	NIL	NIL
d	200	100,400	20.1
ROOF	1250	130,300	162.9
TOTAL			278.9

Figure 3.19. The solar radiation during the heating season on a 25 ft x 50 ft x 8 ft flat-roof building in Lincoln, Nebraska.

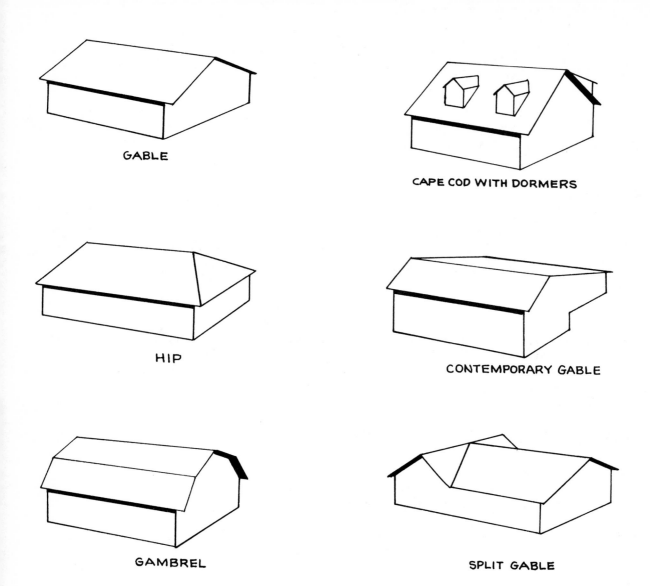

Figure 3.20. Nine basic building roof styles.

Mercator Projections of Building Structures

You will recall from Decision 2 that a Mercator projection is the projection of a three-dimensional object onto a flat surface. That nomenclature is usually reserved for maps of the earth. However, here it will be applied to a building structure. Figure 3.22 is a Mercator projection of the gable house shown in Figure 3.20.

To make this projection, it was pretended that the structure was only a cardboard model. This model was cut along one corner, up the edge of the roof to the ridgepole, and along the length of the ridgepole.

This cut-up model was then flattened out on a surface and resulted in the shapes shown in Figure 3.22. Now the area of each surface, its tilt

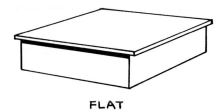

FLAT

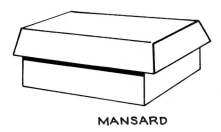

MANSARD

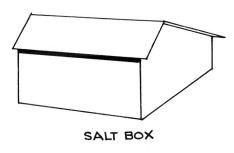

SALT BOX

angle, and the direction that it faces can easily be determined. Note that the ground has been included so that the reflected energy can be calculated.

Determine the Tilt Angles

Vertical walls have a 90° tilt angle. Flat roofs have a 0° tilt angle. Pitched roofs and the ground surrounding the house have unknown tilt angles that you must measure in order to determine the amount of solar radiation striking them. And, where necessary, you must determine the angle of incidence and reflection.

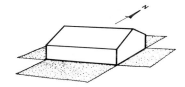

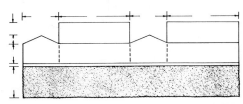

Figure 3.22. Mercator projection of a building structure.

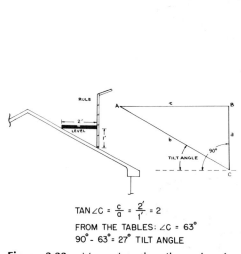

$$TAN \angle C = \frac{c}{a} = \frac{2'}{1'} = 2$$

FROM THE TABLES: $\angle C = 63°$

$90° - 63° = 27°$ TILT ANGLE

Figure 3.23. Measuring the tilt angle of a finished roof.

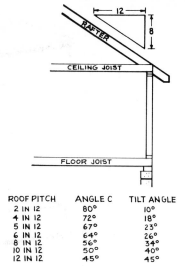

ROOF PITCH	ANGLE C	TILT ANGLE
2 IN 12	80°	10°
4 IN 12	72°	18°
5 IN 12	67°	23°
6 IN 12	64°	26°
8 IN 12	56°	34°
10 IN 12	50°	40°
12 IN 12	45°	45°

Figure 3.24. Determining the tilt angle from the plans.

Measuring Roof Tilt Angles

The easiest way to measure the tilt angle of a roof is with a 2-ft builder's level and a folding 6-ft rule. Proceed as shown in Figure 3.23.

- Set the builder's level on the roof so that it reads level.
- Measure down to the roof with the folding rule from the bottom edge of the level.

You know the two sides of a right triangle: side *a* and side *c* in the illustration. Using the tangent table, angle C = 63°. The tilt angle is the *complementary angle.* Complementary angles are two or more angles whose sum equals 90°. So the tilt angle equals 90° minus angle C, or 27°.

If you have a set of building plans that shows the roof pitch, the tilt angle can quickly be determined from the plans. Roof pitches are stated in inches of rise per inches of ceiling joist run, such as *5 in 12* or *8 in 12*. Look at Figure 3.24. Note that the roof pitch shown, *8 in 12*, gives you the dimensions of the needed triangle. Some common roof pitches and their tilt angles are also shown in Figure 3.24.

Measuring the Ground Tilt Angles

The tilt angle of the ground is measured in the same manner. However, the ground tends to be more uneven. So it is advisable to use a long, straight 2 × 4 or other timber to make your measurement and to make several measurements at several different locations. This is shown in Figure 3.25.

Measuring the Angles of Incidence and Reflection

To obtain the angles of incidence and reflection of the sun, you must know the altitude of the sun and the tilt angle of the surface. The altitude of the sun is determined from the sun-path diagrams shown in Decision 2. The angle of incidence is then calculated as shown in Figure 3.26.

By the laws of triangles: angle A + angle B + angle C = 180°. Angle B and the incident angle are *supplementary angles.* Supplementary angles are angles whose sum is equal to 180°. Supplementary angles form a straight line.

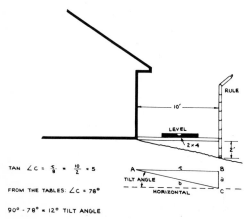

$$TAN \angle C = \frac{c}{a} = \frac{10}{2} = 5$$

FROM THE TABLES: $\angle C = 78°$

$90° - 78° = 12°$ TILT ANGLE

Figure 3.25. Determining the tilt angle of the ground.

So angle B + incident angle = angle A + angle B + angle C. Removing angle B from the equation: *The angle of incidence equals the altitude plus the tilt angle.* As you learned earlier, the angle of incidence equals the angle of reflection.

Measuring the Amount of Reflection

Figure 3.27 shows how to calculate the length of the area that will reflect solar energy against the structure once the angle of incidence (angle *i*), the altitude of the sun (angle *a*), and the tilt angle of the ground (angle *t*) are known.

In the triangle ABC, angle C = the angle of reflection. Angle A = 90° minus the sum of the angle of incidence and the tilt angle.

By the laws of triangles, the length of side *a* equals *c* sin A ÷ sin C. Or: *The length of the ground reflecting onto the building equals the height of the sidewall times the sine of 90° minus the sum of the angle of reflection and the tilt angle divided by the sine of the angle of reflection.*

The width of the area of reflectivity is the length of the building wall that receives the reflected energy. The area that reflects the energy is the length of the ground times the width of the building. The amount of energy that is reflected is the ground area times the percent energy reflected, which can be found in Figure 2.48.

Solar Availability Worksheets

The amount of solar energy striking the building can now be calculated and placed in the solar availability worksheets shown in Figures 3.29, 3.31, 3.32, and 3.34.

Solar availability should be calculated by month. For most locations and purposes, the availability should be calculated separately for the winter and the summer seasons. If you wish, you can subdivide the seasonal worksheets into months or other subdivisions such as a 4-mo heating or cooling season.

Calculating the Roof's Solar Availability

To calculate the availability of solar energy on the roof, proceed as follows:

- Determine the number of square feet in each roof.
- Determine the tilt angle of each roof.
- Determine the orientation of each roof.
- Decide what radiation table is closest to the roof's orientation (Figures 3.5 through 3.8).
- Determine what angle factor must be used to modify the radiation table (Figures 3.11 and 3.12).
- Calculate the amount of radiation striking the roof's surface for each month using the following formula:

$$\text{MMBtu/mo} = \frac{\text{(MMBtu/100 sq ft/mo) (tilt angle factor) (sq ft of roof)}}{100}$$

Figure 3.28 is a worksheet that will help you lay out your figures for easy calculations. Place your final calculations in the roof solar availability worksheet shown in Figure 3.29.

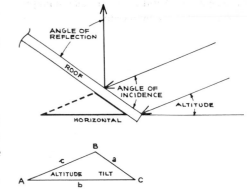

Figure 3.26. The sum of the altitude and the tilt angle equals the incident angle.

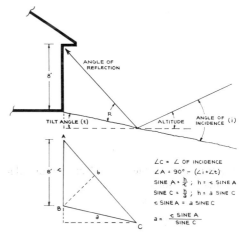

Figure 3.27. Determining the length of the ground area reflecting energy onto a structure's sidewall.

Figure 3.28. Worksheet for determining roof solar availability by month.

WORKSHEET

Item	Roof A	Roof B	Roof C	Roof D
1. Square feet	_____	_____	_____	_____
2. Tilt angle	_____	_____	_____	_____
3. Orientation	_____	_____	_____	_____
4. Radiation table	_____	_____	_____	_____
5. Tilt angle factor	_____	_____	_____	_____

MMBtu/100 sq ft/mo

	Roof A	Roof B	Roof C	Roof D
January	_____	_____	_____	_____
February	_____	_____	_____	_____
March	_____	_____	_____	_____
April	_____	_____	_____	_____
May	_____	_____	_____	_____
June	_____	_____	_____	_____
July	_____	_____	_____	_____
August	_____	_____	_____	_____
September	_____	_____	_____	_____
October	_____	_____	_____	_____
November	_____	_____	_____	_____
December	_____	_____	_____	_____

Figure 3.29. Winter and summer roof solar availability tables.

WORKSHEET

1. Winter Radiation

Month	Roof A	Roof B	Roof C	Roof D	Total
October	_____	_____	_____	_____	_____
November	_____	_____	_____	_____	_____
December	_____	_____	_____	_____	_____
January	_____	_____	_____	_____	_____
February	_____	_____	_____	_____	_____
March	_____	_____	_____	_____	_____
Total	_____	_____	_____	_____	_____

2. Summer Radiation

Month	Roof A	Roof B	Roof C	Roof D	Total
April	_____	_____	_____	_____	_____
May	_____	_____	_____	_____	_____
June	_____	_____	_____	_____	_____
July	_____	_____	_____	_____	_____
August	_____	_____	_____	_____	_____
September	_____	_____	_____	_____	_____
Total	_____	_____	_____	_____	_____

Calculating the Sidewalls' Solar Availability

To calculate the availability of solar energy on the vertical sidewalls of the building, proceed as follows:

- Determine the number of square feet in each sidewall.
- Determine the orientation of each sidewall.
- Choose the proper solar radiation table.
- Calculate the amount of radiation striking each sidewall using the following formula:

$$\text{MMBtu/mo} = \frac{(\text{MMBtu/100 sq ft/mo})\ (\text{sq ft of sidewall})}{100}$$

A worksheet is provided in Figure 3.30. Place your final results in the sidewall solar availability worksheet shown in Figure 3.31. If you wish to calculate the foundation walls separate from the structure sidewalls, place the foundation results in the worksheet provided in Figure 3.32.

Calculating the Ground-Reflected Solar Availability

To calculate the amount of solar energy reflected from the ground to the building's walls, proceed as follows:

- Determine the length of the ground area that will be reflecting the sun's energy for each month.
- Determine the square feet of radiation area for each month.
- Determine the ground's tilt angle.
- Select the proper radiation table.
- Select the proper tilt angle factor.
- Determine the percent reflectance.
- Calculate the amount of radiation striking each sidewall using the formula:

$$\text{MMBtu/mo} = \frac{(\text{MMBtu/100 sq ft/mo})\ (\text{sq ft of ground})\ (\text{tilt angle factor})\ (\%\ \text{reflectance})}{100}$$

A worksheet is provided in Figure 3.33. Place your final results in the solar availability ground worksheet in Figure 3.34.

Figure 3.30. Worksheet for determining sidewall solar availability by month.

WORKSHEET

Item	Wall A	Wall B	Wall C	Wall D
1. Square feet	——	——	——	——
2. Orientation	——	——	——	——
3. Radiation table	——	——	——	——

MMBtu/100 sq ft/mo

	Wall A	Wall B	Wall C	Wall D
January	——	——	——	——
February	——	——	——	——
March	——	——	——	——
April	——	——	——	——
May	——	——	——	——
June	——	——	——	——
July	——	——	——	——
August	——	——	——	——
September	——	——	——	——
October	——	——	——	——
November	——	——	——	——
December	——	——	——	——

Figure 3.31. Winter and summer sidewall solar availability tables.

WORKSHEET

1. Winter Radiation

Month	Wall A	Wall B	Wall C	Wall D	Total
October	——	——	——	——	——
November	——	——	——	——	——
December	——	——	——	——	——
January	——	——	——	——	——
February	——	——	——	——	——
March	——	——	——	——	——
Total	——	——	——	——	——

2. Summer Radiation

Month	Wall A	Wall B	Wall C	Wall D	Total
April	——	——	——	——	——
May	——	——	——	——	——
June	——	——	——	——	——
July	——	——	——	——	——
August	——	——	——	——	——
September	——	——	——	——	——
Total	——	——	——	——	——

WORKSHEET

Figure 3.32. Winter and summer foundation wall solar availability tables.

1. Winter Radiation

Month	Wall A	Wall B	Wall C	Wall D	Total
October	____	____	____	____	____
November	____	____	____	____	____
December	____	____	____	____	____
January	____	____	____	____	____
February	____	____	____	____	____
March	____	____	____	____	____
Total	____	____	____	____	____

2. Summer Radiation

Month	Wall A	Wall B	Wall C	Wall D	Total
April	____	____	____	____	____
May	____	____	____	____	____
June	____	____	____	____	____
July	____	____	____	____	____
August	____	____	____	____	____
September	____	____	____	____	____
Total	____	____	____	____	____

Figure 3.33. Worksheet for determining ground-reflected solar availability by month.

WORKSHEET

Item		Ground A	Ground B	Ground C	Ground D
Jan/Nov	Length	——	——	——	——
	Sq ft	——	——	——	——
Feb/Oct	Length	——	——	——	——
	Sq ft	——	——	——	——
Mar/Sept	Length	——	——	——	——
	Sq ft	——	——	——	——
Aprl/Aug	Length	——	——	——	——
	Sq ft	——	——	——	——
May/July	Length	——	——	——	——
	Sq ft	——	——	——	——
June	Length	——	——	——	——
	Sq ft	——	——	——	——
Dec	Length	——	——	——	——
	Sq ft	——	——	——	——

	Ground A	Ground B	Ground C	Ground D
1. Ground tilt angle	——	——	——	——
2. Orientation	——	——	——	——
3. Radiation table	——	——	——	——
4. Ground tilt angle factor	——	——	——	——
5. Percent reflectance	——	——	——	——

MMBtu/100 sq ft/mo

	Ground A	Ground B	Ground C	Ground D
January	——	——	——	——
February	——	——	——	——
March	——	——	——	——
April	——	——	——	——
May	——	——	——	——
June	——	——	——	——
July	——	——	——	——
August	——	——	——	——
September	——	——	——	——
October	——	——	——	——
November	——	——	——	——
December	——	——	——	——

Figure 3.34. Winter and summer ground solar availability tables.

WORKSHEET

1. Winter Radiation

Month	Ground A	Ground B	Ground C	Ground D
October	——	——	——	——
November	——	——	——	——
December	——	——	——	——
January	——	——	——	——
February	——	——	——	——
March	——	——	——	——
Total	——	——	——	——

2. Summer Radiation

Month	Ground A	Ground B	Ground C	Ground D
April	——	——	——	——
May	——	——	——	——
June	——	——	——	——
July	——	——	——	——
August	——	——	——	——
September	——	——	——	——
Total	——	——	——	——

Calculating the Effects of Solar Shading

If obstacles intrude into the solar window between the hours of 9:00 A.M. and 3:00 P.M., then solar energy will be lost during the shaded period. To determine how much energy is lost, you must calculate how much of the building is shaded and in which months shading occurs.

Because so many different types of shading and shade locations can exist, shading can best be shown by an example. In Figure 3.35, a tree is located to the south of a structure wall. Its height is such that the sun is blocked from November through January. However, from February through October, the sun is high enough in the sky so that the tree does not cast a shadow on the wall.

As the sun moves across the sky from 9:00 A.M. to 3:00 P.M., different parts of the wall are shaded from the sun. So some part of the wall is shaded all day.

The amount of solar energy lost can be calculated by determining the length and height of the shadow on the wall at solar noon and deducting that number of square feet from the wall for the months of November, December, and January.

Obviously thousands of shading problems can exist and may have to be dealt with. Usually some intelligent estimations of the energy lost can be made in a manner similar to the example just shown.

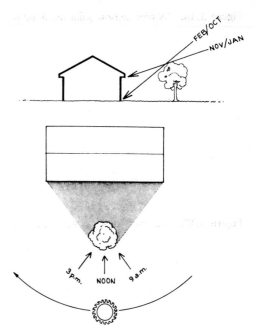

Figure 3.35. A typical shading problem.

Seasonal Solar Availability

The solar energy available for each orientation can now be calculated so that a record of winter and summer solar availability by direction can be gathered. Take the totals from Figures 3.29, 3.31, 3.32, and 3.34 and add them together on the tables in Figures 3.36 and 3.37. This is the key information that you will need to determine which part of your building to modify to collect solar energy or to block it according to your needs.

Figure 3.36. Winter season solar availability.

WORKSHEET

Solar Availability	East	West	North	South
Roof (Figure 3.29)	___	___	___	___
Wall (Figure 3.31)	___	___	___	___
Foundation (Figure 3.32)	___	___	___	___
Ground (Figure 3.34)	___	___	___	___
Total availability	___	___	___	___

Figure 3.37. Summer season solar availability.

WORKSHEET

Solar Availability	East	West	North	South
Roof (Figure 3.29)	___	___	___	___
Wall (Figure 3.31)	___	___	___	___
Foundation (Figure 3.32)	___	___	___	___
Ground (Figure 3.34)	___	___	___	___
Total availability	___	___	___	___

Making a Decision

In this chapter you learned how solar radiation varies, what solar radiation data are required, and how the country can be separated into solar radiation blocks.

You learned how solar radiation tables are laid out and how they can be used to provide accurate monthly, seasonal, and annual radiation data on horizontal, vertical, and tilted surfaces oriented in different geographic directions.

Then you learned how to calculate the size, the tilt angle, and the orientation of each part of your building so that you could calculate the amount of solar energy falling on each surface.

Last you learned how to fill out solar availability tables that will allow you to modify your building properly so that it makes maximum use of the available solar energy.

You should have decided that there is more solar energy available than you thought and that you can collect it from a number of different surfaces throughout the year.

DECISION
4

Determine Your Building's Energy Needs

We stand on the planet Earth, three planets out from the sun—93,000,000 miles away and the source of most of our energy.

Our planet sees temperatures ranging from 40° below zero at the polar caps to 120° above zero at the equator. The humidity of the air that we breathe ranges from 0 to 100%.

But God did not design the human race to endure at these temperature and humidity extremes. People are only comfortable near the average of these extremes. Rarely, if ever, is the outdoor temperature and humidity at a level that humankind finds most comfortable. So the human race seeks shelter to provide the optimum environment for its happiness. Shelter where the temperature ranges from 65 to 75°F and the relative humidity ranges from 25 to 50%.

It takes energy to maintain these closely controlled conditions—thermal energy, or as it is commonly known, heat energy. When the outdoor environment is colder than what people desire, then heat energy has to be added to the shelter. When the outside environment is warmer than what people desire, then heat energy has to be removed from the shelter.

In this chapter you will study:

- Heat, temperature, and how heat energy is transmitted to where you need it.
- How heat is transmitted in building structures.
- How to calculate the heat losses in a building structure during the winter months.
- How to derive the heat transfer coefficients that are used to make these calculations.
- How to calculate the heat gains in a residence during the summer months.

You will start with a definition of heat and temperature so that you can immediately distinguish the difference. This is basic to an understanding of thermal energy.

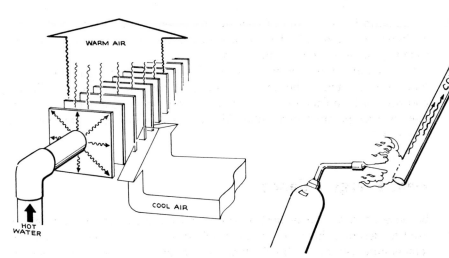

Figure 4.1. Heat is transferred by radiation, conduction, and convection.

Figure 4.2. Heat is conducted throughout a solid object.

Heat and Temperature

Heat and temperature are different. *Heat* is a form of energy. *Temperature* is a measure of hot or cold. Temperature changes are caused by a gain or loss of energy. When large amounts of energy are lost from a small space, large temperature changes are observed. But the loss of the same amount of energy from a larger space results in a smaller change of temperature. For example, an 80-gal water tank holds 664 lb of water. If the tank loses 1333 Btu of heat energy, the temperature of the tank will drop 2°F because it takes 1 Btu to change the temperature of 1 lb of water by 1°F. If a 160-gal water tank lost the same 1333 Btu, the temperature of the tank would drop by only 1°F because the tank contains twice as much water.

Energy is never destroyed or used up. It can, however, be converted from one type of energy into another. An electric motor converts electrical energy into mechanical energy. An electric resistance heater converts electrical energy into heat energy. The burning of a wood log converts the stored solar energy into heat energy.

Energy can be transferred from one location to another. The energy lost from the water tank in the example just cited most likely went to heat up the air surrounding the tank. Heat energy escaping from a building structure goes to heat the outside air.

$$
\begin{array}{r}
80 \text{ gal} \\
\times \quad 8.3 \text{ lb/gal} \\
\hline
= 664 \text{ lb of water}
\end{array}
$$

$$
\begin{array}{r}
1333 \text{ Btu} \\
\div \quad 664 \text{ lb of water} \\
\hline
= \quad 2° \text{ temperature change}
\end{array}
$$

Heat Transfer Principles

Heat energy always seeks equilibrium, just as water seeks its own level. When a hot object is placed in a refrigerator, it cools, transferring its heat to the air in the refrigerator. If two adjoining objects have different temperatures, heat energy flows from the hot object to the cold object in an attempt to equalize the temperature. The phenomena by which heat transfer occurs are *conduction, convection,* and *radiation.* Look at Figure 4.1. Hot water flows into the radiator where the heat is conducted through the metal and radiates to the air. The air next to the radiator is warmed, making it lighter so that it rises and is replaced by cooler air, thus spreading the heat by convection.

Conduction is the transfer of heat through a solid mass. Look at Figure 4.2. The flame from the torch heats one end of the solid rod. The heat is conducted along the rod until the entire rod is the same temperature.

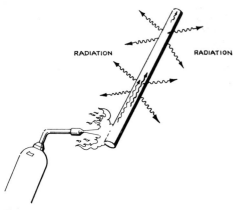

Figure 4.3. A warm object emits rays of heat energy.

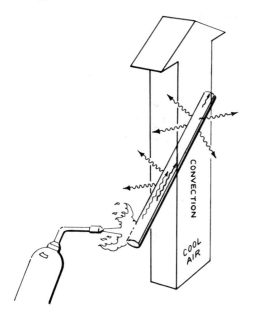

Figure 4.4. A warmed liquid or air rises and convects energy away from an object.

Radiation is the transfer of heat by rays given off by a warm body. This is shown in Figure 4.3. The surface of the rod is warmer than the surrounding air so energy is radiated to the air.

Convection is the transfer of heat by the movement of a liquid or a gas. As heat is radiated to the air surrounding the rod, the air becomes lighter and rises. It is replaced with cooler air. The process continues as long as there is a temperature differential. This convective process is illustrated in Figure 4.4.

Heat Energy Balance

Because energy is never destroyed or used up, a simple formula can be used to describe the total energy required to keep an object at a given temperature. Let the symbol Q stand for heat energy. Then the heat energy balance formula would read: $Q_{total} = Q_{lost} + Q_{retained}$, or $Q_T = Q_L + Q_R$.

The amount of energy needed to keep a building structure and the space within it at a given temperature is therefore a function of the heat loss (or gain) of the building. If the heat loss (or gain) can be minimized, then the amount of energy needed to keep the structure at a comfortable temperature can be lowered. Figure 4.5 illustrates this formula.

The heat energy balance of a building is affected by many diverse factors. Heat is lost by conduction through the walls, floors, and ceilings. Heat is lost by the infiltration of air through the building. Heat is gained from the energy given off by lighting, appliances, and occupants. And heat is gained by the solar radiation that penetrates into the building through the windows and the walls. Some of these factors are shown in Figure 4.6. Conduction, convection, and radiation all contribute to heat losses and gains.

Heat Transmission in Buildings

Heat enters or leaves a building in two ways: *transmission* and *infiltration*. Heat transmission is the movement of heat through the solid walls of the structure. Infiltration is the movement of air through the building's interior.

Heat Transmission

Figure 4.7 shows the three ways that heat is transmitted through building walls, ceilings, and floors. The heat is conducted through the solid part of the wall. It is radiated away from the surfaces, and it is convected away by the air surrounding it.

The amount of heat that is transmitted through 1 sq ft of building wall in 1 hr when a 1°F temperature differential exists between the two sides of the wall is known as the *overall coefficient of heat transmission.*

U is the symbol for the overall coefficient of heat transmission. In the United States, U is expressed in Btu/hr/sq ft/°F; or U = Btu/hr/sq ft/°F.

To find the total amount of heat that would pass through any given area in 1 hr when a 1°F temperature differential exists, the area in square feet must be designated. The symbol A is used to describe the number of square feet of wall being examined.

The term UA is commonly used in the building industry to describe the heat transmission through a given building wall. Obviously, UA is the product of $(U)(A)$ and is obtained by multiplying the two factors together: UA = Btu/hr/°F.

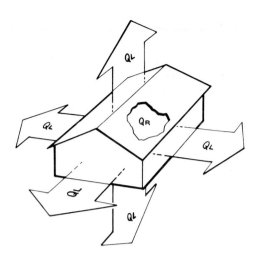

Figure 4.5. Energy balance formula: $Q_{total} = Q_{lost} + Q_{retained}$.

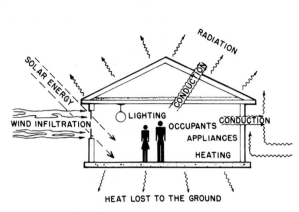

Figure 4.6. Some major factors affecting the heat energy balance of a building structure.

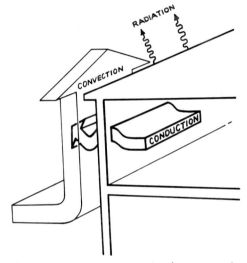

Figure 4.7. Factors governing heat transmission through a solid wall.

The term Δt is used to describe the temperature difference between the two sides of the wall. Δt is expressed *delta t* rather than triangle *t*. Δ is the Greek letter delta. The value of Δt is determined by subtracting the lower temperature from the higher temperature. $\Delta t = °F$.

The formula $UA \Delta t$ is used to describe the heat transmission through a given wall in 1 hr at a given temperature differential. $UA \Delta t = Btu/hr$.

The term T is used to describe the time period under consideration. T is expressed in hours. So to determine the transfer of heat through a wall of any size in any time period at any temperature differential, the formula becomes: Heat loss in Btu = $UA \Delta tT$.

Figure 4.8 reviews the derivation of this formula.

$$U = Btu/hr/sq\ ft/°F$$
$$UA = Btu/hr/°F$$
$$UA \Delta t = Btu/hr$$
$$UA \Delta tT = Btu\ heat\ loss$$

Figure 4.8. Formulas for determining heat transmission.

The Degree Day

A concept known as the *degree day* has been evolved to make heat transmission calculations easier. A degree day is a day when the average outdoor temperature throughout the 24-hr period is 64°F. Degree days is commonly abbreviated as *dd*.

As you learned earlier, the occupants and the appliances within a residence generate heat that adds to the energy contained in a building. Over the years, it has been experimentally determined that this energy contributes about 5°F to the total temperature in the house. Thus the building heat load that must be carried to maintain a comfortable 70°F temperature within the structures drops to 65°F.

65°F − 64°F equals 1 dd. If the outside temperature averaged 35°F over the day, that would be a 30 dd since 65°F − 35°F = 30°.

The degree day concept is important because degree days for each month of the year have been tabulated for all the major locations in the United States. This leads to a very simple formula for determining the heat transmission from a building over a monthly period, namely:

$$\text{Monthly heat loss in Btu} = UA \times 24 \text{ hr} \times \text{No. of dd}$$

As an example of how this is used effectively, let us examine a structure that has a $UA = 600$ Btu/hr/°F in two locations that have different amounts of degree days. Let us use Minneapolis, Minnesota = 1300 dd in February and St. Louis, Missouri = 900 dd in February. The structure will lose 18,720,000 Btu in Minneapolis and 12,960,000 Btu in St. Louis during the month of February.

A similar calculation can be made for the different months of the year for one location. This will describe the annual heat loss by month for the structure. Figure 4.9 shows such a calculation for Minneapolis, Minnesota, using a *UA* of 600 Btu/hr/°F. The total heat load for the year is 113 MMBtu, but about 80% of the heat, or 91 MMBtu, will be needed in the 5-mo period of November through March.

```
       600   Btu UA
    ×   24   hr
    14,400   daily UA
  ×  1,300   Feb dd
= 18,720,000 Btu heat loss

       600   Btu UA
    ×   24   hr
    14,000   daily UA
  ×    900
= 12,960,000 Btu heat loss
```

MONTH ×	DEGREE DAYS ×	24 HR ×	UA =	MMBtu/MO
January	1562	24	600	22.4
February	1310	24	600	18.9
March	1057	24	600	15.2
April	570	24	600	8.2
May	259	24	600	3.7
June	80	24	600	1.2
July	8	24	600	0.1
August	17	24	600	0.2
September	157	24	600	2.3
October	459	24	600	6.6
November	960	24	600	13.8
December	1414	24	600	20.4
Total	7853			113.0

Figure 4.9. Using degree days and *UA* to determine the annual heat requirements by month in Minneapolis, Minnesota.

A table of degree days by month for the cities chosen around the United States as representative of the 24 U.S. geographic areas is shown in Figure 4.10. You can obtain local information by consulting the *ASHRAE 1977 Handbook of Fundamentals* or similar sources at your local library.

How the *U*-Factor is Established

The derivation of *U*, or as it is commonly called the *U-factor*, is relatively complicated. This derivation will be explored shortly. But for most heating load calculations, the U-factor has been calculated for you by the author. Figure 4.11 gives *U*-factors for common constructions. These average *U*-

CITY	JAN	FEB	MAR	APRIL	MAY	JUNE	JULY	AUG	SEPT	OCT	NOV	DEC	ANNUAL
Atlantic City, NJ	905	829	729	468	189	24	0	0	29	230	507	831	4741
San Diego, CA	317	247	223	151	97	43	11	7	24	52	147	255	1574
Phoenix, AZ	474	309	196	74	0	0	0	0	0	22	223	400	1698
Fort Worth, TX	622	446	308	90	5	0	0	0	0	58	299	533	2361
Jackson, MS	535	405	299	81	0	0	0	0	0	69	310	503	2202
Charleston, SC	472	379	281	63	0	0	0	0	0	52	270	456	1973
Tampa, FL	201	148	102	0	0	0	0	0	0	0	60	163	674
Spokane, WA	1243	988	834	561	330	146	17	28	205	508	879	1113	6852
Great Falls, MT	1311	1131	1008	621	359	166	24	50	273	524	894	1194	7555
Fargo, ND	1795	1518	1231	687	338	101	25	41	215	586	1122	1615	9274
Duluth, MN	1758	1512	1327	846	474	178	56	91	277	614	1140	1606	9937
Sault Sainte Marie, MI	1587	1442	1302	846	499	224	109	126	298	639	1005	1398	9475
Caribou, ME	1745	1546	1342	909	512	201	85	133	354	710	1074	1562	10173
Medford, OR	862	627	552	381	207	69	0	0	77	326	624	822	4547
Pocatello, ID	1333	1022	880	561	317	136	0	0	183	487	873	1184	6976
Lincoln, NE	1271	1030	822	401	190	38	0	12	82	340	774	1144	6104
Chicago, IL	1243	1053	868	507	229	58	0	0	90	350	765	1147	6310
Rochester, NY	1249	1148	992	615	289	54	9	34	133	440	759	1141	6863
Blue Hills, MA	1178	1053	936	579	267	69	0	22	108	381	690	1085	6468
Fresno, CA	629	400	304	145	43	0	0	0	0	86	345	580	2532
Grand Junction, CO	1271	924	738	402	145	23	0	0	36	333	792	1132	5796
Wichita, KS	1023	778	619	280	101	7	0	0	32	219	597	915	4571
St. Louis, MO	1017	820	648	297	101	11	0	0	45	233	600	927	4699
Greensboro, NC	806	672	528	241	50	0	0	0	29	202	510	772	3810

Figure 4.10. Average monthly degree days for the 24 cities shown in Figure 3.4.

factors will cover most of your calculations accurately enough for most residential construction.

The U-factor is derived from a figure known as the *R-value*. The R-value is the measure of the materials' resistance to heat flow. The U-factor is the reciprocal of the R-value, or $U = \frac{1}{R}$. R would, of course, equal $\frac{1}{U}$. So a material having an R-value of 10 would have a U-factor of 0.1. The determination of R-values for building structure walls, ceilings, and floors is shown in Appendix B.

$$U = \frac{1}{10} = 0.1$$

Air Infiltration

Infiltration is the leakage of air through cracks and openings, around doors and windows, and through the ceilings, walls, and floors of building structures. Air infiltration in buildings is measured in the *number of air changes per hour*. One air change per hour would be the replacement of all the air in the building in 1 hr.

For human comfort, about 0.7 to 1.5 air changes per hour are required in a building structure used as a residence. With more exchanges, the cost of heating the building would be greater than necessary.

Depending on the outside temperature, the air entering a structure must be either heated or cooled. For the purposes of this discussion, the heating of incoming air will be used.

It takes 0.018 Btu to heat 1 cu ft of air 1°F. Figure 4.12 shows a building containing 10,000 cu ft of air. If the building had one air change per hour, it would take 180 Btu/hr/°F to heat the incoming air. On a day containing 10 degree days, it would take 43,200 Btu to heat the air during the 24-hr period. Obviously, this is an important consideration in determining the total heat transmission.

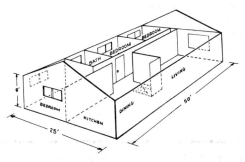

Figure 4.12. This structure would contain about 10,000 cu ft of air.

$$
\begin{array}{rl}
180 & \text{Btu/hr/°F} \\
\times\ 10 & \text{dd} \\
\hline
1,800 & \\
\times\ 24 & \text{hr} \\
\hline
=\ 43,200 & \text{Btu}
\end{array}
$$

CONSTRUCTION	AVERAGE U-FACTORS WHEN INSULATED AS SHOWN				
	NONE	1 IN.	2 IN.	4 IN.	6 IN.
EXTERIOR WALLS					
2 × 4 wood stud sheathed in wood or insulating board and covered with wood siding, shingles, or brick, and sheetrocked or plastered	0.22	0.12	0.09	0.07	
2 × 6 wood stud covered as above					0.05
12-in. concrete block	0.49	0.14	0.08	0.05	
8-in. poured concrete wall	0.70	0.16	0.09	0.05	

	AVERAGE U-FACTORS WHEN INSULATED AS SHOWN				
	NONE	4 IN.	6 IN.	8 IN.	10 IN.
INTERIOR CEILINGS, ROOFS, AND FLOORS					
Ceiling applied directly to wood rafters with wood sheathing covered by asphalt or cedar shingles	0.64	0.08	0.05	0.04	0.03
Horizontal ceiling under a pitched roof with no flooring on the ceiling and roof covered with sheathing and asphalt or cedar shingles	0.32	0.07	0.05	0.04	0.03

There is no heat loss between heated floors. For floors over insulated crawl spaces, use one-half the U-factor shown for ceilings. For floors over vented or unheated crawl spaces, use the U-factor shown. For floors over unheated basements use one-third the indicated U-factor.

Concrete slab floors on grade

In heated buildings, assume the edge loss indicated in the next part of the table per lineal foot of exposed edge around the perimeter.

CONSTRUCTION	AVERAGE U-FACTORS WHEN EDGE IS INSULATED TO DEPTH SHOWN WITH 1-IN. THICK INSULATION			
	NONE	12 IN.	24 IN.	
Concrete slab floors on grade	0.81	0.46	0.21	Per lineal foot

WINDOWS	AVERAGE U-FACTOR	DOORS	AVERAGE U-FACTOR
Single glazed (SG)	1.1	1 in., wood	0.64
Patio doors, SG	1.1	1½ in., wood	0.49
Add storm window to SG	0.45	2 in., wood	0.43
Thermopane (DG)	0.61	1½ in., wood with storm door	0.24
Horizontal skylight SG	1.11	Steel door with urethane core	
Horizontal skylight DG	0.70	and thermal break, 1½ in.	0.19
Basement walls below grade		For uninsulated walls below grade use a U-factor of 0.06. Above the frost line, use the outdoor temperature to calculate the heat loss (degree days). Below the frost line use a temperature differential of 20°F.	
Basement floors below grade		Calculate basement floors to have a heat loss of 1 Btu/hr/sq ft regardless of outside temperature.	

Figure 4.11. Table of typical U-factors for use in residential construction.

Heat Loss Calculations

You now have the basic information that you need to perform heat transmission calculations for your building. These will be called heat loss calculations, which assume that the outside air is cooler than the desired temperature within the structure. The forms from Appendix A of *The Solar Decision Book* (John Wiley & Sons, New York, 1978) will be used to make these calculations.

The method that you will use is easy. First, you will calculate the heat losses through the walls, doors, and windows. Then you will calculate the heat losses through the ceilings and floors. Last, you will add the heat loss from the air changes. This will give you an overall *UA* for the structure.

You will then take this total *UA* and multiply by 24 hr and the number of degree days for each month in order to determine the total heat loss. By using this system, you will be able to determine the heating requirements of the structure by month so that you can compare the need for heat with the availability of solar radiation in your area. The following instructions are reprinted from *The Solar Decision Book* with permission.

Walls, Windows, Doors

Use the sample form shown in Figure 4.13: Wall Heat Loss Calculations. This form will help you calculate the transmission losses through *one* wall. Each wall in the structure should be studied separately. The loss calculations will help identify those walls needing special treatments for energy conservation. The form allows for notation of the wall direction. Usually, you will make calculations for each of four exterior walls. More calculations may be required, depending on the irregularity of the structure. Perform the calculations as follows:

1. Note the direction (N-E-S-W) of the wall.
2. Calculate the *net* wall area. This is the total wall area minus any doors and windows.

Figure 4.13. Form for tabulating wall heat loss calculations. (Reprinted by permission from R. H. Montgomery and J. Budnick, *The Solar Decision Book,* John Wiley & Sons, Inc., 1978.)

WALL HEAT LOSS CALCULATIONS

WALL IDENTIFICATION:			
Portion	**Area, Sq. Ft.**	**U-Factor**	**Heat Loss, Btu/hr/°F**
Above-Grade Sidewall A. Type _____ B. Type _____ C. Type _____	_____ _____ _____	_____ _____ _____	_____ _____ _____
Windows No. A. Single Glazed ____ B. Thermopane ____ C. Storm Window ____	_____ _____ _____	_____ _____ _____	_____ _____ _____
Doors A. 3/4" Wood ____ B. 1 5/8" Wood ____ C. 1 5/8" with Storm ____ D. Other ____	_____ _____ _____ _____	_____ _____ _____ _____	_____ _____ _____ _____
Below-Grade Sidewall A. Type _____ B. Type _____	_____ _____	_____ _____	_____ _____
		TOTAL:	_____

Note. The form allows for entries on three types of above-grade sidewalls. A typical sidewall might include a part of the concrete foundation, a block or brick section, and a wood construction section.

3. Determine the number and type of windows in the wall and calculate the total area for each type.
   Example. There are four windows each 3 ft wide by 4 ft high. The area of one window would be 12 sq ft (12 = 3 × 4). The total area for the four windows would be 48 sq ft (48 = 4 windows × 12 sq ft).
4. Determine the number and type of doors in the wall and calculate the total area for each type.
5. Calculate the area for any below-grade wall sections.
6. Using the heat transmission table in Figure 4.11, enter the appropriate U-factors for the various types of construction.
7. Calculate the heat losses through the above-grade wall sections.
   Note. Heat loss, or UA, = area times U-factor.
8. Add up the total heat losses through the particular wall, then perform the same calculations for other walls in the structure.

Ceilings and Floors

Figure 4.14 is a sample form for calculating ceiling and floor heat losses. This form will help you calculate the heat losses through the ceilings and floors of your structure. You will use the same procedures as those for calculating wall heat losses. Make certain that you enter the correct U-factors. The U-factor can change depending on the location of the ceiling or the floor. (These changes are discussed in the heat transmission tables in Figure 4.11.) For concrete slab floors on grade, the floor area is not used. Instead, the length of the slab perimeter is calculated and then multiplied by the U-factor.

CEILING AND FLOOR HEAT LOSS CALCULATIONS

Portion	Area, Sq. Ft.	U-Factor	Heat Loss, Btu/hr/°F
Attic Ceiling	————	————	————
First-Floor Ceiling	————	————	————
First Floor	————	————	————
Basement Floor	————	————	————
On-Grade Slab (Edge)	————	————	————
	(use lineal ft.)		

Figure 4.14. Form for tabulating ceiling and floor heat loss calculations. (Reprinted by permission from R. H. Montgomery and J. Budnick, *The Solar Decision Book,* John Wiley & Sons, Inc., 1978.)

Note. There is no heat loss in ceilings between heated floors. For floors over insulated crawl spaces, use one-half the U-factor shown in the heat transmission table. For ceilings or floors over vented or unheated crawl spaces, use the U-factor shown. For ceilings or floors over unheated basements, use one-third the U-factor listed in the table.

Infiltration

Infiltration losses are calculated by multiplying the volume of air in the structure by 0.018 Btu/cu ft/°F. This is then multiplied by the estimated number of air changes per hour. For average new construction this would be one air change per hour. For a building that is being constructed to limit air change, use 0.7 air changes per hour. For an older building with poor-fitting windows and doors, use 2 air changes per hour. For easy reference:

Infiltration $UA =$ (cu ft of air in structure)(air changes/hr)(0.018)

CONSTRUCTION	AIR CHANGES/HR
Average	1.0
Tight	0.7
Old and poor	2.0 or more

Total Heat Loss

Enter your calculated heat loss figures in the table shown in Figure 4.15: A Form for Tabulating the Total Heat Loss. When you add these heat losses up, you will have a total heat loss (UA) for the house in Btu/hr/°F.

Heating Requirements

Your heating requirements can be calculated by using the table shown in Figure 4.16: A Form for Tabulating Total Heating Requirements. By using the monthly degree days, the heat required per month can be obtained. By using the annual degree days, the heat required per year can be obtained.

To calculate the maximum amount of heat needed to maintain the structure at a comfortable temperature, use the following formula:

(65°F − design temperature) (Btu/hr/°F) = maximum heat/hr

Design temperature is the lowest temperature at which the structure is expected to heat up to 65°F. Typical design temperatures are:

Northern states   0° to −10°F
Middle states   0° to +10°F
Southern states   +10° to +20°F

Your local building inspector can tell you what design temperature is best for your location.

TOTAL HEAT LOSS

HEAT LOSS SOURCE	HEAT LOSS, Btu/hr/°F
Transmission Losses	
North Wall	_____
South Wall	_____
East Wall	_____
West Wall	_____
Ceilings and Floors	_____
Infiltration Losses	_____
TOTAL:	_____

Figure 4.15. Form for tabulating the total heat loss in Btu/hr/°F (UA). (Reprinted by permission from R. H. Montgomery and J. Budnick, *The Solar Decision Book*, John Wiley & Sons, Inc., 1978.)

MONTH	DEGREE DAYS	X	24 HOURS	X	BTU/hr/°F	=	BTU/MONTH
January	_____		24		_____		_____
February	_____		24		_____		_____
March	_____		24		_____		_____
April	_____		24		_____		_____
May	_____		24		_____		_____
June	_____		24		_____		_____
July	_____		24		_____		_____
August	_____		24		_____		_____
September	_____		24		_____		_____
October	_____		24		_____		_____
November	_____		24		_____		_____
December	_____		24		_____		_____
ANNUAL	_____		24		_____		_____ Btu/Year

Figure 4.16. Form for tabulation total heating requirements. (Reprinted by permission from R. H. Montgomery and J. Budnick, *The Solar Decision Book,* John Wiley & Sons, Inc., 1978.)

Heat Gain Calculations

When the outdoor temperature is higher than the temperature desired within the building, the building gains heat rather than loses it, so the process of heat transmission is reversed. This situation usually occurs above 75 to 80°F.

Residential buildings gain heat from solar radiation, heat conduction through the exterior walls, and heat generation from people, lighting, and appliances.

There are two types of heat gains: *sensible heat gain* and *latent heat gain.* Sensible heat gain is the type of heat gain that raises the temperature of the air. Latent heat gain is the type of heat gain that increases the amount of water vapor in the air.

Cooling a residential building requires two primary functions: the removal of sensible heat to lower the temperature and the removal of latent heat to lower the humidity. The removal of latent heat is known as *dehumidification.* Dehumidification is accomplished by passing the air over a cold surface so that the water vapor condenses out as water droplets.

The Cooling Load

The *cooling load* is the rate at which heat energy must be removed from the structure to maintain a comfortable temperature and humidity. The cooling load in a home is quite variable. It depends on the hour of the day, which determines the solar energy input, and it depends on the activities being carried out within the structure, which determine the internal heat generation.

When you sized the furnace to carry the heat load, you used a minimum design temperature. This ensured that the building would heat to a comfortable temperature under all conditions. If you were to calculate the cooling load in the same manner, you would be investing in an un-

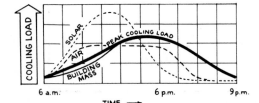

Figure 4.17. The thermal mass of the building's exterior surface delays the conductance of heat into the building and lowers the peak cooling load.

economical cooling system. It is important to use a more sophisticated analysis that will keep the size and the cost of the cooling unit down to a more reasonable level. Figure 4.17 shows why.

The Structure's Heat Storage Capacity

A building structure has a certain weight or mass. This mass has the capacity to gain or lose heat. For example, a concrete wall typically weighs 144 lb/cu ft. Concrete has a *specific heat* of 0.156 Btu/lb/°F. That is, it takes 0.156 Btu to raise or lower the temperature of 1 lb of concrete 1°F. So it takes 22.5 Btu to raise or lower the temperature of 1 cu ft of concrete by 1°F.

$$\begin{aligned} 144 & \text{ lb/cu ft} \\ \times\ 0.156 & \text{ Btu} \\ \hline =\ 22.5 & \text{ Btu/cu ft} \end{aligned}$$

If heat is applied to one side of this concrete wall, it takes time for the heat to raise the temperature of the entire wall because the concrete also has resistance to heat flow through it as measured by its *k-factor*. The *k-factor* of a material is the rate at which energy will be conducted through a 1-in. thickness of the material per square foot of area. So there is a delay between the time when heat, such as solar radiation, is applied to the concrete wall and when the inside of the wall is heated and can add to the heat within the building. The same facts hold true for any solid building material. The amount of delay is a function of the type of material and its configuration.

The building structure's exterior walls act as a heat storage mechanism and as a heat gain delay mechanism. The infiltration of warm, humid air into the structure causes an immediate cooling load. The conduction of heat through the building's exterior surfaces causes a delayed cooling load. The internal heat generation is a combination of immediate and delayed load depending on when it occurs. As the air infiltrating into the structure is typically the warmest at the same time as the solar radiation striking the building is at its peak, the peak cooling load is diminished by the conduction delay.

In large commercial buildings, the calculation of the building's ability to delay heat gain and the calculation of the internal heat generation is complex and difficult. Fortunately, simple procedures have been established for residential cooling load and heat gain calculations.

Residential Cooling Load Calculations

The calculation of the cooling load for a building structure used as a residence uses six assumptions:

- The residence is occupied and cooled every day of the cooling season.
- The majority of the cooling load imposed on the system consists of heat flow through the structure's exterior walls, ceilings, and floors plus the infiltration of air. Internal heat generation is a very minor part of the load.
- There is only one cooling zone within the structure.
- The cooling system uses a small capacity unit with no means to alter the capacity.
- Dehumidification is achieved only when the cooling unit is operating. A temperature control determines when the unit operates (sensible heat controlled).
- The system operates 24-hrs/day, so maximum advantage can be taken of the thermal storage characteristics of the building.

The Total Residential Cooling Load

Five separate heat gains need to be calculated in order to arrive at the total cooling load.

- Heat gains through walls, ceilings, and floors.
- Heat gains through windows.
- Heat gains through air infiltration.
- Heat gains from occupants.
- Latent heat gains (calculated as a percentage of the rest of the load).

The calculations are based on maintaining a thermostat setting at 75°F, allowing a 3°F temperature swing during the day, and operating the system 24 hr a day. No allowance is made for the fact that an individual room will vary in its needs during the day, but the design of the distribution system can compensate for that change.

Heat Gain Through Walls, Ceilings, and Floors

To determine the heat gain through walls, ceilings, and floors, you will need a table of U-factors, a *design temperature,* and the *daily temperature range.* The design temperature is the maximum outdoor temperature at which you expect to cool the house to 75°F. The temperature range is the daily swing of temperature obtained by subtracting the lowest temperature from the highest temperature.

Figure 4.18 is a table of design temperatures and temperature ranges for 24 cities across the United States. The U-factors shown in Figure 4.11 are typical for most common constructions.

Figure 4.19 is a design equivalent temperature difference table reprinted by permission from the *ASHRAE 1977 Fundamentals Handbook.* This table is used to determine the temperature differential, or the *design Δt.* In

CITY/STATE	DESIGN TEMPERATURE	TEMPERATURE RANGE
1. Spokane, Washington	90	28
2. Great Falls, Montana	88	28
3. Fargo, North Dakota	89	25
4. Duluth, Minnesota	82	22
5. Sault Sainte Marie, Michigan	81	23
6. Caribou, Maine	81	21
7. Medford, Oregon	94	35
8. Pocatello, Idaho	91	35
9. Lincoln, Nebraska	95	24
10. Chicago, Illinois	90	20
11. Rochester, New York	88	22
12. Blue Hills, Massachusetts	86	17
13. Fresno, California	100	34
14. Grand Junction, Colorado	94	29
15. Wichita, Kansas	98	23
16. St. Louis, Missouri	94	21
17. Greensboro, North Carolina	91	21
18. Atlantic City, New Jersey	89	18
19. San Diego, California	80	12
20. Phoenix, Arizona	107	27
21. Fort Worth, Texas	99	22
22. Jackson, Mississippi	95	21
23. Charleston, South Carolina	91	18
24. Tampa, Florida	91	17

Figure 4.18. Summer design temperatures and temperature ranges for 24 U.S. cities.

Design Equivalent Temperature Differences

Design Temperature, °F	85		90			95			100		105	110
Daily Temperature Range[a]	L	M	L	M	H	L	M	H	M	H	H	H
WALLS AND DOORS												
1. Frame and veneer-on-frame	17.6	13.6	22.6	18.6	13.6	27.6	23.6	18.6	28.6	23.6	28.6	33.6
2. Masonry walls, 8-in. block or brick	10.3	6.3	15.3	11.3	6.3	20.3	16.3	11.3	21.3	16.3	21.3	26.3
3. Partitions, frame	9.0	5.0	14.0	10.0	5.0	19.0	15.0	10.0	20.0	15.0	20.0	25.0
masonry	2.5	0	7.5	3.5	0	12.5	8.5	3.5	13.5	8.5	13.5	18.5
4. Wood doors	17.6	13.6	22.6	18.6	13.6	27.6	23.6	18.6	28.6	23.6	28.6	33.6
CEILINGS AND ROOFS[b]												
1. Ceilings under naturally vented attic or vented flat roof—dark	38.0	34.0	43.0	39.0	34.0	48.0	44.0	39.0	49.0	44.0	49.0	54.0
—light	30.0	26.0	35.0	31.0	26.0	40.0	36.0	31.0	41.0	36.0	41.0	46.0
2. Built-up roof, no ceiling—dark	38.0	34.0	43.0	39.0	34.0	48.0	44.0	39.0	49.0	44.0	49.0	54.0
—light	30.0	26.0	35.0	31.0	26.0	40.0	36.0	31.0	41.0	36.0	41.0	46.0
3. Ceilings under unconditioned rooms	9.0	5.0	14.0	10.0	5.0	19.0	15.0	10.0	20.0	15.0	20.0	25.0
FLOORS												
1. Over unconditioned rooms	9.0	5.0	14.0	10.0	5.0	19.0	15.0	10.0	20.0	15.0	20.0	25.0
2. Over basement, enclosed crawl space or concrete slab on ground	0	0	0	0	0	0	0	0	0	0	0	0
3. Over open crawl space	9.0	5.0	14.0	10.0	5.0	19.0	15.0	10.0	20.0	15.0	20.0	25.0

[a]Daily Temperature Range
    L (Low) Calculation Value: 12 deg F.   M(Medium) Calculation Value: 20 deg F.   H (High) Calculation Value: 30 deg F.
    Applicable Range: Less than 15 deg F.   Applicable Range: 15 to 25 deg F.   Applicable Range: More than 25 deg F.

[b]Ceilings and Roofs: For roofs in shade, 18-hr average = 11 deg temperature differential. At 90 F design and medium daily range, equivalent temperature differential for light-colored roof equals 11 + (0.71)(39 − 11) = 31 deg F.

Figure 4.19. Table of design equivalent temperature differences. (Reprinted by permission from the *ASHRAE 1977 Fundamentals Handbook.*)

doing winter heat loss calculations, you used degree days and a single minimum temperature to calculate the maximum heat needed. But in doing summer heat gain calculations, you will use a different design Δt for each type of construction. This allows you to calculate in the time-delay effect of the building's construction on the peak cooling load.

Therefore you must use a $UA\Delta t$ formated table rather than a UA table. This table is shown in Figure 4.20. Proceed to fill out this table as follows:

• Determine the design temperature from the table in Figure 4.18.
  Note. If your location is not listed, obtain the correct figure for your area from either the *ASHRAE Manual* or other local source. Design temperatures are very location-dependent.

• Determine the daily temperature range from the table in Figure 4.18.
  Note. If your location is not listed, obtain the correct figure.

• Decide whether the daily temperature range is low (L), medium (M), or high (H).
  Note. Low is a range of less than 15°F
              Medium is a range of 15 to 25°F
              High is a range of more than 25°F.

• Take the design equivalent temperature difference for each type of construction from the table in Figure 4.19 and tabulate it in Figure 4.20 under design Δt, °F.
  Note. The tables are written in increments of 5°F. Where design temperature falls in between these values, correct the equivalent temperature difference by 1°F for each 1°F difference in the design temperature. For example, design temperature = 93°F. 95° − 93° = 2°F correction. Equivalent temperature difference in table = 17.5°F. Correct to read 15.5°F. (17.5 − 2 = 15.5).

• Calculate the area of each type of construction in square feet and tabulate under area.

WORKSHEET

Portion	Design Δt °F	Area Sq ft	U-Factor	Heat Gain Btu/hr
Above-grade sidewall				
A. _____	_____	_____	_____	_____
B. _____	_____	_____	_____	_____
C. _____	_____	_____	_____	_____
Ceilings and floors				
A. _____	_____	_____	_____	_____
B. _____	_____	_____	_____	_____
C. _____	_____	_____	_____	_____
D. _____	_____	_____	_____	_____
Roofs				
A. _____	_____	_____	_____	_____
B. _____	_____	_____	_____	_____
C. _____	_____	_____	_____	_____
Doors				
A. _____	_____	_____	_____	_____
B. _____	_____	_____	_____	_____
C. _____	_____	_____	_____	_____
			Total gain	_____

Figure 4.20. Heat gains through walls, ceilings, and floors.

- Take the *U*-factor for each type of construction from the table in Figure 4.11 and tabulate it under *U*-factor.
- Multiply (design Δ*t*) (area) (*U*-factor) and tabulate the result under heat gain, Btu/hr.
- Add up the heat gains to obtain the total heat gain through the walls, ceilings, and floors.
  Note. The windows are done separately in the next step.

Heat Gain Through Windows

The heat gain through windows is calculated using a table that gives the number of Btu/hr gained through 1 sq ft of window area depending on the type of glass, the direction in which the window is facing, the amount and type of shading, and the design temperature for the location.

Figure 4.21 shows this table, reprinted by permission from the *ASHRAE 1977 Fundamentals Handbook*. Figure 4.22 is the window heat gain calculation table. To use this table, proceed as follows:

- Determine the types of windows facing north, south, east/west, SE/SW, and NE/NW. Tabulate them under the column titled Type of Window.
  Note. Any windows, or parts thereof, except for NE/NW-facing windows, that are shaded by permanent overhangs should be treated as north-facing windows.
- Determine the shading for each type of window.
  Note. Where different types of shading exist, separate the window types.
- Determine the area of each type of window.
  Note. Use the gross area of the glazed portion.
- From the table in Figure 4.18, determine the design temperature.
- From the table in Figure 4.21, determine the number of Btu/hr/sq ft that pass through the window, and tabulate them under the column titled Btu/hr/sq ft.
- Multiply (area) (Btu/hr/sq ft) for each type of window, and tabulate the results under the column titled Heat Gain.
- Add up all the heat gains to obtain the total heat gain in Btu/hr.

Figure 4.21. Table of heat gains through windows. (Reprinted by permission from the *ASHRAE 1977 Fundamentals Handbook*.)

Design Transmitted and Absorbed Solar Energy and to Air-to-Air Temperature Difference, Btu/(h·ft²)

Outdoor	Regular Single Glass						Regular Double Glass						Heat Absorbing Double Glass					
Design Temp.	85	90	95	100	105	110	85	90	95	100	105	110	85	90	95	100	105	110
No Awnings or inside Shading																		
North	23	27	31	35	38	44	19	21	24	26	28	30	12	14	17	19	21	23
NE and NW	56	60	64	68	71	77	46	48	51	53	55	57	27	29	32	34	36	38
East and West	81	85	89	93	96	102	68	70	73	75	77	79	42	44	47	49	51	53
SE and SW	70	74	78	82	85	91	59	61	64	66	68	70	35	37	40	42	44	46
South	40	44	48	52	55	61	33	35	38	40	42	44	19	21	24	26	28	30
Draperies or Venetian Blinds																		
North	15	19	23	27	30	36	12	14	17	19	21	23	9	11	14	16	18	20
NE and NW	32	36	40	44	47	53	27	29	32	34	36	38	20	22	25	27	29	31
East and West	48	52	56	60	63	69	42	44	47	49	51	53	30	32	35	37	39	41
SE and SW	40	44	48	52	55	61	35	37	40	42	44	46	24	26	29	31	33	35
South	23	27	31	35	38	44	20	22	25	27	29	31	15	17	20	22	24	26
Roller Shades Half-Drawn																		
North	18	22	26	30	33	39	15	17	20	22	24	26	10	12	15	17	19	21
NE and NW	40	44	48	52	55	61	38	40	43	45	47	49	24	26	29	31	33	35
East and West	61	65	69	73	76	82	54	56	59	61	63	65	35	37	40	42	44	46
SE and SW	52	56	60	64	67	73	46	48	51	53	55	57	30	32	35	37	39	41
South	29	33	37	41	44	50	27	29	32	34	36	38	18	20	23	25	27	29
Awnings																		
North	20	24	28	32	35	41	13	15	18	20	22	24	10	12	15	17	19	21
NE and NW	21	25	29	33	36	42	14	16	19	21	23	25	11	13	16	18	20	22
East and West	22	26	30	34	37	43	14	16	19	21	23	25	12	14	17	19	20	22
SE and SW	21	25	29	33	36	42	14	16	19	21	23	25	11	13	16	18	20	22
South	21	24	28	32	35	41	13	15	18	20	22	24	11	13	16	18	20	22

WORKSHEET

Type of Window	Shading	Area	Btu/hr/sq ft	Heat Gain
North-facing				
A. _____	_____	_____	_____	_____
B. _____	_____	_____	_____	_____
C. _____	_____	_____	_____	_____
D. _____	_____	_____	_____	_____
South-facing				
A. _____	_____	_____	_____	_____
B. _____	_____	_____	_____	_____
C. _____	_____	_____	_____	_____
D. _____	_____	_____	_____	_____
East/west-facing				
A. _____	_____	_____	_____	_____
B. _____	_____	_____	_____	_____
C. _____	_____	_____	_____	_____
D. _____	_____	_____	_____	_____
SE/SW-facing				
A. _____	_____	_____	_____	_____
B. _____	_____	_____	_____	_____
C. _____	_____	_____	_____	_____
D. _____	_____	_____	_____	_____
NE/NW-facing				
A. _____	_____	_____	_____	_____
B. _____	_____	_____	_____	_____
C. _____	_____	_____	_____	_____
D. _____	_____	_____	_____	_____
			Total gain	_____

Figure 4.22. Heat gains through windows.

Heat Gains Through Air Infiltration and Ventilation

Air infiltration into buildings in the summertime is typically less than air infiltration in the wintertime. This is because the wind velocity tends to be lower and there is no loss of warm air up chimneys and ventilating stacks. So air infiltration is usually calculated on 0.5 air changes/hr. You may wish to provide some mechanical ventilation to augment this natural air infiltration if your home is stuffy.

The configuration of the structure will also have an effect on the amount of air infiltration during the cooling season. For this reason, the heat gain is calculated as Btu/hr/sq ft of overall exposed wall area of the structure. Figure 4.23 shows the heat gains due to infiltration and mechanical ventilation. This table is reprinted by permission from the *ASHRAE 1977 Fundamentals Handbook*.

Design Temperature, F	85	90	95	100	105	110
Infiltration, Btuh/ft² of gross exposed wall area	0.7	1.1	1.5	1.9	2.2	2.6
Mechanical ventilation, Btuh/cfm	11.0	16.0	22.0	27.0	32.0	38.0

Figure 4.23. Table of heat gains through infiltration and ventilation. (Reprinted by permission from the *ASHRAE 1977 Fundamentals Handbook.*)

Figure 4.24 is the infiltration-ventilation heat gain table. To use this table, proceed as follows:

- Determine the design temperature for your location from the table in Figure 4.18.
- Determine the gross exposed sidewall area of the house. Tabulate this figure under square feet.
- Determine the Btu/hr/sq ft of heat gain from the table.
- Multiply (sq ft) (Btu/hr/sq ft) and tabulate the result under heat gain.
- Determine the number of cubic feet of air being introduced into the residence by any mechanical means in cubic feet/minute. Tabulate this under cubic feet of air/minute.
- Multiply (cu ft of air/min) (Btu/hr/cu ft/min) and tabulate the result under heat gain.
- Add the heat gains to obtain the total heat gain from infiltration and ventilation.

Heat Gains From Occupants

Heat is generated inside a residence by the occupants and by the appliances used. So it is necessary to calculate the internal heat gain when calculating summer heat gains.

Occupants   The average occupant adds about 225 Btu/hr of sensible heat to a residential building. Usually the number of occupants, if unknown, is calculated as twice the number of bedrooms in the residence.

Appliances   An average value of 1200 Btu/hr of sensible heat gain is typically added by the kitchen. Other large heat-producing appliances such as a dryer may also need to be calculated. All heat-producing appliances should be carefully vented to keep the heat gain down.

Figure 4.25 is a heat gain table for occupants and appliances. To use this table, proceed as follows:

- Determine the number of bedrooms.
- Determine the number of occupants. If unknown, use two occupants per bedroom.

- Multiply the number of occupants by 225 to obtain the heat gain.
- Determine the number of kitchens.
- Multiply the number of kitchens by 1200 Btu/hr. Tabulate the result under heat gain.
- Add the heat gains to obtain the total heat gain.

The Total Building Heat Gain

The total sensible heat gain of the structure is the sum of the heat gains from the walls, the windows, the infiltration, and the occupants and appliances. To obtain the total building heat gain, it is necessary to add the latent heat gain to the sensible load.

In this shortcut method of determining residential cooling load, the latent heat gain is determined by adding from 20 to 30% of the sensible heat load to the total sensible load. Twenty percent would be used in dry climates, whereas 30% would be used in climates of average or above average dampness.

Figure 4.26 shows the final heat gain table. To fill it out, proceed as follows:

- Tabulate the heat gains for walls, windows, infiltration, and occupants.
- Add the heat gains to produce the total sensible gain.
- Add from 20 to 30% of the sensible heat gain to obtain the latent heat gain.
- Total the sensible and the latent heat gains to give the total heat gain.

Making a Decision

In this chapter you learned the difference between heat and temperature, the principles of heat transfer, and the heat energy balance formula. This gave you an understanding of the basic mechanisms that you needed to deal with in determining heat transmission within building structures.

Then you went on to learn about heat transmission in building structures. First you studied heat losses during the winter months and how to calculate them. Then you learned how to determine heat gains in a building during the summer months. You learned a shortcut method that only applies to residences. Commercial buildings were not covered.

You should have learned how to calculate the heating and cooling load of a residential building. You should now be equipped to evaluate different types of construction and building materials as to their effect on a building's demand for energy.

WORKSHEET

Item	Sq Ft	Cu Ft of Air/Minute	Btu/hr/sq ft or/cu ft/min	Heat Gain
Exposed wall area	———		———	———
Mechanical ventilation		———	———	———
			Total gain	———

Figure 4.24. Heat gains from infiltration and ventilation.

WORKSHEET

Item	Number	Occupants	Btu/hr	Heat Gain
Bedrooms	———	———	———	———
Kitchens	———	———	———	———
		Total gain		———

Figure 4.25. Heat gains from occupants and appliances.

WORKSHEET

Figure	Item Heat Gain	Btu/hr
4.20	Walls	—————
4.22	Windows	—————
4.24	Infiltration	—————
4.25	Occupants	—————
	Total sensible heat gain	—————
	Latent heat gain	—————
	Total structure heat gain	—————

Figure 4.26. Total structure summer heat gain.

DECISION
5

Build an Energy-efficient Home

The efficient use of energy has never been a subject of concern to most Americans. Why is this? Energy has always cost money. Up until the early 1970s energy was cheap in cost and plentiful in supply, so most Americans had never seen the need to be overly concerned about how efficiently they used the energy that they purchased. Now all that has changed. Energy is tight in supply. It is very costly. It is getting more expensive every day. And it is a major contributor to the rampant inflation that crippled the American economy throughout the 1970s.

The two areas where most Americans have a direct control over energy efficiency are in their choice of automobiles and in their choice of home construction. The federal government has mandated energy-efficient automobiles. Both federal and state governments are beginning to mandate energy-efficient building construction programs in public buildings. Energy-efficient residential construction may be mandated next.

In this chapter you will study what energy efficiency is and how it is achieved. You will study:

- Fuels so that you can make a wise choice from the different types that are available.
- Air infiltration and ventilation so that you can properly control their use to give you comfort without extra cost.
- Moisture in buildings and how its control can contribute to personal comfort and the building's life.
- Thermal insulation and vapor barriers so that you can properly design them for maximum efficiency.
- Thermal insulation practices so that you can use your money wisely when constructing your home.

Last, you will do an analysis of a typical house constructed in three different ways so that you can see for yourself just how important adherence to energy-efficient construction is and how it can benefit your pocketbook over the life of your home.

Energy Efficiency

Energy efficiency is a measure of how well you use the fuel that you purchase. A simple way to express it is effective energy gain divided by total energy purchased. You may buy 100 MMBtu of energy to heat your home over the heating season. But your analysis of heat losses may show that you only need 50 MMBtu to give you the heat that you need. In this particular case, your energy efficiency is only 50%.

$$\begin{array}{r} 50 \text{ MMBtu} \\ \div\ 100 \text{ MMBtu} \\ \hline 0.50 \\ \times\ 100 \\ \hline = 50\% \text{ efficiency} \end{array}$$

It may be possible for you to accomplish that heating job with only 70 MMBtu if you invest in energy-efficient construction. This would raise your efficiency to a little over 71% and save you the cost of 30 MMBtu, which in today's market could be worth up to $450. Why not invest that $450 in measures that will give you increased efficiency? Over the life of a 25-year mortgage that amounts to a savings of $11,250 in today's money. It will be more as inflation continues to increase fuel costs. So let us take a look at how your home can be made more energy efficient.

$$\begin{array}{r} 50 \text{ MMBtu} \\ \div\ 70 \text{ MMBtu} \\ \hline 0.714 \\ \times\ 100 \\ \hline = 71.4\% \text{ efficiency} \end{array}$$

Your Energy Needs

Your need for energy within your home breaks down into three major uses: space heating, water heating, and lighting and appliances. Space heating heats the building structure and the air within it to a comfortable temperature. Water heating supplies the hot water that you need for washing and bathing. Lighting and appliance energy provides the comfort and convenience that you need to perform your household tasks and provide entertainment.

This chapter will discuss the ramifications of space heating. It will touch lightly on how lighting and appliances affect space heating. It will not discuss the heating of water.

How is your energy use broken out? Figure 5.1 shows a typical need for energy within a residence. Fifty percent goes for space heating. Twenty percent goes for water heating. Fifteen percent goes for space cooling. Another 15% goes for lighting appliances. Your needs may be different, but these are typical.

Your purchase of energy may be far different however. Let us assume that the energy in Figure 5.1 was purchased in different fuels: oil heat for space heating, gas heat for hot water, electricity for cooling, and electricity for lighting and appliances as an example. A typical efficiency of an oil burner is 60%. The efficiency of a gas water heater is about 70%. Air conditioning with electricity typically has an efficiency of 250%. Electrical appliances run from 90 to 100% efficiency.

Figure 5.2 shows your purchases of energy under these conditions. You need 83.3 MMBtu of oil energy for heating the space, 28.6 MMBtu of gas energy to heat your water, 6 MMBtu of electrical energy to cool your home, and about 15.8 MMBtu of electrical energy to run your appliances. About 133.7 MMBtu altogether. So your energy efficiency is about 75%.

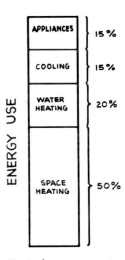

Figure 5.1. Typical energy requirements.

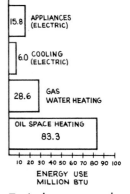

Figure 5.2. Typical energy purchases.

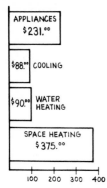

Figure 5.3. Typical 1978 costs.

Your Energy Costs

Each type of fuel that you purchase has a different cost per MMBtu associated with it. For instance, in 1978 the average cost of electricity across the United States was about 4½ cents per kilowatt-hour; or $14.64/MMBtu. The average cost of number 2 fuel oil was about 55 cents per gallon; or about $4.50/MMBtu. The cost of natural gas was about 30 cents per hundred cubic feet; or about $3.15/MMBtu. So the fuel costs for the requirements shown in Figure 5.1 would have been as shown in Figure 5.3. As you can easily see, the cost of heating and cooling the building is a very major energy cost.

Choosing a Fuel

Your choice of fuel depends on supply dependability, convenience of use, economy of purchase, and cost of combustion equipment. Over the past 30 years these factors have been heavily weighed in favor of natural gas, fuel oil, and electricity. But the dependability of supply and the cost of purchase of these fuels have come to be unsatisfactory. So it is necessary to sacrifice some convenience of use and equipment cost to assure supply and economy.

There are five classes of fuel that you can choose from: gaseous fuels, liquid fuels, solid fuels, electricity, and solar energy. Each has its advantages and disadvantages.

Gaseous Fuels For home heating you can choose from two gaseous fuels: natural gas and commercial propane. Both appear to be readily available for the next 20 years. The combustion equipment is relatively inexpensive. They are very clean fuels that are extremely convenient to transport and store. However, you can anticipate that their cost will increase dramatically over the 20-year time period.

Natural gas is the logical choice if you live where it is available. If not, then consider propane in cylinders, bottles, or tanks. Propane is usable throughout the United States as it has a boiling point of −40°F.

Liquid Fuels There are two types of liquid petroleum fuels: *distillates* and *residuals*. The distillates are fuel oils refined from the crude oil, whereas the residuals are the low ends of the crude oil left after gasoline, kerosine, jet fuel, and distillate fuel oils are refined. Residual fuel oils are not satisfactory for home use. They are heavy, thick oils containing sulfur and alkali metals. Residual oils must be preheated to make them flow. They pollute the air unless special equipment is installed.

There are two distillate fuel oils available: grade No. 1 and grade No. 2. Grade No. 1 is a highly volatile, quickly vaporizing fuel for use in pot-type combustion equipment such as room space heaters. It does not require atomization. Grade No. 2 is a heavier distillate for use with atomizing equipment that sprays the oil into the combustion chamber.

For central home heating furnaces, No. 2 fuel oil is the liquid fuel of choice. The combustion equipment is relatively inexpensive. The fuel is slightly dirtier than natural gas but still quite clean. Fuel oils have high flash points and can easily be stored indoors in the home or in an underground tank close to it. The disadvantage to fuel oils is that the price is completely unpredictable, having increased from less than 16¢/gal in 1970 to more than $1/gal in 1980.

Solid Fuels The solid fuels are coal, coke, and wood. Coal was widely used in home heating prior to World War II. But gas and oil replaced it between 1945 and 1970 due to their convenience and cleanliness. There are two types of coal available: anthracite and bituminous. Both have approximately the same heating values. Both are suitable for home heating. Anthracite is cleaner burning and produces less ash, smoke, and soot.

Coal is inconvenient to store. It is dirtier to burn and is less automatic in its combustion process, requiring more labor on the part of the homeowner than either gaseous or liquid fuels. The combustion equipment is readily available and relatively inexpensive. Hauling ashes and disposing of them is necessary. Today coal is generally available. It is competitively priced. However, the increased use of coal by American industry will place it in short supply. Additional mines must be opened. Additional hauling equipment will be needed if the demand grows. The outlook for coal as a source of home heat is questionable over the next 20 years. The cost is expected to rise along with the cost of natural gas and fuel oil.

Coke and wood are not widely used for home heating. Both can be. Automatic equipment is rapidly appearing on the market to reduce the labor of using them. Increased use is expected, especially in rural areas. As wood is a renewable resource, the possible use of it should be explored by the homeowner. The cost of wood is expected to rise with the demand for it. It is hard to transport and store in large quantities.

Electricity The use of electricity as a home heating fuel has only one drawback; it is not affordable. Why is this? Fossil fuels, nuclear fuels, and hydroelectric power are the fuels used to generate electricity. The use of hydroelectric power is very small compared to the use of fossil fuels. The energy efficiency of a fossil fuel electric generating plant is down around 30%. Further losses in efficiency are encountered in transmitting the electrical energy to the home. So although the utility uses residual oils and cheap coals, it must charge a large price for the electricity that it delivers to your home. Additionally, more fossil-fueled utility plants cannot be built if they are to be fueled with gas or oil. The utilities are restricted to coal with its poor supply outlook and to nuclear with its environmental problems. Electricity is clean. It is convenient. The equipment to use it effectively is inexpensive. But you can plan on the cost increasing 10% or more each year over the next 20 years.

There are two types of electrical heating devices: the resistance heater and the *heat pump*. A heat pump can be thought of as an air conditioner mounted backward so that it extracts heat from the outside air and brings it into the house. Resistance heat works at about 100% efficiency. Heat pumps work at about 250% efficiency. But air-to-air heat pumps do not work economically when the temperature of the outside air drops below about 40°F, so they cannot be used economically in the northern states unless they are replacing electric resistance heaters.

Solar Energy "Step right up. Get your solar energy. It's clean. It's ecologically sound. And it's free. You heard me, I said it's free."

These words, taken from a movie distributed by a leading Michigan utility company in 1977, do not tell the whole story. Solar energy is free. It is not going to increase in cost over the next 20 years. It is available across the United States. But the cost of equipment to use it is expensive. A solar system requires a large front-end investment by the homeowner, an investment way beyond that needed for any investment in combustion equipment for fossil fuels. That is a major drawback to its use. On the more positive side, solar energy definitely will continue to be readily available and can contribute strongly to your overall fuel requirements. It does deserve strong consideration.

The Final Fuel Choice

The final fuel choice is up to you after you have studied the alternatives in your location and made some financial calculations about present and future costs. But one fact is very clear; the less fuel you need, the lower your costs. That is why you should own an energy-efficient home.

Building Structure Heat Losses and Gains

To understand building structure heat losses and gains, you must study the principles of infiltration and ventilation, moisture in buildings, thermal insulation and vapor barriers, heat transmission principles, and heat transmission in buildings.

You studied heat transmission in buildings and heat transmission principles in Decision 4. Now you will study the elements of building construction that increase a building's energy efficiency.

Air Infiltration and Ventilation

Infiltration is air leakage through cracks and openings, around doors and windows, and through walls and floors of a structure. The amount of air infiltration depends on how well the building was built, its general condition, and the difference in air pressure between the interior and the exterior of the building.

This difference in air pressure is caused by the wind forces flowing around and over the building. The pressures are positive on the windward side and negative on the leeward side. This causes air to flow through the building.

Buildings can be *naturally ventilated* or *mechanically ventilated*. Natural ventilation is ventilation through windows, doors, and ventilating stacks, whereas mechanical ventilation is ventilation supplied by moving the air with fans and blowers.

When the air inside the building is warmer than the outside air, it flows naturally up through chimneys and ventilating stacks. The air is replaced by cooler air flowing in through cracks and openings. If the wind is blowing, the flow of air tends to increase. If the temperature differential between the inside air and the outside air is increased, the flow of air tends to increase. The higher the flow of air through the building, the more heat that must be supplied or taken away to maintain a comfortable temperature.

Air Changes

The amount of air infiltration is measured in the number of *air changes per hour*. One air change per hour would be the replacement of all the air in a building in one hour. Generally, residences have from 0.7 to 1.5 air changes per hour. But an especially tight house might have as few as 0.5 air changes per hour and a poorly built house in poor condition might have 2 or more air changes per hour.

A certain amount of air change is essential for human comfort. Usually about 0.7 to 1.5 air changes per hour are necessary. More changes result in a house that is expensive to heat. Fewer changes result in a stuffy and/or humid house.

In commercial and industrial buildings, the amount of air that must be exchanged depends on the use of the building. Readers designing commercial buildings are urged to consult the *ASHRAE 1977 Fundamentals Handbook*, Chapter 21, Table 6.

Air Leakage

Air leaks readily through the openings around windows and doors, around sills and foundations, and, to a lesser extent, through the walls themselves. It is also quite common to experience high air leakage where door and window frames join the walls unless the frames are carefully fitted and caulked.

The number of windows and doors in any one room can have a large effect on the air changes per hour in that room. The table in Figure 5.4 shows typical examples.

Figure 5.5 shows typical air infiltration through different types of windows and between window frames and different types of walls. This table shows infiltration in cubic feet of air per hour per foot of *crack*. Crack is the number of feet of opening in the window or the frame. Figure 5.6 shows how crack is measured. Crack in a double-hung window is three times the window's width plus twice the window's height.

	AIR CHANGES PER HOUR	
ROOM TYPE	NO STORM SASH	WITH STORM SASH
No windows or doors	0.5	
Windows and doors on one side	1	0.67
Windows and doors on two sides	1.5	1
Windows and doors on three sides	2	1.34

Figure 5.4. Air changes per hour for different room types.

TYPE WINDOW	AIR INFILTRATION*
A. Double-hung wood window	
Nonweatherstripped, poor fit	150
Nonweatherstripped, average fit	57
Weatherstripped, loose fit	58
Weatherstripped, average fit	30
B. Frame-wall leakage	
Masonry wall, uncaulked	34
Masonry wall, caulked	6
Wood wall, uncaulked	29

*Cubic feet of air per hour per foot of crack with 0.3 in. of water pressure difference.

Figure 5.5. Typical air infiltration through double-hung windows and frame-wall cracks.

Figure 5.7 shows typical air leakage through different types of walls. A poorly constructed, unplastered brick wall will have extremely high leakage. Plastering the wall will eliminate most of that leakage. Lathed and plastered wood-frame walls will have very low leakage. The use of a vapor barrier, such as a polyethylene sheeting, can cut the leakage down even further.

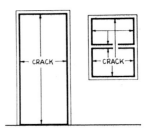

Figure 5.6. Figuring the feet of crack in a window or a door.

Figure 5.8 shows typical infiltration around doors. Good fitting and weatherstripping can cut door air infiltration by a factor of five. Air also infiltrates between the door frame and the wall unless the frame is well fitted and caulked.

Natural Ventilation

Natural ventilation is ventilation achieved by designing the building to promote the flow of air through and around the building. The wind and thermal forces cause air movement. Natural ventilation devices can be arranged to take advantage of and to control these forces.

Natural ventilation devices include windows, doors, skylights, roof ventilators, chimneys, and ventilating stacks. Windows not only ventilate, they also transmit light. Windows can be of many different types depending on the overall needs and design of the structure. Roof ventilators should be mounted where they can receive the full benefit of the draft created by the wind. They should be able to be opened and closed unless they open into an unheated attic. They should be designed to create high air flow and to pivot with changes in wind direction. Chimneys and ventilating stacks must be located where the wind from any direction can act on them. They must have dampers that can be readily opened and closed as required for building interior comfort.

Figure 5.7. Air infiltration through typical wall types.

TYPE WALL	AIR INFILTRATION*
Poor brick wall, 8½ in.	75
Good brick wall, 8½ in.	24
Brick wall plus plaster	0.2
Wood frame wall, lathed and plastered	0.29

*Cubic feet of air per hour with a pressure differential of 0.3 in. of water.

Figure 5.8. Air infiltration around typical doors.

TYPE DOOR	AIR INFILTRATION*
Poor fitting, no weatherstripping	69
Average fitting, no weatherstripping	20
Average fitting, weatherstripped	13

*Cubic feet of air per hour per foot of crack with a 10 mph wind.

For good natural ventilation, observe the following general procedures.

- Design the building for effective ventilation under all wind directions, not just the prevailing winds.
- Do not obstruct the inlets that allow air to flow into the structure.
- Have the same number of square feet of inlet or less as you have air outlet. This will give you the greatest flow.
- Route the air throughout the building. Do not have the inlets and the outlets located close together.
- For cooling a building, locate the air inlets low in the structure and the outlets high in the structure.
- Use devices in each opening that allow you to control the ventilation and to obtain the most favorable effects under all conditions.
- Choose window styles that augment air flow rather than impede it. Casement windows will catch air flowing parallel to the building wall. Awning windows will catch air flowing at right angles to the building wall.

Moisture in Buildings

A typical family of four produces up to 25 lb of water per day from cooking, washing, bathing, breathing, and perspiring. When humidifiers, washers, dryers, and other appliances are used in the home, this production of water greatly increases. This water is generally available as water vapor in the air. Unless it is exhausted from the structure, it can condense and create a serious moisture problem within the building.

Water Vapor In Air

Water vapor in air is a gas that is evenly distributed throughout the air. But it acts independently and can move about through the air independent of the air movement.

A cubic foot of air can only hold so much water. When it holds the maximum amount, it is said to be *saturated*. The amount that can be held is a function of the pressure and the temperature of the air.

Relative humidity is the term that is used to describe the amount of water vapor in the air versus the amount that the air can hold at saturation. If the relative humidity is 40%, then the air is holding 40% of all the water vapor that it can hold. Once the air is saturated with water vapor, any additional water vapor will condense to water droplets and precipitate out of the air as a liquid.

Cool air becomes saturated with water vapor faster than warm air as the cool air will hold less water vapor per cubic foot. So when the air has a high relative humidity and the temperature is dropped, the relative humidity increases until the saturation point is reached.

The temperature at which a given water vapor-air mixture becomes saturated is known as the *dew point temperature*. At the dew point temperature, water will begin to condense out of the air onto cool surfaces as liquid water droplets. If the dew point temperature is below 32°F, then the water will precipitate as frost.

Effects of Water Condensation

Water condensation can have serious effects on a building structure. Therefore it is essential to understand how to control it.

Most common building materials have a strong affinity for water. They can be said to be *hygroscopic*. A hygroscopic material is one that readily absorbs moisture from the atmosphere. Wood, plaster, bricks, stone, and concrete are highly hygroscopic. Mineral fibers and fillers are even more so. Glass and metals are not.

When excess quantities of water are present in wood, it changes in dimension. In fact, it is not uncommon for a typical wood 2 × 4 to gain or lose up to 1/16 in. in width. However, it does not change in length. When large quantities of water are present in wood, it is subject to biologic attack, a condition known as *rot*. So excess moisture must be avoided.

In masonry construction, excess moisture can lead to a condition known as *spalling*. Spalling is the breaking up and the flaking off of layers of the masonry surface due to repeated freeze-thaw cycles. The moisture penetrates the material and freezes. This creates strong forces that peel off the surface layers of the material.

Moisture in insulation, such as vermiculite, perlite, cellulose, and other mineral and fibrous materials, destroys the material's ability to act as an effective insulation. Heat transmission through a water-saturated material is extremely rapid. Over a period of time, insulation treated in this manner will also slump, compact, and become subject to microbiologic decay.

Moisture in building materials markedly affects their heat transmission by creating a better path for heat to flow through the material. When the material is exposed to a *temperature gradient*, that is a condition where one side is colder than the other, the moisture tends to migrate toward the colder side through a process of evaporation, vapor flow, and condensation.

Types of Water Condensation Two types of water condensation occur in buildings: *visible condensation* and *concealed condensation*. Visible condensation is condensation that can be readily observed. Concealed condensation is condensation that is taking place within the walls, ceiling, and roofs that cannot be readily detected with the eye.

Visible condensation occurs when any surface is colder than the dew point of the surrounding air. In the wintertime condensation is usually seen on windowpanes, uninsulated walls, and attic roofs. It can peel paint, loosen wallpaper, and, in extreme cases, start wood rot and plaster or masonry spalling. It is avoided by controlling the relative humidity within the structure and by using good insulation within the walls and the ceiling of the structure. In the summertime visible condensation is normally seen on basement concrete walls, floors cooled by contact with the ground, and uninsulated water pipes. It can be avoided by reducing ventilation, warming the surfaces, or providing dehumidification of the air.

Concealed condensation in heated buildings is caused by the diffusion of water vapor from within the building into the walls, ceiling, and roof. The production of water vapor within the building raises the vapor pressure above that of the surrounding outside air, which provides a driving force to push the vapor through the structure's exterior walls.

A typical well-constructed modern house has about 40% relative humidity in the winter months. An older house typically would have about 25% relative humidity. As would be expected, when the outside temperature warms during the summer months, the interior relative humidity increases into the 50 to 65% range. This increased relative humidity drives the water vapor into the structure's exterior where it condenses as water droplets as it encounters cooler temperatures. The result is concealed condensation within the walls.

In roofs where the exterior of the roof is covered with moisture vapor resistant materials, concealed condensation can cause rapid rot of the lumber. In walls, it swells the wood and damages the heat transmission properties of the insulation. When temperatures go below freezing, it can cause frost damage. Outside paints will peel, and the lumber can rot. In basements and crawl spaces, the condensation can be transmitted through the structure, again causing one or more of these problems.

Concealed condensation is controlled by taking the following steps.

- *Build a vapor barrier into the walls and ceilings near to the warm side of the structure.* In a wood-frame wall, attach it to the warm side of the studs. Polyethylene films, asphalt-laminated paper, and similar materials are generally used. When applying insulation with a vapor barrier attached, be certain that the vapor barrier side of the insulation is closest to the interior of the structure. In a building that has been already constructed and where the vapor barrier has proved to be inadequate, use paints that have good vapor barrier characteristics to add to the barrier.
- *Make certain that any new or existing vapor barriers are continuous.* Use good workmanship. Plug all holes that would allow the convection of air through the wall. Lap edges. Tape around electrical outlets and window and door joints. Seal any holes.

- *Provide good ventilation of the living space.* If you prevent the build-up of moisture vapor within the house, then there will be less moisture to penetrate the walls. In most houses, normal air infiltration will provide adequate ventilation except in the kitchen or bathrooms.
- *Ventilate attic and crawl spaces.* Bare earth should be protected with a heavy vapor barrier. Make sure that these crawl spaces are adequately drained.
- *Use mechanical ventilation or dehumidification devices* where natural ventilation is inadequate.

Thermal Insulation and Vapor Barriers

Thermal insulations are materials that lower the transmission of heat energy. Because they lower this flow, they conserve energy, control surface temperatures, aid in the control of interior temperatures, prevent vapor condensation, and reduce temperature fluctuations.

Water vapor barriers are materials that provide a resistance to the transmission of moisture in the form of water vapor. Because they retard water vapor transmission, they keep the insulation dry, prevent damage from rot, freezing, or corrosion, and reduce the peeling of exterior paints. Typically, the water vapor barrier is part of the thermal insulation material.

Types of Thermal Insulations

There are five basic types of thermal insulation: loose-fill, flexible, rigid, reflective, and foamed-in-place. Typical loose-fill insulations are shredded paper, shavings, expanded perlite, vermiculite, and mineral fibers from rock, glass, or furnace slag. Typical loose-fill insulations have R-values ranging from 2.1 to 3.1/in. of thickness.

Typical flexible insulations are blankets and batts of rock, glass, or furnace slag fibers. Common names are rock wool and fiberglass. They typically range in density from 0.3 to 2.0 lb/cu ft. Their typical R-values range from 2.8 to 3.4/in. of thickness.

Typical rigid insulations are boards or sheets formed from bonded glass fiber, expanded polystyrene, and urethane foam. They typically range from 4.8 to 9 lb/cu ft. They typically have R-values ranging from 4 to 6.5/in. of thickness.

Reflective insulations are generally highly reflective materials such as aluminum foil, often paper-laminated and bonded into multiple sheets with integral air spaces.

Foamed-in-place insulation typically is urethane foam, which has a typical density of about 1.5 lb/cu ft and an R-value of 6.25/in. of thickness.

Properties of Thermal Insulation   Thermal insulations must provide good heat barrier properties in order to retard the flow of heat energy. They must have sufficient structural strength to maintain their integrity for many years. They should not pick up water or water vapor. They should pose no problems to human safety. And they must have low flammability, be nondusting, and nonirritating. Above all, they must last for 20 to 30 yr without decay, rot, or other degradation.

Types of Water Vapor Barriers

The three major types of water vapor barriers are: *structural barriers, membrane barriers,* and *coating barriers.* Structural barriers typically are rigid sheets of reinforced plastics, aluminum, steel, and other rigid insulation materials that are impervious to water flow. They are fastened in place mechanically and their joints caulked or sealed. Membrane barriers include foils, treated papers, coated felts, and plastic films. Quite often they are part of the insulation material. They are nailed or stapled over the wall closest to the interior of the building. Coating barriers typically include asphalt, resinous, and polymeric mastics, which are rolled, brushed, or sprayed in place.

Properties of Vapor Barriers Water vapor barriers are used to reduce the rate of flow of water vapor. This prevents the accumulation of concealed condensation within the walls of the structure. Water vapor barriers must be thermally stable, have good mechanical strength, be inert, and be unaffected by moisture and other deteriorating elements. They must be easily fabricated and applied.

The effectiveness of a vapor barrier depends on its properties, the permanence of these properties, the location of the barrier within the structure, and the care with which it is applied. In a building that requires heating, it is generally placed at or near the surface exposed to the winter-warm side.

If even small openings exist in the barrier, its effectiveness is drastically reduced. Good workmanship is essential. All openings and edges must be sealed or caulked. The effects of aging, building movement, and expansion and contraction must be allowed for.

Thermal Insulation Economics

The primary function of insulation is to reduce the loss of energy from a heated structure or to prevent the gain of heat energy by a cooled structure.

If energy were free, there would be little need for large amounts of insulation. But energy is expensive and growing more expensive every day. So it is wise to use enough insulation to lower energy costs as far as is practical.

However, the use of insulation can be overdone. The simple statement here shows why.

Two inches of insulation pass half as much heat as one inch of insulation. Four inches of insulation pass half as much heat as two inches. Eight inches pass half as much heat as four inches.

In other words, to halve the heat loss through a wall, you must double the existing resistance of the wall by doubling its insulated thickness.

Figure 5.9 is a table illustrating this point. It shows a window that has a resistance to heat flow with a value of one. For illustrative purposes the table assumes that over a certain period of time that window will have 100 Btu flow through it. Compared to the window, an uninsulated wall might have a resistance to heat flow of two. So the heat flow would be cut in half. If 1 in. of fiberglass insulation were added, that heat flow would be

TYPE WALL	Btu'S LOST	RESISTANCE TO HEAT FLOW, R-VALUE
Window	100	1
Uninsulated	50	2
1 in. insulation	25	4
2 in. insulation	12.5	8
4 in. insulation	6.25	16
8 in. insulation	3.12	32

Figure 5.9. Each doubling of insulation cuts heat flow in half.

cut in half again. If 2 in. of fiberglass were added, the heat loss would again be halved. But it will take another 2 in. to halve that heat flow.

Figure 5.10 is a graph showing a plot of these typical heat losses taken from the table in Figure 5.9. A wood-frame sidewall typically has about 4 in. of insulation. Eight inches of insulation are typical of a wood-frame ceiling.

The lesson is clear. Doubling the thickness of the sidewalls by constructing them of 2 × 8 lumber instead of 2 × 4 lumber most likely will not be economical. Using 16 in. of insulation in the ceiling instead of 8 in. is of questionable value if the investment is too large.

Thermal Insulation Practices

It is extremely important to design the thermal insulation carefully during the initial planning of the building. Proper thermal insulation design assures economical and comfortable interior temperatures over the life of the building.

The insulation must be chosen to give good thermal performance, allow water vapor control, prevent structural expansion and contraction, and reduce air infiltration. It is far cheaper to incorporate this insulation during construction than it is to add it later. But in the case of an existing building, insulation can readily be added and may be an excellent investment.

Building Types

Residential construction is typically wood-framed walls, roofs, ceilings, and floors or masonry-constructed walls and floors with wood-framed roofs and ceilings. Metal construction is rarely used. Many combinations of wood and masonry are seen. So in this section you will study the different types of wood and masonry construction and learn the common insulation practices and their effectiveness.

In this section, insulation practices will be labeled as poor, good, and excellent. Each area of the house will be treated separately, and then the house will be treated as a whole. A recommended insulation practice will be provided for both retrofitting an existing house and for new construction.

A Typical Wood-framed House

Figure 5.11 shows a cross section of the typical exterior fabric of a wood-framed house. The details will vary from location to location and from builder to builder, (and the timber sizes are subject to local building codes). The construction shown is typical of good, solid building practice as used in the period of 1940 through 1970 by quality builders. There are no compromises in this frame construction.

The basement consists of a 12-in. concrete block wall protected below grade by a membrane and a tar vapor barrier, a 4-in. poured concrete floor placed over 8 in. of compacted gravel, and a wood sill bolted to the foundation. Both exterior and interior drain tiles or perforated pipe are included to protect against water in the basement. The 12-in. block wall could readily be replaced by an 8-in. poured concrete wall if desired.

The frame of the first floor consists of 2 × 8 floor joists placed on 12- to 16-in. centers depending on the building's width and covered with ⅝-in. Douglas Fir Plyscord; an exterior wall framed with 2 × 4 wood studs placed on 16-in. centers and covered with ½-in. Douglas Fir Plyscord; 2 × 6 ceiling joists placed on 16-in. centers; and an interior finish of ½-in. gypsum wallboard. All joists should be blocked or cross-braced at their midspan points.

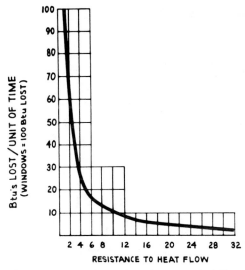

Figure 5.10. Relative heat losses with different thicknesses of a given insulation.

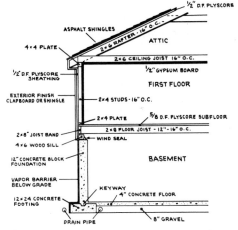

Figure 5.11. Typical wood-framed house built between 1940 and 1970.

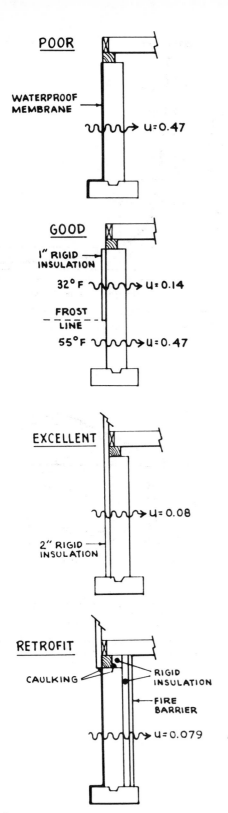

POOR

WATERPROOF
MEMBRANE

$\rightarrow$ U = 0.47

GOOD

1" RIGID
INSULATION

32°F $\rightarrow$ U = 0.14

FROST
LINE

55°F $\rightarrow$ U = 0.47

EXCELLENT

$\rightarrow$ U = 0.08

2" RIGID
INSULATION

RETROFIT

CAULKING

RIGID
INSULATION

FIRE
BARRIER

$\rightarrow$ U = 0.079

Figure 5.12. Some methods of insulating concrete or concrete-block basement walls.

The attic consists of 2 × 6 roof rafters placed 16 in. on center. They should be tied together with a 1 × 8 collar girt every third rafter. An acceptable alternative construction would be the use of trussed construction with the trusses running from 16 to 24 in. on center depending on the span. A minimum of ½-in. Douglas Fir Plyscord should be used on the rafters as exterior sheathing to prevent a scalloped effect between rafters caused by the plywood taking a set with time after encountering live roof loads from ice and snow. The roof should be capped in a thick double-butt asphalt shingle or its equivalent. Alternative roof constructions may be used in certain localities due to local practice. An example might be a wood-shingled roof as is commonly seen in southern California.

Many liberties are taken with this type of quality construction. The outside sheathing is often replaced with ⅜-in. Plyscord or with a tar-impregnated or polystyrene building board. These materials have inadequate strength to withstand lateral forces, provide poor nailing, and cannot be properly straightened to provide a "trued-up" sidewall. The gravel and the inside drainpipe are often eliminated, which can cause the floor to crack under water pressure. The ⅝-in. subfloor is replaced with ½-in. plywood, which can give poor nailing and provides poor resistance to large live loads such as a piano or a waterbed. The membrane barrier on the basement walls is often eliminated in favor of a coat of tar. The joist band is often eliminated to save a few dollars. This practice allows floor timbers to twist under the load of the sidewall.

Hundreds of thousands of homes exist in which the builder has taken these liberties to keep the price down. But the frame of a wood-framed house is the key to its lifetime integrity. No compromises should be accepted.

Even this quality construction can be made more energy efficient. So let us look at the different insulation practices that can be used with this type of construction.

Foundation Walls Concrete and concrete-block foundations have poor insulating qualities. A typical 12-in. block wall loses 0.47 Btu/hr/sq ft/°F, whereas a poured concrete wall 8-in. thick typically loses 0.67 Btu/hr/sq ft/°F. These are high loss rates or *U*-factors.

Losses through concrete or concrete-block walls either above or below grade can best be lowered by covering the wall with rigid slab insulation. Typical products are polystyrene and rigid urethane foamed slab.

Figure 5.12 shows some typical application methods. One inch of insulation can be applied to the outside of the wall down to the frost line. The frost line is typically 3 ft below the grade line. In a concrete-block wall the heat loss through this portion of the wall would be lowered to 0.14 Btu/hr/sq ft/°F or less depending on the material chosen. The loss rate on the lower portion of the wall would not change. But the temperature of the ground below the frost line remains fairly high throughout the year, so overall losses are far less.

Two inches of insulation applied from the top of the joist band to the footing would lower the overall losses to 0.08 Btu/hr/sq ft/°F or less. This is an excellent technique.

In existing buildings where it is not possible to place insulation on the exterior walls, slab insulation can be used on the interior wall to obtain the same results. Figure 5.13 shows a table of *U*-factors and *R*-values obtained by using a polystyrene insulation. Factors are included to convert these figures to 8-in. poured concrete walls.

Whenever using polystyrene or urethane insulation, certain precautions must be taken to protect the insulation and the building:

	INCHES OF INSULATION			
CONSTRUCTION ITEM	NONE	3/4 IN.	1 IN.	2 IN.
Outside surface	0.17	0.17	0.17	0.17
Concrete block*	1.28	1.28	1.28	1.28
Polystyrene†	—	3.35	5.0	10.0
Inside surface	0.68	0.68	0.68	0.68
Total *R*-value	2.13	5.48	7.13	12.13
Derived *U*-factor	0.47	0.18	0.14	0.08

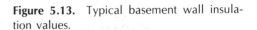

Figure 5.13. Typical basement wall insulation values.

*If using an 8-in. poured concrete wall, change this value to 0.64.
†If using polyurethane slab insulation, change this value to 6.25/in. of insulation thickness.

- Neither material has good ultraviolet light resistance. Therefore, above grade it must be coated to protect against its destruction with time.
- Certain petroleum-based solvents attack it. Always carefully check a small portion of the insulation against the wall's waterproof membrane before installing it.
- Both materials are flammable. When used indoors, they must be protected with a material such as ½-in. gypsum board that has low flammability.**
- Some urethanes have poor below-grade durability. Check out the manufacturer's application data carefully.

Good construction practice demands that four steps always be included to gain maximum value from insulating basement walls with slab insulation:

- Do not eliminate the waterproof membrane on the below-grade part of the wall.
- Caulk the wood sill where it meets the foundation with a flexible caulk to prevent infiltration.
- Use a metal flashing or a silicone caulk to prevent water from entering behind the insulation.
- Protect the basement insulation above-grade with an ultraviolet resistant coating such as silicone rubber latex. Figure 5.14 illustrates these practices.

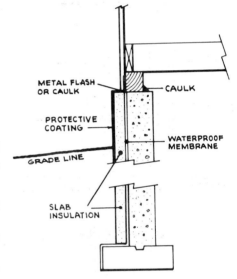

Figure 5.14. Four steps that must be taken to ensure maximum efficiency from exterior slab insulation.

Wood-framed Sidewalls

A typical wood-framed sidewall is shown in Figure 5.15. Two-by-four studs are erected on 16-in. centers using a 2 × 4 bottom plate and a 4 × 4 top plate. The outside of the wall is sheathed in ½ in. Douglas fir plywood covered with wood shingles or clapboards. A vapor barrier is placed on the inside surfaces of the studding from floor to ceiling. One-half inch gypsum wallboard is nailed over the vapor barrier. This construction leaves a 3½-in. air cavity in the center of the wall that can be filled with insulation.

A wood-framed wall constructed in this manner would have a resistance to heat flow of about *R* = 4 to 4.5 if no insulation were placed in the air cavity. The replacement of the shingles or clapboards by a stone or brick veneer would not markedly change this heat flow resistance. Nor would the replacement of the plywood by a building board or the replacement of the gypsum wallboard by plaster.

What will change the thermal resistance of the wall is the filling of the air cavities with good insulation. Sound building practice calls for 3½ in.

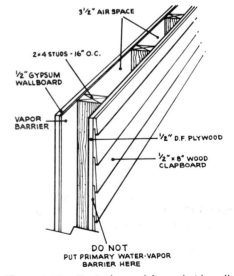

Figure 5.15. Typical wood-framed sidewall.

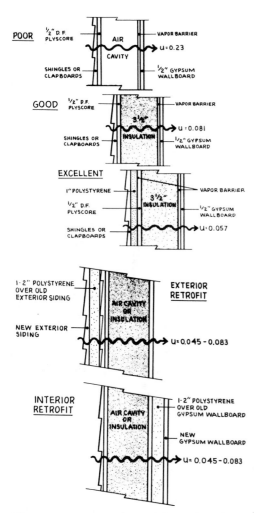

Figure 5.16. Typical wood-framed wall insulation practices.

of fiberglass, mineral fiber, or urethane foam. In extreme climates, a 1-in. thickness of slab insulation, such as polystyrene board can also be added between the sheathing and the exterior clapboards or masonry veneer. Figure 5.16 illustrates some good practices.

The filling of the air cavity is the best practice to follow in a new house. This increases the R-value of the wall by about $R = 8$. The heat flow is decreased by two-thirds. In a retrofitting situation, it is often both practical and economical to blow loose rock wool or fiberglass insulation under pressure into existing uninsulated walls. However, complete filling is never achieved due to blockages within the walls. And no vapor barrier against the wallboard is added if none exists. Good pressure filling is essential because the loose insulation will settle if not firmly packed. Cellulose products such as shredded paper and shavings should be avoided in these applications. They are fair insulation, but they settle badly with time and the labor required to accomplish the job is the larger part of the expense. It is also possible to foam urethane within existing walls, but sometimes this leads to nail popping of the wallboard. Urea formaldehyde products have had odor problems, so they should be very carefully evaluated before considering them.

One to two inches of polystyrene slab or board can be added to either a new or an existing wall. In new construction, 2 in. of slab is rarely needed when the air cavity is also filled. In old construction, where no insulation exists within the walls, 2 in. of polystyrene slab would result in excellent insulation.

Exterior retrofit and interior retrofit are both acceptable. In both cases it is necessary to cover the insulation slab. On the exterior, where the slab is generally applied right over the exterior clapboards, the new exterior covering protects the slab against ultraviolet degradation and provides a pleasing exterior. In the interior, the new wallcovering is needed as a fire-resistant covering and as a base for either painting or wallpapering.

Urethane foam can also be used effectively to fill the air cavities in new construction and offers high insulation qualities with an R-value of about 6.25/in. of thickness. Figure 5.17 shows typical R-values and derived U-factors for wood sidewalls insulated in the manner just described. Generally, sidewalls should have an R-value ranging from $R = 12$ to $R = 22$ for good effectiveness in lowering heat flow.

CONSTRUCTION ITEM	UNINSULATED CAVITY	INSULATED CAVITY	PLUS 1 IN. POLYSTYRENE	PLUS 2 IN. POLYSTYRENE
Outside surface	0.17	0.17	0.17	0.17
Wood siding	0.81	0.81	0.81	0.81
½ in. Douglas Fir Plyscord	0.62	0.62	0.62	0.62
3½ in. air cavity*	1.68	—	—	—
3½ in. fiberglass*	—	9.68	9.68	9.68
Polystyrene slab	—	—	5.00	10.00
½ in. gypsum board	0.45	0.45	0.45	0.45
Inside surface	0.68	0.68	0.68	0.68
R-value	4.41	12.41	17.41	22.41
Derived U-factor	0.23	0.081	0.057	0.045

Figure 5.17. Typical R-values and U-factors for wood-framed sidewall constructions.

*These values allow for 20% wood studding in the wall.

**The Dow Chemical Company has thoroughly researched this application for their product Styrofoam brand insulation. Complete application information can be obtained by writing to Dow Chemical U.S.A., Styrofoam Brand Products, Midland, Michigan 48640.

A word about vapor barriers. The primary vapor barrier should be on the winter-warm side of the wall. This typically means applying it to the interior surface of the studding. Generally, blanket insulation comes with a vapor barrier attached. It is considered excellent practice to stretch polyethylene film over the installed insulation before applying the wallboard. The film should be about 4-mil thick and be well-stapled or taped to the edge of the openings in the wall and to the top and bottom plates.

In the past the use of a vapor barrier on the exterior of the wall has been considered ill-advised. However, recent research by the Dow Chemical Company indicates that a second vapor barrier on the exterior of the wall has no ill effects. Again it should be stressed that wherever possible, the *primary* vapor barrier belongs on the winter-warm side of the wall.

The other things that should be considered in the insulating of sidewalls are orientation and window area. Obviously north-facing walls require much more intensive treatment. And if the wall has an extremely high percentage of window area, money spent on excessive wall insulation might better be spent in providing insulated glass or storm sash for the windows.

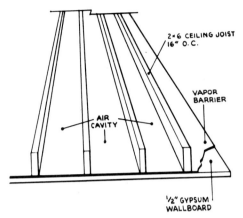

Figure 5.18. Typical conventional ceiling construction.

Wood-framed Ceilings Under Pitched Roofs

Figures 5.18 and 5.19 show typical constructions of wood-framed ceilings under pitched roofs. Figure 5.18 shows conventional construction of 2 × 6 ceiling joists on 16-in. centers. In this type of construction, ½-in. gypsum wallboard is nailed directly to the ceiling joists over a vapor barrier. Figure 5.19 shows trussed construction where 2 × 4 or 2 × 6 trusses are placed 16 to 24 in. on center. Again the ½-in. gypsum board is nailed directly to the ceiling joist part of the truss over a vapor barrier.

If loose fill or batt insulation is to be used in the ceiling, a good vapor barrier must be installed over the bottom of the ceiling joists prior to nailing up the gypsum board. Four-mil polyethylene sheeting can be used. Or foil-backed gypsum board can be installed. If the insulation is installed prior to installing the gypsum board, then paper-backed blankets with a vapor barrier are normally used. This blanket must be installed with the vapor barrier face stapled to the lower portion of the joists. Many houses have been built where this ceiling vapor barrier has been either eliminated or improperly installed because a ceiling vapor barrier is labor-intensive to install.

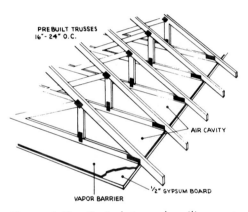

Figure 5.19. Typical trussed ceiling construction.

Considerable care should be taken to insulate the ceilings. The square foot area of the ceiling is large, usually as large as, or larger than, the sidewall area. The heat within the living area is highest at the ceiling level, giving the highest temperature differential between the inside and outside of the structure. Natural convection favors high air infiltration through the ceiling when the structure is warmer than the outside air.

Figure 5.20 shows three insulation practices. In the section labeled poor, no insulation is used. In the section labeled good, the air cavity is filled with fiberglass or mineral wool batts. In the section labeled excellent, an additional layer of batts has been installed over the ceiling joists. These should be laid so that they run at right angles to the first layer to ensure as few air voids as possible.

The results of this type of insulation practice is seen in Figure 5.21. Ninety percent of the heat losses through the ceiling can be eliminated by fully insulating it. Generally, fully insulating the ceiling is an economical practice in both new and retrofit situations. Insulation is inexpensive, and very little labor is needed to install batts on a horizontal surface.

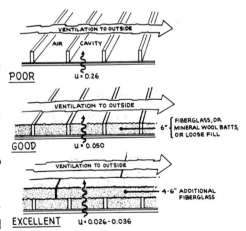

Figure 5.20. Typical ceiling insulation practices.

The use of loose-fill insulation such as perlite or vermiculite in ceilings is not recommended by the author. Nor is the use of polystyrene or polyurethane foam. The loose-fill is often highly hygroscopic. The foam may be a fire hazard.

Good ventilation between the pitched roof and the ceiling is an absolute necessity to prevent the insulation from becoming saturated with water and to keep the attic cool in the summer months. When the rafters of a pitched roof are also used as the ceiling joists, the same details of insulation apply.

CONSTRUC-TION ITEM	UNINSU-LATED	4-IN. INSULA-TION	6-IN. INSULA-TION	8-IN. INSULA-TION	12-IN. INSULA-TION
Inside air	0.61	0.61	0.61	0.61	0.61
½-in. gypsum board	0.45	0.45	0.45	0.45	0.45
2 × 6 joists*	2.14	2.14	2.14	2.14	2.14
Fiberglass batts*	—	8.80	15.20	24.00	35.00
Attic air	0.61	0.61	0.61	0.61	0.61
R-value	3.81	12.61	19.01	27.81	38.81
Derived U-value	0.26	0.08	0.05	0.036	0.026

Figure 5.21. Typical R-values and U-factors for ceilings under pitched roofs.

*Allows for 20% framing, 80% cavity.

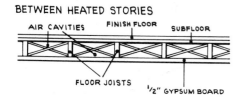

BETWEEN HEATED STORIES

AIR CAVITIES FINISH FLOOR SUBFLOOR

FLOOR JOISTS ½" GYPSUM BOARD

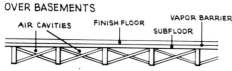

OVER BASEMENTS

AIR CAVITIES FINISH FLOOR VAPOR BARRIER SUBFLOOR

Figure 5.22. Typical wood-framed floors.

Wood-framed Floors

Two typical wood-framed floors are shown in Figure 5.22. The top illustration shows a floor between the first and second story of a two-story house. If both floors are heated, no insulation is needed. If only one story is heated, the cavity between the joists should be filled with fiberglass batts in the same manner as a ceiling under a pitched roof.

The bottom illustration shows a floor between a basement and the first floor. No insulation is generally required over a full basement where a central furnace is installed. When no central heating unit is used, insulation should definitely be considered.

Figure 5.23 shows a floor over a crawl space. Unless the crawl space is heated, the floor should be fully insulated. *A vapor barrier should face the crawl space to protect the insulation.* With plywood subfloors, no additional vapor barrier is needed under the finished floor. (This recommendation does not agree with older, published information, but it is correct.) A second vapor barrier should be placed over the crawl-space floor to prevent moisture condensation.

Floors over unheated rooms such as garages and porches should be treated in a similar manner. These floors will have R-values similar to those previously shown for ceilings.

Flat-Roof Block Houses

During the 1930s and into the 1940s, thousands of houses were built using cinder-block walls and flat roofs. Figure 5.24 shows some typical construction details. In almost all cases, these homes were inadequately insulated and have very high heat losses.

Retrofit insulating these houses is feasible. Figure 5.25 shows some ways to proceed with exterior retrofit. The sidewalls should be strapped with ¾-

in. by 1½-in. wood strapping on 16-in. centers. Over this, 1 to 2 in. of polystyrene slab insulation should be fastened. Then an exterior sheathing should be installed. This procedure will raise the R-value of the wall up to 8 to 13.

The roof should have 4 to 6 in. of urethane foam sprayed in place over the present roof. This should then be protected with an exterior roof coating. The resulting roof will have R-values ranging from 29 to 42. Figures 5.26 and 5.27 detail the different R-values before and after these changes are made.

Interior retrofit can also be undertaken with good results by installing 1 to 2 in. of polystyrene slab insulation over the plaster and covering it with ½-in. gypsum board. Either interior or exterior retrofit gives good results. Sidewall fastening in interior retrofit may be a problem, depending whether the block was plastered directly or whether the wall was wood-strapped first. Before proceeding with interior retrofit, carefully determine how door and window finish can be properly handled.

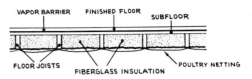

Figure 5.23. Typical insulation practices over unheated crawl spaces.

CONSTRUCTION ITEM	UNINSULATED	1-IN. POLYSTYRENE	2-IN. POLYSTYRENE
Inside air	0.61	0.61	0.61
¾-in. plaster	0.12	0.12	0.12
8-in. cinder block	1.72	1.72	1.72
Polystyrene slab	—	5.00	10.00
New sheathing	—	0.81	0.81
Outside air	0.17	0.17	0.17
R-value	2.62	8.43	13.43
Derived U-value	0.38	0.12	0.07

Figure 5.26. Typical R-values and U-factors for cinder-block walls.

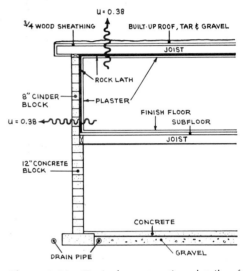

Figure 5.24. Typical construction details of cinder-block flat-roof houses built in the 1930 to 1940 era.

CONSTRUCTION ITEM	UNINSULATED	4-IN. URETHANE	6-IN. URETHANE
Inside air	0.61	0.61	0.61
¾-in. plaster	0.12	0.12	0.12
2 × 8 joist with air cavity	2.25	2.25	2.25
¾-in. sheathing	0.81	0.81	0.81
Tar and gravel roof	0.33	0.33	0.33
Urethane foam	—	25.00	37.50
Outside air	0.17	0.17	0.17
R-value	4.29	29.29	41.79
Derived U-value	0.23	0.034	0.024

Figure 5.27. Typical R-values and U-factors for flat roofs.

Two Troublesome Areas

There are two areas in wood-frame construction that traditionally are inadequately protected. The first area is at the junction of the wood sill and the joist band at the floor level. Typically, cement mortar has been used to seal the crack between the wood sill and the concrete foundation. With time, the wood sill shrinks and a linear crack around the structure's perimeter opens, allowing gross air infiltration. Additionally, the joist band is rarely insulated. Figure 5.28 shows how this area can be handled. The crack at the bottom of the sill should be carefully caulked on the inside

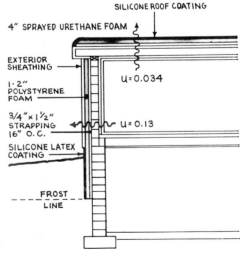

Figure 5.25. Typical exterior retrofit insulation procedure for Cinder-Block Flat-Roof houses.

and the outside. The joist band should be insulated with 3½ in. of fiberglass or mineral wood insulation.

The second area is where the ceiling joist, the rafter, and the sidewall join. It is important to extend the ceiling insulation carefully out over the sidewall into the rafter cavity.* This is shown in Figure 5.29.

Any interior walls between heated and unheated rooms, such as a garage and living quarters, should be fully insulated as standard practice.

*Authorities disagree on this practice. A duct that allows ventilation from the soffit to the attic above the insulation is advisable.

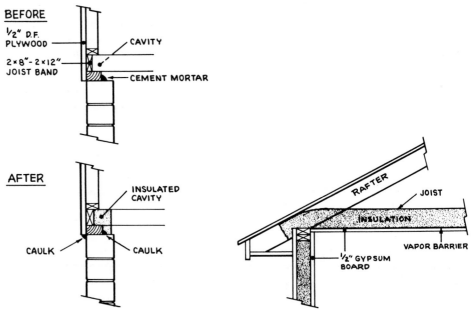

Figure 5.28. The area around the sill must be carefully treated.

Figure 5.29. The cavity at the top of the sidewalls must be fully insulated.

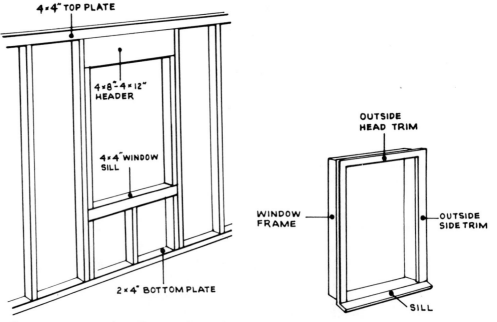

Figure 5.30. Typical window rough opening in a wood-framed sidewall.

Figure 5.31. Typical window frame as seen from outside the house.

Any floors or ceilings over unheated spaces should be fully insulated if heated space is contained over them.

The main purpose of thermal insulation is to provide an unbroken barrier between heated and unheated spaces in order to slow heat transmission. When a building structure is insulated correctly, a *thermal envelope* is created. The effectiveness of this thermal envelope determines the heat loss rate from the building.

Door And Window Insulation Practices

The choice of door or window construction, the style, and the quality has much to do with the insulating value of the item itself. But the installation of doors and windows is also critical to prevent infiltration and moisture damage.

Figure 5.30 shows a typical 2 × 4 wood-stud wall from the inside of the house. Window openings should always be double-framed with 4 × 4 construction and a header large enough to support the roof load. Note that both the window sill and the window header are constructed in such a manner as to provide load-bearing support by the short or "cripple" studs. The 4 × 4 construction all-around is required to provide good nailing for the window frame and its trim.

Figure 5.31 shows a typical window frame for a double-hung window. The sash has been left out for clarity. Although there are many different styles of windows, almost all windows are constructed in this general manner. The outside trim is nailed and glued to the frame and sill to provide a solid and square unit. The trim in many window styles projects in beyond the frame to supply a stop to hold the upper sash in place. The sill is angled down somewhat to encourage the water that collects on the sash and trim to run off. The illustration depicts the window as seen from the outside of the house.

Figure 5.32 shows the same window frame as seen from the inside of the house. Note that the outside trim extends out beyond the window frame. The window is held in place on the sidewall by placing it in the wall opening, leveling and squaring it, and nailing the outside trim securely to the sheathing of the house prior to installing the exterior finish.

To allow the window to be mounted properly, the opening in the wall must be somewhat larger than the window frame. Usually the rough opening for the frame is made about 2 in. larger than the outside frame in width and about 1 to 1½ in. larger than the height. The result, as you will see in Figure 5.33, is an air space all around the window. This air space must be stuffed full of insulation to prevent heat transmission and air infiltration.

Figure 5.34 shows how the window is mounted. Asphalt-impregnated building paper is fastened to the plywood sheathing on the sides of the opening and flush to its edges. The window is then fastened to the wall in the manner previously described. A metal flashing is nailed in place over the header trim, and the exterior sheathing is butted up to the trim sides, trim top, and trim bottom. After the exterior sheathing is applied, a flexible caulk or sealant is used to ensure a completely water- and air-tight joint. Then when insulating the sidewalls, the air cavities around the window are filled. After the gypsum board is applied inside the house, a final inside trim is nailed to the inside of the frame.

Today most windows come completely assembled except for the inside trim. Before 1950, most window frames came knocked down for site-assembly by the builder. Following frame and trim assembly, the builder planned and fitted the sash individually. At that time sash weights were

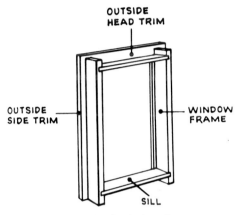

Figure 5.32. Typical window frame as seen from inside the house.

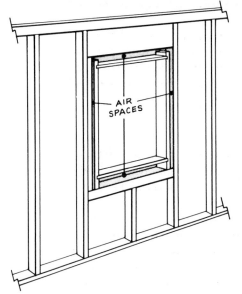

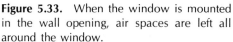

Figure 5.33. When the window is mounted in the wall opening, air spaces are left all around the window.

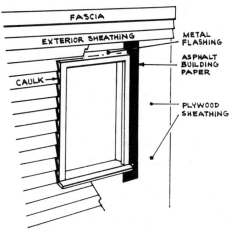

Figure 5.34. How an average wood window is mounted in a frame wall.

used to counterbalance the windows for opening and closing. This precluded insulating the air cavities, because the sash weights had to move up and down in a hollow space. As a result, this is a common source of air infiltration and excess heat transmission in old houses.

The older house can be retrofitted by removing the inside top and side trim, removing the sash weights, and filling the cavities with insulation. Retrofit kits are available to spring-load the sash sideways in order to counterbalance their weight for opening and closing them. A source of smoke, such as a cigarette or a candle can be used to determine whether this procedure is indicated. Pick a windy day when the draft will blow the smoke readily.

The average door is treated in the same manner. Again, today most doors come preassembled and weatherstripped. Up until the 1950s, most exterior door frames came disassembled and the door was planed and fitted by hand.

Aluminum and steel sashes can pose many of the same types of problems in wood-framed walls. In masonry walls, they are usually mortared into the wall so air cavities are nonexistent. However, metals are good conductors of heat, and generally steel and aluminum windows tend to transmit large amounts of energy through their metal parts. The best solution for this in new construction is to stay away from their use. In retrofit situations, one of the best solutions is to make and mount wood-framed storm windows that insulate the metal from the interior air space. Such windows can be manufactured to be placed on either the inside or the outside of the metal sash.

Doors and windows are higher transmitters of heat than are solid ceilings, floors, and walls. Figure 5.35 shows some typical *R*-values and *U*-factors for different window glazings. Single-glazed windows are the poorest insulators; triple-glazed windows are the best insulators. However, the heat transmitted by a single-glazed window with a good fitting storm sash is typically equal to the heat transmitted by a double-glazed window.

In retrofit situations, the storm window should always be considered before replacing a single-glazed window with an insulated unit at higher cost.

WINDOW TYPE	U-FACTOR	R-VALUE
Single-glazed	1.10	0.9
Double-glazed	0.62	1.6
Triple-glazed	0.39	2.6
Storm window*		2.0

*Add this R-value to the R-value of the window used.

Figure 5.35. Typical R-values and U-factors for window types.

Figure 5.36 shows some typical R-values and U-factors for exterior doors. One-and-one-half-inch doors are standard exterior construction. They have an R-value of about 2. Adding a storm door to this construction increases the R-value to about 3.7.

DOOR TYPE	U-FACTOR	R-VALUE
1-in. solid wood	0.64	1.6
1¼-in. solid wood	0.55	1.8
1½-in. solid wood	0.49	2.0
2-in. solid wood	0.43	2.3
1¾-in solid, steel clad, urethane foam-filled with thermal break	0.19	5.3
Storm door*		1.7

*Add this R-value to the R-value of the door used.

Figure 5.36. Typical R-values and U-factors for door types.

A new door has recently been marketed. It consists of a urethane core inside a steel interior and exterior panel. To prevent metal conductance, the two steel panels are separated by thermal spacers. This door has a high R-value of about 5.3. Coupled with a storm door, this makes it possible to obtain a door opening with an R-value of about 7. It is a good investment.

With both doors and windows, quality of construction of the unit is most important. They must be carefully fitted and weatherstripped to prevent air infiltration.

The Insulation Values for an Energy-Efficient House

Figure 5.37 shows the typical insulation values that should appear in poor, good, and excellent energy-efficient construction. In a mild climate with warm winters and cool summers, good construction is adequate. In northern climates with very cold winters and in southern climates with very hot summers, excellent construction practices should be carefully considered. Figure 5.38 shows the changes that must be made to move to an excellent energy-efficient construction. Although it is possible to go even further, economy usually prevents it. Removing the polystyrene slab insulation on the sidewalls and the top 6 in. of fiberglass ceiling insulation would constitute good energy-efficient construction.

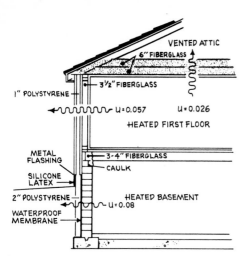

Figure 5.38. Typical construction that leads to excellent energy efficiency.

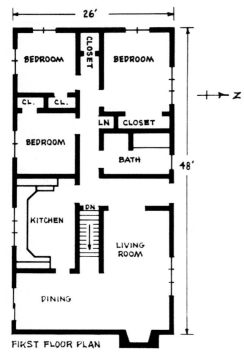

Figure 5.39. Floor plan of a 1248 sq ft ranch house.

CONSTRUCTION ITEM	INSULATING VALUES					
	POOR		GOOD		EXCELLENT	
	R	U	R	U	R	U
Basement wall	2.1	0.47	7.0	0.14	12.0	0.08
Wood sidewall	4.4	0.23	12.4	0.08	17.5	0.057
Wood ceiling	3.8	0.26	12.6	0.08	38.5	0.026
Doors	2.0	0.49	4.0	0.25	5.3	0.19
Windows	0.9	1.10	2.9	0.34	3.6	0.28
Hourly Air Changes	2		1.5		0.7	

Figure 5.37. Typical heat transmittance values for poor, good, and excellent construction.

Energy-Efficient Construction Pays Off

Figure 5.39 shows the floor plan of a 26 ft by 48 ft single-story ranch house. Figure 5.40 shows a basement plan. Figure 5.41 shows some sketches of the front, rear, and sides of this house. The heat loss of this 1248 sq ft structure is a function of its construction.

To show how important energy-efficient construction is, and how it pays off, the heat losses from this structure will be calculated using the U-factors developed in Figure 5.37 for poor, good, and excellent construction.

The tables developed in Decision 4, with some minor modifications, are used for these calculations. The details of the calculations are shown in Figures 5.42 through 5.47. They are summarized in Figure 5.48.

PART OF SIDEWALLS	AREA, SQ FT	U-FACTOR			HEAT LOSS		
		POOR	GOOD	EXCELLENT	POOR	GOOD	EXCELLENT
Wood frame	311	0.23	0.08	0.057	71.5	24.9	17.8
Concrete (above frost level)	135	0.47	0.14	0.08	63.5	18.9	10.8
Concrete (below frost level)	216	0.47	0.14	0.08	101.5	30.2	17.3
Windows	61	1.1	0.34	0.28	67.1	20.7	17.1
Doors	21	0.49	0.25	0.19	10.3	5.3	4.0
Totals	744				313.9	100.0	67.0

Figure 5.42. Estimated heat losses from the north sidewall with three different types of construction.

The estimated heat loss of the house that has construction that results in poor energy efficiency is about 1988 Btu/hr/°F. The estimated heat loss of the house with good energy-efficient construction is about 925 Btu/hr/°F, a savings of 53% in the amount of energy required to heat the house. The estimated heat loss of the house that has excellent energy-efficient construction is about 477 Btu/hr/°F, which is a savings of 76% in the amount of energy required to heat the house.

For every 1000 degree days that the location of this house sees, the cost of fuel can be shown by using the following formula:

$$\text{Cost} = (\text{Btu/hr/°F}) (24 \text{ hr}) (1000 \text{ dd}) (\text{net fuel cost}).$$

PART OF SIDEWALLS	AREA, SQ FT	U-FACTOR			HEAT LOSS		
		POOR	GOOD	EXCELLENT	POOR	GOOD	EXCELLENT
Wood frame	294	0.23	0.08	0.057	67.6	23.5	16.8
Concrete (above frost level)	135	0.47	0.14	0.08	63.5	18.9	10.8
Concrete (below frost level)	216	0.47	0.14	0.08	101.5	30.2	17.3
Windows	57	1.1	0.34	0.28	62.7	19.4	16.0
Glass door	42	1.1	0.34	0.28	46.2	14.2	11.8
Total	744				341.5	106.2	72.7

Figure 5.43. Estimated heat losses from the south sidewall with three different types of construction.

PART OF SIDEWALLS	AREA, SQ FT	U-FACTOR			HEAT LOSS		
		POOR	GOOD	EXCELLENT	POOR	GOOD	EXCELLENT
Wood frame	160	0.23	0.08	0.057	36.8	12.8	9.1
Concrete (above frost level)	126	0.47	0.14	0.08	59.2	17.6	10.1
Concrete (below frost level)	117	0.47	0.14	0.08	55.0	16.4	9.4
Total	403				151.0	46.8	28.6

Figure 5.44. Estimated heat losses from the east sidewall with three different types of construction.

PART OF SIDEWALLS	AREA, SQ FT	U-FACTOR			HEAT LOSS		
		POOR	GOOD	EXCELLENT	POOR	GOOD	EXCELLENT
Wood frame	184	0.23	0.08	0.057	42.3	14.7	10.5
Concrete (above frost level)	78	0.47	0.14	0.08	36.7	10.9	6.2
Concrete (below frost level)	117	0.47	0.14	0.08	55.0	16.4	9.4
Windows	24	1.1	0.34	0.28	26.4	8.2	6.7
Total	402				160.4	50.2	32.8

Figure 5.45. Estimated heat losses from the west sidewall with three different types of construction.

PART	AREA, SQ FT	U-FACTOR			HEAT LOSS		
		POOR	GOOD	EXCELLENT	POOR	GOOD	EXCELLENT
Attic ceiling	1248	0.26	0.08	0.026	324.5	99.8	32.4
First floor (none, basement heated)							
Basement floor (none figured)							

Figure 5.46. Estimated heat losses from the floors and ceilings with three different types of construction.

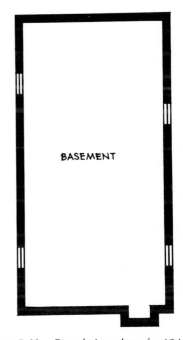

Figure 5.40. Foundation plan of a 1248 sq ft ranch house.

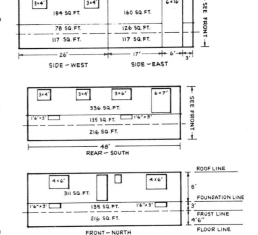

Figure 5.41. Exterior dimensions of the 1248 sq ft ranch house.

PART	CU FT OF AIR	AIR CHANGES PER HOUR			HEAT LOSS		
		POOR	GOOD	EXCELLENT	POOR	GOOD	EXCELLENT
First floor	9672	2	1.5	0.7	348.2	261.1	121.9
Basement	9672	2	1.5	0.7	348.2	261.1	131.9
Total	19344				696.4	522.2	243.8

Figure 5.47. Estimated heat losses from air infiltration with three different types of construction.

HEAT LOSS SOURCE	HEAT LOSS IN BTU/HR/°F		
	POOR	GOOD	EXCELLENT
North wall	313.9	100.0	67.0
South wall	341.5	106.2	72.7
East wall	151.0	46.8	28.6
West wall	160.4	50.2	32.8
Ceilings & floors	324.5	99.8	32.4
Air infiltration	696.4	522.2	243.8
Total	1987.7	925.2	477.3
% Savings		53%	76%

Figure 5.48. Total estimated heat losses from three different types of construction.

The table in Figure 5.49 shows those costs when the net fuel costs are $15.00/MMBtu. You can readily see that in the northern part of the country where between 5000 and 7000 degree days are normal that the savings mount up rapidly and quickly pay for the cost of building an energy-efficient house.

EFFICIENCY RATING	ANNUAL LOSSES MMBTU	COST AT $15/MMBtu
Poor	47.7	$715.50
Good	22.2	$333.00
Excellent	11.5	$172.50

Figure 5.49. Cost of heat losses per 1000 degree days when the net fuel cost is $15.00/MMBtu from three different types of energy-efficient construction.

Making a Decision

In this chapter you studied fuels. You learned that choosing the right fuel is an important factor in determining your final energy costs.

You studied air infiltration, ventilation, moisture control, and thermal insulation. From this you learned what type of construction yields an energy-efficient house.

Last, you calculated the heat losses in three different types of construction. From these calculations you learned that energy-efficient construction quickly pays for itself.

You are now equipped to check out your present home for steps that you should take to increase its energy efficiency or to specify the type of construction that should be used in building a new residence.

DECISION
6

Estimate Your Future Fuel Costs

Historians will record that 1974 marked the end of an era. An era when hydrocarbon-based fossil fuels were cheap and plentiful. From the mid-1950s until the early 1970s, the cost of fossil fuels rose only 5%. But during the 1970s the cost of these same fossil fuels rose almost 500%. In 1979 the Bureau of Labor Statistics forecast that an annual 6%/yr compounded cost increase could be expected during the decade of the 1980s. This means that in 1990 fuel that cost only $1.00 as late as 1969 will cost almost $9.00.

To obtain the energy required to heat your home or your hot water, you must purchase more than fuel. You must purchase a device to burn the fuel. You must install that device. You must operate and maintain it. And you must replace that device when it wears out.

You must describe all these expenses in order to estimate your future energy costs. This chapter will teach you how to make this assessment. You will learn:

- How to convert the purchase price of fuel to a net energy cost.
- How to cost out fossil-fueled energy-producing devices.
- How to estimate the future price of fuels.
- How to calculate the cost of a solar system.

When you are finished, you will be able to compare the financial costs of following different energy paths in the future.

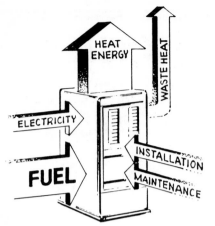

Figure 6.1. Net cost of energy is the sum of these costs.

The Net Cost of Energy

The net cost of the energy that you require is a function of the fuel that you burn, the operational costs that you incur, the installation cost of your furnace, and the system's maintenance costs. Figure 6.1 depicts these costs.

Your fuel efficiency will vary from 50 to 100% depending on your choice of fuel and furnace. The cost of running the burners, fans, or pumps within that furnace will depend on the type that you choose. The costs of installing and maintaining the device depend on the furnace type and your fuel choice.

The two major costs that you will incur are the cost of the device and the cost of the fuel. You may purchase a furnace for only 700 or $800. By the time it is installed and maintained, that cost can double or triple. However, over its lifetime, which can be 20 yr or longer, you may have to feed it with $50,000 in fuel in order to produce the heat that you need.

It is important to understand these costs if you are to consider the solar energy option. The solar energy option changes the ratio of the cost of the device and the cost of the fuel. When you decide to heat with solar energy, you are making a decision to invest perhaps 10,000 to $20,000 in the device in order to use a fuel that costs nothing. That is a major decision, one that you should be well-informed about before you move ahead with it. This chapter will show you how to determine whether solar is a wise decision.

Making Fuel Cost Comparisons

When you purchase a fuel, you may pay for it by the gallon, by the pound, by the cubic foot, or by the kilowatt-hour. The measurement that is used depends on the type of fuel that you purchase, so it is hard to draw a direct comparison in purchase costs between fuels.

You must reduce these costs to a common denominator for accurate comparison. The common denominator in thermal energy cost comparisons is *dollars per million Btu*. This is commonly written as $/MMBtu.

A simple formula is used to convert purchase price to $/MMBtu:

$$\$/\text{MMBtu} = \frac{\text{Cost/unit purchased} \times 1,000,000 \text{ Btu}}{\text{number of Btu in one unit}}$$

Let us assume that a kilowatt-hour, or kWh, of electricity costs $0.05 and contains 3413 Btu. Then the cost per MMBtu is $14.65.

Figure 6.2 shows the thermal energy contained in a unit of fuel, the number of units per MMBtu, and the most common unit of sale. By using this table you can simplify the calculation. Just use this formula:

$$\$/\text{MMBtu} = \text{units/MMBtu} \times \text{cost/unit}$$

In the example just presented, the simplified calculation becomes:

$$
\begin{array}{r}
\$0.05 \\
\times \quad 293 \\
\hline
= \$14.65
\end{array}
$$

$$
\begin{array}{r}
\$0.05 \\
\times \ 1,000,000 \\
\hline
50,000 \\
\div \ 3413 \\
\hline
= \$14.65/\text{MMBtu}
\end{array}
$$

FUEL	THERMAL ENERGY	UNITS/MMBtu	UNITS OF SALE
Natural gas	1000 Btu/cu ft	1000 cu ft	$/CCF
LPG (propane)	21,560 Btu/lb	46.4 lb	$/lb
Gasoline	125,000 Btu/gal	8 gal	$/gal
Kerosene	135,000 Btu/gal	7.4 gal	$/gal
No. 2 fuel oil	138,000 Btu/gal	7.25 gal	$/gal
Coal (average)	11,375 Btu/lb	88 lb	$/ton
Crude oil (typical)	138,000 Btu/gal	7.25 gal	$/barrel
Red oak	5,500 Btu/lb	182 lb	$/cord
Electricity	3413 Btu/kWh	293 kWh	$/kWh

Figure 6.2. Some common average fuel values and units of sale.

Converting Your Gas Bill Most gas utility bills read in *dollars per hundred cubic feet,* or $/CCF. One hundred cubic feet of natural gas contains about 100,000 Btu. So 10 CCF = 1 MMBtu.

Your gas bill will most likely read like this:

Number of units	500 CCF
Cost	$180

So your cost is $0.36/CCF, or $3.60/MMBtu.

$$\begin{array}{r} \$180 \\ \div\ 500\ \text{CCF} \\ \hline 0.36\ \$/\text{unit} \\ \times\ 10\ \text{CCF/MMBtu} \\ \hline = \$3.60/\text{MMBtu} \end{array}$$

Converting Your Electric Bill Most electric utility bills read in *dollars per killowatt-hour,* or $/kWh. One kilowatt-hour of electricity contains 3413 Btu. Two hundred ninety-three kWh equals 1 MMBtu.

Your electrical bill will most likely read like this:

Number of units	1000 kWh
Cost	$50.00

So your cost is $0.05/kHw, or $14.65/MMBtu

$$\begin{array}{r} \$50 \\ \div\ 1000\ \text{kWh} \\ \hline 0.05\ \$/\text{unit} \\ \times\ 293\ \text{kWh/MMBtu} \\ \hline = \$14.65/\text{MMBtu} \end{array}$$

Converting Your Propane Bill Propane gas is sold as a liquid. It is usually measured by the pound. One pound of propane, or LPG, contains 21,560 Btu. So 46.4 lb of liquified LPG equals 1 MMBtu. If you paid $15.00 for 100 pounds of LPG, then your delivered fuel cost is $6.97/MMBtu.

$$\begin{array}{r} 100\ \text{lb} \\ \div\ 46.4\ \text{lb/MMBtu} \\ \hline 2.15\ \text{MMBtu} \end{array} \qquad \begin{array}{r} \$15.00 \\ \div\ 2.15\ \text{MMBtu} \\ \hline = \$6.97/\text{MMBtu} \end{array}$$

Converting Your Fuel Oil Bill Fuel oil is sold by the gallon. One gallon of No. 2 fuel oil contains about 138,000 Btu. So 7.25 gal of fuel oil equals 1 MMBtu. If you paid $100 for 100 gal of fuel oil, then your cost is $7.25/MMBtu.

$$\begin{array}{r} 100\ \text{gal} \\ \div\ 7.25\ \text{gal/MMBtu} \\ \hline 13.8\ \text{MMBtu} \end{array} \qquad \begin{array}{r} \$100 \\ \div\ 13.8\ \text{MMBtu} \\ \hline = \$7.25/\text{MMBtu} \end{array}$$

Converting Your Coal Bill Coal is generally sold by the ton. A ton equals 2000 lb. One ton of coal contains about 22.75 MMBtu. 88 lb of the average coal is equal to 1 MMBtu. If you paid $120 for a ton of coal, then your cost is $5.29/MMBtu.

$$\begin{array}{r} 2000\ \text{lb} \\ \div\ 88\ \text{lb/MMBtu} \\ \hline 22.7\ \text{MMBtu} \end{array}$$

$$\begin{array}{r} \$120 \\ \div\ 22.7\ \text{MMBtu} \\ \hline = \$5.29/\text{MMBtu} \end{array}$$

The use of cost/MMBtu allows you to compare directly the cost of purchasing different fuels. But these fuels burn at different efficiencies. So next you must examine the efficiency at which the various fuels commonly burn.

Comparing Fuel Efficiencies

When fuel is burned carbon dioxide, water vapor, and heat are generated. The heat released must heat the incoming air and fuel, break down the fuel, heat up the combustion process, and radiate heat to the surroundings. The heat needed to support and continue the combustion process cannot be used to supply useful energy to heat your home. So an efficiency factor must be calculated into the cost of the fuel that you purchase.

Fuel Oil Efficiency Generally, fuel oils offer about 50 to 70% efficiency. An improperly sized and maintained furnace will generally operate down around 50 to 55% efficiency. If the furnace is properly sized and maintained, it is possible to operate it at 65 to 70% efficiency. But it is a rare furnace that ever achieves a steady 70% efficiency. Higher efficiencies are not possible because of the chemical nature of the fuel and the combustion process. So in calculating your true cost of fuel oil, you must plan on an efficiency factor. The author recommends 60% as reasonable for the average residence.

Natural and LPG Gas Efficiency Natural and LPG gas are cleaner burning than fuel oils, but they contain more hydrogen. So the top efficiency is about 70% because more hydrogen means more water vapor formation. The fact that they are cleaner burning means that they will perform better and longer with less maintenance. Generally about 55% efficiency is the lowest seen. A fuel efficiency factor of 65% is reasonable for the average residential application.

Electrical Efficiency The efficiency of electricity will depend on the nature of the application. For resistance baseboard heating or for ceiling or floor radiant heating, an efficiency factor of 95 to 100% is generally used.

When air-conditioning units or heat pumps are used, an extremely high efficiency factor comes into the picture. In these cases, the electrical energy is used to compress a gas that extracts heat from either water or air and then pumps it either into or out of the building. The actual heat energy moved is obtained from the water or the air. So it is possible to obtain fuel efficiencies of 200 to 250%. In some cases for short periods under favorable conditions, these efficiencies can rise to 300%.

It is reasonable to use a 100% efficiency factor for baseboard resistance heating, a 95% efficiency factor for ceiling or floor resistance heating, and a 225 to 250% efficiency factor for air-conditioning and heat pump applications. Figure 6.3 is a table of efficiencies that you can use for reference in these applications.

Figure 6.3. Common residential fuel efficiencies.

FUEL	% EFFICIENCY RANGE	AVERAGE EFFICIENCY
Fuel oil	50-70	60
Natural gas	55-70	65
LPG	55-70	65
Electricity	95-100	95-100
Heat pump	200-250	225

293 kWh = 1 MMBtu

1 MMBtu
× 2.50 efficiency
= 2.5 MMBtu

1 MMBtu
× 0.95 efficiency
= 0.95 MMBtu

How Fuel Efficiency Affects Fuel Costs

Take electricity as an example of how fuel burning efficiency affects your fuel costs. You learned that 293 kWh of electricity contained 1 MMBtu as supplied. If that electricity is used to run a 250% efficient heat pump, then you will receive 2.5 MMBtu of useful energy from the electricity. On the other hand, if you used that electricity to run a 95% efficient resistance heater, you would receive 0.95 MMBtu of useful energy.

If the cost for that electricity was $0.05 kWh, then the energy received would have cost $14.65. The cost of usable energy received from the heat pump would have been $5.86/MMBtu. The cost of usable energy received from the resistance heater would have been $15.42/MMBtu. As you can see, the efficiency at which you use the fuel has a marked effect on the final fuel cost.

$$\begin{array}{r} 293 \ \text{kWh} \\ \times \ 0.05 \ \text{\$/kWh} \\ \hline = \$14.65 \ \text{/MMBtu received} \end{array}$$

$$\begin{array}{r} \$14.65 \text{/2.5 MMBtu useful energy} \\ \div \ 2.5 \ \text{MMBtu} \\ \hline = \$5.86 \text{/MMBtu} \end{array}$$

$$\begin{array}{r} \$14.65 \text{/0.95 MMBtu useful energy} \\ \div \ 0.95 \ \text{MMBtu} \\ \hline = \$15.42 \text{/MMBtu} \end{array}$$

Costing Energy-producing Devices

There are two major costs associated with producing usable heat energy within a building structure. One cost is the purchase of fuel. The other cost is the purchase of the device within which to burn the fuel. The most common devices that are used are furnaces, water heaters, and heat pumps or air conditioners.

Fuel-burning devices have a finite life. Over their lifetime they are called on to produce a finite amount of usable energy. Therefore they have a known cost per unit of energy produced, although that cost per unit can vary widely from one installation to another. So the cost of purchasing, installing, operating, and maintaining the combustion unit can, and should, be added to the cost of purchasing fuel in order to arrive at an overall usable-energy cost.

Furnaces

Furnaces are space-heating devices. The residential furnace is generally one of two types. It is either a forced circulation warm-air furnace or a hot water boiler with forced water circulation.

The unit generally is regarded as having two main parts: the combustion unit with the circulation fan or pump and the distribution system, which may be either air-carrying ductwork or water-carrying piping with room heat exchangers.

For the purposes of analyzing costs, only the costs that are associated with the combustion unit will be considered. The distribution system life is generally long enough so that it can be considered infinite for cost analysis purposes.

Two mail-order houses, Sears Roebuck and Montgomery Ward, engage heavily in providing units of this type directly to the consumer, so their catalog prices will be used as a purchase costing reference. The consumer purchase price for combustion equipment from these sources as of January 1, 1980, is shown in Figures 6.4 and 6.5. The figures do not include shipping or installation costs. A perusal of these tables shows that the cost of the unit is a function of size, fuel source, and whether the unit heats air or water. The units chosen were of equal quality.

$$\begin{array}{r} \$4.92 \text{/MBtu} \\ \times \ 150 \ \text{MBtu} \\ \hline = \$738.00 \ \text{purchase price} \end{array}$$

$$\begin{array}{r} 150 \ \text{MBtu input} \\ \times \ 0.70 \ \% \ \text{efficiency} \\ \hline = 105 \ \text{MBtu output} \end{array}$$

$$\begin{array}{r} 65°F \ \text{interior design temp.} \\ - \ (-10)°F \ \text{exterior design temp.} \\ \hline = 75°F \ \text{temp. differential} \end{array}$$

$$\begin{array}{r} 105 \ \text{MBtu output} \\ \div \ 75°F \ \text{differential} \\ \hline = 1400 \ \text{Btu/hr demand} \end{array}$$

The Cost Analysis As the furnaces are all different sizes, an analysis was performed to determine the average cost of a furnace per thousand Btu (MBtu) of rated fuel input per hour. An eyeball analysis of the two tables in Figures 6.4 and 6.5 indicates that an average cost of $4.92/MBtu is a reasonable analysis figure, with larger units costing less and smaller units costing more.

For purposes of analysis, the author has chosen a cost of $738.00 for a 150,000 Btu/hr input furnace. Such a furnace should readily heat a well-constructed 1500 sq ft house in a northern climate. It should be expected to produce a maximum hourly output of about 105,000 Btu at the point-of-use within the building structure. This would satisfy a UA demand of 1400 Btu/hr when the temperature of the outside air was −10°F.

FUEL	Btu/HR FUEL INPUT	PURCHASE COST	COST/1000 Btu/HR INPUT
Gas	105,000	$590	$5.62
Gas	210,000	$860	$4.10
Oil	105,000	$610	$5.81
Oil	210,000	$1039	$4.94

Figure 6.4. Typical warm-air furnace prices, January 1980. (*Source:* Sears, Roebuck & Company.)

FUEL	Btu/HR FUEL INPUT	PURCHASE COST	COST/1000 Btu/HR INPUT
Gas	112,500	$630	$5.60
Gas	262,500	$920	$3.50

Figure 6.5. Typical hydronic boiler prices, January 1980. (*Source:* Montgomery Ward Stores.)

$$
\begin{array}{r}
1400 \quad \text{Btu/hr} \\
\times\ 24 \quad \text{hr} \\
\hline
= 33,600 \quad \text{Btu/day} \\
\times\ 6000 \quad \text{dd} \\
\hline
201.60 \quad \text{MMBtu/yr output} \\
\div\ 0.60 \quad \text{\% efficiency} \\
\hline
= 336 \quad \text{MMBtu/yr fuel input}
\end{array}
$$

$$
\begin{array}{r}
336 \quad \text{MMBtu fuel input} \\
\times\ 20 \quad \text{yr} \\
\hline
= 6720 \quad \text{MMBtu lifetime fuel input}
\end{array}
$$

$$
\begin{array}{r}
202 \quad \text{MMBtu energy output} \\
\times\ 20 \quad \text{yr} \\
\hline
= 4040 \quad \text{MMBtu lifetime energy output}
\end{array}
$$

$$
\frac{738}{4\ \text{billion}} = \$0.18/\text{MMBtu}
$$

$$
\frac{738}{6.7\ \text{billion}} = \$0.11/\text{MMBtu}
$$

If the heat loss of the house were 1400 Bth/hr and if the geographic area contained an average of 6000 dd, then the furnace would be called on to produce 202 MMBtu/yr. That would require 289 MMBtu of fuel input if the furnace were operating at 70% efficiency. It would require 336 MMBtu of fuel when an efficiency of 60%, which is most likely over the life of the unit, is experienced.

The life of a quality furnace is deemed to be at least 20 yr if it is properly serviced and maintained. Few expire sooner and many last well in excess of that time. So multiplying your yearly fuel use by 20 yr shows you that this furnace will burn about 6.7 billion Btu over its lifetime and produce about 4.0 billion Btu of useful heat energy.

So the purchase price of $738.00 must be spread across either a 4 billion Btu output or a 6.7 billion Btu input. The cost on the energy output equals $0.18/MMBtu. The cost on the fuel input equals $0.11/MMBtu. Figure 6.6 is a table on which you can make your own fuel price calculations using either the input or the output figures. You must use either one or the other. You cannot mix the figures.

Shipping and Installation Shipping the furnace to your home and installing it are two major costs. But as they are locally incurred, no one estimate will be correct for the entire country. Chances are that the shipping and installation costs will be equivalent to the purchase cost. You must check locally, however, for an accurate estimate. For illustrative purposes, the author will use $738.00 in his final cost assessment. So these costs, as a function of fuel input and energy output, are also, respectively, $0.11/MMBtu and $0.18/MMBtu.

Maintenance and Repair Furnaces contain mechanical devices such as pumps, fans, and controls. These are generally not designed to last the life of the furnace. At some point, they may have to be replaced. In the case of a circulating water pump or a fan in a warm-air furnace, the new units can cost from 75 to $125. From 2 to 4 hr of labor are required to replace such units, which adds 30 to $60 to the replacement cost. Again, such costs can vary widely.

For purposes of analysis, the author has chosen to have two major repair incidents over the life of the furnace that cost $145 each. So the lifetime cost of repairs is $290.

To maintain its efficiency, your furnace should be serviced and adjusted annually. Filters must be changed, burner and damper adjustments must be checked, and the unit must be cleaned. Many times homeowners can perform many of these maintenance tasks themselves. An annual service

WORKSHEET

Furnace purchase price	$ _____	
Rated hourly fuel input	_____	MBtu/hr
Percent efficiency	× _____	% efficiency (express as decimal)
Furnace hourly energy output	= _____	MBtu/hr
Design temperature differential (inside air minus ambient air)	÷ _____	°F
Maximum hourly heat loss that the furnace will service	= _____	Btu/hr/°F
Your home's hourly heat loss	_____	Btu/hr/°F
Number of hours in a day	× 24	hr
Your home's daily heat loss	= _____	Btu/day/°F
Number of degree days per year	× _____	dd
Your annual need for energy	= _____	MMBtu/yr
Percent efficiency of furnace	÷ _____	% efficiency (express as decimal)
The fuel required annually	= _____	MMBtu/yr
Furnace purchase price	$ _____	
MMBtu energy output over lifetime	÷ _____	Annual × 20 yr
Cost/MMBtu of output to purchase	$ _____	
Furnace purchase price	$ _____	
MMBtu fuel input over lifetime	÷ _____	Annual × 20 yr
Cost/MMBtu of energy purchased	$ _____	

Figure 6.6. Table for calculating the purchase price of a furnace on the fuel purchased and the energy received.

call might cost as little as $15 or as high as $35. Or again, it may be provided free by the fuel dealer or the utility. The author has chosen to use a $15 service call on a biannual basis for his cost analysis. This appears to be a minimal figure. It represents a cost of $150 over the life of the furnace.

Operational Costs Furnaces generally contain at least one pump or fan. In a large residence, they may contain more. Such devices are electrically operated. Their motors generally range from $1/6$ to $1/3$ horsepower. A $1/4$ horsepower motor is a typical average device. It generally runs for 10 to 16 hr/day over the heating season. In the case of an air circulating fan, it may be run daily for ventilation during the spring, summer, and fall. A $1/4$ horsepower motor uses about 420 W/hr. So running for 160 days, 10 hr/day, it would use 672 kWh of electricity per year. At 5¢/kWh, it would cost $672 to run the furnace for 20 yr.

How It All Adds Up Purchase cost, installation cost, repair costs, and operational costs all add up to a goodly sum. Figure 6.7 shows the author's example. The total cost of the device over its lifetime calculates out as $2588.00.

$$
\begin{array}{rl}
420 & \text{W/hr} \\
\times\ 10 & \text{hr} \\
\hline
4200 & \text{Whr} \\
\times\ 160 & \text{days} \\
\hline
672{,}000 & \text{Whr} \\
\div\ 1000 & \\
\hline
672 & \text{kWh} \\
\times\ 20 & \text{yr} \\
\hline
13{,}440 & \\
\times\ \$0.05 & \text{\$/kWh} \\
\hline
=\ \$672 &
\end{array}
$$

Figure 6.7. Typical total lifetime furnace cost.

ITEM	COST
Purchase price	$738
Shipping and installation	$738
Maintenance and repair	$440
Operational expense	$672
Total device costs	$2588

The author also calculated that the device would require 6720 MMBtu of fuel over its 20-yr life and that the device would produce 4040 MMBtu of energy from that fuel. So by simple division, you will see that the device's cost over its lifetime is 39¢/MMBtu of fuel purchased and 64¢/MMBtu of energy received. These costs must be added to the cost of purchasing the fuel to determine the true cost of heating the structure.

Fuel oil in January 1980 was costing about $1.00/gal. At 7.25 gal/MMBtu, the cost to purchase the 6720 MMBtu that this furnace will require over its lifetime is $48,720. That is an uninflated cost in 1979 dollars. The actual costs will be much greater.

Figure 6.8 puts the costs all together. In 1979 dollars, ignoring any inflation or cost increases, the total cost of heating for 20 yr will be $51,308. That is most likely close to what the contractor spent to build the house in which the furnace is installed. Ninety-five percent of the total cost is in fuel, whereas 5% of the total cost is in the device.

$$
\begin{array}{rl}
\$2588 & \\
\div\ 6720 & \text{MMBtu} \\
\hline
\$0.39 & \\
\\
\$2588 & \\
\div\ 4040 & \text{MMBtu} \\
\hline
=\ \$0.64 & \\
\\
\$1.00 & \text{\$/gal} \\
\times\ 7.25 & \text{gal/MMBtu} \\
\hline
7.25 & \text{\$/MMBtu} \\
\times\ 6720 & \text{MMBtu} \\
\hline
=\ \$48{,}720 &
\end{array}
$$

Figure 6.8. Uninflated total heating cost for the 20-yr life of a typical furnace.

ITEM	OIL		
Fuel input MMBtu	6720		
Cost/MMBtu	$7.25		
Ten-year fuel cost	$48,720		
WITH OIL			
Cost of fuel	$48,720	95% of total cost	$7.25/MMBtu
Cost of device	$ 2,588	5% of total cost	$0.39/MMBtu
Total cost	$51,308		$7.64/MMBtu

Water Heaters

Domestic water heaters are generally gas-fired or electric-resistance heated. Oil-fired units are also available but are not in general use.

A typical use of a domestic water heater is to heat 20 gal of water per day per person in the household. Assuming an average family of four, the heater is called on to produce 80 gal of hot water per day. On the average, the water must be heated from 55 to 140°F, or 85°. So the unit must produce 56,644 Btu/day or 20.7 MMBtu/yr. That is an energy output of 207 MMBtu over the 10-yr average life of a hot water heater.

If the unit is electric-resistance heated, its efficiency is about 95%, so the fuel input would be about 218 MMBtu. If the unit is gas-fired, the efficiency is about 65%, so the fuel input would be about 318 MMBtu.

Many water heaters are poorly insulated. Up to one-third of the energy put in the water can be lost through the jacket. These *Stand-By losses* have not been included in these calculations.

Equipment-related Costs Figure 6.9 shows the purchase prices of four typical domestic water heaters. The data is from Sears Roebuck & Company. These are Sears' best units. They are designed for a service life of 10 yr. The average cost of these units in January 1980 was $270.

20	gal	
× 4	people	
80	gal/day	
× 8.33	lb/gal	
666.4	lb/day	
× 85	°F/Temp. rise	
56,644	Btu/day	
× 365	days/yr	
20.7	MMBtu/yr	
× 10	yr	
= 207	MMBtu/10 yr	

207	MMBtu output	
÷ 0.95	electric eff.	
= 218	MMBtu of fuel	

207	MMBtu output	
÷ 0.65	gas eff.	
= 318	MMBtu of fuel	

FUEL	SIZE (GAL)	PURCHASE COST
Electric	42	$230
Electric	82	$310
Gas	40	$255
Gas	65	$295
Average		$270

Figure 6.9. Purchase price of four typical water heaters, January 1, 1980. (*Source:* Sears, Roebuck & Company.)

Shipping and professional installation would add from 100 to $200 to the purchase price. These costs can vary widely. The author will use $150 in his analysis.

These units rarely have to be serviced or repaired. An electric element may burn out or a thermocouple on a gas-fired unit may fail. So one service call over the life of the heater will most likely be average. Labor and parts would most likely run under $50. There are no operational costs. You may wish to add stand-by losses to your calculations. The author has not done so because a solar water heater would have equivalent stand-by losses.

Typical Lifetime Total Costs Figure 6.10 shows the typical lifetime costs associated with a water heater. They add up to $470.

Figure 6.11 shows a typical uninflated total heating cost over the 10-yr life of the water heater. With a gas-fired heater, the fuel cost is low and the cost of the device is high. With an electric resistance heater, the cost of the fuel is higher, but the cost of the device per MMBtu of fuel input is lower.

ITEM	COST
Purchase price	$270
Shipping and installation	$150
Maintenance and repair	$ 50
Operational	0
Total costs	$470

Figure 6.10. Typical total lifetime water heater cost.

ITEM	GAS		ELECTRIC
Fuel input MMBtu	318		218
Cost/MMBtu	3.60		14.65
10-yr fuel cost	$1144.80		$3193.70
WITH GAS			
Cost of fuel	$1145	71% of total cost	$3.60/MMBtu
Cost of device	$ 470	29% of total cost	$1.48/MMBtu
Total cost	$1615		$5.08/MMBtu
WITH ELECTRIC			
Cost of fuel	$3194	87% of total cost	$14.65/MMBtu
Cost of device	$ 470	13% of total cost	$ 2.16/MMBtu
Total cost	$3664		$16.81/MMBtu

Figure 6.11. Uninflated total heating cost for the 10-yr life of a typical water heater.

Go back and compare the cost of a water heater per MMBtu of fuel input or energy output with the cost of a furnace per MMBtu of fuel input or energy output. You will see that the water heating device is much more expensive than the furnace per MMBtu. The cost of heating water for 10 yr with a gas-fired unit adds up to $1615 at 1979's costs. With electricity, it adds up to $3664 at today's costs. Yet the device only costs $420 to purchase and install.

The True Cost of Obtaining Your Energy

Water heater costs, furnace costs, labor costs, and fuel costs are rising rapidly. Inflation must be factored into any calculations of your future energy costs.

Much has been written about the future cost of energy and the rising cost of living. Some of this information is biased. Some of it is erroneous. But there is one piece of information that is highly regarded as reliable. This is the forecast of wholesale prices by the Bureau of Labor Statistics (BLS).

Over the years, the Bureau of Labor has analyzed both retail and wholesale prices across the United States. Their results are published as the *Wholesale Price Indexes* and the *Consumer Price Indexes*. You are most likely familiar with the *Consumer Price Index*. This is the best known Bureau of Labor Statistics forecast.

Figure 6.12 shows the Bureau of Labor Statistics, October 1979 forecast of the wholesale price index for all fuel and power. Here is how this index is read. All BLS indexes are calculated to read 1967 = 100. This is known as the base year. The cost for each previous and for each succeeding year is calculated in percentages of the base year. For instance, in 1968 the cost of a unit of fuel was 98.9% of the 1967 price. In 1975 the cost of a unit of fuel was 245.1% of its cost in 1967. To determine how much fuel costs rose from one year to another, say from 1974 to 1975, subtract the cost in 1974 from the cost in 1975 and then divide by the cost in 1974 and multiply by 100. This shows that the cost of a unit of fuel rose 17.7% in that 1 year.

What will your fuel cost be in 1990 if the forecast is correct? Assuming that you use your 1980 cost as the base, then you will experience a 77% cost increase. Multiply your 1980 cost by 1.77 and you will have a fuel price estimate for 1990.

```
  245.1  1975
− 208.3  1974
───────
   36.8  difference
÷ 208.3  1974
───────
  0.177
× 100
───────
= 17.7 % change


  867  1990
− 490  1980
─────
  377  difference
÷ 490  1980
─────
 0.769
× 100
─────
= 77 % change
```

FUEL AND POWER	BLS INDEX
1957	99.1
1958	95.3
1959	95.3
1960	96.1
1961	97.2
1962	96.7
1963	96.3
1964	93.7
1965	95.5
1966	97.8
1967	100.0
1968	98.9
1969	100.9
1970	105.9
1971	114.2
1972	118.6
1973	134.3
1974	208.3
1975	245.1
1976	265.5
1977	302.2
1978	322.5
1979	406.0
1980	490.0
1985	672.0
1990	867.0

Figure 6.12. Estimate of the wholesale price of all fuel and power. (*Source:* U.S. Bureau of Labor Statistics, October 1979.)

To find the price of fuel for the years where no index is available, you must plot a graph that shows the annual increase. Figure 6.13 shows such a graph for the BLS Fuel and Power Wholesale Price Index. The author has extended the estimate at the same rate to the year 2000. This may or may not be correct. No one knows at this time. The annual cost index may now be taken directly from this graph for your fuel cost calculations.

The BLS Wholesale Price For Heating Equipment, Excluding Electric Equipment has also been calculated on this graph. The figures were taken from a May 1979 BLS forecast covering 1960 to 1978, as shown in Figure

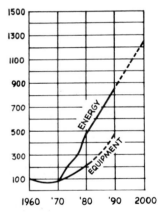

Figure 6.13. Wholesale price indexes for energy and heating equipment. (*Source:* U.S. Bureau of Labor Statistics, 1979; extended by the author, see text.)

HEATING EQUIPMENT	BLS INDEX
1960	105.8
1961	101.8
1962	100.5
1963	100.2
1964	99.2
1965	98.9
1966	99.8
1967	100.0
1968	102.7
1969	105.4
1970	110.6
1971	115.5
1972	118.2
1973	120.4
1974	135.0
1975	150.7
1976	158.1
1977	165.5
1978	174.4

Figure 6.14. Estimate of the wholesale price of heating equipment, except electrical equipment. (*Source:* U.S. Bureau of Labor Statistics, May 1979.)

6.14. They were extended to 1982 using an industry forecast from the June 1979 issue of *Purchasing* Magazine. The author then extended the forecast to 1990 with a trend line, which again may or may not be accurate.

One thing is very clear from these estimates. The cost of fuel and power will rise much higher than the cost of heating equipment. But the rate of increase for both will be about the same in the 1980s.

Calculating Your Future Energy Costs

You are now in a position to estimate your future fuel costs from fossil-fueled or electrical-fueled heating equipment. Figure 6.15 is a calculation table for you to use.

- Calculate the amount of energy in MMBtu that you will need and place the figure in item 1.
- Determine the average efficiency that your heating device will operate at over its lifetime from Figure 6.3. Convert this to a decimal (60% = 0.60) and place the figure in item 2.
- Divide item 1 by item 2. Place your answer in item 3. This will give you the MMBtu of fuel that you need to purchase each year.
- Determine the number of fuel units in 1 MMBtu. This figure will be found in Figure 6.2. Insert this figure in item 4.
- Multiply item 3 by item 4. Insert your answer in item 5. This will give you the number of units of fuel that you must purchase each year. For example: 20 MMBtu × 7.5 gal of oil equals 150 gal/yr.
- Determine the cost of fuel per unit that you are paying. Insert this in item 6.
- Multiply item 5 by item 6 and place your answer in item 7. This will give you the cost of fuel in the first year.

Note. How you figure your annual fuel cost inflation is important. The BLS figures do not take into account the declining value of the dollar, so they do not include inflation in the cost of living. When you use them, you are calculating the cost of future fuel in 1980 dollars if that is your year of analysis. The author suggests that this is advisable, as in the next section you will be calculating your solar energy costs in 1980 dollars (assuming that you are working with 1980 costs).

If you use the BLS figures, the average rate of increase compounded for the period 1980 through 1990 is 6%/yr. If you calculate over 20 yr, the average rate of increase compounded is 3½%/yr.

- Assuming that you are doing a 10-yr analysis, insert the figure you arrived at in item 7 into yr 1 and then multiply each succeeding year by 1.06 to arrive at each year's cost. Example: yr 1 = 100, then yr 2 = 100 × 1.06, yr 3 = yr 2 × 1.06 or 106 × 1.06 = 112.36, yr 4 = yr 3 × 1.06 or 112.36 × 1.06 = 119.10. Continue on in this manner for the full 10-yr analysis and place each year's cost on the correct line.
- Add up the cost of fuel over the life of the device and place your answer in item 10. This gives you a lifetime cost of fuel in constant dollars as of the year of analysis.
- Place the purchase price of the device in item 11.
- Place the cost of shipping and installation in item 12.
- Place the cost of maintenance and repair in item 13.
- Place the cost of operation in item 14. You may want to calculate inflation into operational costs as these are energy costs.

WORKSHEET

1. Your annual energy requirement _____ MMBtu

2. Efficiency of the combustion device (decimal) ÷ _____ efficiency

3. Your annual fuel purchase requirement _____ MMBtu

4. Units of fuel per MMBtu (see Figure 6.2) × _____ units/MMBtu

5. Annual fuel units required _____ units of fuel

6. Cost of fuel per unit × _____ $/unit

7. Total cost of fuel in first year _____ $

8. Annual fuel inflation factor (decimal) _____ %

9. Cost to purchase fuel in each year. (Compound item 7 by multiplying the first year's cost by the inflation rate. *Ex:* 6% inflation, use 1.06 as the multiplier. If the first year's cost were $100, the second year's cost would be $106 and the third year's cost would be $112.36, and so on.) If you go by the BLS figures shown in Figure 6.13, use 6%/yr cmpd for a 10-yr analysis and a 3.5%/yr cmpd for a 20-yr analysis.

   yr 1 _____ yr 11 _____
   yr 2 _____ yr 12 _____
   yr 3 _____ yr 13 _____
   yr 4 _____ yr 14 _____
   yr 5 _____ yr 15 _____
   yr 6 _____ yr 16 _____
   yr 7 _____ yr 17 _____
   yr 8 _____ yr 18 _____
   yr 9 _____ yr 19 _____
   yr 10 _____ yr 20 _____

10. Total cost of fuel estimated over 20 yr (add up the fuel costs for each year) _____ $/lifetime

11. Purchase price of combustion device + _____ $

12. Shipping and installation costs + _____ $

13. Maintenance and repair costs + _____ $

14. Operation costs (factors in inflation) + _____ $

15. Your true cost to obtain the energy that you need (Items 10 + 11 + 12 + 13 + 14) _____ $

Figure 6.15. A method of determining the true cost to obtain the energy that you need in the future. The method uses uninflated dollars.

- Add items 10, 11, 12, 13, and 14 together. Insert your answer in item 15. This is your true cost of obtaining your energy calculated in today's dollars.

Calculating the Cost of a Solar Energy System

A solar energy system must be subjected to the same type of cost analysis. There is a purchase cost, an installation cost, a maintenance and repair cost, and an operational cost that must be considered. However, there is no fuel cost.

You must also look at the cost of investing your money. If you left that money in an investment, it would earn money for you. Of course money invested in solar systems is money invested in real estate. Generally real estate investments have been excellent consumer investments over the past 40 years. Most likely they will continue to be good investments.

There is the cost of borrowing money if you use a loan to pay for the solar system. Interest must be paid annually. How much the real interest is over the rate of inflation must be calculated in order to arrive at the true cost of the money.

And there is the need to still place a conventional heating system in your structure. A solar heating system simply cannot provide all of your energy and be built at an economical cost. In the end analysis, your total energy cost will be a combination of solar costs and conventional costs.

The Value of Money

The basic concept of investing in a solar heating system is the concept that if you invest in the heating system now, you will save money in the future that you would have otherwise spent for electricity or fossil fuels.

That being the case, then it is essential that you know how to determine the value of money with time. Money invested gains value with time. In an inflationary economy, money left idle loses value with time as prices rise.

Two tables are used to show how money gains or loses value with time: a *compound interest table* and a *present value of money table*. Figure 6.16 shows a compound interest table. This table shows how much money $1.00 will earn if left invested at a given percentage for a given period of time. For example, $1.00 invested for 20 yr at 8% becomes $4.66 at the end of that period. If that $1.00 were invested at 16% for 20 yr, it would become $19.46.

YEAR	2%	4%	6%	8%	10%	12%	14%	16%
2	1.040	1.082	1.124	1.166	1.210	1.254	1.300	1.346
4	1.082	1.170	1.262	1.360	1.464	1.574	1.689	1.811
6	1.126	1.265	1.419	1.587	1.772	1.974	2.195	2.436
8	1.172	1.369	1.594	1.851	2.144	2.476	2.853	3.278
10	1.219	1.480	1.791	2.159	2.594	3.106	3.707	4.411
12	1.268	1.601	2.012	2.518	3.138	3.896	4.818	5.936
14	1.319	1.732	2.261	2.937	3.797	4.887	6.261	7.988
16	1.373	1.873	2.540	3.426	4.595	6.130	8.137	10.748
18	1.428	2.026	2.854	3.996	5.560	7.690	10.575	14.463
20	1.486	2.191	3.207	4.661	6.728	9.646	13.743	19.461

Figure 6.16. Typical compound interest table.

Figure 6.17 shows a present value of money table. This table shows the value of a dollar at some time in the future as prices increase if the dollar is left idle. For example, $1.00 left idle for 10 yr in an economy that is inflating at 6% compounded will only have a value of $0.56 in 10 yr and a value of only $0.31 in 20 yr.

YEAR	2%	4%	6%	8%	10%	15%	20%	25%
5	0.906	0.822	0.747	0.681	0.621	0.497	0.402	0.328
10	0.820	0.676	0.558	0.463	0.386	0.247	0.162	0.107
15	0.743	0.555	0.417	0.315	0.239	0.123	0.065	0.035
20	0.673	0.456	0.312	0.215	0.149	0.061	0.026	0.012
25	0.610	0.375	0.233	0.146	0.092	0.030	0.010	0.004
30	0.552	0.308	0.174	0.099	0.057	0.015	0.004	0.001
40	0.453	0.208	0.097	0.046	0.022	0.004	0.001	—
50	0.372	0.141	0.054	0.021	0.009	0.001	—	—

Figure 6.17. Table showing the present value of money.

To obtain the value of any sum of money with these two tables, you merely multiply the number of dollars that you are discussing times the change in value for $1.00.

Using the Money Tables

The use of these two tables can best be shown by example. The following example shows how they are used to calculate the value of an investment.

First, some assumptions must be made. You must assume a rate of economic inflation. This example will use a rate of 6% compounded annually.

Inflation rate: 6% cmpd annually

Second, you must assume an investment rate. This example will use 8% compounded annually.

Investment rate: 8% cmpd annually

Third, you must assume an amount of money. This example will assume $5000. If $5000 were invested for 10 yr at 8%/yr compounded annually, then it would yield $10,795.

If at the same time the economy inflated at 6%/yr, compounded annually, then the value of that $10,795 in today's dollars would only be $6023.61.

Investment sum: $5000

$5000	$10,795	$6023.61
× 2.159	× 0.558	÷ $5000.00
= $10,795	= $6023.61	= 1.204

That is an effective yield of slightly under 2%/yr compounded annually. This figure is found by dividing the sum invested into the yield and referring back to the compound interest table, which shows that $1.00 invested at 2% for 10 yr yields $1.219.

Determining the Value of the Energy Produced

If you invested your $5000 in a solar system that produced energy, then you would earn money on your investment. Again, this can best be shown by example.

First, assume that your system yields 40 MMBtu of energy per year. Second, assume that your present cost to purchase alternative fuel is $8.00/MMBtu net. Third, assume that the cost of purchasing that alternative fuel is inflating at 6%/yr compounded plus the inflation rate of 6%/yr compounded, for a total increase of 12%/yr compounded cost increase.

Annual energy produced: 40 MMBtu

Cost to purchase energy: $8.00/MMBtu

$8.00/MMBtu
$\times$ 40 MMBtu/yr
= $320.00 1st yr cost

You cannot use the compound interest table to calculate your total fuel cost because you are making your fuel investment during the 10 years, not at the front end. So you must take the $320 first year cost of fuel and calculate each year's cost by 12% compounded.

Compounded at 12%

yr 1 = $320.00
yr 2 = $358.40
yr 3 = $401.41
yr 4 = $449.58
yr 5 = $503.53
yr 6 = $563.95
yr 7 = $631.62
yr 8 = $707.41
yr 9 = $792.30
yr 10 = $887.38
Total = $5615.58

$5615.58
$\times$ 0.558
= $3133.49

$5000 invested
+ $3133 earnings
8133
$\div$ $5000
= 1.627 yield

5%/yr compd annually

Under these assumptions, your 10-yr cost for fuel would be $5615.58. To find the value of this fuel in present dollars, you must use the present value table. The present value of that fuel is $3133.49.

So your investment of $5000 has earned you about 5%/yr compounded in fuel savings at today's values. This is real value after counting the increase in the cost of living during that period. Assuming that your system holds its $5000 value, this is a good investment.

Determining the Total Future Value of the System

The total future value of your system is the sum of its value at any given point in time plus the fuel savings that you have enjoyed up to that point. To arrive at the figure, the following formula can be used:

(Replacement cost) (% life left) + (accumulated energy savings) =
future value in inflated dollars

This formula assumes that the sales value of the system is equal to that of a new system built at that time multiplied by the amount of service left in the present system.

Here is a typical example of the use of this formula. Assume that the system has a 25-yr life. Solar systems properly built and maintained should have lives of 30 yr or longer. With a 25-yr life estimate, the system's life must be reduced 4% for each year that it is in operation. So at the end of 25 yr, the value of the investment is zero.

Assume that the cost of installing a new solar system increases at an inflation rate of 6%. Then the replacement cost is $5000 compounded at 6%/yr. Assume that the cost of fuel rises at 12%/yr compounded. That would, of course, include inflation. It is also most likely a high figure for a 25-yr analysis. But in this example it will be used.

Figure 6.18 shows what happens when these assumptions are placed in a table. The future value of the system rises each year for the full life of the system as shown in column 7. In the 25th yr, the system has a lifetime value of $43,410. In column 8 of this table, the future value of the system has been deflated at 6%/yr compounded to arrive at the future value of the system in terms of today's dollars.

It is not the author's intent to determine the value of a solar system for the reader in this analysis but merely to show some of the things that should be considered in making a solar investment.

1 YEAR	2 REPLACEMENT COST	3 % LIFE LEFT	4 $ SALES VALUE	5 $ ENERGY SAVED	6 CUMULATIVE $ ENERGY SAVED	7 TOTAL FUTURE VALUE	8 DEFLATED TO PRESENT VALUE
1	5000	100	5000	320	320	5320	5017
2	5300	96	5088	358	678	5766	5132
3	5618	92	5169	401	1079	6248	5248
4	5955	88	5240	450	1529	6769	5361
5	6312	84	5302	504	2033	7335	5479
6	6690	80	5352	564	2597	7949	5604
7	7091	76	5389	632	3229	8618	5731
8	7516	72	5412	707	3936	9348	5861
9	7967	68	5418	792	4728	10146	6006
10	8445	64	5405	887	5615	11020	6149
11	8952	60	5371	993	6608	11979	6313
12	9489	56	5314	1112	7720	13034	6478
13	10058	52	5230	1245	8965	14195	6657
14	10661	48	5117	1394	10359	15476	6840
15	11301	44	4972	1561	11920	16892	7044
16	11979	40	4792	1748	13668	18460	7273
17	12698	36	4571	1958	15626	20197	7493
18	13460	32	4307	2193	17819	22126	7744
19	14268	28	3995	2456	20275	24270	8033
20	15124	24	3630	2751	23026	26656	8317
21	16031	20	3206	3081	26107	29313	8618
22	16993	16	2719	3451	29558	32277	8973
23	18013	12	2162	3865	33423	35585	9323
24	19094	8	1528	4329	37752	39280	9702
25	20240	4	810	4848	42600	43410	10115

Figure 6.18. Typical determination of the future value of a solar system.

Operational and Maintenance Costs

Perhaps a fully passive system can be operated for 25 years without any operational or maintenance costs. After all, passive systems, by definition, do not have any mechanically driven devices. Yet often to build a completely passive system is to not make best use of the sun's energy. Some active components do have to be installed. These will require energy to operate, and they will wear out with time. So some operational moneys will certainly be required.

Very few building materials can be left to weather in the sun for 25 years. Plastics will lose their ability to transmit the energy. Paints will weather, chalk, and peel. And caulking will generally harden and fall out over that period of time. So even a fully passive solar system will have maintenance costs. These costs have to be deducted from the energy savings or added to the system's installed costs. There is no way to generalize what these costs will be unless the details of the system are fully known. So no detailed method of analysis will be presented. But be certain that these costs are added to your financial analysis.

Financing Costs

If the system is large and involved, you may have to borrow either short-term home improvement money or long-term mortgage money to pay for your solar system. Again these are costs that must be added to the system cost. Do not leave them out. As has been shown, money has a time value. This is true whether it is your money or the money belonging to some financial institution.

Keep your eye on your monthly cash flow. If the solar system you borrow on does not promise to reduce your monthly cash flow over its life, then it has doubtful value. After all, one of your goals in considering a solar system is to reduce your costs by replacing fossil fuels or electricity.

Keep your eye on your real estate investment. Placing a $20,000 solar system on a 40,000 to $50,000 home usually will not pay if you decide to sell the property at some time in the future. Your investment should be tempered by the real estate values in your neighborhood.

Making a Decision

In this chapter you learned how to convert the purchase price of fuel to $/MMBtu of energy produced. You learned that an important part of your energy costs is the purchase, installation, operation, and maintenance of your energy conversion device such as a furnace or a water heater.

You learned that your energy costs are expected to continue to rise rapidly. And you were taught a method of calculating what that increase is expected to be. Then you examined the value of money versus time. You learned that the investment in a device to burn the free fuel obtained from the sun must be looked at carefully in order to determine its real value.

You should now be able to make an intelligent financial decision on how you will obtain your energy in the future and on how to determine how much that energy should cost you.

DECISION
7

Orient Your Building to Utilize the Sun

America's homes can be characterized as urban, suburban, and rural. The urban home is the product of the first 40 years of this century. The homes are located for good public transportation. They are placed on very small lots close together. Often they are multifamily.

The suburban home is the product of the post-World War II building boom caused by the existence of the GI mortgage and by the popularity and availability of the mass produced, reasonably priced automobile. The suburban home is characterized as single-family, larger plot, away from the city and public transportation. It spelled a more affluent America with a dream of living independence.

The rural home spans the mid-1880s through to the present. It was solely the home of the farmer and rancher until after World War II when this segment of the population was joined by some of the more affluent who desired country living. It is not possible to characterize the rural home. It varies too much.

The average urban multifamily home does not lend itself well to reorientation for the better utilization of solar energy. The building lots are generally tiny, the houses are close together, and there is no opportunity to make any large changes. The average rural home presents few problems in taking remedial steps to more fully utilize the sun. There is generally enough room around the structure to allow any desired changes.

It is the suburban subdivision, where the bulk of America's population lives today, that represents the solar orientation challenge.

In this chapter you will study building orientation as it relates to suburban subdivisions. Much of what you learn can be translated to rural and urban locations. You will:

- Examine the typical suburban subdivision and learn why it may not be solar-oriented. You will start with the land parcel, go through the subdivision process, and look at the building

lots that are derived. The problems of existing subdivisions will become clear to you.
- Redivide the subdivision into a solar-oriented subdivision. This will teach you what to look for in locating your next home.
- Plan a solar subdivision. By learning about the planning process, you will equip yourself to purchase or retrofit a building lot properly.
- Study the thermal orientation principles of solar utilization. You will learn what data are needed and how all the factors come together to produce the final product.
- Study how to control wind and shade through the use of hedges, fencing, and trees to improve existing building performance.
- Finally, you will revisit Winesap Farms, your original subdivision, in order to replan its orientation for solar energy.

The Existing Suburban Subdivision

There are about 55 million single-family residences in the United States. The majority of these homes are in suburban subdivisions. Most of these suburban subdivisions were created without considering the use of solar energy.

The subdivision developer takes a parcel of land, subdivides it into building lots, builds streets, installs water and sanitary services, and then either sells off the lots or proceeds to construct houses on the lots.

Real-estate subdivision development is a high risk, entrepreneurial enterprise that is highly competitive. The developers must read the marketplace and create the right product for the right price. They must do this in a politically regulated atmosphere where zoning laws and building restrictions tightly circumscribe their actions. So it is of little wonder that, in the past, orientation for the utilization of the sun's energy has not received much attention.

In the following pages you will study Winesap Farms, a typical urban subdivision of the early 1960s—a subdivision that was created without considering the use of solar energy. Then you will study how Winesap Farms could have been laid out for full utilization of the energy from the sun.

The Land Parcel

In the early 1960s a parcel of land known locally as the Winesap Farm came onto the real estate market in Tuburgh, Massachusetts. Figure 7.1 shows this land parcel.

The land had been farmed extensively since the 1920s when Mr. Winesap acquired it. In the intervening years, the city of Tuburgh had grown up around it. The parcel was purchased by Jack Sullivan, a local real estate developer who wished to subdivide it into building lots.

The parcel lies between Park Road and Valley River. It is about 750 ft wide by 750 ft long. Between the river and Park Road, the parcel rises about 40 ft in a steady, gentle slope. Looking from the river to Park Road, one faces north. So the parcel is a south-facing gentle hill.

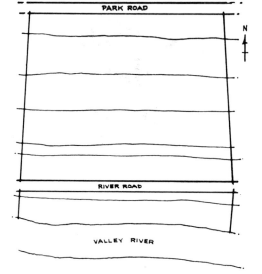

Figure 7.1. The Winesap Farm land parcel.

The city of Tuburgh had passed a number of subdivision rules and regulations in the late 1950s, so Sullivan was faced with lot size and use restrictions. The building lots had to be a minimum of 10,000 sq ft with 80-ft frontage on a developed road. The developer was required to install the finished roads, water, and sewers.

Jack Sullivan studied his housing market and, based on the subdivision regulations and his assessment of the market for homes, drew up the subdivision plan shown in Figure 7.2.

The Subdivision

Sullivan decided that the building lots bordering the river would be the choicest lots and command the highest price, so he planned lots of about 12,000 sq ft along the river. To reach River Road, which would be the frontage road for these lots, he constructed three streets, which he named Elm, Fir, and Hemlock, 600 ft in from Park Road. This allowed him to develop 10,000-ft lots that were basically 100 ft by 100 ft.

The subdivision plan yielded 44 lots with about 2550 lineal feet of road. Only 12 corner lots with double frontage were created. Water and sewer lines were kept to a minimum. River Road was opened to connect on both ends with feeder roads that had dead-ended at Winesap's farm prior to its development.

The Winesap Farms subdivision may look very familiar to you. There are thousands of suburban housing developments that were built across America in the last 30 years that are very similar to Winesap Farms.

There was no energy problem apparent when Jack Sullivan planned this subdivision, so no consideration was given to the orientation of the lots to take maximum advantage of solar energy. The largest problem that Sullivan faced was how to keep the cost of the development competitive.

Chances are that your subdivision was also planned without giving much thought to using solar energy. If so, then the problems that you will see by examining Winesap Farms will most likely be similar to the problems that you face with your house if it is built in a suburban location.

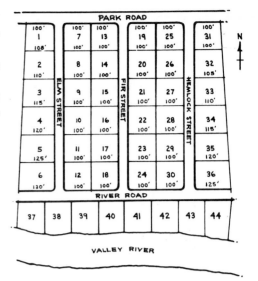

Figure 7.2. The Winesap Farms subdivision.

The Building Lots

Lots 37 through 44, which border on the river, have an east/west frontage. So most likely the houses on these lots were built to face north or south. This orientation is good for the use of solar energy.

The houses facing Park Road could have been built with either an east/west orientation or with a north/south orientation because they are corner lots. The same is true for the six houses on the north side of River Road.

Most likely the houses on Elm, Fir, and Hemlock were built to face east or west. This makes it very hard to benefit properly from the sun's energy. Let us look at why this is so.

Figure 7.3 shows the zoning regulations that Tuburgh uses for single-residence areas such as Winesap Farms. The lot must contain 10,000 sq ft. It must be 80 ft wide. The house must be set back 30 ft from the street, 10 ft from the side lot lines, and 20 ft from the rear lot line. The house cannot be more than 35 ft high, and it cannot cover more than 30% of the lot. These are typical zoning regulations for subdivisions such as Winesap Farms.

MINIMUM LOT AREA (SQ FT)	MINIMUM LOT WIDTH (FT)	MINIMUM YARDS (FT)			MAXIMUM LOT COVERAGE (% TOTAL)	MAXIMUM HEIGHT OF BUILDING (FT)
		FRONT	REAR	SIDE		
10,000	80	30	20	10	30	35

Figure 7.3. Tuburgh's zoning regulations for the Winesap Farms residential area.

As a result of these regulations, there is only a 4000 sq ft area in the center of a lot such as lot 16 where the builder can place the house. This area is shown in Figure 7.4. It is easiest for the builder to line up all the homes with a 30-ft setback facing the street. This placement promotes a harmonious appearance when looking down Fir Street. So most likely the houses on Fir Street are built like the house on lot 17, with the front of the house facing to the east. The house on lot 17 is a 1300-sq-ft ranch with an attached garage. The garage is on the north side, which helps protect the house from the cold northern exposure. But the long sides of the house face to the east and west where they do not receive the full benefit of the sun. Only 26 ft of the house's perimeter faces to the south. So the amount of solar energy that can be collected is minimal.

Lot 18 is a corner lot. The builder wanted to place the same ranch house on this lot, but a double setback was required. So the builder elected to build the house in an L shape. To make it more impressive, obtain a better floor plan, and have it harmonize with Fir Street, he set a breezeway between the garage and the house.

This house has a good solar exposure. The 50-ft-long front wall of the house faces south. The two sides have good afternoon or morning solar exposure. Almost half of the north side of the house is protected by the garage and breezeway from the cold northern exposure.

If the builder had elected to face the house on Fir Street with the breezeway and the garage on River Road, then the solar exposure would have been much poorer.

The Shading

Tuburgh's zoning law states that a structure may be built up to 35 ft high. Figure 7.5 shows the implications of this ruling. A 35-ft-high wall, 50 ft long and only 10 ft from the adjoining lot's southerly line would cast a shadow 62 ft onto the adjoining lot at solar noon on December 21.

Most likely the adjoining lot would not be shaded to that extent, although it legally could be. A typical one-story house is less than 18 ft high. A typical two-story house is less than 26 ft high. The typical residence is only 24 to 30 ft wide. The adjoining lot may only see shading to the extent shown in Figure 7.6, which is much less severe.

The Southerly Lot Line

There are no restrictions at Winesap Farms on lot-line fencing or plantings. So the lot owner may elect to build a fence or plant trees along the lot line to give privacy or to provide a windbreak. Fences are generally 6 ft or less. A 6-ft fence would cast a shadow 12 ft onto the adjoining lot. But if evergreen trees were planted, they could easily grow to a height of more than 20 ft in a fairly short period of time. These would cast a shadow up to 41 ft onto the adjoining lot. Figure 7.7 shows the details.

You can readily see that the owners of an east-facing or west-facing building lot, which has an adjoining lot on the south side, must give a great amount of attention as to how much sun they are legally entitled to.

Figure 7.4. Typical subdivision home siting used prior to the energy shortage.

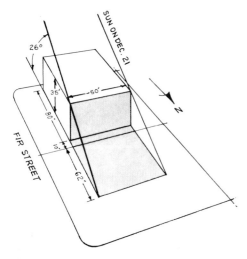

Figure 7.5. Tuburgh's zoning laws allow the northerly adjoining lot to be badly shaded.

The zoning laws, if loosely drawn, will not give them the protection that they need.

The Solar-oriented Subdivision of the 1980s

Winesap Farms could have been developed differently. Figure 7.8 shows one way. This plat assumes that the zoning laws allow the creation of cul de sac lots with lower frontage. This is not an uncommon regulation.

Fir Street would remain, as would River Road. Elm Street and Hemlock Street would be changed to courts ending in cul de sacs. Forty-four building lots can still be created. But the average lot is larger, ranging from 11,000 to 12,500 sq ft. Only 1850 lineal feet of road are required. Four corner lots are eliminated. All the lots except four are north/south oriented. The four lots that are not north/south oriented may be built-on with orientation within 20° of south.

This is a good subdivision plan. The courts are short and present no major dead-ended problems. There is more privacy. The building lots allow larger backyards. The biggest compromise comes with the river lots, where the frontage was cut to maintain a full 44 lots. Of course the developer could have elected to settle for 42 lots and maintain 100-ft frontage if that were more suited to the market. The zoning laws might also have prevented the creation of lots 17 and 18.

But one fact is certain. The developer has created a subdivision that is more suited to the utilization of solar energy without compromising the quality of the subdivision or increasing the roads and services. So the economics would be good.

Solar Subdivision Planning

Orienting your home to utilize solar energy begins with good subdivision planning. The subdivision planner must analyze and weigh all the factors pertaining to the social, economic, engineering, climatic, and aesthetic features and emerge with a balanced land use plan.

Zoning

Local subdivision zoning ordinances are designed to regulate the use of land. They usually cover density of population and buildings, usage of the building lots, and the general size of the building structure.

The two measurements that are used to determine the density of population and space are the number of dwellings per acre and the number of people per acre. If the zoning laws call for minimum 10,000 sq ft lots and single family residences, then a maximum of 4.35 houses may be built per acre as an acre contains 43,560 square feet. And a maximum of 4.35 families may occupy an acre. If there are an average of five people per family, then only 22 people can live on an acre of land.

These measurements are extremely important to local government. They spell out what services the town or city must supply, such as schools, water, and sewers. By creating land use density laws, local government can plan for the future with some degree of confidence.

At Winesap Farms, the zoning ordinance called for 10,000-sq-ft lots and single-family dwellings. Winesap Farms consists of 13.3 acres of land. So the maximum number of houses that could legally be built was 57. The

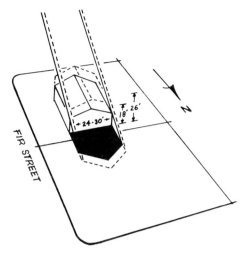

Figure 7.6. Shading problems will generally be less severe on the northerly adjoining lot.

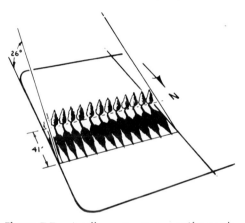

Figure 7.7. A tall evergreen or conifer north lot-line planting can shade the northerly lot.

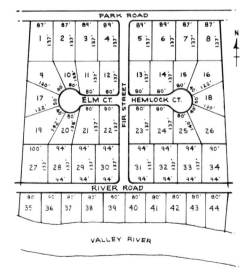

Figure 7.8. Winesap Farms subdivided for good solar orientation.

maximum number of people that the town could expect to have occupy those houses was 285. But roads had to be built that occupied much of the land. So Winesap Farms ended up with 44 building lots and the likelihood that 220 people would occupy them. If two-family houses had been allowed and the average family was a family of four, then 352 people would be living there. This would have made considerable difference in the services that the town would have to provide. If the lot size had been changed, then the number of people would have also changed. So density laws are most important to future planning.

Land Survey Once the developer has determined the zoning laws that regulate the use of the land, he must obtain an accurate survey of the land parcel. A typical land parcel survey will show the boundary lines, the easements, the street locations, the utilities, the ground elevations, the subsoil and drainage conditions, and the important natural features of the parcel such as trees and rock outcroppings. The survey should also show some details about the adjacent property's land use and features.

For a solar subdivision, the developer should also obtain a complete weather analysis. This analysis should include the monthly average air temperature and relative humidity, the monthly average wind direction and speed, and the monthly average solar radiation for horizontal and vertical surfaces. Figure 7.9 shows a table for this data.

Physical Land Inspection

A personal inspection of the site should be made once the survey has been received. This visit allows the developer to record graphically any features of the parcel and the surrounding parcels that impinge on its successful development.

The developer should check the land's slope and gradient; the condition, location, and size of any buildings; the existence of power lines, railroads, highways, industrial plants, or public nuisances nearby; the nonresidential use of any adjoining property; and the plans to make any future public improvements such as a new highway or a sewage plant.

Preliminary Platting

The developer is now in a position to do some preliminary *platting* of the subdivision. Platting is the act of drawing up a sketch of the development.

The preliminary plat covers the grading, the drainage, the utilities, the streets, the building lots, and the land improvements.

A contour or grade plan must be determined that will provide proper drainage of surface water, minimize the need for retaining walls, and make all the building lots suitable for construction.

Water, sewer, electric, and gas utilities must be planned and located. Any necessary street lighting must be planned. And the streets must be planned and profiled.

Each building lot must be located and sized to meet the local zoning ordinances and land use restrictions. Proposed land improvements such as walls, fences, trees, plantings, and parks or recreational facilities must be detailed.

For a solar subdivision, the developer must adhere to a number of self-imposed restrictions in making the preliminary plat. Where it is desired to use solar energy, the lots should be laid out so that houses can be built facing north and south.

When solar heating is needed, the lot-line restrictions on fences, walls, trees, and other plantings must be carefully considered so as not to shade

WORKSHEET

1. Latitude _____ °N   2. Elevation _____ min _____ max

3.

Month	Temp. °F	R.H. %	Wind direction	Wind speed	Horiz. radiation	South-vertical radiation
Jan	—	—	—	—	—	—
Feb	—	—	—	—	—	—
March	—	—	—	—	—	—
April	—	—	—	—	—	—
May	—	—	—	—	—	—
June	—	—	—	—	—	—
July	—	—	—	—	—	—
Aug	—	—	—	—	—	—
Sept	—	—	—	—	—	—
Oct	—	—	—	—	—	—
Nov	—	—	—	—	—	—
Dec	—	—	—	—	—	—

Figure 7.9. Typical solar subdivision monthly weather analysis.

adjacent lots. Yet ample provision to shelter the houses from the winter winds needs consideration. When solar cooling is indicated, the lot-line restrictions change. They should promote shading and the movement of the air through the action of the wind.

The side-yard setbacks on the northerly lot lines may have to be revised where solar shading of the adjacent lot is undesirable. The sunrights of each lot owner may have to be spelled out in some detail.

The Final Subdivision Plat   The final subdivision plat is a legal document that, when properly prepared and filed in the public land records, firmly establishes a legal description of the streets, the building lots, the other land uses, and the restrictions. It must be carefully prepared and checked prior to its final filing.

Orient Your Building

Any building must fit into the pattern of its location if it is to be in harmony with its surroundings and provide a satisfactory home. It must be aesthetically pleasing. It must be politically situated to meet the zoning codes. It must be socially acceptable to the immediate neighborhood. The more urban the area, the greater the need for the building to conform to the other structures in the immediate vicinity.

Both physiological and psychological needs must be taken into account. Physiologically, the thermal, visual, and noise problems must be dealt with. Psychologically, needs for privacy, visual communication, and pleasing surroundings must be satisfied.

Site Standards

When building one- and two-family residences, there are a number of site standards that are generally considered to be critical. These standards relate to building design, site conditions, lot coverage, yard dimensions, access to streets and utilities, and the finished grade elevation.

Houses must be designed to fit within the available building space as mandated by the zoning laws. They must conform to the local building codes.

The site must be free of any hazards that would adversely affect the health and safety of the occupants. Land subsidence, poor drainage, land erosion, floods, and fire hazards must be carefully assessed and taken into consideration.

The structures must not cover more of the land than the regulations allow. They must not protrude into the mandated side-, rear-, or frontyard setbacks. The site must have the minimum frontage required. There must be good access to the street, to the utilities, and to the rear yard without intruding onto adjoining property.

The finished grade of the building site must provide good drainage without erosion or intruding on adjoining sites. It also needs to be harmonious with the surroundings.

Thermal Site Standards

The climatic forces become all-important for the proper utilization of solar energy. The wind, the temperature, the relative humidity, the topography, and the solar radiation all play an important role in setting solar site standards.

Where winter heating is the most important consideration, buildings should typically be oriented to receive the maximum sunlight and the least wind. Where summer cooling is most important, buildings should typically be oriented to receive the minimum sunlight and the most wind.

At first glance, you would think that these statements mean that houses in the lower latitudes of the United States should be oriented differently from houses in the upper latitudes. Such is not the case. Studies from Princeton University show why. Victor Olgyay, an associate professor at the School of Architecture at Princeton shows some of the important solar orientation principles in *Architectural Graphic Standards* (John Wiley & Sons, New York, 1981.)

Figure 7.10 shows a graphic representation of the solar energy received by houses in Minneapolis, New York City, Phoenix, and Miami for January and July. In these diagrams, the air temperature variation is represented by the outside concentric circles. Each circle stands for a 2°F temperature difference from the lowest daily temperature. The direction of the impact is indicated according to the sun's direction as temperatures occur. Note that the low temperatures are easterly whereas the high temperatures are westerly. The total direct and diffuse radiation is indicated with arrows. Each arrow represents 250 Btu/sq ft/day.

These diagrams show that in the upper latitudes the south side of a building receives nearly twice as much solar radiation in the winter as in the summer. In the lower latitudes, the south side of the building sees almost four times as much radiation in the winter as in the summer. They also show that in the upper latitudes the east and west sides receive about 2½ times more radiation in the summer than in the winter. But in the lower latitudes the east and west sides only see about twice as much radiation in the summer than in the winter.

In all latitudes, the north side sees very little radiation. And the north side sees most of this radiation in the summer. Also note that in Phoenix the north and the south sides of the house see about the same amount of radiation in the summertime whereas in Miami the north side of the house sees almost twice as much radiation as the south side in the summertime.

In the upper latitudes, the roof sees very little solar radiation in the wintertime but receives very large amounts in the summertime. The same trend is seen in the lower latitudes, but the difference is not quite so great.

Olgyay also conducted experiments on the thermal behavior of buildings exposed to different orientations at Princeton University's Architectural Laboratory. Figure 7.11 shows the summer results of north, south, east, and west exposures.

When the building is oriented to the west, there is a wide swing in temperature over the daytime hours with the room being very hot in afternoon and evening hours. When the building is oriented to the east, the temperature climbs rapidly in the morning and remains high into the evening. When the building is oriented to the south, the temperature climbs at the same rate as a west orientation in the hours of 6 A.M. to 3 P.M. but remains about the same temperature as the east orientation into the evening. When the building is oriented to the north, the temperature remains the coolest throughout the day.

From these calculations and experimental observations, Olgyay drew three basic conclusions about building orientation:

• The optimum year-round building orientation will lie near south, but it will differ in the various regions and will depend on the daily temperature variation.

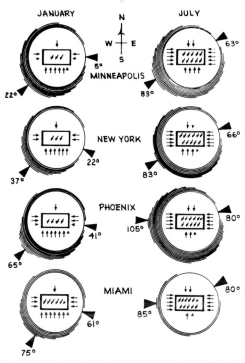

Figure 7.10. Graphic representation of solar radiation and temperature at four different building sites. (Redrawn by permission from *Architectural Graphic Standards,* John Wiley & Sons, New York, 1981.)

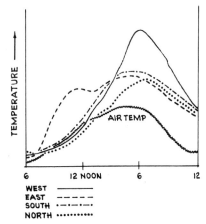

Figure 7.11. Room temperature in differently oriented houses. (Redrawn by permission from *Architectural Graphic Standards,* John Wiley & Sons, New York, 1981.)

WORKSHEET

1. Latitude of building location   _____ °N

2. Elevation of building lot (above sea level)   _____ ft

3. Air temperature and relative humidity

	Temp. °F	R.H. %
Dec to Feb	_____	_____
Mar to May	_____	_____
June to Aug	_____	_____
Sept to Nov	_____	_____

4. Wind direction and speed

	Speed mph	Direction
Dec to Feb	_____	_____
Mar to May	_____	_____
June to Aug	_____	_____
Sept to Nov	_____	_____

5. Horizontal and south-vertical radiation

	Horizontal	Vertical
Dec to Feb	_____	_____
Mar to May	_____	_____
June to Aug	_____	_____
Sept to Nov	_____	_____

6. Building lot dimensions

North lot line	_____
South lot line	_____
East lot line	_____
West lot line	_____

7. Building lot shading problems:

_____

_____

_____

Figure 7.12. Typical thermal forces that must be considered in building siting and orientation.

- In all regions, an orientation east of south gives a better yearly performance and a more equal daily heat distribution. Westerly orientations perform poorly with unbalanced heat impacts.
- The thermal orientation has to be correlated with the local wind directions.

Thermal Orientation Data Needs Figure 7.12 shows the data that you need to gather to make some intelligent thermal decisions. You can locate the latitude of your building location from an atlas or even a local road map. The elevation of your building is usually shown on the lot or subdivision plan. If not, it can generally be obtained from the building department of your city or town.

The air temperature or the relative humidity that is experienced in your area can be located in a number of reference books. *The U.S. Climatic Atlas* will list a location close to you. So will the *ASHRAE 1977 Handbook of Fundamentals*. Or get in touch with your local weather bureau or newspaper.

The building lot dimensions can be taken from the lot or subdivision plan. Again, these are on file at the building department office in your local city or town if you are in an established location and do not have the lot or subdivision plan readily available.

The Thermal Plot Plan The thermal considerations can be visualized better if placed on a plan of the building plot. Figure 7.13 shows such a plan. The building lot faces west. It is lot 1 from block 6. The lot contains 12,500 sq ft. Its basic dimensions are 100 ft by 125 ft. The zoning laws call for a front setback of at least 30 ft, a rear setback of at least 20 ft, and

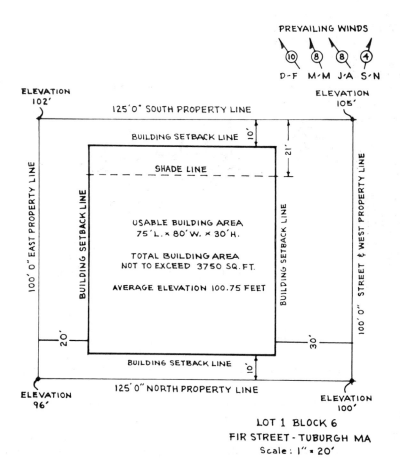

Figure 7.13. Typical thermal plot plan.

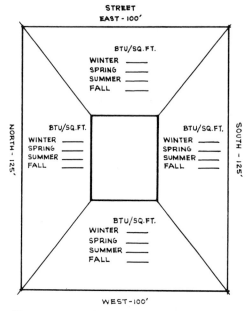

Figure 7.14. Climatic map of your building lot.

Figure 7.15. Typical chain-link metal fence.

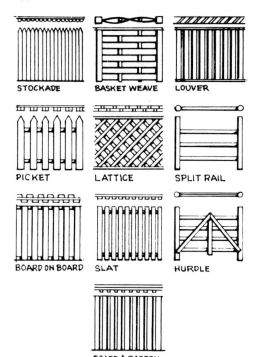

Figure 7.16. Ten types of wood fences.

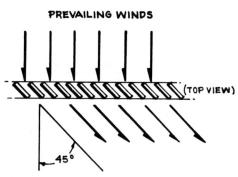

Figure 7.17. How a vertical louvered fence can be used to bend the wind's direction sideways.

side setbacks of 10 ft. So the usable building area is 75 ft long by 80 ft wide. A building cannot be built higher than 35 ft above the average elevation, which is 100.75 ft above sea level. Only 30% of the lot, or 3750 sq ft, may be built on.

The prevailing wind in the winter, spring, and summer is from the northwest. But in the fall it shifts to directly out of the north. There is a possible shade problem from the adjoining lot extending 21 ft in from the south lot line, which leaves 11 ft of the possible building area shaded on the south side.

You could also add the solar radiation for a square foot of horizontal surface and for a south-facing vertical surface to this map along with the seasonal temperatures. Or you could place them on a separate climatic map as shown in Figure 7.14.

Controlling Wind and Shade

Often the wind currents and the solar radiation patterns fight each other. The solar radiation pattern cannot be changed, but shade can be provided where necessary. The wind patterns cannot be changed either. But again these patterns can be controlled. The two devices that are used to accomplish these purposes are fencing and trees.

Fencing

There are many types of fencing to consider. They break down into two general categories: wood fences and metal fences.

Generally, metal fences are not used for the purpose of wind control or to provide shading. Instead they are used to provide privacy and to control the wanderings of small children and pets.

The average metal fence is a fencing known as chain-link. Figure 7.15 shows a fence of this type. It usually ranges from 3 to 4 ft high. Occasionally it may range up to 12 ft in height for specific purposes such as enclosing tennis courts. About the only way that shading can be accomplished with this fence is to weave metal lattice strips through the wire mesh.

Wood fences come in all styles and variations. Their style and height are only limited by the designer's imagination. Figure 7.16 shows 10 types of typical residential fences. These fences can range anywhere from 3 to 8 ft high. A typical height would be 5 to 6 ft.

Lattice, hurdle, and split-rail fences do little to control the wind. Picket, slat, and board-on-board fences do an excellent job of reducing the wind's velocity. Often their use will result in snow-drift or sand-drift control without completely blocking the breeze.

Stockade, board and batten, and basket-weave fences generally act to block and change the wind patterns completely. The louvered fence is one of the most useful designs in changing wind patterns. If the fence is set perpendicular to the prevailing wind direction, then the louvers can be arranged to bend the wind into the desired direction. It is possible to change the wind direction up to about 45° by installing a fence like the one shown in Figure 7.17, which is a vertical louvered fence, or like the fence in Figure 7.18, which is a horizontal louvered fence.

A right-angled solid fence, such as the one shown in Figure 7.19, can be used to divert the wind away from a structure. A solid fence placed at a 45° angle will slip the wind in one direction around or away from the structure.

Such fences are extremely useful in reconciling the wind patterns with the solar radiation patterns. When installed with good advance planning, they can add measurably to the looks of a building lot.

Hedges

Fencing need not be restricted to manufactured materials. Nothing looks nicer than a green or living fence. Such fences add measurably to the appearance of the building lot. Deciduous plantings, which shed their leaves in the winter provide good control in the summer but do little in the winter. Evergreen plantings act year round to control the wind currents. Exam-

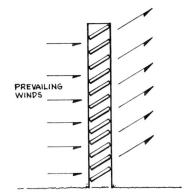

Figure 7.18. How a horizontal louvered fence can be used to bend the wind up or down.

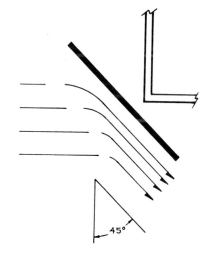

Figure 7.19. Using solid fences to break the wind.

Orient the Building **125**

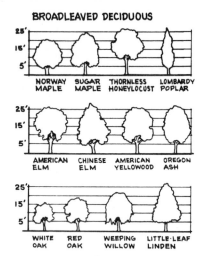

Figure 7.20. Some broad-leaved deciduous trees.

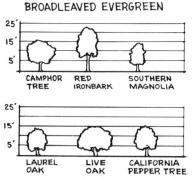

Figure 7.21. Some broad-leaved evergreen trees.

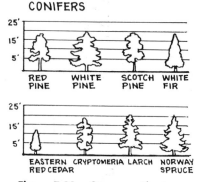

Figure 7.22. Some conifer trees.

ples of deciduous plantings that can be used for this purpose and that are adaptable to pruning for control are dogwood, witch hazel, privet, lilac, chokeberry, flannel bush, spirea, viburnum, barberry, and forsythia. Examples of evergreen shrubs are juniper, yew, rhododendron, myrtle, nerium, dwarf box, english ivy, and pachysandra.

The suitability of these shrubs to your local climate will vary. You should consult closely with local nurseries to help choose the best shrub for your soil and location.

Shading

Shade control on the building lot is best accomplished with major trees. Here again you have many different trees to choose from. Trees can be divided into four major groups: broad-leaved deciduous, broad-leaved evergreen, conifers, and palm trees.

Broad-leaved deciduous trees are trees such as maples, honey locust, poplar, elms, yellowwood, ash, oak, willows, and linden. Broad-leaved deciduous trees shed their leaves in the winter, so they offer excellent summer shade without interfering with the use of the winters' sun. The various trees have different shapes and heights. Figure 7.20 shows the average height and silhouettes of the most popular trees in this class after 10 years of growth. In general they range from 15 to 30 ft in height.

Broad-leaved evergreen trees are trees such as camphor, ironbark, magnolia, live oak, laurel oak, and the California pepper tree. These trees hold their leaves year round so they offer year round shade. The heights and shapes of these trees after about 10 years of growth are shown in Figure 7.21.

Conifer trees are trees such as pine, fir, cypress, cedar, cryptomeria, larch, spruce, arborvitae, yew, and hemlock. The conifer tree tends to be tall and skinny in shape. Conifers may be planted close together to make living lot-walls. They hold their leaves year round and are fast growing. Figure 7.22 shows some common conifer trees.

Palm trees, which are restricted to the lower latitudes, hold their leaves year round and grow quite tall. They are generally characterized by bare trunks and spreading top foliage. Figure 7.23 shows the common palm trees. Like shrubs, trees have certain geographic planting considerations. You should consult with local nurseries about which ones are best for your part of the country.

Improving Existing Building Performance

Figure 7.24 shows a 26 ft by 48 ft ranch house with an attached garage on the north side. The building is oriented with the long side facing to the east/west. This is a poor solar orientation. The winter winds come from the northwest and sweep against the long west side of the building whereas the summer breezes come from the southwest.

The sun rises in the front of the house, travels across the south end and sets over the rear lot line. The 9 A.M. to 3 P.M. sun lines, which describe the sun's direction in the sky at those times, lie along the south lot line.

A review of Olgyay's work shows that the rooms at the rear of the house, or the west, will remain hot through the late evening whereas the rooms in the front of the house, or the east, will warm up early in the day and remain hot in the summer months.

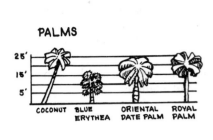

PALMS

COCONUT · BLUE ERYTHEA · ORIENTAL DATE PALM · ROYAL PALM

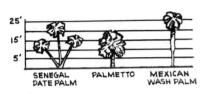

SENEGAL DATE PALM · PALMETTO · MEXICAN WASH PALM

Figure 7.23. Some palm trees.

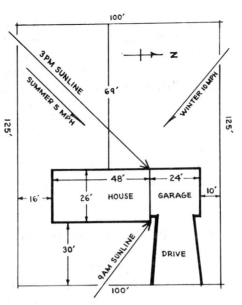

Figure 7.24. A poorly oriented house for solar radiation can be improved with changes in the building lot plantings.

Some Remedial Steps

Figure 7.25 shows some of the steps that can be taken to improve the solar utilization on this building lot. First, summer shade could be provided by the planting of six large deciduous trees such as maple, elm, yellowwood, or ash in the locations shown. These would provide summer shade to ward off the radiation in the summer but would not interfere with the impingement of solar energy on the house in the winter. As the sun is high in the sky in the summer, the four trees near the house should be kept close, so as to also provide shade for the roof. But beware of planting them too close. These broad-leaved deciduous trees are extremely large when fully mature. The trees at the back of the lot are important. They prevent the evening sun's rays from creeping under the high branches of the close-in trees.

A tall hedge, fence, or row of conifers along the northwest corner and up the side and rear lot line will blunt the winter winds. Tall yews or junipers make good shrubs. Slender conifers such as pine, spruce, hemlock, or fir planted close together will work well. So will solid fencing. A row of evergreen shrubs along the north side of the drive will complete the windbreak. But be certain to leave an exit to funnel the summer breezes between the planting and the edge of the garage.

Any foundation plantings should be carefully chosen. Deciduous planting should be used to the south, west, and east sides of the house. Evergreens would be better on the north and around the garage. The rule of thumb that should be followed in this orientation is deciduous plantings on the southerly part of the lot and evergreen plantings on the northerly part. On larger lots in more suburban locations, it is also generally possible to use the grade of the building lot to provide the windbreaks required.

Plantings and fences need not be restricted to poor solar orientations. Figure 7.26 shows a north/south orientation where plants have also provided some improvements in the utilization of solar energy. Hedges along

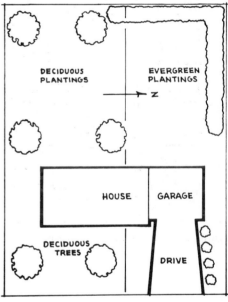

Figure 7.25. Some typical lot changes that improve solar use with an east-west orientation.

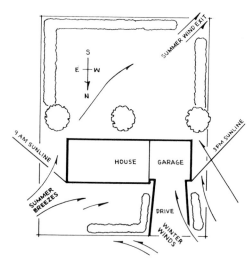

Figure 7.26. Some typical lot changes that improve solar use with north-south orientation.

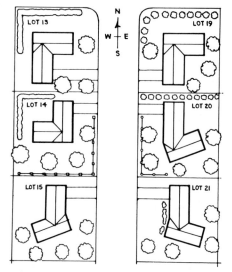

Figure 7.27. Winesap Farms revisited.

the drive and in front of the house break up the winter winds. Deciduous trees off the rear corners and along the rear of the house provide summer shade but permit good winter solar radiation.

Be certain that you restrict the plantings or fences in the rear yard to a height that will not block the winter sun. Leave exit spaces for the summer breezes. Use deciduous foundation plantings in the rear and along the sides. Use evergreens in the front. Again, use the same basic rule of thumb of deciduous plantings on the southern side of the lot and evergreen plantings on the northern side.

All these remedial steps are quite basic. Many things can be done on your building lot once you sit down and start planning.

Winesap Farms Revisited

Many subdivisions exist that are platted and approved but are not yet developed. Quite often reopening the planning to make drastic changes would subject the developer to making expensive changes in the plans due to zoning changes passed subsequent to the subdivision's approval.

Much can be done with east/west oriented building lots to utilize solar energy effectively and with some imagination. Some examples of how Fir Street could be treated are shown in Figure 7.27.

Lot 13 is a corner lot that faces on both Fir Street and Park Road. The house was faced north/south with the rear yard placed on Park Road, protected with a dense hedge that blunted the winter winds and provided privacy.

A breezeway was added to the garage, and the combination was moved to the rear of the lot at right angles to the house. The L shape of the house now faces southeast, which is a good solar orientation. Deciduous broadleaved trees are strategically placed to provide summer shade.

The house on lot 14 has been pushed to the northwest rear of the lot. The rear yard is now a small private area. A hedge or fencing protects it against the winter winds and provides privacy. The house faces to the south with the garage on Fir Street. A continuous roofline is utilized on Fir Street to harmonize the house with the street. Again, deciduous trees are strategically located to protect against the summer sun. A 40 ft by 100 ft frontyard is opened on the south side. Fencing can be utilized to make this a great family area, as the house is located well back from the southerly lot line.

On lot 15, the house has been cocked at an angle and moved to the south with a small breezeway. This opens the rear yard further, gives a southeasterly solar exposure, and provides a better view of the river. The front yard still provides many possibilities.

Lot 19 utilizes a very similar orientation to lot 13. The garage and breezeway are brought forward to create a southeasterly exposure. The house faces on Park Road. A line of conifer trees on Park Road and Fir Street provides privacy and protection against the winter winds.

Lot 20 is an unusual approach that utilizes an oversized breezeway as a front entry and faces the house southeasterly down the rear lot lines. An approach of this type would have to be carefully fitted into the overall subdivision planning. But it presents a number of architectural possibilities.

Lot 21 takes a southwesterly approach to orientation and faces the main house looking down Fir Street to the river. The orientation fits well with the house on lot 20, and it opens a larger rear yard.

Certainly these orientations are different from lining up the homes to face on Fir Street. The addition of breezeways adds some costs to the housing. But such changes would be both refreshing and more conducive to the use of the sun.

Making a Decision

In this chapter you studied building orientation. You started by examining one of America's many existing subdivisions that was not oriented to make maximum utilization of solar energy. This gave you some insight as to the practical problems faced by the real estate developer.

Then you saw how that subdivision could have been laid out to utilize the sun. You learned that streets running from east to west generally give the best solar orientation.

You studied the steps of subdivision planning. You learned that the land survey is followed by a physical examination, a preliminary platting, and a final full subdivision plat.

Then you learned the principles of thermal orientation of buildings by studying thermal standards, thermal data needs, thermal plot plans, and final orientation. You learned how to employ trees, fencing, and hedges to give wind and shade control. And you learned the major remedial steps that could be taken with existing structures.

Finally, you revisited Winesap Farms and saw how an existing platted, but unbuilt, subdivision that was not solar-oriented could be made solar-oriented.

You now have the basic principles of solar orientation to guide you. You should be able to make a decision on how you will solar orient your new home or increase the solar orientation of your existing home.

DECISION
8

Plan Your Building's Interior

A home must provide for four main functions: the function of sleeping, bathing, and dressing; the function of daily eating, living, and entertaining; the function of vehicle and implement storage; and the function of housing the mechanical devices that heat, cool, light, and supply water and sanitary services for the structure.

Generally, these four functions are carried out in different parts of the home. So a home can be split into four functional modules: the sleeping module, the living module, the transportation module, and the mechanical module.

A review of these four functions shows that each requires about the same amount of space within the home. This means that three bedrooms and two baths take up about the same square footage as the living, dining, and kitchen area. A two-car garage requires a similar amount of space. The mechanical module can be smaller, but it usually is most convenient when it is of a similar or a larger size so as to also provide room for laundry functions, hobbies, and crafts.

In this chapter you will study:

- The requirements for lighting, space, furnishings, heating, cooling, and privacy in a home.
- The basic modules for the four main functions of a home and the requirements for each of these modules.
- How the four modules can be fitted together to form many different home designs.
- How the modular concept can be used to orient the interior for good solar thermal performance on most building lots.

The Functional Building Module

The basic functional building module measures 22 ft by 22 ft, 24 ft by 24 ft, 26 ft by 26 ft, 28 ft by 28 ft, or 30 ft by 30 ft. Note that these modular sizes are square. If four-sided structures are to be built, then the maximum number of square feet can be placed in a square module.

Modules 22 ft to 26 ft wide generally use 2 × 8 to 2 × 10 floor joists ranging from 12 to 16 in. on center over a center girder such as shown in Figure 8.1. Modules 26 to 30 ft wide typically require 2 × 10 to 2 × 12 floor joists over a center girder with 12 to 16 in. spacing. There is usually little to be gained by building wider.

The square module is in no way sacred. Quite often a rectangular module fits the design requirements better. When it does, it should be used. But more perimeter walls are needed to enclose the same amount of space, so costs increase as a result.

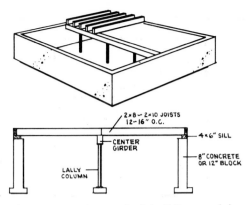

Figure 8.1. How typical building modules are framed.

Combining the Building's Modules

Using square modules does not mean building square homes. Quite to the contrary, the modular ranch usually ends up at a width to length ratio of 1 to 2, or 1 to 3. A straight ranch composed of three 24-ft modules placed end-to-end, with the mechanical module located in the basement would measure 72 ft long. If a 26-ft module were used, this configuration would end up being 78 ft long.

If an L-shaped ranch were to be created, using 26-ft modules, then the building would be 52 ft by 52 ft. With a split-level design using sleeping module over transportation module alongside living module over mechanical module, the building would end up at 26 ft by 52 ft. Some typical examples are shown in Figure 8.2.

The modules do not all have to be the same size. Perhaps it is desired to build a four bedroom home with only a living, dining, and kitchen area. In this case, a 30 ft by 30 ft sleeping module combined with a 26 ft by 26 ft living module may work out well.

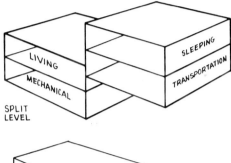

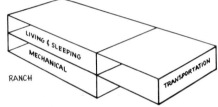

Figure 8.2. Typical ways in which building modules are combined.

However, when building one module over another, the modules must be the same length and the top module can only be up to 2 ft wider or the building will not go together properly. An example, shown in Figure 8.3, is the two-story colonial, which can readily have a garrison overhang, provided it is properly framed for it.

Why not build the house completely square, if a square building is the most economical? Many designers will tell you, "This rarely can be done. Such a house has poor natural lighting, poor ventilation, oversized timbers and joists, a cumbersome roof structure, and many of the rooms would not have an exterior wall. Very few building codes would allow such a structure even if it made sense." And as for solar orientation, a square house is poor. A 2 to 1 or 3 to 1 length to width ratio gathers more sun when it is properly oriented on the building lot. However, such is not always the case as you will see in later chapters. Square solar designs do make good sense.

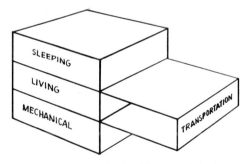

Figure 8.3. How the building modules fit together in a two-story colonial house.

The Exterior Appearance of Modular Interior Design

The use of the modular design concept does not in any way cause the exterior of the house to suffer. Nor does it create a development of look-alikes. The house design process proceeds like this in using the modular interior approach: The number of rooms and the amount of space needed in each module is determined. The modules are designed. The basic style

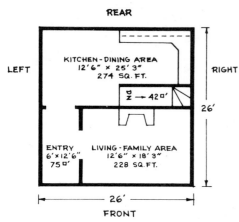

Figure 8.4. Typical 26 ft by 26 ft living module.

of house—ranch, split-level, or two story—is determined. The modules are fitted together. Any modifications to meet the needs of the final structure are made. The exterior design is determined and drawn. At that point any reconciliation of the interior/exterior appearance is made.

Modular interior design is only a way of proceeding with the design process. Throughout the process, preliminary decisions about orientation, style, and exterior are being fed into the process.

The Living Module

The living module contains the kitchen, the living room, the dining room, and the family room. These may be separate rooms or they may be functionally combined.

Figure 8.4 shows a typical 26 ft by 26 ft living module. This module lends itself well to being combined with several configurations of sleeping and transportation modules. The mechanical module is presumed to be in a full basement under the living module. No exterior doors and windows are shown. Their locations will depend on the final house configuration. The room layout is designed so that there are two options for window location in each room. It is designed so that there is only one entry and exit from the kitchen and living room, which ensures that they will not become high traffic areas.

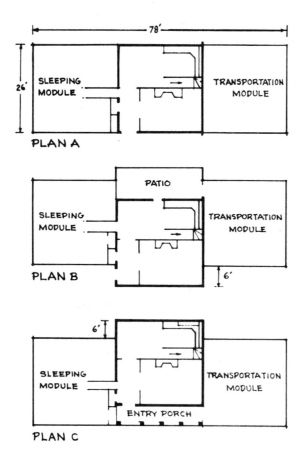

Figure 8.5. Typical in-line ranch module combinations.

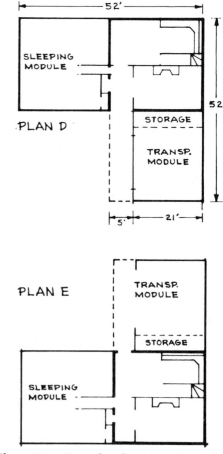

Figure 8.6. Typical L-shaped ranch module combinations.

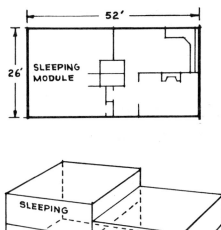

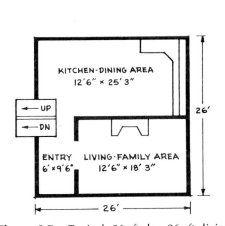

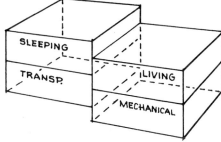

Figure 8.7. Typical 26 ft by 26 ft living module modified for a split-level configuration.

Figure 8.8. Typical split-level configuration using the 26 ft by 26 ft living module.

The sleeping module is designed for the left of the plan. It can be entered at any point along the left wall. The transportation module may be placed on any of the other three sides. The module is designed without a front hall closet. A closet can be easily added to the front hall if a side entry is used. Or the closet can be placed in the sleeping module and entered from the left wall. An interior fireplace is used. It could be shifted to the right wall of the living room if desired.

Figure 8.5 shows some typical in-line ranch module combinations using the basic living module shown. In Plan A, the three modules are in one unbroken line. There is no entry to the transportation module except through the garage door. The transportation module may be entered from either the rear, the right side, or the front as desired.

Plan B is similar except that the living module has been pulled forward by 6 ft to create a space for a patio or porch at the rear of the module. A door from the patio to the transportation module is now possible. The transportation module may again be entered from the front, the rear, or the right side. The entry may be entered from the front or from the left side. A door to the patio has been placed in the rear wall.

Plan C has the living module set back 6 ft to create a covered entry porch. The roofline would have to be raised to provide for a 32 ft width. The transportation module should not be entered from the front in this style in most cases. Either side- or rear-wall entry/exit to the backyard can be employed.

Figure 8.6 shows typical L-shaped configurations. For both of these configurations, the front wall of the garage has to be pulled back about 5 to 6 ft for entry into the living module. The 26-ft roof width is maintained to provide for a covered entry. The transportation module cannot be entered from the front or the rear due to the final sizing of 21 ft by 26 ft. Either left or right entry is satisfactory.

The Living Module Modification for a Split-level

The same 26 ft by 26 ft living module works quite well in a split-level design if the staircase is moved as shown in Figure 8.7. In a side-by-side

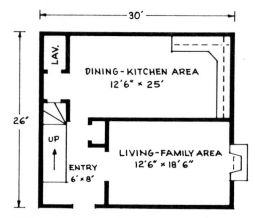

Figure 8.9. Typical 26 ft by 30 ft living module for a two-story house.

split-level design, one-half of the staircase typically appears in the adjoining module. This can be seen better by referring to Figure 8:8, which shows a typical split-level design with the sleeping module stacked on the transportation module and the living module stacked on the mechanical module. The grade of the lot is normally at the floor line of the transportation module. The same forward and backward movements of the side-by-side modules can be employed as was seen in the ranch configurations.

The Living Module Modification for a Two Story

The two-story house is best approached by adding 4 ft to the module's length to hold the staircase. Figure 8.9 shows how this is done. The additional 4 ft ensures the designer of having room for a first-floor lavatory and a hall closet. In a 26-ft length module, these would not be possible because of space limitations.

It should be noted that a center-hall two-story house cannot be designed into a 30-ft long module. The center hall with the staircase uses 7½ ft of width. This would only leave room for 10½-ft wide rooms, which is way out of proportion. So a center-hall two-story house should be designed at least 32 ft in length.

Planning the Living Module

All planning for the living module begins with the number of occupants. Therefore the basic decision as to how many people the sleeping module will accommodate must be made first. A two-bedroom home will house two to four occupants. A three-bedroom home will house from three to six occupants. And a four-bedroom home will house from four to eight occupants.

The ages of the occupants is important because activities vary with age. A convenient grouping of age brackets is preschool age, school age, and adult. A fourth category of senior citizen is also helpful to establish in custom planning.

Figure 8.10 shows a list of typical daily activities for each of the three major age groupings and the modules in which the activities would typically take place. Of course, in custom planning the list could be much longer and more specific.

Examination of the activity list shows that the living module must be planned for about 10 different activities if all age groups are to be accommodated.

PRESCHOOL CHILDREN	LIVING	SLEEPING	TRANSPORTATION	MECHANICAL
Feeding	x			
Snacking	x			
Play	x	x		x
Television/reading	x			
Sleep/nap		x		
Dressing		x		
Toilet	x	x		
Toys	x	x	x	x
Coats and accessories	x	x		

Figure 8.10. List of typical activities in the home that must be planned for.

SCHOOL CHILDREN	LIVING	SLEEPING	TRANSPORTATION	MECHANICAL
Dining	x			
Snacking	x			
Enertainment	x			
Television/reading	x	x		
Private conversation	x			
Homework		x		
Telephone	x	x		
Hobby				x
Vehicle			x	
Sporting goods		x	x	x
Sleep		x		
Dressing		x		
Toilet	x	x		

ADULT	LIVING	SLEEPING	TRANSPORTATION	MECHANICAL
Dining	x			
Snacking	x			
Enertainment	x			
Television/reading	x	x		
Private conversation	x			
Sexual congress		x		
Paperwork	x	x		
Telephone	x	x		
Hobby				x
Vehicle			x	
Implements			x	
Sleep		x		
Dressing		x		
Toilet	x	x		

The Kitchen

The basic kitchen equipment necessary in all residences is sink, range, and refrigerator. Any number of other appliances can be added to this list such as range hood, oven and broiler, cooking top, freezer, disposal, dishwasher, trash compactor. Figure 8.11 shows the typical dimensions of most of this equipment for your planning purposes.

BASIC KITCHEN EQUIPMENT	DIMENSIONS (IN.)		
	WIDTH	DEPTH	HEIGHT
Sink	28-46	16-25	5-10
Range	20-40	24-27½	35-36
Refrigerator	24-48	23-30	55-69½
Range hood	24-72	12-27½	5½-8½
Oven and broiler	21-24½	21-24	23½-50½
Cooking top	12-48	18-22	2-3
Freezer	28½-32	24½-33	56½-71
Disposal	7-10½	7-10½	12-16
Dishwasher	23-24	25-25½	34¼-34½
Trash compacter	14-15	20-24½	34¼-35
Microwave oven	16½-24	15½-21	12½-16
Washer	25-27	25-29	35½-36½
Drier	26½-31½	25-29	35½-36½

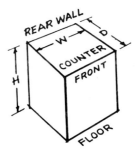

Figure 8.11. Typical dimensions for major kitchen appliances.

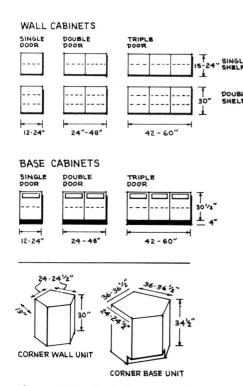

WALL CABINETS

SINGLE DOOR · DOUBLE DOOR · TRIPLE DOOR

15-24" SINGLE SHELF

30" DOUBLE SHELF

12-24" · 24"-48" · 42-60"

BASE CABINETS

SINGLE DOOR · DOUBLE DOOR · TRIPLE DOOR

30½"

4"

12-24" · 24-48" · 42-60"

24-24½"
36-36½"
36-36½"
30"
24-24½"
34½"

CORNER WALL UNIT

CORNER BASE UNIT

Figure 8.12. Typical preassembled kitchen cabinet dimensions.

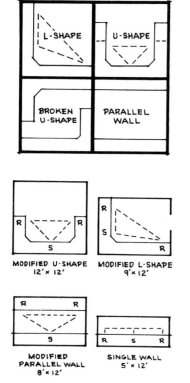

L-SHAPE · U-SHAPE

BROKEN U-SHAPE · PARALLEL WALL

MODIFIED U-SHAPE 12' x 12'

MODIFIED L-SHAPE 9' x 12'

MODIFIED PARALLEL WALL 8' x 12'

SINGLE WALL 5' x 12'

Figure 8.13. Different kitchen configurations in a 12 ft by 12 ft room.

The kitchen cabinets can be built-in-place on site, or preassembled cabinets may be grouped and built onto the walls. Preassembled cabinets are supplied in 3-in. increments from 12 to 84 in. wide.

Generally there are two depths of cabinets. Upper wall cabinets range from 13 to 16 in. in depth; base units that fit under the counter range from 24 to 24½ in. in depth. Base units generally run 34½ in. high before the counter top is applied; wall units vary from 15 to 30 in. high. Figure 8.12 shows typical units for planning purposes. It is generally best to obtain the manufacturer's specifications before drawing the final plan.

Special cabinets such as corner units, oven cabinets, utility closets, and two-sided peninsula cabinets are generally available. So are filler strips to fill any odd spaces less than 3 in. wide.

Kitchen Space Planning There are five basic floor space configurations used in kitchen planning: the single wall, the parallel wall, the L shape, the U shape, and the broken U shape. These basic shapes are shown in Figure 8.13 with the exception of the single wall shape, which is drawn in Figure 8.14 to show some typical dimensions.

In Figure 8.13, all the kitchen configurations were placed in a 12 ft by 12 ft room so that they could be compared. The L shape gives 22 ft of counter space and an excellent kitchen eating area. It can be served by one or two doors. The U shape gives 28 feet of counter space, allows for one or two doors, but leaves no room for kitchen dining. Six feet of counter, as indicated by the dashed lines, has to be removed if kitchen dining is desired. This leaves the same 22 ft of counter as shown in the L shape.

The broken U shape gives 34 ft of counter space, allows for two doors, and leaves no room for kitchen dining. The parallel wall space leaves 8 ft between the two counters, which is undesirable. It allows for one or two doors. Kitchen eating is possible.

You can learn a number of things from this simple comparison. First, the U shape modified for 22 ft of counter space is an excellent design. The traffic pattern, which is shown by the dashed triangle, is short and compact. Each corner of the triangle contains a work center such as the cooking center, the sink center, or the refrigerator center. There is no cross-flow of traffic from people passing through the room. There is enough room for two people to work in the area without getting in each other's way. And there is ample room for an eating area.

Second, the L shape is a satisfactory plan. Its main disadvantage is the long traffic pattern from one end of the L shape to the other. But there is room for two or three people to work. And a good kitchen dining area is available.

Suppose the room were only 9 ft by 12 ft. If only one door were employed, the eating area could still be maintained. The traffic pattern would be more satisfactory. But a U-shaped kitchen would not work out in this narrow room.

Third, when the room is 7 to 8 ft wide and requires doors at each end, then the parallel wall kitchen works out well. The traffic pattern is closed. However, this type of kitchen receives high cross-traffic through the room. If only one door is required, then an L shape would work better. When the room is less than 7 ft, a single wall kitchen must be used. In the 8-ft room, one of the parallel counters could be replaced by an eating area and a single-wall kitchen if the occupancy was only two or three people.

Last comes the broken U shape. It obviously is too much kitchen for a 12 ft by 12 ft room. It has 34 ft of counter space, much more than any of the other kitchens. It has room for two or three people to work. But it has a bad cross-traffic pattern and a long work triangle.

The broken U shape kitchen lends itself admirably to a large family residential kitchen for serious cooks and for families with kitchen help. Figure 8.15 shows such a kitchen in a 14 ft by 14 ft configuration with a 4 ft by 4 ft food and serving preparation area in the center of the room.

Food is received at the service entrance and stored. Food preparation starts at the refrigerator area and proceeds through the cleaning and cooking operation and is maintained ready to serve at the right of the range. Dishes, silver, and other equipment come from the serving area where they do not interfere with the cook. Clean-up is accomplished between the sink and the service door, effectively separating clean-up and serving. The preparation table serves the cook during the food preparation time and as a place for dirty tableware during the clean-up or between courses.

What you should have learned from this discussion is that kitchen planning is a function of the space available, the types and numbers of kitchen workers, and the family's eating preferences.

Think of a kitchen as containing three individual work centers: a refrigerator center where food is received and prepared, a range center where food is cooked and served, and a sink center where food preparation and clean-up is accomplished. Figure 8.16 shows typical layouts for each of these centers reprinted from *Architectural Graphic Standards*. The sink center should be between the refrigerator and the range center where it is convenient to both. The refrigerator center should be close to the entry of the kitchen, and the range center should be close to the dining area.

For storage area you should provide 18 sq ft of cabinet plus 6 sq ft for each occupant normally served. Typical residential kitchen layouts, reprinted from *Architectural Graphic Standards*, are shown in Figure 8.17.

The use of corner-cabinet units is a *must*. When corner units are not used, a blind corner, good for nothing except long-term storage, is created. Removing items from blind corners is frustrating for the cook.

The top shelf in the wall cabinets should not be more than 6 ft off the floor for people of average height. This allows the contents to be seen before attempting to remove them.

Figure 8.16. Typical layouts for range, refrigerator, and sink centers. (Reprinted by permission from *Architectural Graphic Standards*, John Wiley & Sons, New York, 1981.)

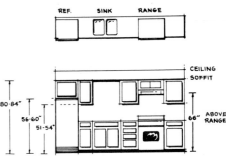

Figure 8.14. Some typical small kitchen measurements.

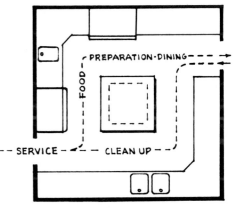

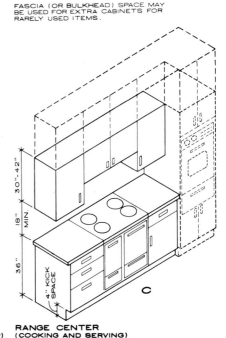

Figure 8.15. The broken U shape in a 14 ft by 14 ft large residential kitchen.

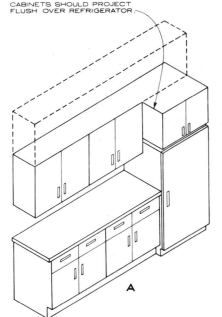

REFRIGERATOR CENTER
(RECEIVING AND FOOD PREPARATION)

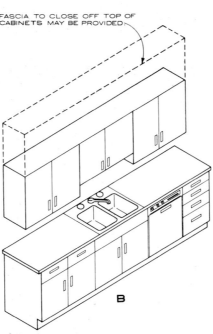

SINK CENTER
(FOOD PREPARATION, CLEANING AND CLEAN-UP)

RANGE CENTER
(COOKING AND SERVING)

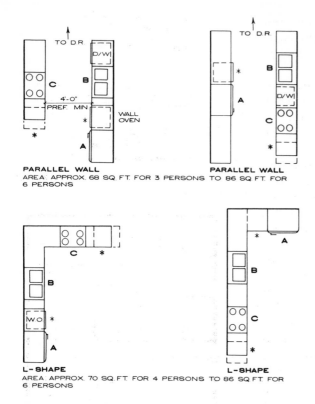

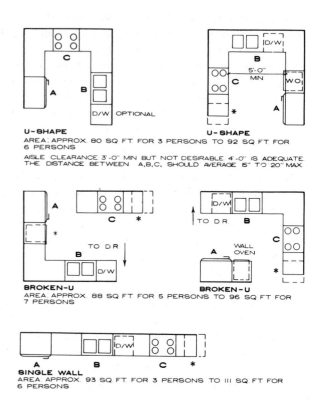

PARALLEL WALL
AREA: APPROX. 68 SQ. FT. FOR 3 PERSONS TO 86 SQ. FT. FOR 6 PERSONS

PARALLEL WALL

L-SHAPE
AREA: APPROX. 70 SQ. FT. FOR 4 PERSONS TO 86 SQ. FT. FOR 6 PERSONS

L-SHAPE

U-SHAPE
AREA: APPROX. 80 SQ. FT. FOR 3 PERSONS TO 92 SQ. FT. FOR 6 PERSONS

U-SHAPE

AISLE CLEARANCE 3'-0" MIN. BUT NOT DESIRABLE. 4'-0" IS ADEQUATE. THE DISTANCE BETWEEN A,B,C, SHOULD AVERAGE 15" TO 20" MAX.

BROKEN-U
AREA: APPROX. 88 SQ. FT. FOR 5 PERSONS TO 96 SQ. FT. FOR 7 PERSONS

BROKEN-U

SINGLE WALL
AREA: APPROX. 93 SQ. FT. FOR 3 PERSONS TO 111 SQ. FT. FOR 6 PERSONS

Figure 8.17. Typical residential kitchen layouts. (Reprinted by permission from *Architectural Graphic Standards,* John Wiley & Sons, New York, 1981.)

Counter top height is ordinarily 36 in. off the floor. This can be changed from 34 to 37 in. for custom planning in the case of tall or short occupants.

Lighting of the work areas is extremely important. A work light should be located over the sink, over the stove, and over any food preparation area. Using only central ceiling fixtures casts a shadow on the counter top that precludes satisfactory vision.

Windows for normal lighting are most often placed at the sink area where a view is provided and the space for wall cabinets is least disrupted. The wall cabinets should be held back from the windows about 6 to 8 in. if room natural lighting is desired.

Ventilation of the kitchen work area is desirable. The usual practice is to include a hood over the cooking top or the range that includes a ventilation fan and lighting for cooking. Choose the fan carefully. Some fans have very loud noise levels that are quite distracting.

The Kitchen Orientation Kitchens oriented between east and south receive the benefit of the early morning sun but are shaded in the afternoon and evening. Kitchens oriented between west and south are dark in the morning hours and tend to receive too much solar energy in the afternoon and evening hours. This can cause them to overheat. Kitchens oriented on the north side of the building tend to be dark and receive little winter sun. You should typically seek an east to south orientation for this room.

The Dining Room

A complete complement of dining room furniture is a table, chairs, china closet, and a side buffet. Less furniture can be used. But for a formal dining room, it is best to plan for this full complement.

Dining room tables typically are rectangular, although they may be designed in all shapes. A table seating four to six people generally ranges

30 in. wide by 60 to 66 in. long. A table seating six to eight people typically ranges from 36 to 42 in. wide and from 78 to 90 in. long.

Dining room tables are quite often capable of being lengthened and shortened through the addition or subtraction of center leafs or drop leafs. This is very handy for making dining rooms multipurpose.

In a three- or four-bedroom home, you should plan to accommodate from six to eight people in the dining area. So planning calls for a table 36 in. wide to 78 in. long or larger.

Dining room side chairs without arms average 20 in. in width and 22 in. in depth. Armchairs average 23 in. by 23 in. Often armchairs will not fit under the table. Typical planning calls for two armchairs and four to six side chairs.

The back of a chair is normally 18 in. from the edge of the table when it is occupied. For serving and getting to and from the table, another 30 to 36 in. behind the chair is required.

A typical sideboard or buffet is 66 to 78 in. long and 18 in. deep. Two inches should be allowed between the sideboard and the wall, giving a 20-in. overall depth. China closets can be corner cabinets, hutch styles over sideboards, or rectangular types of furniture. Hutch styles over sideboards need no additional floor space. Corner china cabinets generally take up about 30 in. along the wall.

Figure 8.18 shows a dining room dimension plan that will accommodate eight people without any compromises. A 36 in. by 78 in. table is used. Eighteen inches is left all around for chair space, except at the corners. Thirty inches is allowed behind the chairs for service, entrance, and egress.

If corner buffets and china closets are used, this room should be a minimum of 11 ft by 14½ ft. If rectangular sideboards and china closets are planned, then the room must be expanded to 12½ ft by 14½ ft or to 11 ft by 16 ft.

Compromises may be made in this planning. A drawleaf table could be placed against one wall, saving 48 in. and deleting one person from the table. The table could be 42 in. wide, which would accommodate two at one end to replace the lost end. The 27-in. service area resulting would not be too cramping. Or the room could be widened by 6 in. Drawleaf tables that collapse against the wall lend themselves well to multipurpose rooms that allow formal dining on special occasions.

If you plan to use a round table, then plan a 3½-ft diameter table for four to five people, a 4½-ft diameter table for five to six people, and a 6-ft diameter table for seven to eight people.

The Living Room

The living room and the family room can be approached together for design purposes. Both are living areas. The family room tends to be less formal and used more by the family, whereas the living room tends to be held for visitors and company. But these are only generalizations. There are dramatic differences from family to family in the design and the use of the living areas.

Planning starts by deciding what functions are to be carried out in each room. Figure 8.10 gave a series of activities that occur in the living area. A series of questions should be asked using this list as a frame of reference.

First, what is the split of activities between the living room and the family room? A typical activity split is shown in Figure 8.19. Nine activities have been listed. The living room will be used to entertain guests, to read, for quiet conversation, and for playing musical instruments. The family

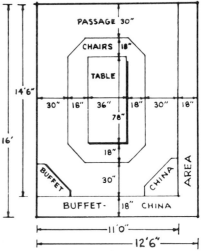

Figure 8.18. Typical dining room plan that will accommodate eight people with no compromises.

room will be used for telephoning, homework, the family's paperwork, and family entertainment.

LIVING ROOM	FAMILY ROOM
Reading	Television watching
Private conversation	Homework
Formal entertaining of guests	Telephoning
Music playing and listening	Paperwork
	Family entertaining

Figure 8.19. Typical split of living activites between the family room and the living room.

Second, what is needed to carry out each activity? Each of these activities requires certain furniture and fixtures. In the living room, reading and conversation require a corner grouping of at least two comfortable armchairs with good lighting, a bookcase, and a magazine rack. The formal entertainment of guests requires additional chairs and perhaps a sofa. These furnishings must be grouped for easy and relaxed conversation. Music playing or listening requires either a musical instrument or a stereo.

At least one desk is needed in the family room. This may or may not act as the telephone center. A table and two to four chairs may be needed for playing family games. A television set and comfortable chairs must be grouped for easy vision and listening.

Third, how much space is needed to contain the furniture and fixtures and to carry out the activities? This must be determined by listing the pieces needed. Figure 8.20 gives a list of typical furniture sizes for each type of furniture and fixture.

FURNITURE PIECE	TYPICAL DIMENSIONS (IN.)		
	WIDTH	DEPTH	HEIGHT
Benches	48-72	23	31
Bookcases	24-48	12	30-72
Cabinets	24-48	15-18	36-84
Chairs			
Arm	23	23	31
Side	20	22	31
Lounge	30	25-40	31
Chests	36-72	18	31
Desks	60	30	29
Lamps		-vary-	
Organs			
Spinet	44-47	25-29	35-38
Console	53	30	43
Theater	58-63	42-46	49
Pianos			
Spinet	58	25	36
Studio	58	25	40
Baby grand	62	58	45
Sofas	48-112	29-37	30
Stereos, console	48-72	16-20	31
Tables			
End/side	21-42	19-28	17-28
Corner	24-32	24-32	28
Coffee	40-60	24	17
Televisions, console	32-48	18	30
TV/stereo combinations	68-72	21	31

Figure 8.20. Typical living room furniture dimensions.

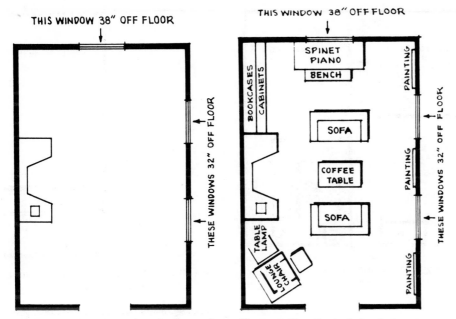

Figure 8.21. Typical scale drawing for placement of furniture.

Figure 8.22. Typical furniture arrangement arrived at by using scaled furniture cutouts.

Fourth, what is the best arrangement for the furniture that the rooms must contain? The arrangement is best determined by making a scale plan of the rooms and placing scaled cutouts of the furniture on the plan. One-quarter-inch scale is usually used.

Figure 8.21 shows a scale drawing of a typical living room taken from the house in Figure 8.4. Note that the height of the windows off the floor is shown. This is an important dimension for planning purposes. Furniture that sticks up into the window is unsightly.

Figure 8.22 shows a typical placement of furniture in this room. A spinet piano is desired. There is only one place in the room that it will fit, under the window that is 38 in. off the floor. So the piano has been centered under this window.

There is no wall space for a long sofa. But there is a fireplace that makes a natural focal point. Two 4-ft sofas, with a coffee table between them, have been grouped in front of the fireplace. This space serves as a walk-through.

An open bookcase with cabinets under it has been placed to the left of the fireplace. A comfortable lounge chair with side table is located to the left of the fireplace.

No furniture is grouped along the front exterior wall, although some could be. For instance, three wall panels exist between the windows. Three large paintings or photographs would make excellent conversation pieces. So would display tables or cases holding family collections.

This arrangement satisfies the furniture and fixture needs outlined for the functions that will be carried out in this living room. Is it the best arrangement? Most likely not. Each family will have ideas of its own. But the arrangement shown is a typical one. And it was arrived at by using a scale drawing and scale furniture cutouts.

If your favorite piece of furniture ruins the room layout, you may have to change your activity schedule. Obviously a grand piano would not fit into this room. As it is, the spinet piano dictates much of the room arrangement.

Planning for the family room proceeds in the same manner.

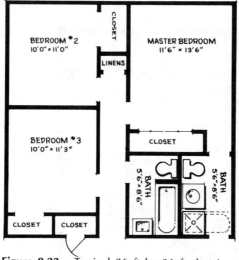

Figure 8.23. Typical 26 ft by 26 ft sleeping module.

Figure 8.24. A one bathroom design that yields a larger master bedroom.

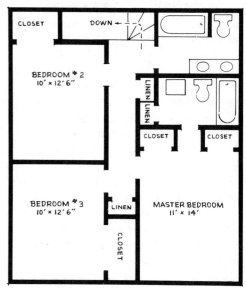

Figure 8.25. Typical 26 ft by 30 ft sleeping module for a two-story house.

Living Module Orientation Obviously the orientation of the living module should be such as to conform to the needs of the occupants. Here are some of the general considerations:

- Kitchen orientation should be considered first.
- Family rooms need good winter sun but tend to overheat in the afternoon and evening hours.
- Living rooms are used most in the evening hours, particularly if the structure contains a family room. Plan the orientation for maximum comfort after 3 P.M.
- Do not neglect visual outdoor communications in the orientation of the living module. A lake or a waterfall hidden from view does not present a pleasing orientation.

Solar utilization is only one of many factors in determining the proper orientation of the living module. If you cannot achieve the proper compromise of benefits that you desire with your present set of building plans, most likely you should change the plan now rather than live with the results over the next 10 to 20 years.

The Sleeping Module

The sleeping module contains the bedrooms, the bathrooms, the clothes closets, and the linen storage area. Figure 8.23 shows a typical 26 ft by 26 ft sleeping module.

A center hallway, leading from the living module, opens into three bedrooms and a bath. A second bath is located so that it can be entered from the master bedroom, from the kitchen-dining area, or from both. When only the bedroom entry is used, a bathtub can replace the shower if desired.

The two-bathroom arrangement compromises the layout of the master bedroom. It shortens the bedroom by 2 ft and it eliminates 3 ft of closet. Figure 8.24 shows a one bathroom layout that yields a better master bedroom design.

If the hall closet were eliminated, the closets for the second and third bedrooms could be placed on the common interior wall. The closet at the end of the hall could be used for the master bedroom. Three layouts are possible that would fit well into this size sleeping module. The same layouts will work for split-level designs with only minor modifications.

Both the master bedroom and bedroom 3 will accept twin beds. Bedroom 2 will not. Bedrooms 2 and 3 both have 5-ft closets, which are ample. The master bedroom closet is 8½ ft, which is minimal. There is no linen storage in either bathroom.

Figure 8.25 shows a 26 ft by 30 ft sleeping module for a two-story house. The module is entered from a set of stairs originating in the entry hall of the living module. A full bath is located at the head of the stairs. A central hall, jogged back from the landing, leads to the three bedrooms. There is ample room for bed and bath linens. This is important in a two-story house.

The master bedroom again suffers somewhat from the inclusion of a second bath. Three feet of closet space are lost. Five feet of bedroom length are lost. A single bath arrangement would yield 11 ft of closet and a 19½-ft long bedroom. Twin beds may be placed in bedroom 2 but not in bedroom 3. Both bedrooms have ample closet space.

Planning the Sleeping Module

A two-bedroom home, as previously mentioned, will house from two to four occupants. A three-bedroom home will house from three to six occupants. And a four-bedroom home will house from four to eight occupants.

The basic furniture required in a bedroom is a bed, a dresser, and 2 ft of hanging closet space for each occupant. However, life-styles vary. Children of the same sex, and close in age, often sleep together. Husband and wife often share the same bed. Adults, and some teenagers, need more closet space. A desk is often indicated for study purposes.

The Beds

There are six standard sizes of bed mattresses. They range from a 76 in. wide by 84 in. long king-sized mattress to a 33 in. wide by 75 in. long

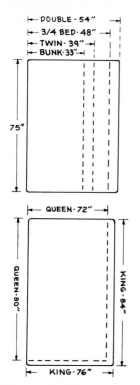

Figure 8.26. Standard bed mattress sizes.

bunk-bed mattress. Figure 8.26 shows these six sizes of standard mattresses.

Figure 8.27 shows a pair of twin beds separated by an 18-in. nightstand. Twelve inches has been allowed on either side of the beds so that they can be made-up easily. The beds have been pulled out 5 in. from the wall. Such an arrangement will require a space that is at least 10 ft in width and 6 ft 8 in. long.

A king-sized bed takes up a space 9 ft 8 in. wide by 7 ft 5 in. long. A queen-sized bed takes up a space 9 ft 4 in. wide by 7 ft 1 in. long. The details are shown in Figure 8.28.

Figure 8.29 shows the minimum space required by a double bed. This space is 7 ft 6 in. wide by 6 ft 8 in. long when 18 in. is allowed on either side of the bed and the bed is pulled out 5 in. from the wall.

The beds are the largest pieces of furniture required in a bedroom, so you can use these dimensions to determine what types of beds each bedroom will comfortably hold.

The Dressers

The average bedroom dresser is 18 to 20 in. in depth, 34 to 60 in. high, and from 32 to 98 in. in width. A space of 3 ft is needed in front of the dresser in which to stand and open the drawers. A single occupant needs at least four drawers that are 30 in. wide to accommodate his or her clothing. Figure 8.30 illustrates the space requirements.

The Critical Bedroom Size

An analysis of the space requirements just discussed indicates strongly that there is a critical minimum bedroom size. When a three-quarter bed is used, the critical minimum dimensions are about 9 ft by 11½ ft as shown in Figure 8.31. When a double bed is used, the critical minimum dimensions are typically about 9½ ft by 11½ ft. With twin beds and double occupancy, the critical minimum dimensions increase to about 13 ft by 11½ ft. These dimensions allow for desk room and two dressers.

How the room is laid out is important. If in Figure 8.31 the door were moved to the corner of the room at the upper left of the drawing, dresser space would be lost.

It is advisable to make scaled cutout furniture that conforms to the list of activities that are to be carried out in the bedroom. This will allow you to work out a satisfactory room arrangement on a scale drawing of the room.

The Master Bedroom

Bedrooms are not only for sleeping. Many other activities need to be planned for. The master bedroom is a good example. Here consideration needs to be given to grooming, television, sexual habits and needs, and similar activities. Each activity must be planned for. Space and furniture must be allotted to carry out the occupant's needs and desires comfortably.

Chests and Storage

The clothes closet should be at least 24 in. in depth when finished. In hanging closets, the clothes rod should be 12 in. from the rear wall and about 60 in. off the floor. A 12-to-14-in. wide shelf should be mounted at about 64 to 66 in. off the floor.

Five to six coats or suits can be hung on 1 ft of closet rod. So can 12 to 14 shirts or blouses. Shoes and slippers need a 12-in. wide shelf. One pair

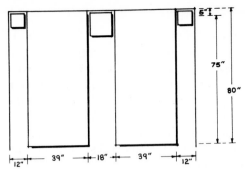

Figure 8.27. The minimum space needed for twin beds is 10 ft by 6 ft 8 in.

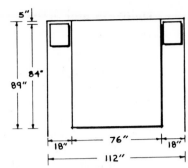

Figure 8.28. The minimum space needed for a king-sized bed is 9 ft 8 in by 7 ft 5 in. A queen-sized bed could be placed in a space 9 ft 4 in. by 7 ft 1 in.

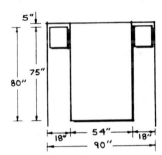

Figure 8.29. The minimum space needed for a double bed is 7 ft 6 in. by 6 ft 8 in. A three-quarter bed could be placed in a space 7 ft by 6 ft 8 in.

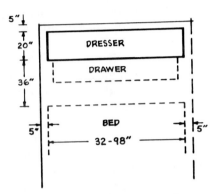

Figure 8.30. A dresser requires a space about 5 ft in depth and a minimum of 3 ft in length per occupant for comfortable use.

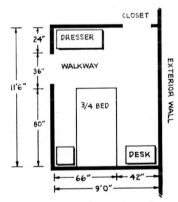

Figure 8.31. Critical dimensions for a single occupant bedroom using a three-quarter bed.

of shoes takes up about 9 in. in width. Special arrangements should be made for evening gowns. A clothes rod about 72 in. off the floor is recommended.

Linen closets for sheets and towels range from 12 to 18 in. in depth. The shelving is normally placed from 10 to 14 in. apart. Blanket closets should range from 18 to 24 in. in depth.

Many built-in units can be purchased or created. *Architectural Graphic Standards* should be consulted for details.

Hallways and Stairs

The hallways in the sleeping module should range from 34 to 42 in. in width. The longer the hall, the wider it should be. If paintings, pictures, or small furniture are planned for hallway placement, the hall should be widened to about 48 in. It is unwise to skimp on hallway width to gain bedroom space. Use as wide a hall as is practical and that still adheres to the critical minimum bedroom dimensions.

Staircases should be 36 to 42 in. wide. The stair risers should not be more than 9½ in. in height. It is wise to place a smoke alarm in all halls and stairwells. Good lighting is also important.

The Transportation Module

The transportation module typically contains the vehicle storage area, the outdoor equipment storage area, and room to work on the transportation equipment.

Generally not enough time and effort are spent in planning the transportation module. Instead, a minimum one or two car garage is tacked on to the remainder of the house. This type of planning results in an unsatisfactory transportation module.

America's cars are becoming smaller. As a result, vehicle storage area needs are decreasing. The modules in this book were laid out using the cars of the mid-1970s. A reduction of 6 in. in width and 1 ft in length may be safely made for compact vehicles manufactured after 1980.

The transportation modules are presented as fully enclosed building structures. They may easily be converted to carports or partial-walled structures since the space requirements will typically be the same.

Planning the Transportation Module

The first decision in planning the transportation module is to decide whether it will house one or two cars. Figure 8.32 shows the minimum dimensions needed for a single car garage. The garage must be at least 15 ft by 22 ft.

A two-car garage can have one large single door or two smaller doors. A garage with two doors needs to be 2 ft wider than a garage with a single door. The single door two-car garage needs to be at least 22 ft wide by 22 ft deep whereas the double door, two-car garage needs to be 24 ft wide by 22 ft deep. These two garages are illustrated in Figures 8.33 and 8.34.

Note that all the minimum garages use an 8 ft wide or a 16 ft wide door. The 8-ft door is a minimum size for the pre-1980 car. A 9-ft door is more desirable.

These minimum garages are just that—minimum garages. A true transportation module must be larger. The transportation module is approached in Figure 8.35. This module was designed for the home mechanic. The module has been widened to 28 ft so that the mechanic can work around the car. The module has been lengthened to 30 ft so that a workbench and a work space can be included. The doors have been widened to 9 ft so that the cars can be maneuvered to different positions within the module.

Another approach to a transportation module is shown in Figure 8.36. The module was widened to 32 ft to allow for a home-craft shop. A curtain separates the cars from the shop to prevent covering the cars with

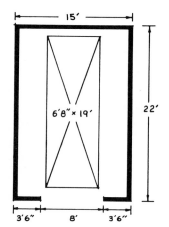

Figure 8.32. Minimum dimensions for a single car garage.

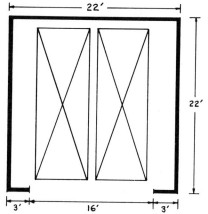

Figure 8.33. Minimum dimensions for a single-door two car garage.

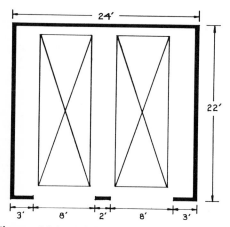

Figure 8.34. Minimum dimensions for a double-door two car garage.

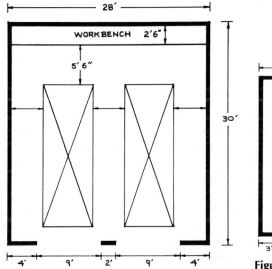

Figure 8.35. A garage for the mechanic.

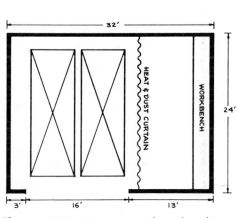

Figure 8.36. A garage for the home craftsperson.

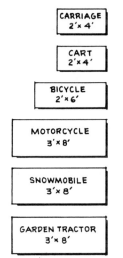

Figure 8.37. Some transportation vehicle storage space requirements.

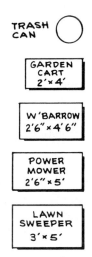

Figure 8.38. Some garden equipment storage space needs.

sawdust and to allow for shop heating in the winter months. A single 16-ft door was used to crowd the automobile storage space over to one side. The building was lengthened by 2 ft so that the engine compartment, be it front or rear, could be worked on.

Neither of these two designs satisfies the need for storage space. Transportation module storage space often needs to be relatively large. The family may own other transportation vehicles such as motorcycles, bicycles, or snowmobiles. Figure 8.37 shows the storage space required for those vehicles.

Most families have garden equipment that needs to be stored such as wheelbarrows, lawn mowers, and trash cans. Figure 8.38 shows typical storage area requirements for these items. A 22 ft deep by 30 ft wide transportation module will easily accommodate a large amount of storage. Figure 8.39 shows such a module. A 30 ft by 30 ft transportation module, such as shown in Figure 8.40, will easily provide a most satisfactory com-

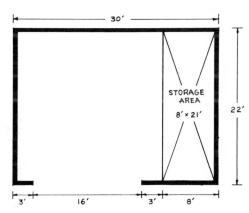

Figure 8.39. Two car garage with good storage area.

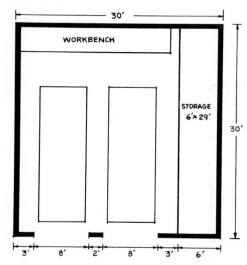

Figure 8.40. Typical complete transportation module with work space and good storage.

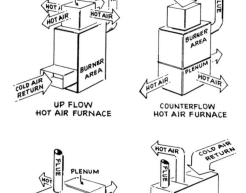

Figure 8.41. Typical styles of hot air furnaces.

plete module for just about any family. If the family owns compact cars, a 28 ft deep by 29 ft wide module will work just as well.

You may have problems in obtaining the space that you desire in your transportation module if your home is designed as a split-level or with the module located in the basement. But by careful advance planning, you can make the best use of your available space.

Safety Considerations Provide good lighting for the desired activities. Whenever possible, include windows for good natural lighting. Beef up the roof rafters and ceiling joists if overhead hoisting equipment is to be used. Slope the floors toward the doors to provide good drainage and prevent the build-up of gas fumes. If automobiles are to be run in the module, provide an exhaust hose and a door or wall cutout to exhaust any carbon monoxide fumes. Mount a large dry powder fire extinguisher near the door. Keep the floor at least 6 in. below the floor of the home. Do not store fuel oil or gasoline in the module. Do not locate furnaces or heaters with open pilot flames in the module. Provide a fire wall between the transportation module and the house. Build the floor of noncombustible materials.

Orientation Considerations Transportation modules belong as buffer zones between the winter cold and the house in northerly locations. In southerly climates they can be located as buffer zones to prevent the summer sun from overheating the house. Locate the transportation module where it will take some of the burdens imposed by climate away from the rest of the home.

The Mechanical Module

The mechanical module contains all the equipment required to power, heat, and cool the building. This includes the furnace, the hot water heater, the air conditioner, the electrical center, the sanitary center, the drainage pumps, and the fuel supply.

It is also common practice to use the mechanical module for a laundry center, a hobby workshop center, a children's play area, and for storage purposes.

Planning the Mechanical Module

Planning the mechanical module begins with planning the heating equipment. Most structures generally use a central furnace in the mechanical room and a hot air or hot water distribution system that blows or pumps the heated air or water to the different rooms.

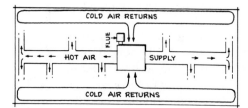

Figure 8.42. Typical center-wall forced hot air delivery system.

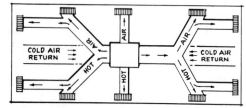

Figure 8.43. Typical perimeter-wall forced hot air delivery system.

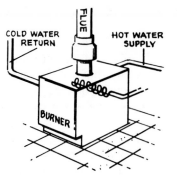

Figure 8.44. Typical hydronic boiler with a tankless heater coil.

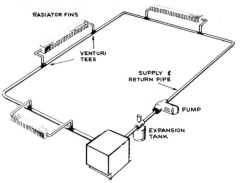

Figure 8.45. A one-pipe hydronic system.

The Forced Hot Air Heating System

The forced hot air system typically consists of a furnace, a distribution duct system, a fan, a fuel supply, and a chimney or stack for flue gases.

There are four major types of hot air furnaces: the up-flow furnace, the counterflow furnace, the horizontal flow furnace, and the lowboy furnace. Figure 8.41 shows how the air flows through each of these types.

The distribution of the hot air usually takes place from a chamber known as the *hot air plenum*. The plenum is a sheet-metal chamber located on the furnace. Distribution ducts are led to each room from the plenum.

Two types of distribution systems are generally seen: the center-wall distribution system and the perimeter-wall distribution system. Figure 8.42 shows a typical center-wall distribution system. The hot air is blown through a distribution trunk located along the center wall of the building. Smaller ducts lead to interior outlets within each room. The cold air is collected along the exterior walls of the structure and is returned to the furnace for reheating.

The advantage of the center-wall distribution system is that a minimum of hot air ductwork, which is more expensive than cold air ductwork, is needed. This holds down the expense of installation. But the system does not supply the hot air to the outside walls where the room is the coldest.

Figure 8.43 shows a perimeter-wall forced hot air system. Here the ductwork supplies the hot air to the outside walls of the structure. The cold air is returned along the center wall. A perimeter system gives more even temperatures throughout the building, but it is more expensive to install.

The Forced Hot Water Heating System

The forced hot water heating system typically consists of a hydronic boiler, a water distribution system, radiators, a circulator pump, an expansion tank, a fuel supply, and a chimney or stack for flue gases. A copper coil, known as a *tankless heater coil*, may be included to provide hot water for the home. Figure 8.44 shows a typical hydronic boiler with a tankless heater coil.

There are three major ways to pipe a hydronic distribution system. Figure 8.45 shows a one-pipe system. This is the simplest system of piping. Water at about 160 to 180°F is pumped around the loop. Special fittings, known as *venturi tees*, draw off hot water. The water circulates through the radiator and returns cooled to the main loop. In a one-pipe system, the

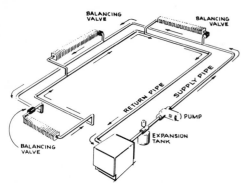

Figure 8.46. Two-pipe hydronic system with direct return. Balancing valves must be used on each radiator.

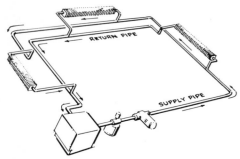

Figure 8.47. Two-pipe hydronic system with reverse return. No balancing valves are needed.

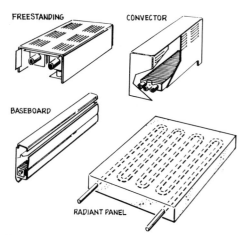

Figure 8.48. Some common types of hydronic radiators.

radiator that is farthest from the boiler water feed operates at the coldest temperature.

Figure 8.46 shows a two-pipe hydronic system with direct return. Here the radiators are all fed from a main supply pipe. All the radiators return the cooled water to a separate return pipe, so the hot supply water is the same temperature in each radiator. But the length of pipe between the boiler and each radiator varies. The water flows faster in the radiators with the least amount of piping. So those radiators get hotter. Balancing valves are usually used to equalize the flow of water.

In Figure 8.47, a two-pipe hydronic system with reverse flow has been used. In this system, the amount of pipe between the boiler and the radiators is the same for each radiator. So the flow equalizes. Balancing valves are not needed.

Each distribution system has its application merits. All three are used. In larger systems, two or more circulating loops are often used. This allows different parts of the structure to be heated to different temperatures.

Hydronic Radiators In forced-circulation hot air systems, the air in the house is moved to the furnace, heated, and returned to the rooms. So all the air in the house is moved to the furnace for heating.

In forced-circulation hot water systems, hot water from the boiler is supplied to each room where it heats up a radiator. This radiator then heats up the air in the room by radiation and convection. The air does not have to leave the room to be warmed. This is an important difference between hot water and hot air heating.

There are many different types of radiators. The most common type is baseboard radiation. Other common types are convector cabinets, radiant floors, ceiling panels, wall panels, and freestanding convection units. Some common types of radiators are shown in Figure 8.48.

Heating System Space Requirements

In forced-circulation hot air furnaces, the style of furnace that you choose will have a decided effect on the amount of space needed. Lowboy units and horizontal units will require more floor area than up-flow or counter-flow units.

For up to 84,000 Btu/hr output, plan on 4.2 to 6.3 sq ft of floor area. From 84 to 120,000 Btu/hr, plan on 6.6 to 9.9 sq ft. For units producing from 120 to 200,000 Btu/hr, plan on 13.1 to 19.7 sq ft of floor area.

Room must also be left for combustion air to reach the furnace because large quantities of air are needed to burn the fuel. You should leave typically from 18 to 24 in. around the furnace free of any combustible materials.

Supply ductwork for the hot air furnace can run along the basement ceiling, can be installed in crawl spaces, and can be designed into a floor slab. All the ductwork that passes through an unheated area should be well insulated. Cold air return ductwork can use the spaces between floor or ceiling joists as the actual duct. This lowers the cost of installation.

Hydronic boilers typically take up less room than do hot air furnaces. Most boilers used in residences will fit into an area 2 ft by 3 ft. The same precautions on the storage of combustibles and the availability of combustion air must be taken.

Some Recent Advances A number of new devices have recently been made available that can help increase your fuel efficiency. You should consider a clock-driven thermostat that automatically regulates the temperature in your home at different levels according to your need for heat.

In gas furnaces, electric ignition devices are available to replace pilot flames. Thermostatically controlled flue dampers can be used to lower the fuel needs. And you can consider whether using outside air for combustion will lower your air infiltration.

If your home is heated with oil, you should look into a new furnace that recirculates the unburned gases back through the combustion chamber. Some excellent increases in efficiency have been reported for these pieces of equipment.

Other Heating Systems

There are many other types of heating systems, but their use is less widespread than forced hot air or hot water central heating systems, except perhaps for the use of electric resistance heating.

Electricity has been used to heat many homes over the past 20 years. The favorite method of using electricity has been the use of electrical resistance baseboard heaters. Electric baseboard heating is clean, can be controlled by individual room thermostats, requires no central furnace, and is inexpensive to install. Today, however, the high cost of buying electric power makes the use of baseboard resistance heating uneconomical.

Other common forms of electrical heating include unit resistance heaters, radiant heating panels and cable, and electrically fired boilers. All these units have a high fuel cost and tend to be uneconomical in residential applications.

The Heat Pump One electrical powered unit, the heat pump, shows good economy. It has much to recommend it when conditions are right.

A heat pump operates on the same principle as an air conditioner. Electric power is used to drive a gas compressor. The compressor cycle is shown in Figure 8.49. A suitable gas, such as Freon, is placed in a sealed system that contains a compressor, an indoor heat exchanger, an expansion valve, and an outdoor heat exchanger.

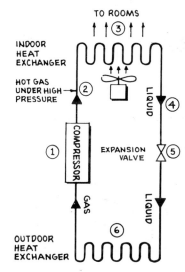

Figure 8.49. An electrically driven heat pump.

When the compressor is started up, the gas is compressed under high pressure: ① This compression heats up the gas within the building area. ② The hot gas passes through a heat exchanger where it gives up heat to the room. ③ The loss of heat causes the gas to condense to a liquid. ④ This liquid passes through a constricted valve, known as an expansion valve. ⑤ The expansion valve allows the Freon to escape slowly into an outdoor heat exchanger. ⑥ The Freon vaporizes into a gas in the outdoor heat exchanger. In order to change from liquid to gas, it must draw in heat from the outside air, or a water source, surrounding the heat exchanger. So it extracts the heat from the air or liquid surrounding the exchanger. The gas goes back to the compressor and the cycle is repeated.

The system extracts heat from the outside air or a water source and pumps it into the house where it can be used to heat the rooms. This is a highly efficient process because the only power used is the electrical power used to run the compressor. The actual heat energy comes from the outside air or water source.

Heat pumps will usually work efficiently down to outside air temperatures of about 40 to 45°F. They typically produce 2½ Btu of energy for each Btu of power required to run the compressor. This makes the electricity costs competitive with natural gas and fuel oil in many areas of the country.

In the northern half of the United States, the air temperatures are too cold to run air-to-air heat pumps in the winter months. So water-to-air heat pumps must be used. A source of water that is above 45°F in temperature must be available.

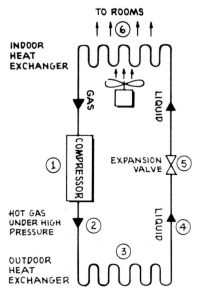

Figure 8.50. An air conditioner works the same as a heat pump, but the cycle is reversed.

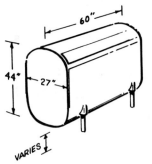

Figure 8.51. Typical 275-gal fuel oil storage tank.

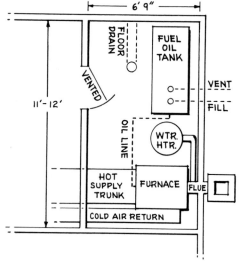

Figure 8.52. Typical furnace room placed in the end of a mechanical module.

An air conditioner works on the same principle as a heat pump, but the cycle is reversed so that heat is extracted from the building air and pumped outdoors. This is shown in Figure 8.50. Most modern heat pumps are built so that they can be used either as heat pumps or air conditioners by reversing the flow of the refrigerant through internal valves.

Solid Fuel Furnaces and Stoves Prior to 1940, solid fuels were in general use across the United States to heat homes. Both coal and wood were used extensively. Today, with the high cost of fuel oil and natural gas, the use of solid fuels is coming back.

For automatic operation, wood and coal are best used in combination with oil or gas. A number of companies have introduced combination forced-circulation hot air furnaces that use two separate combustion chambers: one for the solid fuel and one for the gas or fuel oil. These units occupy about twice the space as a regular up-flow hot air furnace.

Fuel Storage Requirements

Natural gas and electricity need no storage space. Fuel oil needs a storage tank. This tank can be placed either indoors or outdoors. Generally a 275 to 500 gal tank is used. Figure 8.51 shows the space requirements for a 275-gal indoor fuel oil storage tank.

Fuel oil tanks located in the mechanical module must be carefully installed to be safe. The tank must be vented to the outdoors. The delivery system to the furnace must have a spring-loaded, heat-activated shut-off valve that closes in the case of a fire in the structure. A sump should be provided in case the tank springs a leak. The tank fill pipe should be fitted with an audible alarm that prevents overfilling. Liquified petroleum gas (LPG) should always be stored outdoors. It must not be stored in the mechanical module.

Handling Flue Gases

All furnaces, except those run by electricity, require a stack or chimney to exhaust the flue gases generated by the combustion process from the building. Most furnaces used in residences require a minimum flue of 8 in. by 8 in. or an 8 to 10 in. round flue. The stack must extend from the combustion chamber of the furnace to a point 1 to 2 ft over the ridge of the roof in order to draw the gases off properly.

The Furnace Room

The space required for a furnace room will vary depending on the equipment chosen to heat the home. Figure 8.52 shows a typical furnace room that will accommodate an oil-fired, medium-sized circulating hot air furnace. Note that the water heater, which in this case is gas-fired, has been placed next to the furnace so that it may be vented into the stack. A separate opening into the stack is typically required.

This furnace room has been designed for the end of the building where it is close to the chimney. The furnace is placed along the center girder of the house so that the hot air supply trunk can be run alongside the girder through the center of the house. The cold air return runs alongside the hot air supply trunk. The fuel oil tank is placed in the corner of the building with an outside vent and fill pipe.

In this location, the furnace room can be easily enclosed by placing a wall under the center girder and a wall across the mechanical module.

One wall must be vented to allow combustion air to reach the furnace. It is important to leave enough room in front of and around the equipment to inspect and service it. Fire retardant construction is recommended. A floor drain is included to keep the area dry and to handle any leaks from the equipment.

Solar Heating Requirements

When active solar systems are incorporated into the residence, the space requirements increase dramatically. Active solar systems require a mechanical center and a heat storage facility. The storage facility must be large if heat is to be stored for 2 or 3 days of cloudy weather. Solar system requirements will be covered in detail in Decisions 9 through 11.

The Water Supply

Water can be supplied to the home from a municipal water system or from a private water system. When a municipal water system is used, the equipment required in the home will consist of a supply pipe, a shutoff valve, and a meter. A water softener may be desired if the water is hard.

If a private water supply is used, a pump and storage tank must be added to the mechanical module or placed in an outside location. Equipment will vary depending on the well capacity, the type of pump, and the need for storage.

A typical installation might be a deep well using a jet pump, 120 gal of storage, and a water softener. Such a well should be capable of producing not less than 50 gal of water per occupant per day at a rate of not less than 5 gal/min.

The well should be located at least 50 ft from any septic tank and at least 100 ft from any sewage disposal field. It should be cased with steel pipe to prevent any surface water or sewage contamination. The water should be periodically tested for any pathogenic bacteria or disease-producing organisms. Your local or state health department most likely provides these testing services.

Figure 8.53 shows a typical well installation. The wellhead is located in a concrete sump. It is insulated against freezing or slightly heated in the winter. Often a single 100-watt bulb will give off enough heat to prevent freezing. The sump extends well above the grade to prevent surface water contamination. The well pipe is located below the frostline and leads to the pump in the mechanical module.

The water is stored in an air-cushion tank that provides water pressure to move the water around the house. A water softener has been installed ahead of the tank and before the water service to the house. Such an installation would occupy a space of about 3 ft wide by 6 to 7 ft long in the mechanical module.

The Hot Water Heater

Hot water heated to about 120 to 140°F is required in most homes. A supply of about 20 gal per day per person plus 20 gal for an automatic washer and 15 gal for an automatic dishwasher is considered typical.

Water heaters vary from 30 gal capacity to 120 gal capacity in most homes. The larger heaters are generally electrically powered heaters that use off-peak electricity to heat the water at night when power is the cheapest. A 40 to 62 gal heater is generally used when a gas-fired unit is chosen. Such a unit generally has a fast recovery rate of about 30 to

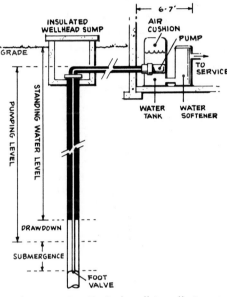

Figure 8.53. Typical well installation.

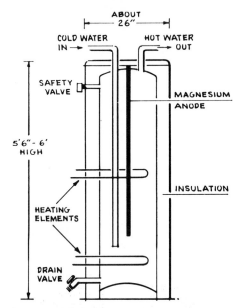

Figure 8.54. Typical 120-gal electric hot water heater.

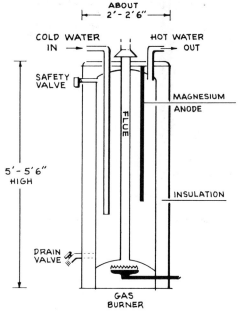

Figure 8.55. Typical 62-gal gas-fired hot water heater.

$$\begin{array}{r} 200 \ \text{A} \\ \times \ 220 \ \text{V} \\ \hline = 44{,}000 \ \text{W} \end{array}$$

40,000 Btu/hr when the hot water is exhausted. Figures 8.54 and 8.55 show typical hot water heaters. They range from 5 to 6 ft high and from 2 ft to 2½ ft in diameter.

Cold water is supplied to the bottom of the tank, and hot water is drawn from the top of the tank. When no water is being drawn, the hot water tends to concentrate in the top of the tank, whereas the cold water stays in the bottom. In the electrically heated tank, the element in the center of the tank is used during peak hours when electricity is expensive. During nonpeak hours, the lower element, or both elements together, is used to heat the tank.

Most hot water tanks are steel. The inside is typically coated with heat-glazed ceramic frits. This is called a *glass-lined tank*. The lining slows the galvanic corrosion of the tank that occurs because of the copper water lines. A magnesium anode is generally also placed in the tank to slow corrosion. Magnesium is a more anodic, or active, metal than either iron or copper. So the anode will corrode away first.

Some tanks are stone-lined. These tanks generally have a much longer life than a glass-lined tank. But they are more costly.

When a hydronic boiler is used to heat the house, a tankless coil can be inserted into the boiler water to replace a separate water heater. Cold water is drawn into a copper water pipe coiled in the boiler water. The water in the coil is heated by the boiler water and sent to the faucet in the house that is demanding hot water. Such tankless coils typically provide from 3 to 4 gal of hot water per minute, which is ample for most residential needs. But the boiler must be kept hot at all times for the tankless heater to work. This is expensive in the summertime. It is also common to place a storage tank in series with the tankless heater. A circulator pump circulates water from the tank to the coil and thus provides greater storage capacity. Figure 8.56 shows such a set-up.

The Electrical Center

Most residences are wired with a 220 V (volt), three wire, single-phase electrical system. Two of the wires are live, wire Ⓐ and wire Ⓒ in Figure 8.57. An electrical potential of 220 V exists between them. The third wire, wire Ⓑ in Figure 8.57, is grounded at the utility pole. An electrical potential of 110 V exists between wire Ⓐ and wire Ⓑ and between wire Ⓒ and wire Ⓑ.

Typically, the three wires are fed into an insulated head mounted on the top of a heavy metal conduit attached to the house. The wires are fed through the conduit to an electrical meter and then passed to a fused main switch on the electrical service board. Wire Ⓑ is again grounded either at the meter to a long copper rod driven into the ground or to a strap mounted on the cold water service pipe where it enters the house. Every outlet, switch box, and appliance in the house is also grounded back to the main switchboard through the home's internal wiring system.

The service board shown in Figure 8.57 is designed to handle 200 A (amperes) of electrical current. *Amperes* refers to the amount of electrical current that will flow in the circuit between either wire Ⓐ or Ⓒ and wire Ⓑ or between wires Ⓐ and Ⓒ.

In electrical parlance, the electrical potential (volts—V) times the electrical current (amperes—A) equals the power (watts—W). The residence served by the 200 A, 220 V electrical service shown in Figure 8.57 can handle 44,000 W of power.

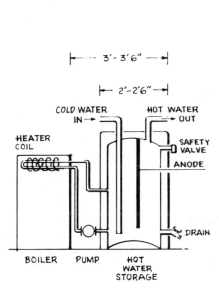

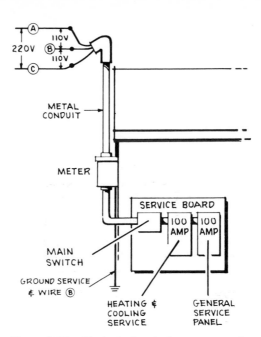

Figure 8.56. Tankless heater coil with a hot water storage tank.

Figure 8.57. Typical electrical entrance and service center.

The electrical service board is generally divided into two sections: the heating and cooling apparatus service and the general electrical apparatus service. The heating and cooling service is typically only needed when the house contains electrical heating or central air conditioning. A 150 A general service will handle almost any home's requirements when it is heated with fossil fuels.

The electrical service panel shown is a maximum size. Without the heating and cooling service, it could be reduced in width by 18 in. If the main switch were incorporated into the general service panel, the width could be reduced to about 2 ft.

It is best, however, not to skimp in electrical service board size. Additional power centers may need to be added at a later date. Wires must be fed from the box to each individual circuit in the house. These wires must all be securely fastened to the service board for safety. Figure 8.58 shows how a completed 100-A service board might look.

A ¾-in. plywood panel makes an excellent electrical service board. It must be securely mounted to the wall or hung from the floor joists. For convenience, it is best mounted with its center about 66 in. off the floor. The panel can be concealed in the wall or it may be surface mounted. There can be heat build-up in a service board, so in concealed installations, allowance for heat dissipation should be made.

The Laundry Center

The laundry center can be located in the sleeping module, the living module, or the mechanical module. It is quite often located in the mechanical module.

An automatic washer or dryer takes up a maximum space of about 30 in. deep and 27 in. wide, as shown in Figure 8.59. The tops of the units are generally about 36½ in. off the floor. There usually is a backsplash containing a control panel that projects up about 6 to 8 in. over the top. This gives the unit a total height of about 42½ to 44½ in.

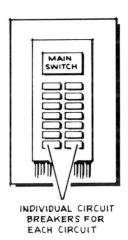

Figure 8.58. Typical completed 150 A electrical service board.

Figure 8.59. Washer and dryer dimensions.

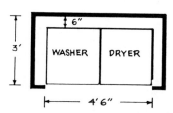

Figure 8.60. A typical washer and dryer closet is 3 ft deep with a 4 ft 6 in. opening in the front.

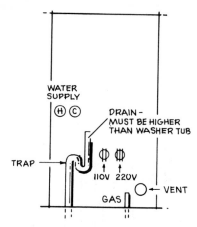

Figure 8.61. The washer and dryer area needs a water supply, a trapped drain, a dryer vent, a 100 V electrical outlet, and either a gas supply or 220 V to provide heat to the dryer.

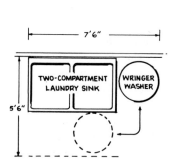

Figure 8.62. Typical space requirement for a wringer washer with set tubs.

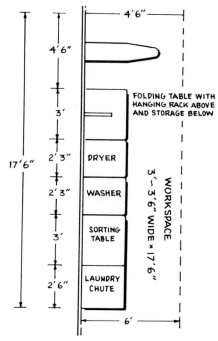

Figure 8.63. Typical complete residential laundry layout.

Figure 8.60 shows a typical closet for a washer and dryer such as would be found in a sleeping or living module. An automatic washer and dryer placed in such a closet will require an opening of about 4½ ft for access. The closet needs to be 3 ft deep so that it can accommodate the services required to power the units.

Figure 8.61 shows the services required for an automatic washer and dryer. Hot and cold water taps are needed for the washer. A 2- to 2½-in. trapped drain that extends to the top of the washer's tub must be installed. And a grounded 110 V electrical outlet is needed.

A 4-in. vent to the outdoors must be supplied for the dryer. If the dryer uses electrical power, it must have a 220 V service. If the dryer is gas-powered, it must have a gas service outlet and a 110 V service plug to power the motor.

These services should typically be placed on the rear wall behind the units. The faucets should be about 48 in. off the floor. The electrical plugs can be placed behind the unit where it is convenient. The washer drain should be about 36 to 38 in. off the floor.

When a wringer washer is used, it is generally used in combination with a set of laundry sinks. A double compartmented sink (set tubs) usually is desired. This combination together with workspace takes up a floor area of about 7 ft 6 in. wide by 5 ft 6 in. deep. Figure 8.62 shows the typical space requirement for a wringer washer with set tubs.

The Complete Laundry Center

A complete laundry center is shown in Figure 8.63. It contains a laundry chute, a clothes-sorting table, a washer, a dryer, a clothes-folding table, a rack for hanging garments, storage for folded clothes, and an ironing board. Such a laundry center takes up a space about 17 ft 6 in. wide and 6 ft deep. If the person who will do the ironing is left-handed, the ironing board should be placed on the left end of the center rather than on the right end.

Making a Decision

In this chapter you studied the requirements for laying out the interior of your home. Then you studied the four basic modules within a residence and the requirements for each module. You learned how the four modules can be fitted together to form many different home designs. You saw how the modular concept can be used to orient the interior for good thermal performance on most building lots.

You should now be able to make the correct decisions on how to design the interior of your home.

DECISION
9

Collect the Available Solar Energy Efficiently

There are two ways to bring solar energy into your home. You may cut light-transmitting openings, such as windows, into the walls and roof so that the sun's energy can enter directly. Or you may place solar collection devices on the outside of the walls and the roof that convert the sun's energy into thermal energy that you can then blow or pump indoors.

There are advantages and disadvantages to each method. Light-transmitting openings will transmit 70 to 80% of the sun's energy. But light-transmitting openings have very low insulating values. Much of the collected energy will pass back outdoors during non-sunlight hours.

Solar collection devices are less efficient. They typically transmit only 30 to 50% of the sun's energy. But solar collection devices can be mounted on walls and roofs that have very high insulating values. And the collected energy can be kept within the structure.

In new construction, light-transmitting openings tend to be less expensive to install. But in renovating buildings, solar collection devices tend to be less expensive to install because they can be added to the building without extensive remodeling.

In this chapter you will study the various ways to collect the available solar energy efficiently.

You will study:

- *Fenestration:* The arrangement, proportioning, and design of light-transmitting openings such as doors, windows, skylights, and clerestories.
- *Solar Collectors:* Devices that collect the sun's radiant energy and convert it to thermal energy.
- *Solar Shades:* Devices that prevent the sun from entering the building during the summer hours.
- *Solar Reflectors:* Devices that reflect the solar energy striking the ground to the collectors where it can be utilized.

Once you have learned the principles of how these devices work, then you will study how to blend them together for efficient solar energy collection and utilization.

Finally, you will study how to construct typical devices.

Solar Energy for Heating Buildings

People are most comfortable when the temperature of the air surrounding them ranges from 65 to 75°F. But in most temperate climates, the temperature of the air ranges from well below zero to well above 90°F at various times throughout the year. This wide temperature range creates the need for heating and cooling the buildings that people occupy so that they are comfortable year round.

In Decision 3, you learned how to calculate the amount of solar energy striking the building's surfaces. In one example, you saw that a 25 ft by 50 ft building located in Lincoln, Nebraska, received about 279 MMBtu of solar energy during the heating season.

A building of that size in that geographic location would typically have a need for about 100 to 150 MMBtu of energy to heat it. So certainly enough solar energy is available at the building to fill much of the heating requirements. It is only necessary to collect and store the energy efficiently.

In Decision 4 you learned how to calculate the heat losses in a building. You learned that windows and doors had very little insulating value and high heat losses. You also learned that walls, ceilings, and floors could be constructed to have low heat losses and to provide a good thermal envelope.

In Decision 5 you learned how to construct an energy-efficient home with this good thermal envelope. Chances are that you also learned that the thermal envelope of your present home could be improved at a relatively low cost.

You must keep the principles that you learned in these three chapters firmly in mind as you study how to collect solar energy efficiently. You can only collect the energy that is available. You can only use what your building demands. And you must not destroy the thermal envelope of the building in order to utilize the radiant heat of the sun.

The Comfort Zone

A building that varies in temperature from 55 to 85°F provides adequate shelter, but it is not very comfortable. Most people would not be happy living in such a building. A building that varies in temperature from 60 to 80°F has a higher degree of comfort. Some people would be willing to settle for such a home. A purely passive solar home of the type being built today, and over the past 5 years, typically fits into this category.

A building that varies in temperature from 65 to 75°F provides excellent comfort. Most people would prefer to live in a home that can provide this narrow comfort zone.

Throughout this book you will be learning how to provide a building that will operate in the narrow 65 to 75°F comfort zone. Often this requires more than purely passive design. Some active solar devices must

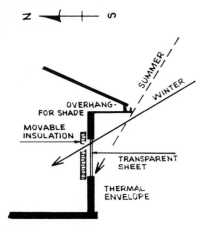

Figure 9.1. Five design elements must be present to build an efficient solar light transmitting device.

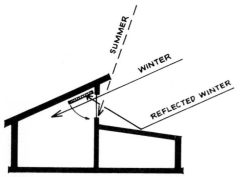

Figure 9.2. A clerestory window makes an efficient solar energy transmitting device.

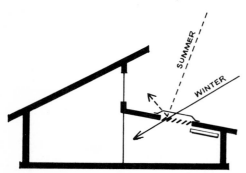

Figure 9.3. A skylight in a south-facing roof can be an efficient solar energy transmitting device, but it is very difficult to provide summer shading.

generally be incorporated into the planning, design, and construction of the building in order to achieve this comfort zone.

Passive Systems Versus Active Systems

A *passive solar system* is a solar system that uses no external power to run the system. An *active solar system* is a solar system that requires external power to run the system. In the past designers tended to lump light-transmitting openings into the passive classification and solar collectors into the active classification. This is a major technical error. Solar collectors that *thermosyphon* are passive solar systems. A thermosyphon system is a system that conveys energy by natural convection. It works due to the fact that hot air or water is lighter than cold air or water and rises. Light-transmitting openings that use external power to move insulation in front of them during nonsunlight hours are active solar systems. Even human power is external energy. *A device that needs human energy is not a passive device.*

Collecting Solar Energy   Solar energy is collected by placing solar collectors and light-transmitting openings in areas where the sun strikes the building. Additional energy is added by using *solar reflectors* on the ground and the adjacent building surfaces to reflect the solar energy into the light-transmitting openings and the solar collectors. A solar reflector is any surface that efficiently reflects the sun's energy. Reflectors can range from high efficiency mirrors to a white shingled roof or white painted wall.

Retaining Solar Energy   Solar energy is retained in the building by having a thermal envelope that surrounds the space within the building. The better the thermal envelope, the longer the energy is retained.

Denying Solar Energy   Solar energy is denied to—or prevented from entering—the building by using *solar shades* and by having a good thermal envelope surrounding the building. A solar shade is a device that shades the building so that the sun's energy does not penetrate its thermal envelope.

The Building's Elements   A building consists of five major structural elements: the foundation, the walls, the floors, the ceilings, and the roof. When all these elements are treated properly, an aesthetically-pleasing, energy-efficient, and comfortable building is created.

Fenestration

The purpose of fenestration is to place openings within the structural elements of the building that allow people, heat, ventilation, and vision to pass.

Consider, for instance, a building without adequate windows. The occupants would be cut off from communicating with their surroundings. Natural light would be denied entrance. Ventilation from the wind could not cool the house. Windows provide visual communication, admit solar light and heat, provide ventilation, provide emergency entrance and exit, and enhance the architectural appearance of both the interior and the exterior of the building. But they only provide these benefits well when they are carefully studied and understood.

Windows must be oriented to the sun and to the surroundings. They must be combined with shading devices to keep out the summer sun.

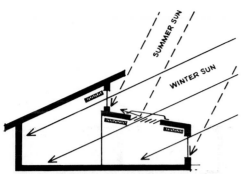

Figure 9.4. The wall window, the skylight, and the clerestory can be combined to bring solar energy into the entire house.

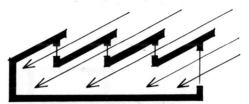

Figure 9.5. The repeating clerestory makes a sawtooth roof and allows solar energy to reach into the entire house.

They must be combined with insulating systems that can be moved in front of them during nonsunlight hours.

Five design elements must be present to provide an efficient solar light-transmitting device such as a solar window. First, the device must face the sun. Second, a transparent or translucent sheet such as glass or plastic must cover the opening. Third, the opening must be in the thermal envelope of the structure so that the energy can pass into the building. Fourth, some type of movable insulation must be available to put in front of the opening when the sun is not shining. Fifth, shading against the summer sun must be provided. Figure 9.1 shows these design elements in a wall window opening.

A *clerestory* window can become an excellent solar energy transmitting device when all five of the design elements are adhered to. A clerestory is an outside wall of a room or building that rises above an adjoining roof and contains windows. Figure 9.2 shows an example in which the roof beneath the clerestory also makes an excellent solar reflector. Note also that the slope of the upper roof conforms to the altitude of the sun in the winter months.

A *skylight* window, when properly designed and oriented, can also be an efficient solar energy transmitting device. A skylight is an opening in the building's roof that is covered with a transparent or translucent material. But skylights are hard to shade in summer months and particular attention must be paid to a tight-fitting movable insulation. Figure 9.3 shows a skylight placed in the lower roof of a clerestory-designed building.

Clerestories, skylights, and wall windows can be designed into a new structure so as to bring solar energy into the entire house as shown in Figure 9.4. Or a sawtooth clerestory design, such as shown in Figure 9.5, can be used to perform the same task.

The designs shown in the last few figures differ markedly from average existing house construction. Remodeling existing houses to use skylights and clerestories is a major undertaking. But it can be done. Figures 9.6 and Figure 9.7 show a cross section of a house before and after such remodeling.

The remodeling consists of five steps. First the ridgepole of the roof is posted. (A load-bearing partition should be located within 1 ft of directly under the ridgepole.) Second, the ceiling is removed over the area where the sunlight is to enter. (To maintain structural integrity, a doubled-up ceiling joist must be left every 4 ft across the opening.) Third, the ceiling thermal envelope is relocated to up between the roof rafters. Fourth, the

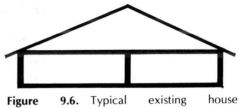

Figure 9.6. Typical existing house construction.

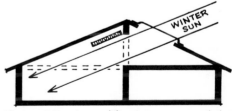

Figure 9.7. A modification to an existing house to use skylight-clerestory principles.

BEFORE

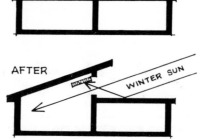

AFTER

Figure 9.8. A modification to an existing flat-roofed house to use clerestory principles.

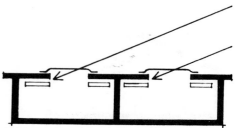

Figure 9.9. Skylights may be cut into a flat-roofed house to admit the sun.

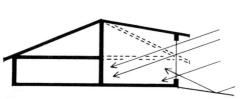

Figure 9.10. The use of a south-facing dormer clerestory.

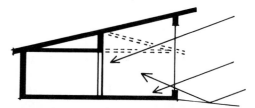

Figure 9.11. Houses with low-pitched roofs can be modified by carrying the roofline back to form a south-facing clerestory.

skylight is installed on the rear roof. The existing rafters should be left intact. Fifth, the movable insulation is constructed and hung so that it can be swung down against the roof-posting partition.

Although the material costs for this modification are modest, the labor costs are extremely high. Great care needs to be taken to protect the building's structural integrity. This type of remodeling should not be undertaken lightly. As you will see in the solar collector section of this chapter, there are less disruptive ways to bring solar energy into the northern half of an existing house.

Figure 9.8 shows a similar modification made to an existing flat-roofed house. The same general remodeling steps are followed. A skylight could also be added to this type of structure. It would represent less of a remodeling chore. Figure 9.9 shows a typical example.

Another modification, which is architecturally aesthetic and adds dramatic interest to the interior of the house, is the south-facing dormer clerestory. This is illustrated in Figure 9.10. A shed dormer is built on the south roof, and a 10- to 12-ft window is constructed on the outside wall. Such dormers should be limited in width to maintain structural integrity. Modifications more than 4 ft wide will require posting of the ridgepole. Clerestories more than 6 ft wide will be hard to insulate. This modification should only be employed in houses having a 6-in. or higher roof pitch. The shed dormer must maintain at least a 2-in. pitch roof.

When the structure has a low-pitched roof, it is possible to build the dormer by extending the front roofline. Again, the same structural considerations and width restrictions should be observed. The effect of such construction on the overall appearance of the house's exterior should be carefully examined before proceeding. Figure 9.11 shows an example.

It is also possible to combine a skylight on the lower edge of the south-facing roof with a south-facing window wall. Such an application is shown in Figure 9.12. You should keep these roof modifications down to 4 ft wide when remodeling. You must maintain the structural integrity of the building. If you have any question about this, you should consult an architect or an experienced builder.

In making any of these fenestration modifications, keep these five rules firmly in mind:

- The fenestration device must face south plus or minus 45°.
- A transparent or translucent material must cover the opening.
- The opening must be in the building's thermal envelope.
- Some type of movable insulation must be provided to cover the opening during nonsunlight hours.
- Shading against the summer sun must be provided.

Materials for Covering Light-transmitting Openings

Materials used to cover light-transmitting openings are called *glazings*. Two types of materials are generally used as glazings in residences: glass and plastics.

There are a number of design factors that you must take into consideration in making a wise decision on which glazing to choose. These factors relate to light transmittance, human comfort, sound control, safety, thermal performance, and cost.

Windows must transmit sunlight in order to provide natural light to the building and to allow visual communication with the outdoors. The need for light and visual communication must be traded-off versus the need for energy transmittance and for personal privacy.

Too much solar heat gain, too many cold drafts, and too much heat loss through large light-transmitting openings destroys the comfort of the home. Both the summer cooling problem and the winter heating problem must be carefully considered when choosing the right material.

Sound penetrates through light-transmitting openings more easily than it does through thermal envelopes. Large widows or skylights facing the street will intensify traffic noises. Large expanses of windows or skylights on the rear or the side of the house will bring in the outside noises and can destroy the home's privacy.

Large expanses of light-transmitting openings can produce safety problems. The materials must be chosen for good structural performance against wind-loading, thermal stress, or accidental mechanical damage. Careless human behavior must also be guarded against.

The material chosen must give a good thermal performance. It must admit the proper amount of solar energy by radiation. It must prevent excess heat loss by reradiation and conduction. And it must not be adversely affected by the extremes of temperature that it will see over the annual temperature cycle.

Finally, when the proper materials are decided on, the cost of each alternative material must be considered if the wisest choice is to be made.

Solar Heat Gain

The solar radiation that strikes the glazing material is either transmitted through the glazing, absorbed by the glazing, or reflected off the surface of the glazing as shown in Figure 9.13.

The amount of energy transmitted, absorbed, or reflected is dependent on the wavelength of the energy, the physical characteristics of the materi-

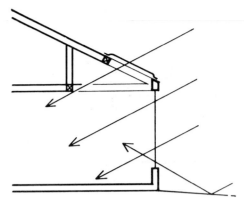

Figure 9.12. A skylight on the lower edge of the roof can be combined with a window wall to admit additional solar energy.

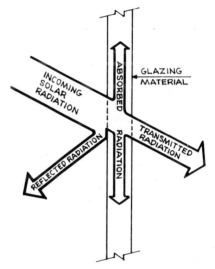

Figure 9.13. Energy striking the glazing material is either reflected, absorbed, or transmitted by the glazing.

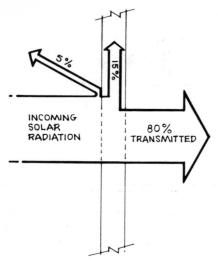

Figure 9.14. Clear ¼-in. glass transmits about 80% of the incident energy striking the glazing at a 90° angle.

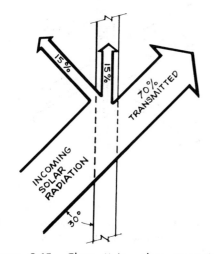

Figure 9.15. Clear ¼-in. glass transmits about 70% of the incident energy striking the glazing at a 30° angle.

al, the thickness of the material, and the angle at which the radiation strikes the surface of the material.

Figures 9.14 through 9.16 show the effect of changing the angle at which the solar radiation strikes the glazing. From an angle of about 90° to an angle of about 30°, only about a 10% loss of the energy transmitted is seen. But at a 20° angle, the transmission is cut in half from a 30° angle.

Figure 9.17 shows the effect of changing the physical characteristics and the thickness of the material. Double-strength (DS) glass is thinner than ¼-in. glass, so it absorbs less energy. The reflectance is the same at the three angles shown. One-quarter inch glass, tinted to absorb energy, greatly increases the absorptance and cuts down slightly on the reflectance.

Figure 9.18 shows the effect of wavelength on a glass glazing material. Glass transmits short-wave radiation extremely well. Solar radiation is short-wave radiation. Glass transmits long-wave radiation very poorly. Thermal radiation is long-wave radiation. So the solar radiation passes through the glass, hits a solid surface, and heats the surface up. This heated surface emits long-wave thermal radiation, which cannot escape back through the glass. In solar language, this is known as the *greenhouse effect*.

Most solar radiation lies below a 3.0 micron wavelength. Most thermal radiation lies above 3.0 microns. Figure 9.19 shows the wavelengths of thermal and solar radiation.

The energy that is absorbed by the glazing material heats it. This heat then flows both inward and outward from both sides of the glazing material by convection and radiation, as shown in Figure 9.20. The total heat transmitted into the structure due to solar energy consists of the transmitted solar radiation plus the inward flow of absorbed heat from the glazing.

Calculating Solar Heat Gain

So many factors relate to solar heat gain through a glazing that a computer program has been developed by ASHRAE to describe this heat gain. This program is called the *Solar Heat Gain Factor Program*.

Appendix D gives the ASHRAE solar intensity and solar heat gain factors for 24, 32, 40, and 48°N latitude. The tables take the normal solar radiation striking a horizontal surface each hour on the 21st day of each month and from this value calculate the number of Btu/hr/sq ft that would pass through a double-strength sheet of glass with 86% transmittance, 8% reflectance, and 6% absorptance located in a vertical wall. *Note.* The tables

GLAZING	INCIDENT ANGLE	TRANSMIT- TANCE % TOTAL	REFLECTANCE % TOTAL	AB- SORPTANCE % TOTAL
DS, clear glass	90	88	6	6
	30	80	12	8
	20	46	46	8
¼-in. clear glass	90	79	7	14
	30	70	12	18
	20	36	46	18
¼ in. tinted heat-absorbing glass	90	46	4	50
	30	36	9	55
	20	16	42	42

Figure 9.17. Effect of incident angle changes on the transmittance of solar radiation through different types of glass.

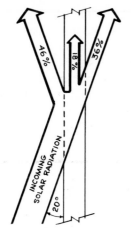

Figure 9.16. Clear ¼-in. glass transmits about 36% of the solar energy striking the glazing at a 20° angle.

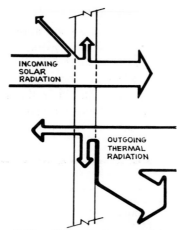

Figure 9.18. Glass glazing material transmits short-wave or solar radiation but does not transmit long-wave or thermal radiation.

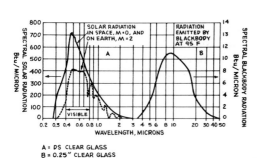

A = DS CLEAR GLASS
B = 0.25" CLEAR GLASS

Figure 9.19. Solar and thermal radiation wavelengths.

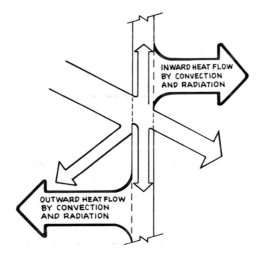

Figure 9.20. Absorbed energy heats the glazing and heat flows inward and outward by convection and radiation.

assume 365 cloudless days, so they cannot be used to calculate annual heat gain without using a correction factor, which you will study shortly.

To learn how to use these tables, turn to Appendix D, Figure D-3. This table shows the solar heat gain factor for 40°N latitude. Look at the column labeled S for south at the top of the chart. Under January 21, note the horizontal line titled Half-day Totals. Read across to the S column, and you will see that between the hours of 7 A.M. and noon the windows will provide 813 Btu/sq ft of area. This figure is the sum of the hourly heat gains shown for 7 A.M. until noon.

Now note the table titled Solar Time, P.M., on the far right-hand side of the page. Look down to the bottom of the chart. Here you will see afternoon orientations listed. Find the column labeled S. Read up to the half-day total listed in the column. The half-day total for the afternoon hours is also 813 Btu/sq ft. So the total daily solar gain is 1626 Btu/sq ft. However, if your orientation were SE, then the morning total reading down would be 904 Btu whereas the afternoon total, reading up, would be 273 Btu. The daily total would be 1177 Btu/sq ft.

1626 Btu
× 31 days
= 50,406 Btu, Jan

January has 31 days. So multiply 1626 Btu/sq ft/day times 31 and you will obtain a good approximation of the monthly heat gain if all the days are sunny. That would equal 50,406 Btu/sq ft for the month of January for a vertical south-facing double-strength glass window.

When you perform that calculation for each month and add the months up, you will obtain the annual solar heat gain through 1 sq ft of a south-facing, double-strength glass window *assuming 365 cloudless days.* The result is shown in Figure 9.21. It is 446,290 Btu/yr.

MONTH	DAYS	DAILY SHG	MONTHLY SHG
January	31	1626	50,406
February	28	1642	45,976
March	31	1388	43,028
April	30	976	29,280
May	31	716	22,196
June	30	630	18,900
July	31	704	21,824
August	31	948	29,388
September	30	1344	40,320
October	31	1582	49,042
November	30	1596	47,880
December	31	1550	48,050
Annual	365		446,290

Figure 9.21. The solar heat gain (SHG) in Btu through a 1-sq-ft piece of south-facing double-strength clear glass at 40°N latitude. *Note:* This table assumes 365 days and must be corrected for estimating true solar heat gain.

The solar heat gain table gives values for each major compass orientation and for horizontal surfaces. So any size vertical window facing in any direction or any horizontal window can have its solar heat gain calculated from these tables if it is glazed with a single thickness of double-strength glass. Again this assumes 365 cloudless days. *You must apply a correction factor for cloud cover.*

The Shading Coefficient

Not all windows are single thicknesses of double-strength glass. Many other materials are used. So a table of *shading coefficients* has been devel-

TYPE OF GLASS	THICKNESS (IN.)	% TRANSMIT-TANCE	SHADING COEFFICIENT
Clear, single pane	1/8	84	1.00
	1/4	78	0.95
	3/8	72	0.91
	1/2	67	0.88
Heat absorbing single pane	1/8	64	0.84
	1/4	46	0.71
	3/8	33	0.62
	1/2	24	0.56
Clear, double-glazed	1/8	71	0.88
	1/4	61	0.82
Double-glazed with heat-absorbing glass on the outside and clear glass on the inside	1/4	36	0.57

Figure 9.22. Some typical average shading coefficients for single- and double-glazed glass units.

oped to allow you to calculate the solar heat gain for other common types of glazings.

For any other glazing material, the solar heat gain is equal to the shading coefficient for that type of glazing times the solar heat gain for a single thickness of double-strength glass. Some typical shading coefficients are shown in Figure 9.22 for single glass and for *insulating glass units*. An insulating glass unit is a factory-fabricated double-glazed unit or a single-glazed unit with a storm window added on site.

For double-glazed units using ¼-in. glass, the shading coefficient, or the SC, equals 0.82 from the table in Figure 9.22. So the annual solar heat gain factor shown in Figure 9.21 for double-strength glass (⅛ in. thick) would drop from 446,290 Btu/yr to 365,958 Btu/yr.

Figure 9.23 gives typical shading coefficients for some plastic glazings. Note that the shading coefficient in the tinted glazings is a direct function of the amount of tint as shown by the solar transmittance. If there is any doubt in your mind about the transmittance of any glazing material that you plan to use, consult the glazing material manufacturer for his tested shading coefficient for that glazing.

$$
\begin{array}{r}
446{,}290 \text{ Btu} \\
\times\ 0.82 \text{ SC} \\
\hline
= 365{,}958 \text{ Btu}
\end{array}
$$

TYPE PLASTIC	% TRANSMITTANCE	SHADING COEFFICIENT
Acrylic		
Clear	85	0.98
Gray tint	27	0.52
	41	0.63
	55	0.74
	62	0.80
	74	0.89
Bronze tint	20	0.46
	35	0.58
	56	0.75
	62	0.80
	75	0.90
Reflective	12	0.21
Polycarbonate, ⅛		
Clear	82	0.98
Gray	57	0.74
Bronze	57	0.74

Figure 9.23. Typical shading coefficients for plastic glazings.

Correcting the Solar Heat Gain Table

Many authors of passive solar books have neglected to correct the solar heat gain table for local weather conditions. As a result, the use of their data will result in a gross overstatement of the role that solar heat gain plays in the heating of a residence. *The solar heat gain table must be corrected for local weather conditions.* Most locations have some cloudy weather—not 365 days of sunshine. This correction is an extremely important step in determining the amount of solar heat that you will gain from a light-transmitting opening.

Figure 9.24 shows how to correct the solar heat gain table for use in Lincoln, Nebraska. The horizontal incident solar, assuming 365 cloudless days, in the ASHRAE program can be calculated by adding up the column titled Direct Normal Btuh/ft² in Table D-3 and doubling it to obtain the full day's incident solar. These figures for 40°N latitude have been tabulated in the column titled Monthly Normal Incident Solar ASHRAE in Figure 9.24.

The horizontal incident solar for Lincoln, Nebraska, 41°N latitude, can be obtained from Figure 3.9 in Decision 3. These values are tabulated in the column titled Monthly Incident Solar F-Chart. Note that they are much smaller. That is because they take the local cloudiness into account.

MONTH	MONTHLY NORMAL INCIDENT SOLAR F-CHART	÷	MONTHLY NORMAL INCIDENT SOLAR ASHRAE	=	% ACTUAL SOLAR	×	MONTHLY SOLAR HEAT GAIN	=	CORRECTED SOLAR HEAT GAIN
January	21,700		76,756		28		50,406		14,114
February	26,300		81,200		32		45,976		14,712
March	39,700		99,944		40		43,028		17,211
April	46,900		101,520		46		29,280		13,469
May	56,700		106,764		53		22,196		11,764
June	60,300		103,800		58		18,900		10,962
July	61,400		103,416		59		21,824		12,876
August	58,100		99,138		59		29,388		17,339
September	45,600		89,940		51		40,320		20,563
October	37,100		85,188		44		49,042		21,578
November	22,900		72,420		32		47,880		15,322
December	19,700		70,184		28		48,050		13,454
Annual	496,400		1,090,270				446,290		183,364

Figure 9.24. Correcting the ASHRAE solar heat gain table for local weather conditions.

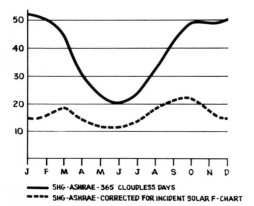

Figure 9.25. When F-Chart weather correction is applied to ASHRAE solar heat gain calculations, the window performance levels out.

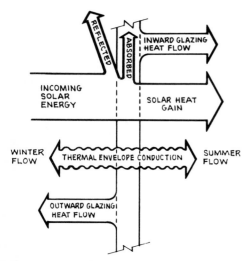

Figure 9.26. The total heat balance through a glazing material is complex. Six types of heat flow are taking place simultaneously.

If the F-Chart solar total is divided by the ASHRAE solar total, then a percentile based on actual weather data is obtained. This is tabulated in the column titled % Actual Solar.

The monthly solar heat gain calculated from the ASHRAE table is listed in the column titled Monthly Solar Heat Gain. Multiply the monthly solar heat gain by the percent actual solar and you will arrive at a corrected monthly solar heat gain for Lincoln, Nebraska.

The importance of taking this corrective step can be immediately seen by examining the results in Figure 9.24. *The actual heat gain for Lincoln, Nebraska, is only about 41% of the heat gain calculated in the ASHRAE tables.* You will also note that the monthly performance of the south-facing window levels out when the local weather correction is applied. This is shown graphically in Figure 9.25.

Conduction Gains and Losses

There are six types of heat flow occurring through the glazing material during the sunlight hours. These are shown in Figure 9.26. The solar heat gain tables cover five of these types of heat flow: the solar radiation, the transmittance, the reflectance, the absorptance, and the inward and outward flow of the heat absorbed by the glazing.

The glazing material is part of the building's thermal envelope. As you learned in Decision 4, heat is conducted through the thermal envelope throughout the day and night. The amount of heat lost is a function of the glazing's U-factor, the area of the glazing, and the difference in temperature between the building's air and the outdoor air. You learned to calculate this gain or loss in heat by using the formula: $UA \Delta t$ = heat loss (or gain).

In the winter months, heat losses are encountered. The outdoor air is the coldest. In the summer months, heat gains are experienced. The building air is the coldest.

To calculate the total heat exchange through the glazing, you must calculate the solar heat gain and add or subtract the conduction heat losses or gains. This formula shows how:

Solar heat gain factor × shading coefficient ± thermal envelope heat flow = total glazing heat gain

The only heat flow occurring during nonsunlight hours is conduction through the thermal envelope. In the winter months of December through

February, the sunlight hours at 40°N latitude are from about 8 A.M. until about 4 P.M. That is a total of about 8 hr. So there are about 16 hr when the thermal envelope's conduction is the only heat exchange occurring. The average temperatures occurring in those months are typically in the range of 28 to 34°F.

Assuming an average temperature of 30°F for outdoor air and an average temperature of 65°F for building air, a square foot of single-glazed double-strength glass can be expected to lose about 27,720 Btu/mo. Over the heating season, this would amount to 83,160 Btu.

This is a substantial loss, as can be seen by looking at Figure 9.27, which tabulates solar heat gain and thermal envelope conduction losses for the glazing that was located in Lincoln, Nebraska. The table shows that the glazing ends up with a net loss of 15,460 Btu during the December-February period.

	1.1	U-factor
	× 1	sq ft
	1.1	Btu/hr/sq ft/°F
	× 35	temp. diff.
	38.5	Btu/hr/sq ft
	× 720	avg hr/mo
	= 27,720	Btu/mo loss

MONTH	DAYS	SOLAR HEAT GAIN	−	THERMAL ENVELOPE HEAT LOSS	=	NET HEAT GAIN (OR LOSS)
December	31	19,700		28,644		(8944)
January	31	21,700		28,644		(6944)
February	28	26,300		25,872		428
Total	90	67,700		83,160		(15,460)

If the glazing were doubled through the use of an insulating glass unit, the seasonal heat loss would be cut by a little over one-half to 37,422 Btu.

Insulating glass would also cut down the solar heat gain to 59,576 Btu. So now the glazing produces a net heat gain of 22,154 Btu during the heating season.

Go one step further. If an insulating panel with an R-value of 10 were placed over the glazing during the nonsunlight hours, then the heat conduction losses would be lowered drastically. The glazing would be an excellent solar heat producer. The results of this decision are shown in Figure 9.28. The structure ends up with a net heat gain of 41,806 Btu or 62% of the energy that entered the glazing during the sunlight hours.

Figure 9.27. A double-strength, clear glass single-pane glazing located in Lincoln, Nebraska, facing south shows a net heat loss over the heating season.

	0.5	
	÷ 1.1	
	= 0.45	
	83,160	Btu
	× 0.45	
	= 37,422	Btu heat loss

MONTH	DAYS	SOLAR HEAT GAIN	−	HEAT LOSS SUNLIGHT HOURS	−	HEAT LOSS NONSUNLIGHT HOURS	=	NET HEAT GAIN (OR LOSS)
December	31	19,700		7161		1758		10,781
January	31	21,700		7161		1758		12,781
February	28	26,300		6468		1588		18,244
Total	90	67,700		20,790		5104		41,806

To be an effective solar device, the glazing must be insulated during nonsunlight hours with at least R-5 insulation but preferably with R-10 or better insulation.

Making a Total Heat Gain Estimate

The total heat gain can be estimated and tabulated by using the tables shown in Figures 9.29 through 9.31.

Figure 9.29 is a worksheet that shows how to estimate the glazing-corrected monthly solar heat gain for 1 sq ft of glazing oriented in the proper direction. One of these worksheets must be filled out for each month.

Figure 9.30 shows how to estimate the conduction heat gain (or loss) through 1 sq. ft. of any common glazing. One of these worksheets must be

Figure 9.28. When R-10 insulation is placed over the same glazing for 18 hr/day, a large heat gain is seen over the heating season.

	67,700	Btu
	× 0.88	SC
	59,576	Btu solar gain
	59,576	
	− 37,422	
	= 22,154	net gain in Btu

filled out for each month. Heat will be lost during the winter months and gained during the summer months.

Figure 9.31 is a worksheet that tabulates the net heat gain for each month and for the year using the figures developed in Figures 9.29 and 9.30. The worksheet is self-explanatory.

To obtain the total heat gain, multiply the net heat gain for 1 sq ft of glazing by the area of the glazing in square feet. You will want to separate the winter results from the summer results. And you will want to calculate the effects of any summer solar shading that you incorporate to keep the summer sunlight off the glass.

WORKSHEET

Orientation ——————— Month ——————— Glazing ———————

Item	Value	Source or Procedure
1. Monthly horizontal incident solar, F-Chart	———	Decision 3
2. Half-day horizontal incident solar-ASHRAE SHG table	———	Direct normal Btu/hr/sq ft sum from Appendix
3. Full-day horizontal incident solar ASHRAE SHG table	———	Item 2 × 2 = item 3.
4. Monthly horizontal incident solar ASHRAE SHG table	———	Item 3 × the number of days in the month.
5. Percent actual solar	———	Item 1 divided by item 4.
6. Morning solar heat gain	———	Solar heat gain factor half-day total using orientation at the top of the table.
7. Afternoon solar heat gain	———	Solar heat gain factor half-day total using orientation at the bottom of the table.
8. Monthly solar heat gain	———	Add items 6 and 7 and multiply the result by the number of days in the month.
9. Location corrected monthly solar heat gain	———	Multiply item 5 by item 8 and divide by 100.
10. Shading coefficient	———	Take from table in Figure 9.21 or 9.22.
11. Glazing-corrected monthly solar heat gain factor for 1 sq ft of glazing	———	Multiply item 9 by item 10.

Figure 9.29. Table for estimating the monthly solar heat gain through 1 sq ft of any common glazing.

WORKSHEET

Orientation _____ Month _____ Glazing _____

Figure 9.30. Table for estimating the monthly conduction heat gain or loss through any common glazing.

Item	Value	Source or Proceedure
1. Glazing *U*-factor	_____	Decision 4. Btu/hr/sq ft/°F.
2. Average monthly outdoor temperature	_____	Appendix, °F.
3. Indoor building design temperature	_____	Use 75°F for summer months. Use 65°F for winter months.
4. Temperature difference	_____	Item 3 minus item 2 in winter (loss), Item 2 minus item 3 in summer (gain).
5. Hourly heat gain or loss	_____	Item 4 multiplied by item 1.
6. Number of hours of sun daily	_____	Appendix.
7. Monthly heat gain or loss during sunlight hours	_____	Multiply item 5 by item 6 and multiply the result by the number of days in the month.
8. *R*-value of glazing	_____	1 divided by item 1.
9. *R*-value of glazing insulation	_____	User determined.
10. Total *R*-value	_____	Item 8 plus item 9.
11. Insulated *U*-factor	_____	1 divided by item 10
12. Hourly heat gain or loss during nonsunlight hours	_____	Multiply item 11 by item 4.
13. Number of hours of nonsunlight/day	_____	Twenty-four minus item 6.
14. Monthly heat gain or loss during nonsunlight hours	_____	Multiply item 12 by item 13 and multiply the result by the number of days in the month.
15. Total monthly heat gain or loss	_____	Add item 7 to item 14.

WORKSHEET

Orientation _____ Glazing _____

Month	Solar Heat Gain	±	Conduction Heat gain or loss	=	Net heat gain
January	_____		_____		_____
February	_____		_____		_____
March	_____		_____		_____
April	_____		_____		_____
May	_____		_____		_____
June	_____		_____		_____
July	_____		_____		_____
August	_____		_____		_____
September	_____		_____		_____
October	_____		_____		_____
November	_____		_____		_____
December	_____		_____		_____
Total	_____		_____		_____

Figure 9.31. Table for estimating the monthly and annual net heat gain from 1 sq ft of any common glazing.

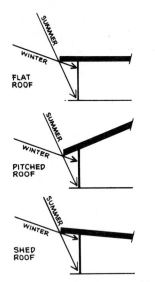

Figure 9.32. A properly engineered building overhang excludes the direct rays of the summer sun.

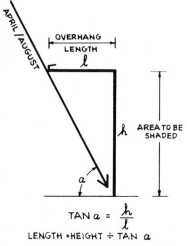

$$\text{TAN } a = \frac{h}{l}$$

LENGTH = HEIGHT ÷ TAN a

Figure 9.33. The length of the overhang required to shade the wall can be determined with this formula.

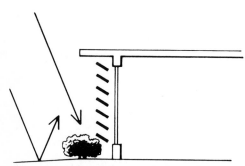

Figure 9.34. Using horizontal louvers, planting low shrubs, and slanting the grade away from the building will help control summer ground reflection and sky glare.

Solar Shading

Fenestrations that allow the solar radiation to enter the building year round are not always the most satisfactory fenestrations. Many buildings need solar heat in the wintertime, but they do not need it in the summertime. In these cases, *solar shades* are employed to help control the penetration of the solar radiation. A solar shade is any device that helps to control the penetration of the sun's rays. Solar shades are used to exclude the direct rays of the sun, to control the glare from the sky, and to control the reflection from the ground and the adjacent building surfaces.

Solar shades such as building overhangs, louvers, screens, or trees are located outside the thermal envelope of the structure. Shades such as venetian blinds, roller shades, and draperies are located inside the thermal envelope. In the case of insulated glass units, shades can be placed between the two glazings so that they become part of the thermal envelope.

Exterior Solar Shades

A properly designed roof overhang will exclude the direct rays of the summer sun. Overhangs may be placed on most types of roofs, as shown in Figure 9.32. The length of the overhang can be easily calculated by the formula shown in Figure 9.33. It is best to limit roof overhangs to under 18 to 24 in. Use the lowest monthly altitude of the sun for the season that you wish to shade for. On an existing building, awnings can easily be used in the place of overhangs.

Although roof overhangs exclude the direct rays of the sun, they do not control reflection from adjacent surfaces nor do they control the glare from the sky. Summer reflection from the ground can be controlled by slanting the grade away from the sidewall and planting low shrubs in front of the window. Exterior horizontal louvers can also be used, but they tend to block the view. The exterior horizontal louver will also help cut down the glare from the sky. Figure 9.34 illustrates these shading methods.

The summer sun is low in the sky during the early morning and late evening hours, so building overhangs facing east or west are ineffective. For east/west facing solar shades, the horizontal louver or trees and tall shrubs will control the sun the best. Use evergreen plantings to exclude both the winter and the summer sun. Use deciduous plantings to exclude only the summer sun.

Vertical louvers can also be used effectively on the east and west sides of the house as shown in Figure 9.35. They can be adjusted to reflect the winter sun into the structure or to deflect the summer sun.

Figure 9.36 shows the advantages and disadvantages of three typical south-facing overhangs and louvers. The solid overhang effectively blocks the direct rays of the sun, but it does not control reflected radiation or sky glare. And heat can build up under the overhang.

The louvered overhang also excludes the sun's rays, but it diffuses them. Some of the light passes through in a diffuse fashion. Heat cannot build up under the overhang, but ground reflectance and ground glare are still uncontrolled.

A slotted solid overhang, combined with hanging horizontal louvers, controls the direct radiation, the ground reflection, and the sky glare. The slot prevents the build up of heat under the overhang.

Figure 9.37 shows a typical use of vertical louvers on the east or west side of the building. If the louvers are set east-west, they help collect direct radiation in the early or late hours and they provide some diffuse reflected sunlight in the late morning or early afternoon. If the louvers are set to the southeast or the southwest, they allow the direct rays to penetrate during the early morning or late evening and they reflect-in solar radiation during the morning and the afternoon. If the louvers are set to the northeast or the northwest, they deflect away the solar radiation during the entire morning and afternoon.

Figure 9.38 shows vertical and horizontal louvers combined into an egg-crate louver. Egg-crate louvers shade a window from summer sun, from early morning and late afternoon sun, from sky glare, and from ground reflection. They tend to admit only the direct rays of the winter sun when the sun is in the orientation of the vertical louvers. The vertical louvers, the horizontal louvers, or both can be tilted up or down or from side to side to favor summer or winter sun or an easterly or westerly direction.

The design of effective exterior solar shading requires that you carefully define the altitude and the orientation of the sun throughout the day and that you carefully define the orientation of the fenestration that is to be shaded. Once these three factors are defined, the design of the shading device can proceed accurately.

Interior Solar Shades

Interior solar shades typically consist of draperies, roller shades, and venetian blinds. The effectiveness of interior solar shades depends on their ability to reflect the solar radiation back out the glazing before it can be absorbed and converted into heat within the building. So interior shading devices are considerably different from exterior shading devices that prevent the radiation from entering the building. They are not as effective in controlling solar heat gain.

Shading coefficients have been developed for typical draperies, roller shades, and venetian blinds. Representative values are shown in Figure 9.39. These values vary. They should only be used for rough estimates. A complete list of shading coefficients can be found in the *1977 Fundamentals Book* published by ASHRAE.

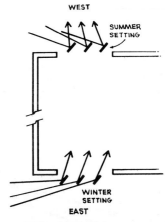

Figure 9.35. Vertical louvers work well on the east and west. They can be set to reflect in the winter sun and to reflect away the summer sun.

Figure 9.36. Typical south-facing shading devices and their general characteristics.

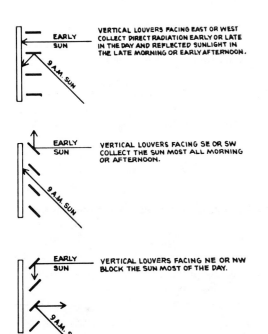

Figure 9.37. Typical east- or west-facing vertical louvers and their general characteristics.

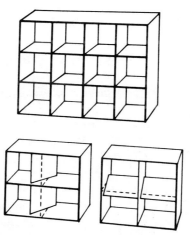

Figure 9.38. Combined vertical and horizontal louvers. Either or both louvers may be tilted.

GLAZING SYSTEM	VENETIAN BLINDS	ROLLER SHADES	DRAPERIES
Single thickness, clear	0.60	0.40	0.40-0.75
Double thickness, clear	0.54	0.40	0.37-0.66

Figure 9.39. Typical shading coefficients for interior shading devices used with clear glass glazings.

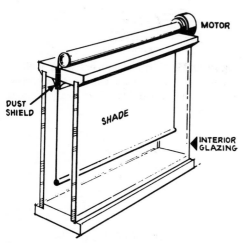

Figure 9.40. A roller shade mounted between the glazings.

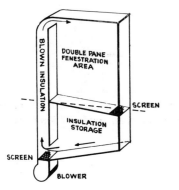

Figure 9.41. An insulated window unit with an insulation storage compartment and blower.

Draperies can be classified by their solar reflectance, the openness of the weave, and their solar transmittance. Tightly woven, light-colored, smooth fabrics will have high shading characteristics of 0.35 to 0.50, whereas loosely woven, dark, rough fabrics will have low shading characteristics of 0.55 to 0.75. Doubled draperies provide a reduced U-value as well as a higher solar shading characteristic. The air space between the two sets of drapes adds a good insulating barrier.

Roller shades can be dark or light-colored. They can also be translucent or opaque. The light-colored, translucent shade will have a superior shading coefficient.

Venetian blinds can be vertical-slatted or horizontal-slatted. The horizontal-slatted blinds will have lower air convection rates. The two styles have about the same shading coefficients.

Between the Glass Solar Shades

When two or more layers of glass are used in a light-transmitting opening, a number of new shading and insulating possibilities arise. It is possible to build the unit so that a venetian blind or a roller shade can be used between the inside and the outside glass. It is possible to put draw draperies between the layers of glass. And it is possible to fill the space between the two layers of glass with insulation during nonsunlight hours.

Locating the shading device in this location has some attractive features. The solar radiation has only partly penetrated the structure and thus is easier to contol. The shading device operates in a dead air space and is not as apt to be disturbed by air convection currents. If loose insulating material is used for shading, a very tight shade that is not subject to air infiltration is created. On the other hand, units of this type must be motorized. And there needs to be a way to clean the inside surfaces of the two glazings periodically.

Figure 9.40 shows how a motorized shade or venetian blind might be constructed. A window unit is constructed with a slot at the top; a weighted, motorized shade is fed down through a dust shield into the window.

Fenestration Insulation

Earlier in this chapter you learned that an effective solar fenestration required insulation placed over it during the winter nonsunlight hours so that the heat would not be lost by conduction out through the thermal envelope. You should also have reached the conclusion that in certain climates insulation is needed at times to prevent too much solar radiation from entering the structure. Solar shades help deflect the solar radiation, but they do not prevent the conduction of heat through the glazing to any great extent. These facts should have led you to the logical conclusion that insulation that can be placed in front of the glazing is an integral part of an effective solar fenestration.

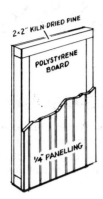

Figure 9.42. Typical high quality panel of movable insulation.

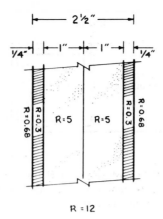

Figure 9.43. Cross section of a typical high quality movable insulation using a wood panel exterior and a Styrofoam interior.

Movable Insulation

Figure 9.41 shows how a between-the-glazing insulated window might be constructed. The insulated window unit is constructed with a storage compartment beneath it. This storage compartment is filled with lightweight insulation such as polystyrene beads.

An air passage with a blower is installed alongside the unit. Two movable screens are inserted; one at the bottom of the glazing compartment and one at the bottom of the storage compartment.

To fill the glazing area with insulation, the top screen is closed. The bottom screen is dropped over the blower, and the blower is started up. The combination of gravity and air pressure moves the insulation into the bottom of the air tube where it is carried up into the window and fills the cavity between the two glazings.

To empty the glazing area, the lower screen is raised to cover the opening from the storage compartment to the air tube and the upper screen is swung down against the side of the storage compartment. Gravity plus air pressure created by the blower moves the insulation back into the storage compartment.

A device such as this can turn the fenestration into a highly efficient part of the thermal envelope. Three inches of polystyrene would have an *R*-value of about 8. This would give the entire fenestration an *R*-value of close to 9.5 or 10.

Movable insulated panels can also be easily constructed and mounted inside the structure as very effective fenestration insulation. Figure 9.42 shows the general construction of such a panel. The panel consists of 2 in. of polystyrene slab insulation placed inside a frame consisting of ¼-in. plywood paneling, chosen to complement the home interior, and a 2 in. by 2 in. kiln-dried pine frame. Properly glued and nailed, this would represent an excellent lightweight, warp-resistant insulating panel. Figure 9.43 shows a cross section of this panel. It has an *R*-value of about 12.

Figure 9.44 shows this panel mounted on sliding rails for large fenestration areas. During the day, the panel is slid aside to expose the fenestration. During nonsunlight hours, the panel slides over the fenestration and up against an insulated stop to prevent air infiltration. Smaller panels

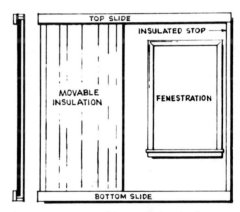

Figure 9.44. Movable insulation for large areas can be mounted on sliding rails for convenience and easy opening and closing.

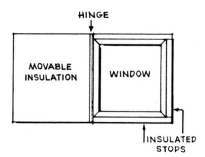

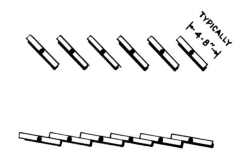

Figure 9.45. Movable insulation for small areas can be hinged on the side, the top, or the bottom to swing shut.

Figure 9.46. Venetian-blind-type devices can also be constructed of lightweight insulating materials to form fairly effective movable insulation. These work well for skylights.

could be hinged to the side, top, or bottom of the fenestration and swung shut against insulated stops when needed as shown in Figure 9.45.

It is also possible to construct venetian blinds from lightweight insulating materials as shown in Figure 9.46. These are particularly effective for skylights because the amount of solar radiation can also be controlled during the day. The slats in such blinds would be much larger than in ordinary window-type venetian blinds. Each slat would typically range from 4 to 8 in. in width.

Outdoor shutters, doors, and other insulating devices can also be used with wall and roof fenestrations, but their use requires going outdoors to open and close them. This is not always convenient.

Solar Reflectors

In Decision 2 you studied sun angles and solar reflectance. You learned that the angle of incidence equaled the angle of reflection. And you learned that different types of surfaces had different reflectances. Figure 2.48 tabulated the typical reflectance values for different types of surfaces.

You learned that concrete surfaces had reflectances ranging from 25 to 35%, that green grass has a reflectance of 20 to 30%, that clean snow has a reflectance of 65 to 75%, and that a white shingled roof has a reflectance of 70 to 80%.

The solar heat gain tables in Appendix D assume that your fenestration sees 20% reflectance. So for reflective surfaces less than 20%, you do not need to calculate any additional solar energy coming from reflectance on the glazing. However, you should add solar radiation when the reflectance is higher.

What makes a good reflecting surface for solar energy? First, the surface should be smooth so that the radiation is reflected in a uniform manner rather than being scattered and diffused. Second, the surface should be a poor transmitter of solar wavelengths. This means that it must be opaque not translucent. And third, it must be a poor absorber of solar energy. This means that it should be dense and light in color. Figure 9.47 illustrates these points. Also remember that the reflector can only add to the building's solar heat gain when it is at the correct angle to reflect the energy into the fenestration.

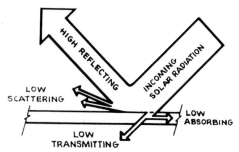

Figure 9.47. A good reflecting surface is smooth, opaque, and nonabsorbing.

Typical Reflectance Values

All the solar radiation striking the surface of any material must be absorbed, reflected, or transmitted. A good glazing material has high transmission, low absorption, and low reflectance. A good reflecting surface is opaque and has little or no transmission. You must be concerned with how much energy is absorbed and how much energy is reflected.

The absorptance values of most common materials are available. Assuming that the reflector is opaque, then the reflectance can be estimated by the simple formula:

$$100\% - \% \text{ absorptance} = \% \text{ reflectance}$$

These materials have high reflectance values:

MATERIAL	TYPICAL REFLECTANCE VALUE
Magnesium carbonate	0.90-0.96
White plaster	0.87-0.93
White paint	0.75-0.80
Snow	0.65-0.75
White enamel	0.55-0.75
Aluminum paint	0.50-0.55
Ice	0.67-0.69
White sand	0.55
Asbestos felt	0.75
Brass, copper, lead	0.60-0.80
Aluminum foil	0.85

These materials have low reflectance values:

MATERIAL	TYPICAL REFLECTANCE VALUE
Green paint	0.45-0.50
Gray paint	0.20-0.25
Red paint	0.20-0.25
Black paint	0.10-0.15
White asbestos board	0.35-0.40
Concrete	0.20-0.35
Grass	0.20-0.30
Bare ground (typical)	0.17-0.24

In using these tables, keep in mind that surface smoothness is an important factor in reflecting solar energy uniformly without scattering it. You can expect to lose 5 to 15% of the reflected energy in light scatter if the surface is not uniformly smooth. Also remember that 20% reflectance is already included in the solar heat gain tables, so reduce the reflectance value by 20% when adding to the solar heat gain if you are using the ASHRAE tables in Appendix D.

Typical Reflecting Surfaces

Figure 9.48 shows a clerestory-type structure. The lower roof below the clerestory fenestration can be an excellent reflecting surface provided that it is pitched at the correct angle and covered with a highly reflective surface. The same is true of the ground area below the south-facing first-story windows. Note also that the underside of the ceilings in both stories make good secondary reflectors and help move the radiation around within the house.

The importance of these reflective surfaces can be illustrated by example. Suppose that the roof is receiving 150 Btu/hr/sq ft, that it has a reflectance of 70%, that the clerestory ceiling has a reflectance of 70%, that and the glazing has a solar transmittance of 87%. The amount of extra solar radiation entering the building would be about 65 Btu/hr/sq ft. That is

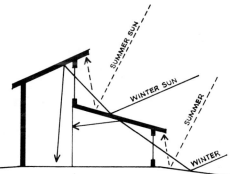

Figure 9.48. The lower roof below a clerestory and the ground below a wall window make excellent reflecting surfaces that can add more solar heat gain.

150	Btu/hr/sq ft
× 0.50	net reflectance
75	Btu/hr/sq ft
× 0.87	glazing SC
65.25	Btu/hr/sq ft
× 0.70	reflectance
= 45.67	Btu/hr/sq ft

about 43% of the energy striking the roof. About 46 Btu/hr/sq ft would be reflected to the floor of the building. That is about 31% of the solar radiation striking the roof.

This is a substantial energy gain. It is obtained at little or no cost by designing the roof at the proper angle and covering it with a highly reflective surface. In the summer months, when the sun is high in the sky, most of the solar radiation will be reflected away from the clerestory fenestration.

Vertical walls over skylights on either flat or pitched roofs make very poor winter reflectors. But in the summer, when the energy is most likely not needed, they may reflect high amounts of energy into the building, so these walls should be shaded against the summer sun or treated to make them poor reflectors. Figures 9.49 and 9.50 illustrate this.

Fenestration Orientation

The orientation of your building fenestration for solar radiation collection depends on the use that you plan for the collected energy. Figure 9.51 shows why.

If you want winter heat gain in Lincoln, Nebraska, then a 1-sq-ft south-facing window sees about 190,000 Btu over the heating season. An east- or west-facing window sees about 100,000 Btu over the heating season. And a north-facing window sees almost no radiation. So a south-facing wall window would be about twice as effective as an east- or west-facing window whereas a north-facing window would supply almost no energy. A skylight would be about 30% more effective than an east- or west-facing window, but it would be only about 68% as effective as a south-facing window.

All this suggests that for maximum winter heat gain, you had best design your building so that the major fenestration areas are located from southeast to southwest and that the use of skylights to augment wall windows is highly feasible.

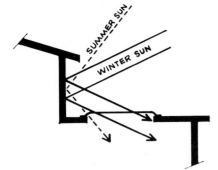

Figure 9.49. Vertical walls above pitched roof skylights do not generally make good solar reflectors for winter sun.

Figure 9.50. Vertical walls above flat roof skylights can make fair solar reflectors for winter sun.

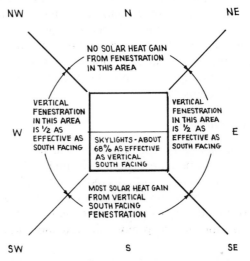

Figure 9.51. Where fenestration should be located for good solar heat gain in Lincoln, Nebraska.

Making a Fenestration Decision

Up to this point, you have been studying the direct gain of solar energy through fenestration. You should have learned that there are three basic fenestration devices: the clerestory, the skylight, and the wall window. You should have learned that solar heat gain calculations require a solar heat gain table, a shading coefficient, a local weather correction, and a estimate of conduction heat gains and losses. You should have mastered the principles of fenestration shading to prevent excessive heat gain during certain times of the year and the use of movable insulation to make fenestration an effective solar collection device. You should know that reflecting surfaces can add measurably to solar heat gain and that solar fenestration needs to to be oriented southward for maximum effectiveness.

If the use of fenestration were the only way to admit solar energy into your house, you would have enough information to make a good solar collection decision. But fenestration is not the only way to collect energy. Indirect gain through solar collectors is another way that is very effective. You must study the use of solar collectors before you complete your fenestration decisions.

Solar Collectors

The sun's energy can also be captured outside the thermal envelope, converted to thermal energy, and pumped or blown through the thermal envelope into the building. The device used to perform this task is the *solar collector*. A solar collector is a heat exchanger specifically designed to capture the sun's radiation and convert it to thermal energy.

Fenestration devices provide high solar heat gain, but they also lose much thermal energy during nonsunlight hours. This limits their efficiency. When too much fenestration area is used in a building, the building's thermal envelope is destroyed. The building ends up having a net thermal loss rather than a thermal heat gain. This is not so for solar collectors. They mount outside the thermal envelope of the building, so they do not suffer heat conduction losses during nonsunlight hours.

The truly effective solar building uses both fenestration and solar collectors to provide the maximum solar heat gain. Fenestration is used where heat gain plus natural lighting and visual communication is desired. Solar collectors are used when the sole purpose is to collect heat. The marriage of the two devices results in the most effective and harmonious building.

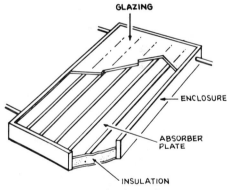

Figure 9.52. Typical solar collector.

How Solar Collectors Work

Figure 9.52 shows a cutaway of a typical solar collector. The solar collector has four major parts: a weather-tight enclosure, a transparent surface glazing, an insulated back and sides, and a thermal absorber plate. The thermal absorber plate has a highly absorptive coating on its surface and contains either air passages or liquid passages to carry away the heat and bring it into the building.

The solar collector is a rather complex device even though it looks quite simple. The complexity comes in the number of things that happen within the collector once the solar radiation hits it.

Figure 9.53 shows what happens to the solar radiation striking the glazing. It is either transmitted through the glazing, absorbed by the glazing, or reflected off the glazing. Some of the transmitted energy is reflected off the

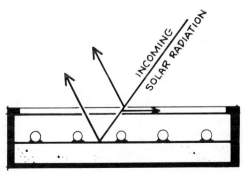

Figure 9.53. Incoming solar radiation is either transmitted, absorbed in the glazing, or reflected off the surface.

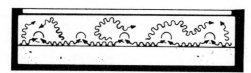

Figure 9.54. Thermal energy generated within the collector is transmitted to the air or liquid in the passages or is emitted to the air space between the glazing and the absorber where it heats it up.

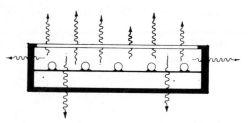

Figure 9.55. The heated collector loses thermal energy through the glazing, the edges, and the back.

absorber plate back through the glazing. The solar energy that is absorbed by the absorber plate coating is the useful energy. It is converted to long-wave thermal energy.

Figure 9.54 shows what happens to the thermal energy that is generated. It heats up the air or liquid in the absorber plate passages and is emitted to the air space above the absorber plate. But because it is long-wave energy, most of it is trapped and does not pass out through the glazing. This emitted thermal energy therefore heats up the collector hotter than the air surrounding it.

Because the collector is hotter than the surrounding air, there are conduction losses through the glazing, the sides, and the back of the collector. So a complex exchange of heat phenomena of three different types is taking place simultaneously within the collector. Figure 9.55 illustrates the conduction losses.

Collectors are designed so that the maximum amount of solar radiation is passed on to the air or liquid circulating through the collector plate. This air or liquid, which is called the *heat transfer fluid,* can be either pumped or blown into the building. It carries the thermal heat generated by the solar radiation with it.

The Solar Collector Heating Cycle

If no heat is removed from the solar collector, it will eventually reach equilibrium with the outside air. As much heat will be lost as is gained. The collector will remain at a constant temperature despite the incoming solar radiation.

The solar collector must be made part of a system that moves the heat indoors. Figure 9.56 shows the simplest type of system that can be used. A duct from the top of the collector leads into the house at a point higher than the top of the collector. Another duct leads back into the collector from a point near the floor of the room.

When the sun heats up the collector, the air in the collector becomes lighter and rises into the house. It is replaced by cooler air entering into the bottom of the collector from the house. The cycle continues as long as the sun shines unless the temperature within the house reaches the temperature within the collector.

Figure 9.57 shows a similar system. But in this system a liquid is used to move the heat into the house. When a liquid is used, a device known as a *liquid-to-air heat exchanger* must be added to the system. A liquid-to-air heat exchanger is a device that transfers the heat in the liquid to air without mixing the air and the liquid. The automobile radiator is an example of a liquid-to-air heat exchanger that you are most likely familiar with. This heat exchanger looks and acts in the same manner as the radiator in your car. The pipes containing the liquid have fins attached to them. The fins are heated by the liquid in the pipes. Air passing over the fins cools

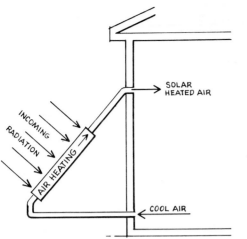

Figure 9.56. A simple air collector system.

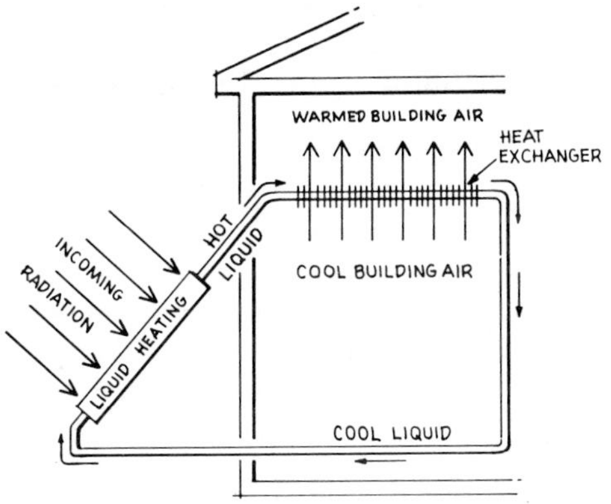

Figure 9.57. A simple liquid collector system.

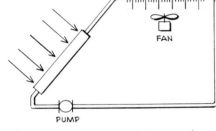

Figure 9.58. Pumps and fans can be added to the system to move the water or the air faster.

the fins while warming the air.

There are a number of ways to increase the efficiency of the two systems just described. More heat will be transferred if the liquid or the air is moved faster through the collector. Or, in the case of the liquid system, if the building air is moved across the fins of the heat exchanger faster.

In Figure 9.58 a pump has been added to the liquid side of the loop and a fan has been added to the air side. Of course, in Figure 9.56 a fan could be placed in the air duct to move the building air through the collector faster.

Systems that do not use fans or pumps are called *thermosyphon systems*. Thermosyphon systems are also known as passive solar systems because they use no external energy to run them. They operate purely on the principle that a hot gas or fluid weighs less than a cold gas or fluid and consequently will rise.

A thermosyphon system will only thermosyphon into the building when the hottest point in the system is within the building. So the collectors must be mounted lower than the ceiling of the room. This is not always possible. Many times the collectors must be mounted on the roof to catch the sun. In these cases, pumps and fans must be used to move the hot

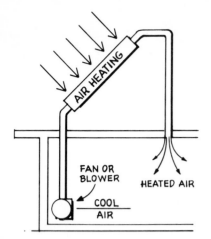

Figure 9.59. When the collector is higher than the building, a fan or blower must be used to push the lighter heated air into the building.

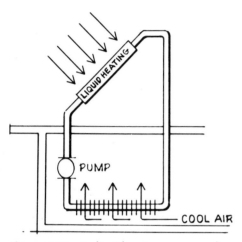

Figure 9.60. In liquid systems, a pump is required when the collector is higher than the building.

liquid or air from the collector into the building. Figure 9.59 shows this principle for an air system. Figure 9.60 shows it for a liquid system.

Some Typical Collection Systems

Figures 9.61 through 9.64 show four typical collection systems. None of the technical details are shown.

Figure 9.61 shows a typical sidewall thermosyphoning air collector. In this system several layers of an air-passing material, such as black painted aluminum screen wire, serve as the absorber plate. Double-strength window glass set in an aluminum or a wood framework serves as the glazing. The wall of the building and its thermal envelope act as the insulation. Vents with dampers over them are cut into the wall.

During the sunlight hours, the dampers are opened. The air in the collector is heated from the sun's radiation and rises into the building through the top vents. Cool air from the floor of the building is drawn into the collector to replace the heated air passing into the structure. The cycle will continue as long as the air in the collector is hotter than the air in the building. When the sun goes down, the dampers are closed to prevent the heated building air from going back outdoors.

Figure 9.62 shows a typical liquid-type thermosyphoning sidewall collector. In this system, copper absorber plates with integral liquid passages are mounted on the wall of the structure. The piping is joined together and led to a large radiant heating panel. This panel must be mounted near the ceiling and higher than the collector. The system is charged with a nonfreezing liquid. An expansion tank is placed in the system to handle fluid thermal expansion. A valve is placed in the lines so that the system may be turned on and off.

During the sunlight hours, the valve is opened. The hot liquid in the collectors rises into the radiant heating panel. The heat moves by convection and radiation off the surface of the panel into the room air. The cooled antifreeze sinks down the return pipe and goes back to the collector to be reheated. At night, or when no heat is desired, the valve is turned off and stops the flow of the liquid.

Figure 9.63 shows a roof-mounted forced-air system. The collectors in this system are higher than the area to be heated, so the system will not thermosyphon. A blower must be added to move the hot air out of the collector and into the building. A controller is required to tell the blower when to operate.

The controller contains two *temperature sensors.* A temperature sensor is a device that constantly reads the temperature at its location. An electronic measuring system, located within the controller, compares the temperature of the two sensors. One sensor is located at the top of the collector. The other is located in the room that is being heated. The controller turns the blower on when the sensor at the top of the collector is about 15 to 20°F hotter than the sensor in the room. The controller turns the blower off when the temperature of the collector drops down to about 5°F hotter than the room. The blower contains a damper that automatically closes when the blower is not running. This prevents the system from *reverse thermosyphoning,* which is the gravity movement of the hot building air back up to the collector. This would cool the room off during nonsunlight hours.

Figure 9.64 shows a liquid system that operates in a similar manner. In the liquid system, a pump replaces the blower. The automatic damper is replaced by a check valve. A radiant ceiling panel is added as a heat exchanger. The system's controller operates in the same fashion.

Many configurations of these basic systems are possible. The configura-

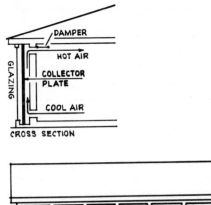

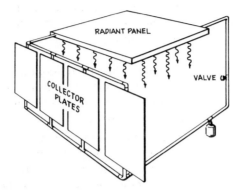

Figure 9.61. Typical sidewall thermo-syphoning air collector.

Figure 9.62. Typical liquid-type thermo-syphoning sidewall collector.

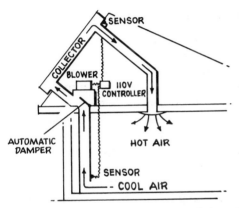

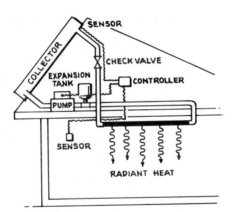

Figure 9.63. Typical roof-mounted forced-air system.

Figure 9.64. Typical roof-mounted pumped-liquid system.

tion will depend on what is right for the home. The sidewall systems may contain a pump and controller for better control and higher efficiency. The liquid heat exchanger may be a convection type exchanger. The exchanger may be located on the wall as well as on the ceiling. It may even be buried in the floor in some systems.

But the principles of the systems do not vary. The solar radiation is collected outside the thermal envelope, converted to thermal energy, and brought into the building through pipes or ductwork. Such a system does not lose heat back to the outdoors as does a fenestration. So the systems have considerable merit in the overall design of solar heat gain systems for both new and retrofitted buildings.

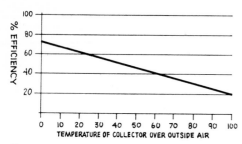

Figure 9.65. Typical efficiency curve for a solar collector.

$$\begin{array}{r} 85°F \text{ turn-on} \\ -\ 50°F \text{ air} \\ \hline = 35°F \end{array}$$

$$\begin{array}{r} 110°F \text{ turn-on} \\ -\ 50°F \text{ air} \\ \hline = 60°F \end{array}$$

$$\begin{array}{r} 85°F \text{ turn on} \\ -\ 30°F \text{ air} \\ \hline = 55°F \end{array}$$

$$\begin{array}{r} 105°F \text{ turn-on} \\ -\ 30°F \text{ air} \\ \hline = 75°F \end{array}$$

Solar Collector Efficiency

Most solar collectors are less efficient than most fenestrations in collecting solar heat. You can visualize this by examining the efficiency graph in Figure 9.65. When this collector is the same temperature as the outside air, it is about 72% efficient. But as the collector gets hotter than the outside air, its efficiency drops because there are more thermal losses out the glazing, the sides, and the back of the collector. This particular collector has only 20% efficiency when the collector is 100°F hotter than the outdoor air.

Assume that the outdoor air is 50°F and that the building temperature is 70°F. The system blower or pump will not operate until the collector is about 85°F. When the collector is at 85°F, it is 35°F hotter than the outside air. Its efficiency is about 55%.

On a hot, sunny day around noon, the air or liquid typically cannot be moved fast enough to keep the collector temperature that low. The collector temperature typically might rise to 110°F. So on a 50°F day the typical system efficiency with this collector is down to 40%.

On a 30°F day system turn-on still occurs at about 85°F, so the maximum efficiency that can be obtained would be about 43%. If the collector temperature rose to 105°F, its efficiency would drop to about 37% according to the graph shown for this collector.

The Collector Temperature Throughout the Day

Figure 9.66 shows what a typical collector temperature might be on a 50°F winter's day. From midnight to 7 A.M. the collector is at the temperature of the outside air. As the sun comes up, the collector starts to heat up. Around 9 A.M. it has reached 85°F. The blower or pump turns on. This causes a drop in temperature as the heat exchanger fluid circulates.

As the sun's radiation becomes stronger, the collector temperature continues to rise. It typically peaks out at about 11 A.M. and remains at this peak until about 1 P.M. During the afternoon the temperature gradually diminishes until around 3 P.M. Then the blower or pump turns off. The collector rises in temperature when the circulation of the fluid stops. But it does not rise high enough to turn the pump or fan back on. The collector cools down and at about 6 to 7 P.M. returns to the temperature of the outside air.

Some Additional Considerations

Solar heat gain either from fenestration or from solar collectors needs to be combined with heat storage devices in order for the systems to be highly efficient. The systems shown in this chapter do not include storage. Storage will be covered in Decision 10. In Decision 11 you will learn how to combine solar heat gain, solar storage, and heat distribution in order to build complete solar systems.

Making a Decision

In this chapter you learned how to collect your available solar energy efficiently. You learned that there were two ways to collect solar energy: through the use of fenestration devices and through the use of solar collectors. You learned that each method has advantages and disadvantages.

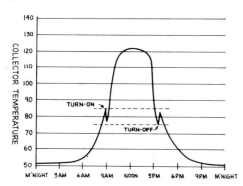

Figure 9.66. Typical collector temperature on a 50°F winter's day.

And you saw that a proper blend of both results in the most efficient energy collection.

You also learned that solar shades are needed to help prevent the gain of too much solar radiation in the summer months and that solar reflectors can be used to reflect additional energy into or away from the building.

You should now be able to decide where to use solar collection devices, where to use fenestration devices, and which device should be used for the application.

DECISION 10

Store the Collected Solar Energy

During the winter months the sun only shines about 8 hr/day in the northern half of the United States. Large amounts of solar energy can only be collected for about 6 hr/day—or from about 9 A.M. to 3 P.M. with a south-facing collector or fenestration. Six hours is only one-quarter of a day.

Many of the days are cloudy during the winter months. Perhaps as many as half of the days see cloudy weather in some locations. So in many locations, solar energy can only be collected for about one-eighth of the time that passes during the heating season. Yet the need for heat goes on 24 hr a day throughout the season. And the need tends to be the greatest when the sun is not shining because that is when the temperature is the lowest.

The available solar energy is often more than is needed at the time that it is available. As a result, it cannot be used effectively unless it is stored for future use.

These facts lead to the simple conclusion that solar energy storage is vital in a solar heating system and that storage must be an integral part of the solar design.

In this chapter you will study how to store the collected solar energy. You will learn about:

* The daily availability of solar energy from season to season and for different compass orientations.
* The thermal energy requirements of buildings and how they relate to the building's thermal mass, the insulation envelope, and the materials from which the building is constructed.
* How thermal mass and building heat loss relate to thermal conductivity and specific heat.

Last, you will learn how solar heat storage units operate. You will study concrete and stone storage, liquid storage, and phase-change media storage.

When you have finished this chapter, you will have learned how to decide what solar storage system is best for your use.

The Availability of Solar Energy

Figure 10.1 shows the solar heat gain factors by the hour for a south-facing fenestration in Lincoln, Nebraska at 40°N latitude during the heating season. Examination of this table shows that 90% of the heat gain comes between the hours of 9 A.M. and 3 P.M., with 71% of the total daily heat gain coming between 10 A.M. and 2 P.M. On a clear, cloudless day, the majority of the heat gain occurs during a 4- to 6-hr period in the middle of the day.

TIME OF DAY	NOV	DEC	JAN	FEB	MAR	AVER-AGE	9 A.M.-3 P.M.	10 A.M.-2 P.M.
7 A.M.	0	0	0	14	22	7	—	—
8 A.M.	72	50	75	94	74	73	—	—
9 A.M.	156	151	160	157	128	150	150	—
10 A.M.	209	210	213	203	171	201	201	201
11 A.M.	240	242	244	231	197	231	231	231
12 noon	250	253	254	241	206	241	241	241
1 P.M.	240	242	244	231	197	231	231	231
2 P.M.	209	210	213	203	171	201	201	201
3 P.M.	156	151	160	157	128	150	150	—
4 P.M.	72	50	75	94	74	73	—	—
5 P.M.	0	0	0	14	22	7	—	—
Total average radiation						1565	1405	1105
Percent total during selected hours							90%	71%

Figure 10.1. The hourly solar heat gain factors for 40°N latitude south-facing windows show that most solar heat gain occurs in a 6 to 8 hr period.

Figure 3.9 shows that the south-facing vertical incident solar in Lincoln, Nebraska, at 41°N latitude is 18.95 MMBtu during the heating season. That is 47% of the annual radiation striking a south-facing vertical square foot of surface in that location.

Figure 3.9 shows that a southeast- or southwest-facing vertical square foot of area in Lincoln, Nebraska, receives 15.65 MMBtu of energy during the heating season. That is 39% of the total radiation striking a surface oriented in those directions.

Figure 3.9 also shows that a horizontal square foot of surface in Lincoln, Nebraska, receives 13.03 MMBtu during the heating season. That is 26% of the total radiation striking a horizontal surface.

So the availability of solar energy for heating purposes in Lincoln, Nebraska, is from about 25 to about 50% of the total annual radiation depending on the tilt angle and the compass orientation of the fenestration or the collector. Ninety percent of that energy falls during the 6-hr period from 9 A.M. to 3 P.M.

You can make this calculation for any area in the country using the tables in Decision 3. And you can make it for any time of the year by month or by season. Knowing solar energy availability sets the stage for designing your building to benefit from its use.

A Building's Thermal Energy Requirements

You must study some basic thermal properties of construction materials in order to understand a building's thermal energy requirements. It is not enough to know only the rate at which the building gains or loses heat.

- First, you must understand how much heat it takes to raise or lower the temperature of a given volume of a given building material. This amount of heat will vary from material to material.

- Second, you must understand how fast a material soaks up or gives off heat. Again this will vary from material to material.
- Third, you must be able to estimate how much of each material is used in the building so that you can estimate how much thermal energy it will take to heat or cool the entire structure, not just the air within it.

The entire thermal mass of the building within the insulation envelope must be heated or cooled to be comfortable. How much energy is needed to do this is a function of the building's mass, its materials of construction, and the difference between the indoor and the outdoor temperature.

The Heat Required to Change the Temperature of a Material

Figure 10.2 shows two basic properties of five common materials used in building construction: *density* and *specific heat*. Density is defined as the mass of a substance per unit of volume. In the English system of measurement, the density of a material is the weight of 1 cu ft of that material.

Specific heat is defined as the amount of heat required to raise one weight-unit of a material by one degree in temperature. In the English system of measurement, the specific heat of a material is the number of Btu required to raise the temperature of 1 lb of a substance by 1°F. You will remember from Decision 4 that a Btu is the amount of energy required to raise the temperature of 1 lb of water by 1°F.

MATERIAL	DENSITY LB/CU FT	SPECIFIC HEAT BTU/LB/°F
Water	62.3	1
Air	0.075	0.24
Concrete	140	0.21
Softwoods	32	0.33
Gypsum board	50	0.29

Figure 10.2. Typical densities and specific heats for five common building materials.

You can calculate and understand some important relationships between common building materials by using density and specific heat. Figure 10.3 shows four common relationships that you need to know.

MATERIAL	DENSITY LB/CU FT	SPECIFIC GRAVITY	SPECIFIC HEAT BTU/LB/°F	HEAT CAPACITY BTU/CU FT	RELATIVE HEAT CAPACITY	RELATIVE VOLUMES
Water	62.3	1	1	62.3	1	1
Air	0.075	0.0012	0.24	0.018	0.00029	3448
Concrete	140	2.25	0.21	29.4	0.47	2.13
Softwoods	32	0.51	0.33	10.56	0.17	5.88
Gypsum board	50	0.80	0.29	14.5	0.23	4.35

Figure 10.3. Some important heat relationships between common building materials.

In Figure 10.3, all substances have been compared to water as a standard. First, look at the column labeled *specific gravity*. Specific gravity is a measure of a material's relative density as compared to water. For example, water weighs about 62.3 lb/cu ft whereas concrete weighs about 140 lb/cu ft. So relatively speaking, concrete is about 2.25 times as dense as water. This was determined by dividing the weight of a cubic foot of water into the weight of a cubic foot of concrete.

Look at the column headed *heat capacity*. The heat capacity of a material is defined as the amount of heat required to raise one unit mass of the material by one degree. The heat capacity of a material is determined by multiplying its density by its specific heat. For example, the specific heat of a softwood is typically 0.33 whereas its density is typically 32 lb/cu ft. So its heat capacity is typically about 10.56 Btu/cu ft.

Now that the heat capacity has been determined for these common building materials, a *relative heat capacity* can be described. Relative heat capacity is defined, by the author, as the amount of heat required to raise a volume of material 1°F compared to the amount of heat required to raise the same volume of water by 1°F. For example, it takes 62.3 Btu to raise the temperature of water 1°F and it takes 14.5 Btu to raise the temperature of gypsum board by 1°F. So the relative heat capacity of gypsum board is 0.23. This was established by dividing the number of Btu needed to raise the temperature of 1 cu ft of water 1°F into the number of Btu required to raise the temperature of 1 cu ft of gypsum board by 1°F.

Now that you know the relative heat capacity, you can describe the relative volumes of materials that require the same amount of heat to raise their temperatures by 1°F. This is done by dividing the relative volume heat into 1, which is the relative volume heat of water. For example, 1 divided by 0.00029, the relative volume heat for air, gives the figure 3448. This tells you that the amount of heat that would raise one volume of water by 1°F would also raise 3448 volumes of air by 1°F.

Why is this important? Suppose that you had 1 cu ft of water in a solar storage unit and 3448 cu ft of air in the building. To increase the temperature of that air by 1°F, the water in storage will have to lose 1°F. If you had 34,480 cu ft of air in the building, the water would have to lose 10°F in temperature to raise the temperature of the air by 1°F.

Now suppose that you wanted to store heat in a building material for later use. If it took 1 cu ft of water to store that heat, then for the same temperature loss you would need 2.13 times the volume of concrete for storage or 5.88 times the volume of a softwood for storage.

Rate of Heat Gain or Loss

The movement of heat through a solid takes place by conduction. The unit of measurement that describes the rate of conduction through a solid is called *thermal conductivity*. The thermal conductivity of a material in the English system of measurement is the number of Btu that will pass in 1 hr through a 1-in. thickness of the material that is 1 sq ft in area and that has a temperature difference of 1°F between its two sides. Figure 10.4 illustrates thermal conductivity.

Figure 10.5 shows the thermal conductivity of various building materials. You will see that heat passes quickly through concrete, sand, and stone, that it passes fairly quickly through brick and stucco, but that it passes slowly through plywood and softwoods, and that it passes very slowly through insulating materials such as shavings and polystyrene.

A *relative thermal conductivity* value, also shown in Figure 10.5, can be calculated for these materials. Relative thermal conductivity, again a term coined by the author, is the amount of heat that will pass through any substance compared to the amount of heat passing through plywood or softwood under the same conditions. Relative thermal conductivity is calculated as follows:

$$\frac{\text{Thermal conductivity of a substance}}{\text{Thermal conductivity of softwood}} = \text{relative thermal conductivity}$$

```
    0.33  Btu/lb/cu ft
  × 32    lb/cu ft
  = 10.56 Btu/cu ft
```

```
    14.5  Btu/cu ft
  ÷ 62.3  Btu/cu ft
  = 0.23  relative heat capacity
```

```
        1
  ÷ 0.00029
  =    3448  relative volume heat of air
```

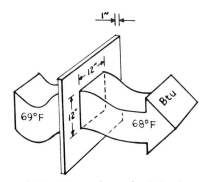

Figure 10.4. Thermal conductivity is measured in Btu/hr/sq ft/°F through 1 in. of a material's thickness.

MATERIAL	THERMAL CONDUCTIVITY	RELATIVE THERMAL CONDUCTIVITY
Common brick	5	6.3
Concrete	12	15
Gypsum plaster	5.5	6.9
Sand	12.5	15.6
Stone	12.5	15.6
Stucco	5	6.3
Plywood	0.8	1
Shavings	0.45	0.56
Softwoods	0.8	1
Polystyrene insulation	0.20	0.25

Figure 10.5. Thermal conductivity of some common building materials.

$$\frac{1}{k} + \frac{1}{k} + \frac{1}{k} + \quad \cdots \quad \frac{1}{k} = \frac{1}{C}$$

$$\frac{1}{12} + \frac{1}{12} + \frac{1}{12} + \frac{1}{12} + \frac{1}{12} = \frac{1}{C} ;$$

$$\frac{1}{C} = \frac{5}{12} ; \qquad C = 2.4$$

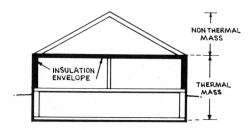

Figure 10.6. Everything that is part of, or within, the insulation envelope is considered thermal mass.

```
   48' 8"  length
×   7' 2"  height
×  23' 8"  width
= 8301.5 cu ft
```

You must also understand the term *thermal conductance*. Thermal conductance is similar to thermal conductivity except that thermal conductance values are calculated for the thickness of the material commonly used rather than for 1 in. of thickness.

Thermal conductivity is represented by the letter k in thermodynamic calculations. Thermal conductance is represented by the letter C. To obtain the thermal conductance, or C, of a given thickness of a substance, the reciprocals of the thermal conductivity must be added together like this:

For example, given the thermal conductivity of concrete at 12, what is the thermal conductance of a 5-in. thick section?

Appendix B contains a more detailed description of deriving thermal conductances and their associated factors.

Now that you understand these important facts about heat and heat capacity, you will study a concept known as thermal mass.

The Building's Thermal Mass

A building's *thermal mass* is the heat capacity of everything in the building that must be heated or cooled. Everything that lies inside the insulation envelope is part of the thermal mass. This includes the building's materials, the building's contents, and the building's air.

Materials that lie outside the insulation envelope are not considered part of the thermal mass because they do not have to be heated or cooled to contribute to the structure's comfort. Figure 10.6 shows an example of what is, and what is not, part of the building's thermal mass in a typical residence. The roof structure lies outside the insulation envelope so it is not part of the thermal mass in this illustration. Everything else is. If the ceiling insulation were to be moved up between the roof rafters, then the roof structure would become part of the building's thermal mass.

The amount of heat that is needed to raise or lower the temperature of the building's thermal mass is a function of the type of materials, the volume of each material, and the heat capacity of each material.

Calculating the Building's Thermal Mass

Figure 10.7 shows a 25 ft by 50 ft by 8 ft flat-roof building with 8-in. concrete walls, floors, and roof. The concrete is also the insulation envelope.

To calculate the thermal mass of this building, proceed as follows:

• Calculate the amount of air in the building by multiplying the inside height by the inside length by the inside width. The building contains about 8302 cu ft of air.

- Multiply the cubic feet of air by the heat capacity of air. The heat capacity of the building's air is 149.4 Btu/°F.
- Calculate the volume of concrete in the floor and the ceiling. Multiply the length times the width times the thickness and double it to include both the floor and the ceiling. The floor and the ceiling together contain 1675 cu ft of concrete.
- Calculate the volume of concrete in the walls. Add up the running feet of wall. Multiply the total by the height to obtain the square feet of wall. Multiply the square feet of wall by the thickness to obtain the cubic feet of concrete. The walls contain 700 cu ft of concrete.
- Total the volume of concrete in the roof, walls, and floor. The building contains 2375 cu ft of concrete.
- Multiply the volume of concrete by the heat capacity of concrete. The heat capacity of the concrete in the building is 69,825 Btu/°F.
- Add the heat capacity for the air in the house to the heat capacity for the concrete in the house to obtain the heat capacity for the total thermal mass of the structure. The thermal mass, or the heat capacity, of the structure is 69,974 Btu/°F.

To heat or cool this building by 1°F would require 69,974 Btu provided that it had no heat loss to the outside air during the time that it was being heated or cooled. However, your previous studies taught you that the building was constantly gaining or losing heat if the indoor and the outdoor temperatures were different. You also learned that the rate of loss followed the formula: $UA\Delta t$ = heat loss, where:

$$U = U\text{-factor}$$
$$A = \text{area}$$
$$\Delta t = \text{difference in temperature}$$

Assume that the indoor temperature is 65°F, that the outdoor temperature is 50°F, that the U-factor is 1.5 Btu/hr/sq ft/°F for the walls, floor, and ceiling and that the area of the outside of the building is 3700 sq ft.

Under these conditions, the building is losing 83,250 Btu/hr. So you need to supply 83,250 Btu/hr just to maintain the building at 65°F.

```
 3700  sq ft
× 1.5  Btu/hr/sq ft/°F
 5550  UA
×  15  Δt
= 83,250  Btu/hr
```

Now suppose that you want to increase the temperature of the building to 70°F over a period of 1 hr. The thermal mass of the building is 69,974 Btu. That is the amount of energy that is needed to heat the building by 1°F. So 349,870 Btu is required to raise the temperature of the building by 5°F.

```
 69,974  Btu
×     5  Δt
= 349,870  Btu
```

But during that 1 hr the building will lose 5500 Btu times the average temperature difference of 17.5°F. That is 96,250 Btu. So a total of 446,120 Btu will be needed to heat the building to 70°F in 1 hr.

```
  5500  Btu            349,870  Btu
× 17.5  Δt           +  96,250  Btu
= 96,250  Btu        = 446,120  Btu
```

```
   8302  cu ft
× 0.018  heat capacity
= 149.4  Btu
```

```
    50'  length
×   25'  width
× 0.67'  thickness
×    2   floor and ceiling
= 1675.0  cu ft
```

```
     50
  +  50
  +  23
  +  23
    146  lineal ft
× 7' 2"  height
1045.36  sq ft
× 0.67   thickness
= 700.4  cu ft
```

```
   1675  cu ft
+   700  cu ft
   2375  cu ft
```

```
   2375  cu ft
× 29.4
= 69,825  Btu/°F
```

```
    149  Btu for air
+ 69,825  Btu for concrete
= 69,974  thermal mass in Btu/°F
```

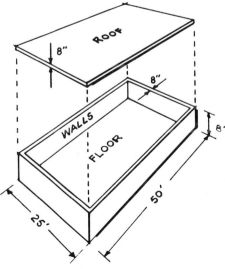

Figure 10.7. Flat-roof concrete building for the problem of calculating thermal mass.

```
  3700  sq ft              3.5  lb
× 0.167  ft thick        × 0.29  Btu/lb
= 618  cu ft             = 1.02  Btu/cu ft/°F


    618  cu ft                69,974
  × 1.02  Btu/cu ft/°F       +    630
  = 630.36  Btu              = 70,604


      10                         1
    + 0.67                   ÷ 10.67
  = 10.67  R-value          = 0.094  U-factor


         3700  sq ft
       × 0.094
         347.8  Btu/°F
        × 17.5  Δt
        = 6086.5  Btu/hr


70,604  thermal mass     353,020  Btu
    × 5  Δt              +   6,087  Btu
= 353,020  Btu          = 359,107  Btu


      446,120  Btu
    − 359,107  Btu
    =  87,013  Btu


      3700  sq ft
    × 0.1  U-factor
      370  Btu/hr/°F
     × 10  °F
    = 3700  Btu/hr


      3700  Btu/hr
    ÷ 630  Btu
    = 5.87  °F
```

The Effect of Insulation

If a 2-in. layer of polystyrene insulation were fastened to the outside of the building, then the heat loss rate would go down, the thermal mass would increase, and fewer Btu would be needed. Here are the calculations:

Volume of polystyrene = 618 cu ft
Weight of polystyrene = 3.5 lb/cu ft
Specific heat of polystyrene = 0.29 Btu/lb/°F
Unit volume heat = 1.02 Btu/cu ft/°F
Thermal mass of polystyrene = 630 Btu
The new thermal mass of the building is equal to 70,281 Btu.

The R-value of 2-in. polystyrene = 10. The R-value of 8-in. concrete = 0.67. The total R-value of the building's skin now becomes 10.67. The U-factor of the skin is 0.094. The hourly heat loss is about 6087 Btu.

The heat required to raise the building's temperature by 5°F is 353,020 Btu. The total heat required to raise the building's temperature by 5°F when the heat loss is included is 359,107 Btu. You will recall that the uninsulated building required 446,120 Btu to heat it 5°F. So with the insulation added, 87,013 Btu are saved.

Insulation lowers the amount of heat lost in a given time period. Maintaining the uninsulated building at a constant temperature requires 5500 Btu/hr/degree difference in temperature between the inside and the outside of the building. Maintaining the insulated building at a constant temperature only requires 348 Btu/hr/of temperature difference, or only 6% as much energy.

The Effect of High Thermal Mass

Another important fact about thermal mass must be taken into consideration. The higher the thermal mass of a building with a given rate of heat loss, or UA, the longer it will take for the building to heat up or cool down.

The insulated building had a thermal mass of 70,604 Btu. It lost 348 Btu/hr. If the difference in temperature were 10°F, the building would lose 3480 Btu in the first hour. That heat loss would only cool the building down by 0.05°F.

If the building were built of only polystyrene insulation and the concrete were eliminated, then the thermal mass of the building would drop to 630 Btu. The U-factor would be 0.1. The hourly heat loss would be 3700 Btu/hr when a 10°F temperature difference existed. The temperature of this building would drop by 5.87°F during the first hour.

The Building Is the Primary Solar Storage Device

The calculations that you just studied should have taught you a very important formula:

$$\frac{\text{Heat loss}}{\text{Thermal mass}} = \text{change in building temperature}$$

This formula leads you to four very important conclusions about buildings.

- A high thermal mass building with a low heat loss rate is an excellent heat-storage building.
- A low thermal mass building with a high heat loss rate is a very poor heat-storage building.

- If you lower the heat loss rate of a building or if you increase its thermal mass, the building will heat up or cool off more slowly.
- If you increase the heat loss rate of a building or if you decrease its thermal mass, the building will heat up or cool off more rapidly.

Your first step in designing buildings to store solar energy is to lower the heat losses through the insulation envelope to the lowest practical level considering the economics of building or remodeling the building.

Your second step is to add thermal mass to your building. That thermal mass must be located inside the insulation envelope of the building. If any storage is outside the insulation envelope, that storage device must be insulated and connected to the inside of the insulation envelope.

General Considerations

There are many things to be considered when you decide to add thermal mass. You must ask yourself:

- Is the structure strong enough to support the added weight?
- Can the solar energy be brought to the thermal mass easily?
- Will the thermal mass give off and pick up heat quickly so that it is instantly available?
- Can the thermal mass be insulated away from the rest of the building so that it can be heated to a higher temperature than the remainder of the building?
- Does the thermal mass need to be contained and protected? Water or other liquids can damage a building or its contents. Salts and other phase-change media may be corrosive or odor-causing.
- How much room is available for the thermal mass?
- Are there space trade-offs to be considered for a given amount of mass?

Doubtless many other questions will occur to you as you study adding thermal mass in order to achieve good solar energy storage.

Heat Storage Mechanisms

Heat can be stored in solids, in liquids, and in solar *phase-change* materials. A solar phase-change material is a material that changes phase, passing from a solid to a liquid or from a liquid to a gas, in the temperature range that solar storage devices normally see.

Phase-change Storage

All substances exist in three physical phases: solid, liquid, and gas. The physical phase that a material is in at any given time depends on the nature of the material, the temperature of the material, and the pressure exerted on the material. As an example, water is a solid at atmospheric pressure below 32°F. From 32° to 212°F, it is a liquid. Above 212°F, it becomes a gas.

Large amounts of energy must be used to make a material change phase. Water again provides an excellent example. It takes 144 Btu to change 1 lb of ice to water. But the material does not change in temperature. It remains at 32°F. Once the ice has melted, the addition of another 144 Btu of energy would raise the temperature of water to 176°F.

The heat that is required to make a material change from a solid to a liquid, or from a liquid to a solid, is called the *heat of fusion*. Every substance has its own unique heat of fusion.

The same phenomenon occurs when a material changes from a liquid to a gas. Water, under atmospheric pressure, changes to a gas at 212°F. It requires the addition of 970 Btu/lb to make this change. This heat is known as the *heat of vaporization*. Steam condensing to water gives up that same 970 Btu/lb. Again, every substance has its own unique heat of vaporization.

Changing the pressure that a material is under changes the temperature at which a material changes phase. But in solar storage devices, the pressures are close enough to atmospheric pressure so that pressure changes can be ignored.

If water changed from a solid to a liquid at about room temperature or slightly above it, then 144 Btu of heat energy could be stored in, or released from, 1 lb of water without changing its temperature. That would be very useful because very little water would be needed to provide large amounts of storage.

Unfortunately, this is not the case. But as you will see, there are materials that do change phase around room temperature. And they do make excellent phase-changing storage materials by using the material's heat of fusion.

At the present time, materials that change from liquids to gases are not generally used in solar storage devices. These materials would use the heat of vaporization. However, in solar collector loops, heat of vaporization materials are often used to help collect and transport the sun's energy.

Specific Heat Storage

You learned earlier that it took energy to raise or lower the temperature of a substance. You learned that the amount of heat needed depended on what the substance was. And you learned that the amount of heat needed to change the temperature of 1 lb of the material by 1°F was called its specific heat.

Heat can be stored by raising the temperature of a substance. That substance can be a solid, a liquid, or a gas. It makes no difference. Typically, the specific heat of a substance is less than its heat of fusion or its heat of vaporization, so more of a substance is required to store the same amount of heat if it does not go through a phase change.

Heat Storage in Solids

A solid substance that would make a good heat storage media would have to have high density, high specific heat, and high thermal conductivity. Such a material would store large amounts of energy in a small space and pick up and release heat quickly. Figure 10.8 shows the common solid materials used for solar heat storage. All of these materials are most satisfactory. Concrete, filled concrete block, stone, and sand appear to be about the best. Brick, stucco, and plaster also appear to be very acceptable.

Solid substances have several distinct advantages over liquid materials as storage media. They are noncorrosive. They neither freeze nor boil. Heat can be added or removed from them without using a heat exchanger. And they can be part of the building's structural walls, roofs, or floors. This allows them to serve a dual purpose economically.

MATERIAL	DENSITY	SPECIFIC HEAT	THERMAL CONDUCTIVITY
Common brick	123	0.20	5
Concrete*	140	0.22	12
Filled concrete block*	110	0.20	12
Gypsum plaster*	105	0.20	5.5
Sand	95	0.19	12.5
Stone	95	0.19	12.5
Stucco	116	0.22	5

Figure 10.8. Common solids used for solar heat storage.

*When using sand and stone aggregate.

Exterior Walls

A vertical wall solar collector can easily be added to the side of a building. Figure 10.9 shows such an addition. Vents are cut through the insulation envelope. During the sunlight hours, the air in the house circulates through the collector for heating. When there is no sun, the vents are closed and no appreciable heat is gained or lost. This is the commonest and the simplest wall collection system.

Figure 10.10 goes one step further. It replaces the insulation envelope on the wall with a concrete or filled concrete block wall. As previously noted, such a wall will quickly absorb much heat. This is called a *Trombe* wall.

In this system, the house air is heated in the collector. The thermal mass of the concrete is heated also. By late afternoon the concrete can reach temperatures of 85 to 95°F. After the sun goes down, the wall continues to radiate heat. Some of the radiation goes back out of the glazing and heat is lost by conduction through the glass. But much of the radiation enters the building if the wall is properly designed and coated.

If such a wall were 10 ft wide by 8 ft high by 8 in. thick, then the wall would have a volume of 53.3 cu ft. Concrete has a unit volume heat of 29.4 Btu/cu ft. So if the wall were heated by the sun to 90°F and if the room were kept at 65°F, then the wall would have stored 39,175 Btu.

$$
\begin{array}{rl}
10 & \text{ft} \\
\times\ 8 & \text{ft} \\
\hline
80 & \text{sq ft} \\
\times\ 0.67 & \text{ft} \\
\hline
=\ 53.3 & \text{cu ft} \\
\\
29.4 & \text{Btu/cu ft} \\
\times\ 53.3 & \text{cu ft} \\
\hline
1567 & \text{Btu/°F} \\
\times\ 25 & \Delta t\text{°F} \\
\hline
=\ 39,175 & \text{Btu stored}
\end{array}
$$

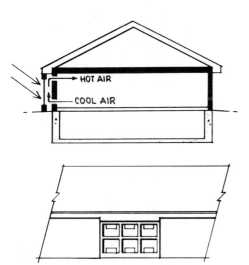

Figure 10.9. A solar collector added to a thermal envelope wall.

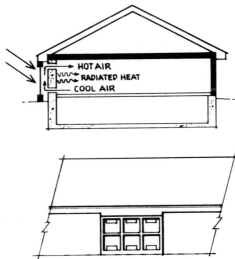

Figure 10.10. A solar collector added to an exterior storage wall.

$$
\begin{array}{rl}
10 & \text{ft} \\
\times\ 14 & \text{ft} \\
\hline
140 & \text{sq ft} \\
\times\ 0.67 & \text{ft} \\
\hline
93.8 & \text{cu ft} \\
\times\ 29.4 & \text{Btu/cu ft} \\
\hline
2758 & \text{Btu/°F} \\
\times\ 25 & \Delta t\text{°F} \\
\hline
= 68{,}950 & \text{Btu stored}
\end{array}
$$

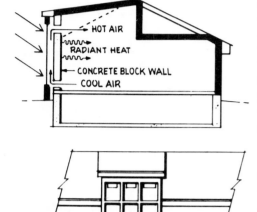

Figure 10.11. A shed dormer solar collector plus exterior storage wall.

Much of this stored energy will enter the house and help to heat it after the sun goes down.

In Figure 10.11 a shed dormer has been added and the insulation envelope of the ceiling has been changed so that a much larger collector and storage wall can be added. Suppose that this wall were 14 ft high. Then it would contain 93.8 cu ft of concrete. Under the same conditions, it would store 68,950 Btu.

Where the Stored Heat Goes

A concrete storage wall such as the walls in Figures 10.10 and 10.11 should be painted black on the glazing side so that it will absorb high amounts of solar energy. It should be painted white on the inside so that it will radiate high amounts of thermal energy to the room. Such a wall will transfer energy into the room at about 2 Btu/hr/sq ft/°F. It will lose energy to the air space next to the glazing at a rate of about 1.25 to 1.5 Btu/hr/sq ft/°F because the black wall has a lower *emissivity* and because less convection should take place in the confined air space of the collector. Emissivity is the capacity of the surface of a material to emit radiant energy. Figure 10.12 illustrates the relative heat transfer.

The glazing system can be designed to further limit the loss of energy to the outdoors by choosing a glazing system that has a U-factor lower than the heat loss of the wall. If a double-glazed window were used that had a U-factor of 0.6 Btu/hr/sq ft/°F, then the storage wall would lose 0.6 Btu/hr/sq ft/°F as shown in Figure 10.13.

How much energy goes where is also a function of the temperature differentials between the wall and the outside air and the wall and the inside air.

Assume that the outside air is 40°F, that the indoor temperature is 70°F, that the wall is 90°F, and that the area of the wall is 80 sq ft. Under these

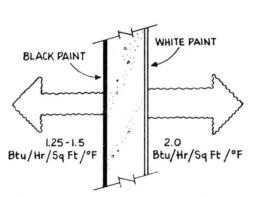

Figure 10.12. A properly designed concrete storage wall will transfer about this much energy.

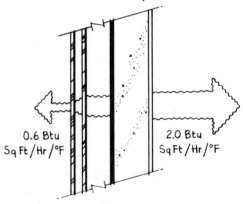

Figure 10.13. Low-loss glazing limits the storage loss to the outdoors.

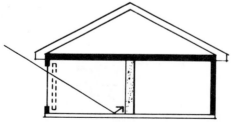

Figure 10.14. This interior storage wall receives no direct solar radiation, so it cannot be heated hotter than the room air.

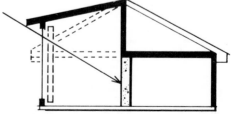

Figure 10.15. This interior storage wall receives direct solar radiation, so it can be heated hotter than the room air.

conditions, the double-glazed collector storage wall will lose 2400 Btu/hr to the outdoors and 3200 Btu/hr to the home's interior.

This is a total loss of 5600 Btu/hr of which 57% of the energy is entering the home. It would take about 6 to 7 hr for the wall in Figure 10.10 to cool down to room temperature. (An exact time estimate would require a more involved calculation because the heat loss rate would decrease as the wall cooled and the temperature difference changed.) So on a 40°F day, the wall would be about 57% efficient. On a warmer day, it would be more efficient. On a cooler day, it would be less efficient assuming that the indoor temperature remained the same for both days.

Interior Walls

Interior walls can also be used for heat storage. The same materials of construction should be chosen. However, an additional problem exists with an interior wall. That problem is the problem of the heating of an interior wall to a temperature hotter than the air temperature desired in the home.

Figure 10.14 illustrates why this is a problem. The interior wall shown is about 12 ft inside the home's perimeter. So only reflected radiation can reach it. Most flooring materials have poor reflectance. In a configuration of this type, the only heat that the wall will receive is from the building's air. So unless the building's air is heated to 85 to 95°F, not much heat can be stored.

Figure 10.15 shows one way to overcome this problem. A shed dormer has been added and the building's insulation envelope has been relocated so that the sun can shine directly on an 8-ft high storage wall. Much of the heat will rise to the top of the dormer and must be mechanically circulated through the house.

Figure 10.16 shows a clerestory design that allows the heating of a 12- to-14-ft high storage wall. In this particular case, the insulation envelope of the entire ceiling area has been relocated at the roofline in order to use the heat storage wall on both sides to its fullest extent.

In Figure 10.17 a different approach has been used. Solar collectors rather than fenestration devices have been used to bring the sun's energy indoors. A radiant heating panel is mounted on the inside of the exterior wall. Thermal energy is radiated through the air without heating it. When the radiant energy strikes a solid surface, it heats that surface hotter than the surrounding air. The radiant energy from the panel heats the walls, floors, and ceiling. Some convection heat exchange takes place also and the air in the room is heated.

A wall-mounted, properly coated metal radiant heating panel has a combined convection and radiant heat transfer of about 2 Btu/hr/sq ft/°F.

	0.6	U-factor
×	50	Δt°F
	30	Btu/hr/sq ft/°F
×	80	sq ft
=	2400	Btu/hr lost outside

	2.0	Btu/sq ft/°F
×	20	Δt
	40	Btu/hr/sq ft
×	80	sq ft
=	3200	Btu/hr gained inside

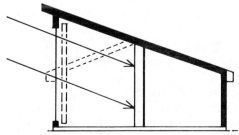

Figure 10.16. This building has a clerestory designed for receiving high amounts of solar radiation on the interior storage wall.

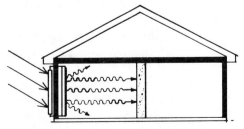

Figure 10.17. This building uses a solar collector plus a wall radiant heating panel to heat the interior storage wall.

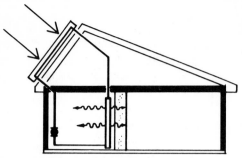

Figure 10.18. This building uses a solar collector plus a wall radiant heating panel mounted on the interior storage wall.

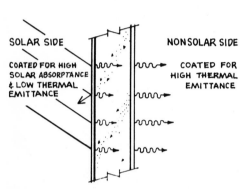

Figure 10.19. An exterior storage wall should be coated with a high solar absorptance/low thermal emittance coating on the solar side and a high thermal emittance coating on the nonsolar side.

Figure 10.20. Typical solar absorptance and thermal emittance values for various surfaces.

Radiant energy at the wavelength of thermal energy drops off rapidly with distance so an alternative approach that provides more energy for the storage wall is shown in Figure 10.18. Here the radiant heating panel has been mounted against the storage wall. About 1.5 Btu/hr/sq ft/°F of thermal energy is passed into the wall from the back of the panel. About 2.0 Btu/hr/sq ft/°F is passed from the front of the panel into the room through convection and radiation. Roof collectors have been used here in a pumped-liquid system. Wall collectors could also be used.

It would also be possible to bury pipes in the center of the wall. These would heat up the wall by conduction. In this case, all the heat collected would be stored. None would be convected to the building's air.

Wall Surface Coatings

Storage walls of concrete or filled concrete block should be treated so that the *absorptance* of solar energy on the solar side is as high as possible, so that the *emittance* of the solar side is as low as possible, and so that the emittance of the interior side is as high as possible.

An exterior concrete storage wall must be designed to absorb the maximum amount of solar radiation on its exterior face. It should be treated to emit the maximum amount of radiation on its interior face. Figure 10.19 illustrates this.

Figure 10.20 shows some typical solar absorptances and thermal emittances for various substances and paint coatings. A bare concrete wall would absorb about 60% of the solar radiation striking it. If the wall were painted with a dull, flat black paint, it would absorb about 94% of the solar radiation striking it. Its thermal emittance would be only slightly affected by painting it.

SUBSTANCE	SOLAR ABSORPTANCE	THERMAL EMITTANCE
Concrete	0.60	0.88
Red brick	0.55	0.92
Dry sand	0.82	0.90
Wet sand	0.91	0.95
Granite stone	0.55	0.44
Black paint	0.94	0.90
Gray paint	0.75	0.90
Red paint	0.74	0.90
Brown paint	0.75	0.90
Green paint	0.50	0.90
White paint	0.25	0.90
Brass, copper, aluminum, galvanized steel, iron	0.4-0.65	0.20-0.30

Other colors could be chosen. Most dark colors would increase the absorptance of the bare concrete. But light colors, such as white or green, would lower the wall's absorptance. In all cases, the thermal emittance would be only slightly affected.

The thermal emittance from the nonsolar side of the wall is also little affected by surface coatings of paint. The interior wall could be painted or left bare at the owner's option.

An interior solar storage wall that receives direct solar radiation should have its solar side treated in the same manner as the exterior wall. An interior wall that is heated by thermal radiant energy can be treated in the same manner as the nonheated side without hurting the wall's thermal performance.

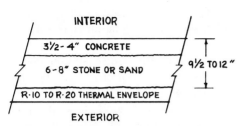

Figure 10.21. Typical thermal storage floor for a building.

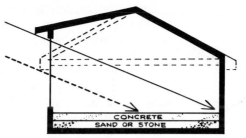

Figure 10.22. The amount of solar energy striking a storage floor depends on the height of the roofline when fenestration is used.

Note that the table in Figure 10.20 also shows solar absorptance and thermal emittance values for metal surfaces. These were included for comparison. Surface coatings are extremely important on metal surfaces if performance is to be maximized.

Floors

Concrete, sand, stone, and brick also make excellent heat storage floors. A typical storage floor is illustrated in Figure 10.21. Its storage capacity can be calculated using the formula: $UA\Delta t$ = heat gain (or loss).

Only 3½ to 4 in. of concrete are needed for strength in most residences. Sand and/or stone can be used under the concrete to provide more storage volume economically. When storage floors are located against the ground, the insulation envelope of the house could run under the storage floor. An unheated thermal storage floor of the type shown loses about 1 Btu/hr/sq ft/°F if it is uninsulated. About R-10 to R-20 insulation is generally satisfactory except in extremely cold climates. The edge of the thermal storage floor *must* be insulated in the same manner to prevent excessive heat loss around the floor's perimeter.

The amount of solar radiation that strikes a storage floor is again a function of the height of the fenestration as well as the width. Figure 10.22 shows the relative difference when a shed dormer is added to the building.

It is also possible to heat the storage floor by using a radiant ceiling panel and liquid-type wall solar panels as shown in Figure 10.23. Or a pumped-liquid system with roof collectors and pipes buried in the sand could be used. Such a system is shown in Figure 10.24.

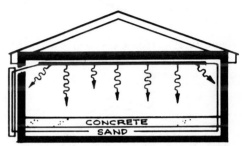

Figure 10.23. A liquid wall or roof collector system can be used to radiate thermal energy to a concrete/sand storage floor.

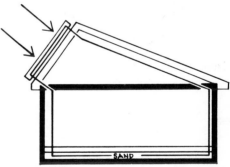

Figure 10.24. A liquid wall or roof collector system can be used with pipes buried in the sand or concrete floor storage to conduct thermal energy into the storage floor or a storage wall.

Rock Storage Bins

Rock storage bins can be made of any building material that is strong enough to hold the rock and that is unaffected by the conditions of use. These conditions of use include resistance to moisture, high humidity, and temperatures to 180°F.

Experience with rock storage beds indicates that there are three problems that occur on an occasional basis that must be guarded against: the invasion of rodents, the growth of mildew or mold, and the seepage of water.

A dead rodent in a rock storage bed can make it necessary to remove and replace all rocks. The build-up of mold or mildew can promote respiratory diseases. The seepage of water encourages the growth of mold and puts highly humid air into the building. All of these problems can be prevented by using the proper construction and taking some precautions.

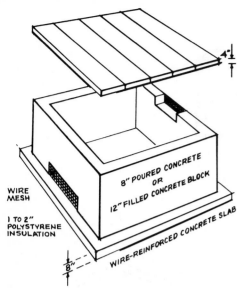

Figure 10.25. Typical concrete or filled concrete block rock storage box designed for air collector systems.

WIRE MESH

1 TO 2" POLYSTYRENE INSULATION

8" POURED CONCRETE OR 12" FILLED CONCRETE BLOCK

WIRE-REINFORCED CONCRETE SLAB

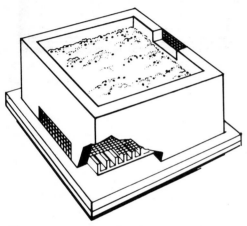

Figure 10.26. Details of construction for a typical rock storage bed.

The author recommends that rock storage bins be constructed of either poured concrete or filled concrete block placed on an insulated slab of wire mesh-reinforced concrete at least 8 in. thick. One or two inches of polystyrene slab make an excellent foundation insulation. General construction is shown in Figure 10.25.

When concrete blocks are used, every fourth course should contain wire reinforcing laid in the mortar courses to prevent cracking. The voids in the blocks should be filled with concrete.

The outside of the bin should be waterproofed. A good grade of asphaltic coating can be used. Then the sides should be well-insulated to R-10 or better. Again, polystyrene board is highly recommended. Two inches of thickness will provide about R-10.

The inside floor and walls of the bin should be sealed to prevent cement dusting prior to filling the bed with rock. The top of the bin should be wire reinforced, precast planks that can be removed if necessary. After the bin is filled, the top should be sealed to the walls with caulk or mastic to prevent any rodent invasion or leakage of air.

It is also possible to place the insulation on the inside of a concrete rock storage bed. Dense, rigid fiberglass with a rating of R-8 or better is recommended. When the bed is built in this manner, the concrete of the bed's walls and floors is not part of the storage, so some storage capacity is lost.

How Rock Storage Beds Work In a rock storage bed the air from the collectors, or from the cold air returns of the house, enters the storage bed. When collector air is flowing through the box, it is giving up its heat to the rocks in the bed. When house air is flowing through the bed, it is gathering heat from the rocks.

Air flow through rock storage beds must be reversible. During the charge cycle when the collectors are adding heat to storage, hot air from the collectors flows into the top of the bed and exits from the bottom. As the hot air passes through the bed, it gives up its heat to the rocks. During the discharge cycle, when the stored hot air is being used to heat the house, air from the heating system's cold air returns enters the bottom of the bed, flows up through it, and passes back into the house from the top of the bed. Where the heated air goes and its direction of flow is determined by the air handler attached to the bed.

Figure 10.26 shows the details of the filled rock storage bed. The bottom 8 in. of the bed contains a concrete block known as a *bond beam block*. Its configuration can be seen in the lower left-hand corner of the figure.

A rigid wire screen with a ½-in. mesh is laid over the blocks. Then 5 to 6 ft of rock is loaded into the box. The rocks must be clean, washed rocks that contain no vegetable matter capable of supporting the growth of bacteria. Sizing is important so that the air can readily pass through the rocks. Rocks that are ¾ to 1½ in. in size are recommended. Larger rocks would present too little surface area for fast heat pick-up and removal. Smaller rocks would give too much resistance to air flow. The top 8 to 10 in. are left empty to form a plenum for the air.

Calculating the Heat Capacity

The heat capacity of the rock storage bed is calculated in the following manner:

- Calculate the cubic feet of concrete contained in the walls, slab, and top of the bin if the bin is made of concrete and insulated on the outside. If the bin is wood or if the insulation is on the inside, skip this step.

- Determine the heat capacity of the concrete in Btu/hr/°F.
- Calculate the space occupied by the rocks. Assume that 30% of this space is air void and calculate the volume of rock based on the rocks being 70% of the total space.
- Determine the heat capacity of the rocks in Btu/hr/°F.
- Calculate the space occupied by the bond beam block. Assume that 65% of this area is air void and calculate the volume of the block based on it occupying 35% of the total space.
- Calculate the heat capacity of the bond block in Btu/hr/°F.
- Total the heat capacity of the concrete enclosure, the rock, and the bond beam block to arrive at the total heat capacity in Btu/hr/°F.

Configuration Restrictions

The heat in rock storage beds stratifies. The top half of the box is much hotter than the bottom half, so it is essential to have vertical air flow through the bed to have it work properly. Horizontal air flow cannot be used.

The optimum size of a rock storage bed is about one-half to three-quarters of a cubic foot of rock per square foot of solar collector. Larger beds will not heat properly. Smaller beds will store too little heat, which will reduce the efficiency of the solar collectors.

The velocity of the air through the bed should be 20 to 30 ft/min. This velocity is obtained by dividing the flow rate of the entering air into the cross-sectional area of the bed.

Building a Rock Storage Bed into the Foundation

Figure 10.27 shows how a rock storage bed could be built into the basement walls during the construction of a new house. In this configuration, the basement walls are used to save on storage bed construction costs. The air from the collectors enters the bed from the outside of the foundation. Proper insulating and protection procedures must be followed. The exits from the beds are located so that good distribution of the heated air to the house can be easily accomplished.

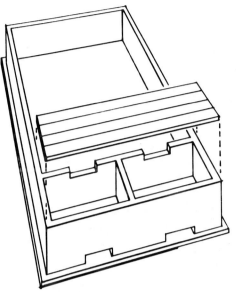

Figure 10.27. A double rock storage bed built into the foundation of a new house uses the basement walls for economy.

Heat Storage in Liquids

Heat may be stored in liquids as well as in solids. Water is generally the liquid of choice because it is cheap, available almost everywhere, and has a high heat capacity.

But water has some drawbacks as a storage media. It can be corrosive. It can freeze and boil. And the containers can leak. But water can store more than three times as much heat as rock storage beds in the same volume. Water is easily moved around the home from the collectors to storage and from storage to the point-of-use. Water pipes take up far less space than air ducts. This makes it easier to remodel with water storage systems.

Figure 10.28 shows the heat capacities of water, rock, and concrete. Note that the heat capacity of water is twice that of concrete and about three and one-half times the heat capacity of stone. This comparison explains why much more energy can be stored in a volume of water versus concrete or stone.

But remember, concrete and stone do not freeze or boil at solar storage temperatures whereas both freezing and boiling must be guarded against

MATERIAL	WATER	ROCKS	CONCRETE	
Specific heat	1	0.19	0.22	Btu/lb/°F
Weight/density	62.3	95	140	lb/cu ft
Unit volume heat	62.3	17.6	30.8	Btu/cu ft/°F
Freeze point	32	Solid	Solid	°F
Boiling point	212	Solid	Solid	°F
Heat of fusion	144	Solid	Solid	Btu/lb
Heat of vaporization	970	Solid	Solid	Btu/lb

Figure 10.28. Comparison of the heat storage properties of concrete, rock, and water in normal solar storage ranges.

with water. Boiling tends to be a very minor problem. But freezing can be a major problem in some geographic areas.

Water Storage Vessels

Water can be used as a static storage media for fenestration or for building space-heating systems. Or water can be used as a dynamic storage media in space heating or hot water heating systems. The storage vessel requirements for each application are different.

Static Storage Media Water stored in tubes can be used in most of the applications shown for concrete storage walls. A typical use is shown in Figure 10.29, where water-containing fiberglass tubes have been placed in front of a south-facing fenestration to absorb the sun's radiation.

Three precautions must be taken when using water storage in this manner. First, the floor and the tube must be engineered to withstand the weight of the water.

A 12-in. diameter tube 7 ft tall contains about 5½ cu ft of water. The water weighs about 343 lb. The load against the floor is about 437 lb/sq ft or about 3 lb/sq in.

Second, the tube must be secured against falling. And third, an unexpected leak should be planned for in advance.

Figure 10.30 shows a typical well-secured and engineered water-tube wall installation. A 6 in. by 8 in. beam has been posted under the floor,

3.14	π
× (0.5)²	radius squared
0.785	area sq ft
× 7	ft
5.495	cu ft
× 62.4	wt cu ft
342.9	lb
÷ 0.785	sq ft
= 436.8	lb/sq ft
436.8	lb/sq ft
÷ 144	sq in/sq ft
3.03	lb/sq in

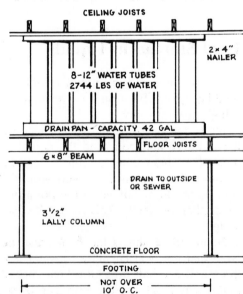

Figure 10.30. Water tubes placed on a frame floor must be supported by a beam posted from the basement footing, drained, and supported against falling.

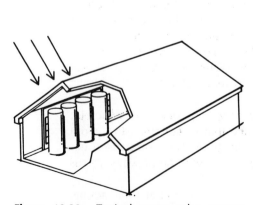

Figure 10.29. Typical water tube storage wall.

held up by 3½ in. Lally columns spaced less than 10 ft apart. The tubes are set in a drain pan that can hold the contents of at least one tube. A drain to an outside sewer or catch basin has been provided. A 2 in. by 4 in. nailer has been secured around the top of the tubes so that they cannot fall.

Translucent fiberglass water tubes have the advantage of passing light through them, so that when they are placed in front of a fenestration, sunlight passes through them into the room. This can be very important in some applications. But fiberglass tubes are expensive. They require a number of precautions in their installation that add to that expense.

When the passage of sunlight is not of major importance, metal containers can be used. There is a wide choice of metal containers available. The least expensive container is typically a 55-gal. steel storage drum such as is used for shipping oil. If closed-head drums are chosen, they can be stood up or laid on their sides in racks. A more expensive container, but one with longer life and more versatility, is the uninsulated water tank such as is used for the storage of water in a well system.

Figure 10.31 shows one way that closed-head steel drums might be used. They could be placed in front of a south-facing patio door to increase the thermal mass of the building and to collect heat. Such a system would work best if the patio door were double glazed and if movable insulation could be placed in front of the glass during the nonsunlight hours. A 55-gal. steel drum filled with 50 gal. of water weighs about 430 lb. It offers storage of about 420 Btu/°F. Five drums placed in front of a 6-ft patio door would provide 21,000 Btu of storage with a 10°F temperature rise.

The drums should be painted a dark color to maximize the absorption of energy. Provision must be made to prevent freezing. About 5% of the drum should be left empty to allow for the water's expansion as it heats. Provision should be made to empty the drums without moving them. The weight must be provided for by posting, if the drums are on a frame floor. Protection against damage to the building from leaks must be taken.

Such a system could be considered as seasonal. The drums could be put in place in the late fall and removed in the early spring so that the door could be used for access during the summer months.

The life of the drums in a system of this type will depend on the interior drum coating and the pH of the water that is placed in the drum. Most drum coatings have pinholes. Acid water will quickly attack the steel and cause rusting.

Each drum would have a surface area of about 5 sq ft that would see the sun. On a clear day with isolation of 300 Btu/hr/sq ft, the five drums would receive about 30,000 Btu between the hours of 10 A.M. and 2 P.M. Much of this energy could be stored for later use when the sun went down.

Steel, glass-lined water tanks can be used in a similar manner. They represent a larger initial investment but will have much longer life and give some flexibility not offered by the steel shipping drum.

A typical steel, glass-lined water storage tank might be a 20 in. diameter tank 36 in. high holding 42 gal of water or a 20 in. diameter tank 62 in. high holding 82 gal of water. The 36 in. high tank would present about 5 to 5½ sq ft of surface area to the sun whereas the 62 in. high tank would present about 8½ to 9 sq ft of area. Three of these tanks would fit in front of a 5-ft or 6-ft patio door. They would offer storage of 1050 to 2050 Btu/°F. Thermal expansion must be allowed for. Freeze protection needs to be provided. However, the chances of leakage are much smaller. And filling and draining are more easily accomplished.

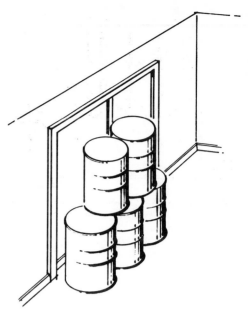

Figure 10.31. The use of steel drums in front of a south-facing patio door to increase the thermal mass of the building.

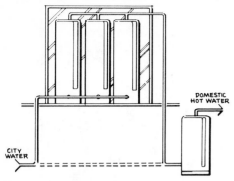

Figure 10.32. Using water storage tanks as preheater tanks for a hot water heater.

Dynamic Storage Media The water storage tank offers the opportunity to use it as a *dynamic storage media*. Water can easily be moved around the house with the use of water pressure or by the use of small centrifugal pumps.

A typical use of the collected energy is shown in Figure 10.32. Three 82-gal tanks are located in front of a south-facing fenestration. They are piped to both the city water line and to the cold water inlet of the domestic hot water heat. City water entering the house at 45 to 55°F goes to the storage tanks. This water is warmed by a combination of the sun's energy and by the warm air in the room. If the water reaches 85°F, then approximately one-half of the energy needed to supply hot water at 120°F has been placed into the water before it reaches the fossil-fueled or electric water heater. As the storage capacity of these preheater tanks is about six times the capacity of a 40-gal hot water heater, the hot water heater could be set to operate at 100°F rather than at 120°F and used straight from the tap without mixing it with cold water. This would result in further savings.

The use of 100 gal of water per day would require about 25,000 Btu to heat the water from 50 to 80°F. If three 82-gal storage tanks were used,

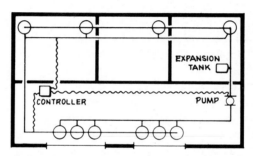

Figure 10.33. Storage tanks can be located on the north-side rooms, and collected energy can be pumped to them.

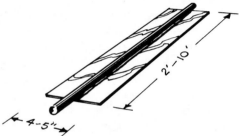

Figure 10.34. A finned water tube absorber plate.

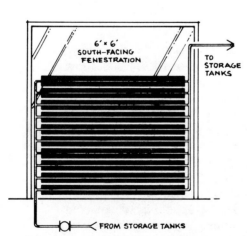

Figure 10.35. Finned tubes manifolded horizontally and placed in front of the lower half of a south-facing fenestration.

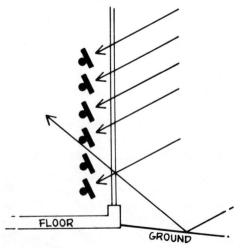

Figure 10.36. When finned tubes are manifolded horizontally, they can be tilted to face the winter sun.

their surface would see about 30,750 Btu, assuming a 15°F temperature rise within the tanks. The water heater would have to supply about 17,000 additional Btu to take the water to 100°F. Without the use of the preheater tanks, the water heater would have to supply about 42,000 Btu of energy or a little over two and one-half times as much energy.

It would also be possible to move the heated water to the north side of the house where the temperature is colder by incorporating some storage tanks and a small pump in a circulating loop around the structure. This is shown in Figure 10.33 where six tanks placed in front of two south-facing fenestrations are connected to four tanks located on the north side in different rooms. A differential thermostat-type controller senses the difference in temperature between the top of the energy-collecting tanks and the bottom of the energy-storing tanks. When the temperature of the collecting tanks is higher than the storing tanks, the controller turns the pumps on and moves the hotter water to the north side of the house.

When a system of this type is used, storage tanks are not needed in front of the south-facing fenestrations. They can be replaced with metal absorbers that will operate more efficiently and that can be installed at a lower cost. Figure 10.34 shows a finned-tube-type absorber. A copper water pipe has had a 4 to 5 in. aluminum or copper fin either soldered or mechanically clamped tightly to it. The tube and the fin are either painted dull black or electroplated with a selective surface.

When this finned tube is exposed to direct sunlight, it picks up large amounts of solar energy and converts it into thermal energy that flows into the water in the copper tube. This water can then be transferred to the storage tanks in another part of the house. This is a simple solar collector absorber plate placed inside the insulation envelope of the house where it does not need to be highly efficient or freeze-protected. Energy that does not enter the water is not lost to the structure but is utilized directly to heat the air within the room where the absorbers are located.

The placement of these finned tubes is somewhat critical. Figure 10.35 shows a typical way in which these finned tubes might be used. Here a series of ten tubes about 5 ft long and with 4-in. fins have been manifolded together and placed in front of a 6 ft by 6 ft south-facing fenestration. Note the reverse manifolding that was used. This ensures that all the fins will receive about the same amount of water flow. By using only the bottom 4 ft of the window, direct radiation is also received through the balance of the window to heat and light the room. The solar energy striking these fins is carried off to the storage tank located on the north side of the house or along an interior wall where it can be used to heat other parts of the building.

When finned tubes are manifolded horizontally, they can be tilted to face the sun if desired. Figure 10.36 shows the configuration. Note that when the tubes are tilted in this manner, the ground-reflected energy tends to enter the house and miss the tubes.

Finned tubes can also be manifolded vertically as shown in Figure 10.37. In this illustration, the tubes are used in front of the fixed sash of a patio door so that they do not interfere with the use of the door. The vertical configuration is quite useful for fenestrations that face from southeast to southwest. The tubes can be angled to face due south as shown in Figure 10.38.

Finned tubes used in this manner are not as efficient as a fabricated solar collector placed on the south-facing exterior wall or roof. Yet they are effective. The energy that is not collected and placed in storage is either radiated or convected to the room in which the tubes are mounted.

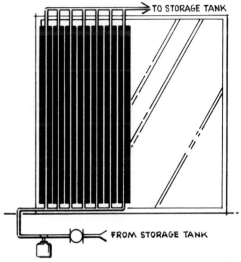

Figure 10.37. Finned tubes can be manifolded vertically to cover the fixed sash of a patio door.

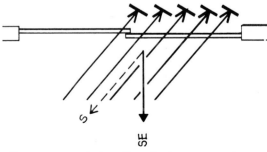

Figure 10.38. When finned tubes are manifolded vertically, they can be oriented south behind a southeast or southwest-facing fenestration.

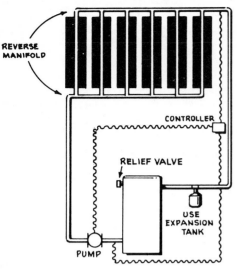

Figure 10.39. Some important points to remember with finned water tubes.

So the net effect is productive. And more than one room in the house receives solar energy.

The use of finned water tubes requires that a few important installation points be adhered to. See Figure 10.39.

- First, the pump must be mounted low on the storage tank so that it always has a head of water to pump from. Centrifugal pumps are not self-priming.
- Second, water expands as it heats up. So an expansion tank should be incorporated into the system.
- Third, reverse manifolding of the finned tubes should be used so as to equalize the flow of the water through the individual tubes.
- Fourth, if the system can see freezing weather, it must be freeze-protected. This can be accomplished by adding common antifreeze to the system.

You should design the system to have 1 to 2 gal of storage for each square foot of finned tube. A temperature and pressure relief valve should be placed on the tank, although it is extremely doubtful that the tank will ever get above 100°F. And you will need a differential controller with sensors mounted on the top manifold and near the tank's bottom in order to have an automated system. This controller will turn the pump on when the finned tubes are hotter than the storage tank.

Heat Storage in Phase-change Materials

Solids and liquids have been used in most instances throughout the 1970s to provide solar storage for residential buildings. They are familiar applications. The materials are easy to obtain and very little can go wrong.

However, as solar systems move into the 1980s, phase-change materials are coming into use. They have some advantages that are important to consider when looking at a solar system. You will remember from the previous discussion of phase-change materials that they depend on the heat required for the material to change state, that generally in solar systems the change in state that is being used is a change from a solid to a liquid, and that the heat stored or given up during that phase-change is called the heat of fusion.

Heat Storage Capability of a Phase-change Salt

Phase-change materials are of three general classes: *salt hydrates, organic solids,* and *eutectic solid mixtures.* A salt hydrate is a mixture of an inorganic metallic salt with water, such as calcium chloride and water to form calcium chloride hexahydrate. An organic solid is a substance containing carbon compounds such as paraffin wax. A eutectic solid mixture is a mixture of two or more compounds that are mixed in the proper proportions so as to give the lowest possible melting point. This melting point is generally below the melting point of any of the materials making up the mixture.

To date, only salt hydrates and organic solids have been used successfully. The most successful material is the salt hydrate known as calcium chloride hexahydrate. So calcium chloride hexahydrate will be used as an example of phase-change materials in this chapter.

Calcium chloride hexahydrate has a melting point of about 84°F. It has a heat of fusion of about 76 Btu/lb. That is, it takes the addition of 76 Btu to melt 1 lb. It has a unit volume heat of 8500 Btu/cu ft.

What this means in terms of energy storage can best be shown on a graph depicting energy stored versus temperature change. Figure 10.40 illustrates such a graph. What this graph shows is that the salt hydrate stores energy at a rate similar to concrete or stone except when it goes through a phase-change from a solid to a liquid. This occurs at about 84°F. From room temperature to 84°F, the salt gains energy of about 5 Btu/lb. So does the concrete, whereas water gains about 14 Btu of energy per pound. Between 84 and 85°F, the salt hydrate then gains another 76 Btu without getting any hotter. So at 85°F it has stored about 81 Btu/lb, whereas water has only stored 15 Btu/lb and concrete has only stored about 5 Btu/lb.

From 85°F up to 110°F, which is about as hot as a passive storage unit will get without compromising comfort, the additional heat storage capacity is about the same as concrete. So at 110°F, a pound of water is storing around 40 Btu/lb. The concrete is storing about 12 Btu/lb, and the salt hydrate is storing about 90 Btu/lb.

Obviously this means that the salt hydrate can offer more energy storage in less space. That is precisely why it is considered an important method of energy storage in solar heating.

Calcium chloride hexahydrate is not the only salt hydrate that has been examined for phase-change properties. Sodium sulfate decahydrate, commonly known as Glauber's salt, has been used with good success. Materials such as disodium phosphate decahydrate, barium hydroxide, and magnesium nitrate decahydrate have been examined, but no commercial results have been reported.

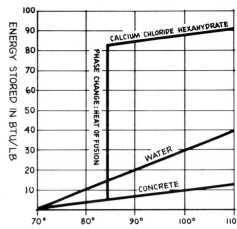

Figure 10.40. Comparison of energy storage in concrete, water, and a common phase-change salt hydrate.

The Potential Problems of Salt Hydrate Energy Storage

Calcium chloride hexahydrate and sodium sulfate decahydrate are low in toxicity, nonflammable, and readily available. These inexpensive materials can easily be used for phase-change energy storage. But they must be used properly or they will not work over long periods of time.

The major problem encountered with these phase-change salts is a phenomenon known as *supercooling*. Supercooling is defined as cooling below the solidification point without solidifying. If supercooling happens, the salt will not give up its heat at the proper temperature but must be lowered in temperature further. This limits its usefulness.

The second problem encountered is the separation of the salt from the *water of hydration* when it is in the liquid state. The water of hydration is the water that the salt is chemically combined with. There is a difference in density, so the water can separate out.

The third problem encountered is the loss of the water of hydration. Unless the salt hydrate is properly packaged, water can be lost from the container when the product is in its liquid form. This generally raises the melting point and lowers the heat capacity of the mixture.

To prevent chemical separation and supercooling, chemicals called *nucleators* are added to the salts. A nucleator is a chemical that will initiate the solidification of the salt hydrate at the proper melting point.

To prevent loss of water of hydration, the salts must be packaged in sealed containers. Metallic salts such as calcium chloride hexahydrate and sodium sulfate decahydrate are active materials that can corrode certain types of containers. Care must be exercised in choosing container materials. Calcium chloride hexahydrate can be packaged satisfactorily in polyethylene containers and in steel cans. Both packages are commercially available. At the time of this writing, no commercial packages for sodium sulfate decahydrate have been reported.

Organic Materials in Phase-change Storage

A number of organic solids have been proposed as phase-change storage materials. Most of the materials proposed have a major drawback. They are either not commercially available, are of moderate to high toxicity, have low density, or are a possible fire hazard.

Paraffin, packaged in small containers, is being used by one major manufacturer as a heat storage material in a moderate temperature heat storage application where solar air collectors are employed in the system. Small metal canisters of the material are placed in an insulated storage chamber that is then heated by passing hot air from the collectors over and around the material. The application is quite successful.

Paraffin melts at 133°F, which is close to ideal for an air-circulating active solar space-heating system. Its heat of fusion is 90 Btu/lb, which is excellent. However, it does have low density and its unit volume heat is only 4490 Btu/cu ft. It is not satisfactory for building storage walls in passive applications because of its higher melting point.

Some Cautions for the Homeowner

The author recommends that unless you are a chemist with a good background in salt hydrates, do not attempt to use salt hydrates by purchasing the raw chemicals and packaging them yourself. There are too many things that you could do wrong. If you purchase packaged materials, be certain that the package has been in general use for several years and that the performance over that period of time has been satisfactory.

Commercial Systems

Some commercial systems are currently available. It is certain that more will appear with time. Phase-change storage does represent an excellent storage method. Technological advances will solve the problems that are currently being cited.

Figure 10.41 shows calcium chloride hexahydrate packaged in a long, slender polyethylene tube that has been heat sealed at both ends. The tube is about 6 ft long and 3½ in. in diameter. It contains about 29 lb of the salt hydrate, is reported to melt at 81°F, have a heat of fusion of 82 Btu/lb, and to store 2378 Btu during change of state. The package is a high density polyethylene with a thermal conductivity of 3.7 and a service range from well below freezing to above 250°F.

Such a "thermal rod," as the manufacturer calls it, has excellent potential for solar storage in direct sunlight. It could also be used in exterior walls and locations in a similar manner to concrete and water storage. The rod is sturdy enough to stand on end. The author recommends that a drain pan be placed under the rods because leakage might be a problem.

Another package that is commercially available is a metal can similar to a large fruit juice can. The material is sealed within the can. These "thermal cans" have properties similar to the "thermal rods." The can is a very versatile package because it can be packed on shelves and placed within enclosures so that the release of the heat can be controlled by the temperature of the home. Again, all the applications previously mentioned for concrete and static water storage lend themselves to the use of this phase-change storage can.

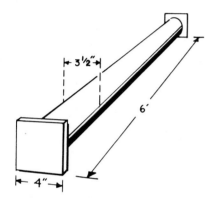

Figure 10.41. A commercial package for a salt hydrate phase-change material.

Making a Decision

In this chapter you have studied the ways in which the solar energy that you collect can be stored for future use.

You reviewed the availability of solar energy, a building's thermal energy requirements, and the effect of the building's thermal mass on its heat storage capability. From this, you learned that the building itself is the primary solar storage device that you need to be concerned with.

Then you went on to study heat storage mechanisms. You learned that the basic storage mechanisms are specific heat storage and phase-change heat storage.

Finally you studied storage in solids, in liquids, and in phase-change materials. You learned that all three types of storage are practical and usable but that there are advantages and disadvantages to each to be considered.

You are now equipped to determine what storage method will work best for you in your particular application.

DECISION
11

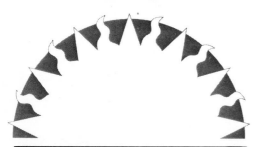

Distribute the Solar Energy

Your home will receive most of the solar energy on the south-facing side of the house. So you will have too much heat on one side of the house and not enough heat on the opposite side.

You must study how to distribute this heat evenly throughout the house. Heat distribution is accomplished either by moving the building's interior air around or by moving heated water around. The method that you use will depend on the solar system that you choose.

In this chapter you will study how this is accomplished.

- First you will study the orientation of the incoming solar energy.
- Second you will study air distribution methods that can be used in both retrofit and new building applications.
- Third you will learn about distributing heat that is stored in water through the use of heat exchangers and fan coils.
- Then you will study how heat is distributed from rock storage beds by using the building's air.
- And last, you will study how heat is distributed from phase-change media with the use of the building's air.

When you are finished, you will be able to choose the best air distribution system for your particular solar application.

The All-Day Distribution of Solar Energy

You learned in previous chapters how solar energy is distributed around a building. In Decision 9 you studied the solar heat gain tables and factors. From these tables you learned that solar heat gain is a function of orientation plus a number of other important factors.

If you took the solar heat gain table for 40°N latitude on January 21 and transferred it to a diagram so that you could study the all-day distribution, you would build two diagrams such as the illustrations shown in Figures 11.1 and 11.2. Figure 11.1 shows the morning solar distribution around a square building. Figure 11.2 shows the afternoon solar distribution around the same building.

Look at Figure 11.1. The northeast-facing room would receive about 845 Btu/sq ft. The southeast-facing room would receive about 3835 Btu/sq ft. The southwest-facing room would receive about 1810 Btu/sq ft. And the northwest-facing room would receive about 306 Btu/sq ft. Analysis of Figure 11.2 shows that in the afternoon the east-facing and the west-facing rooms would change places in the amount of energy received.

On an all-day basis, the north-facing rooms receive the same amount of energy. So do the south-facing rooms. This is shown in Figure 11.3, which also shows that the north side of the house receives 2304 Btu/sq ft while the south side of the house receives 11,290 Btu/sq ft. Eighty-three percent of the total energy striking the vertical sidewalls of the building is received on the south side of the house.

If the structure has a flat roof, then all parts of the horizontal roof receive the same amount of energy. But if the structure has a pitched roof, the amount of solar energy striking each side will also vary.

Obviously, ways to redistribute this solar energy within the structure need to be examined and put into effect if the house is to be comfortable throughout.

The Outdoor Ambient Air Temperature

The outdoor ambient air temperature close to the walls of the structure will also vary. How much it varies is a function of the wind speed, the

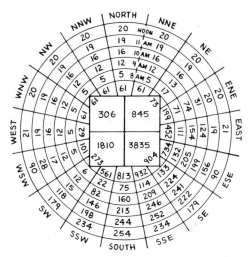

Figure 11.1. Morning solar energy distribution at 40°N latitude on January 21 in Btu/hr/sq ft.

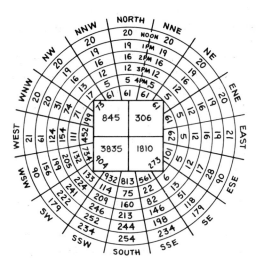

Figure 11.2. Afternoon solar energy distribution at 40°N latitude on January 21 in Btu/hr/sq ft.

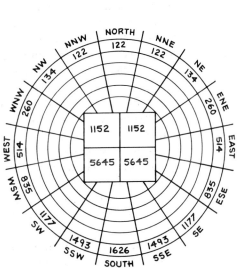

Figure 11.3. All-day distribution of solar energy at 40°N latitude on January 21 in Btu/day/sq ft.

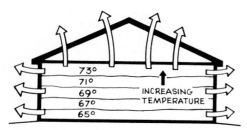

Figure 11.4. How energy leaves a building at night.

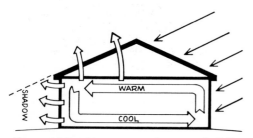

Figure 11.5. How energy leaves a building with no partitions during the day.

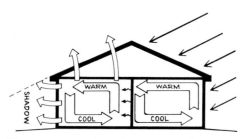

Figure 11.6. When the structure has partitions, the air circulates in separate rooms during the day.

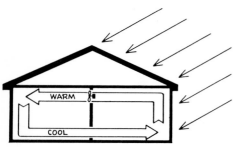

Figure 11.7. A simple way of increasing the interior air circulation between rooms.

shadow location, the reflection of energy from adjacent surfaces, and the size and character of the structure's walls. But large differentials can exist.

The walls of the structure will also vary in temperature due to the difference in the ambient air temperature and due to the presence or absence of direct solar radiation. On a 45°F day, the north-facing wall may be at 45°F while the south-facing wall may be as high as 75 to 80°F.

The temperature differentials of the outside of the walls help determine the heat loss from the building. If the temperature of the north-facing wall is 45°F, then there is a 25°FΔt across the wall when the inside room is 70°F. A high heat loss will be experienced. If the south-facing wall is 70°F, no heat loss will be experienced.

When the sun goes down or when the weather is cloudy, these differences are either nonexistent or very small. So both conditions must be planned for.

The Interior Air Circulation

Figure 11.4 shows how energy moves at night or during nonsunlight hours. The ambient air surrounding the outside of the building is all the same temperature, providing that no strong wind is blowing.

The temperature within the structure will be about the same throughout all the rooms. But the air near the ceilings tends to be the warmest whereas the air near the floor tends to be the coolest. Heat is conducted through the walls, floors, and ceilings in proportion to the $UA\Delta t$. Of course this static condition can be upset or varied by wind currents and air infiltration through the building.

Figure 11.5 shows what happens during sunlight hours. The sun's energy shining on or entering into the building warms the walls and the roof on the south-facing side. This warms the air within these rooms. The heated air rises. It travels across the building's ceiling and is cooled on the north-facing side of the building as heat escapes through the walls and ceiling. The air travels down the inside of the north-facing sidewall and drifts across the floor back to the south side of the building.

If the building contains a center partition running from east to west, then the air will tend to circulate in separate rooms. Figure 11.6 illustrates this condition. The air circulating in the south-side room warms the center partition. Heat is conducted through the partition, and a similar circulation pattern is seen in the north room.

The resistance to heat flow, or R-value, of the center partition is generally high enough so that a large temperature differential will exist between the north and the south rooms. This situation can be corrected by installing mechanical distribution devices such as fans or blowers between the rooms.

Figure 11.7 shows the simplest method of doing this. A fan is installed in the center partition near the ceiling. A return air vent is cut through the partition next to the floor. The fan draws the warm air from the south room and distributes it across the ceiling of the north room. The air travels down the outside north wall and returns back to the south room through the lower vent.

Such a system is not ideal. Noise can also be readily transmitted through the two openings so privacy is lost. The warm air is deposited at the ceiling level of the north room, so it does not warm the walls or floors directly.

Figure 11.8 shows a fan at ceiling level in the center partition with ductwork running down the interior of the partition, under the floor, and

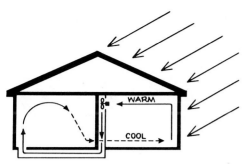

Figure 11.8. This duct system deposits the warm air in the coolest location.

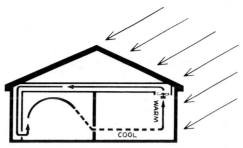

Figure 11.9. This duct system deposits the hottest air in the coolest location.

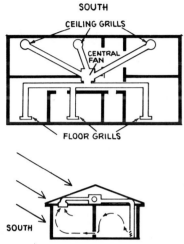

Figure 11.10. Typical five room central fan solar heat distribution system.

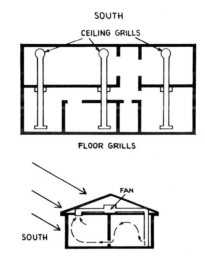

Figure 11.11. Typical five room individual fan solar heat distribution system.

exhausting against the base of the north wall. This method of air distribution deposits the warm air where it will do the most good and results in more even heat distribution throughout the room.

In Figure 11.9, the fan is placed in the ceiling near the outside south-facing wall where the air is the hottest. The ductwork is run across the ceiling. The air is again exhausted at floor level on the inside of the north-facing exterior wall. This system is likely best. The hottest air is being transferred to the coldest area. In all cases, a return air duct needs to be provided in order to get good circulation. This should be baffled where privacy is required.

Most buildings contain more than two rooms. So the system has to be more complex. Figure 11.10 shows a typical central fan layout for a five room, one-story house. Figure 11.11 shows a typical individual fan layout for the same house.

The problem is more complex in a two-story house where the floors are interconnected through an open staircase. Now the warm air rises into the second story. It may concentrate in the south-facing room or perhaps in a center hallway, depending on the room layout. Figure 11.12 illustrates a typical problem. In these cases, a fan is needed in the ceiling of the room where the hot air concentrates. The air should be ducted to the north-facing walls on both the first and second story and exhausted across the floors. Figure 11.13 shows a typical method that can be used.

The rules to be followed in designing such an air distribution system are:

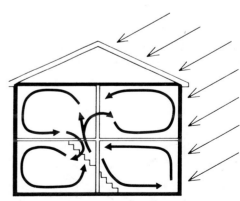

Figure 11.12. When two floors are interconnected, the hot air rises to the ceiling of the top story.

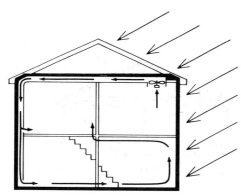

Figure 11.13. Ducting distributes the hottest air to the coldest locations in the structure.

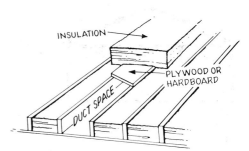

Figure 11.14. General construction of a horizontal duct in a ceiling.

- Duct the hot air from the south-facing rooms at ceiling level to the floor level of the north-facing rooms.
- Provide ample return duct capacity back to the south-facing rooms so that circulation will readily take place.
- Build the system with baffling and turns so that privacy will not be disturbed.

Running the Ductwork

In running ductwork of this type, it is not necessary to install metal ducts. There is no combustion source that can cause a fire. And the air temperatures range from 90°F down. In a two-story house, it is wise to provide automatic dampers that close in the case of a fire in the risers.

The space between ceiling joists or floor joists will make satisfactory ducts when running across the house. These ducts must be insulated when they run outside the thermal envelope so that they are part of or inside the envelope. Figure 11.14 illustrates this.

Interior walls are also generally hollow and contained inside the thermal envelope. They make excellent risers to communicate between stories or to return air from north to south. Figure 11.15 shows how they can be used.

Outside vertical walls should generally not be used for vertical risers. It is hard or sometimes even impossible to insulate the outside wall of the duct properly. Instead, it is necessary to create a duct inside the thermal envelope. Here metal ducts or fiberglass tubes can be used. A number of schemes can be thought of so as to blend with the decor or to fit within the interior of the structure.

Baffling for privacy is accomplished by putting turns and twists into the ductwork. The air stream will follow these twists and turns better than the sound. An example of this is shown in Figure 11.16, where the return duct has been placed in the floor of the two rooms and the air is being led down, around, and back up into the south room. In new construction or where the partition is to be altered, it is also quite practical to lead the air into one stud space at the floor level, let it travel up for 2 to 3 ft, and lead it back down to floor level in the next stud space. This method is illustrated in Figure 11.17.

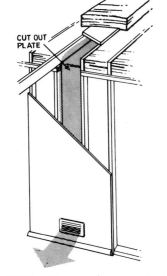

Figure 11.15. How stud spaces in interior walls can be used to make air ducts.

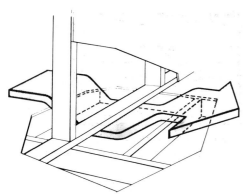

Figure 11.16. How baffling under a center partition is accomplished to decrease noise levels in a cold air return.

Fans

Fans are used to move the air through the ductwork. A *fan* is a rotating device designed to deliver a quantity of air with little or no change in

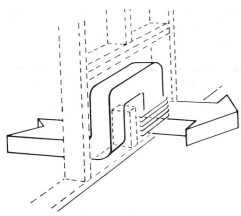

Figure 11.17. How baffling within a center partition can be accomplished to decrease noise levels in a cold air return.

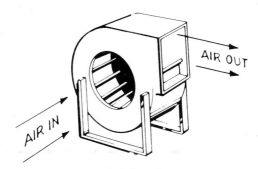

Figure 11.18. Radial-flow fan.

pressure through the use of an impeller using centrifugal or propeller action.

There are two basic classes of fans: the *radial-flow fan* and the *axial-flow fan*. The radial-flow fan is a fan in which the flow of air occurs in a radial direction. Figure 11.18 shows a radial-flow fan. Radial-flow fans are also known as centrifugal fans and squirrel-cage blowers.

The axial-flow fan is a fan in which the flow of air occurs along the axis of the impeller. Figure 11.19 shows a typical axial-flow fan. Axial-flow fans are also known as propeller fans. Axial-flow fans can be *tube-axial-flow* and *vane-axial-flow* types. A tube-axial-flow fan is a propeller fan mounted in a tubular housing or circular duct. A vane-axial-flow fan is an axial-flow fan with stationary vane guides mounted in a tubular housing. Figure 11.20 shows a tube-axial-flow fan. Figure 11.21 shows a vane-axial-flow fan.

Pressure

In working with fans, you need to be concerned with pressure drops. The pressure is the load against which the fan is working. Pressure has two components: static pressure and velocity. When they are added together, they give the total pressure or load that the fan must work against.

In residential hot air systems or in large commercial installations, pressure drops are very important in sizing ductwork and the fans required to move the air. But in the type of work that you will be doing for solar air distribution, pressure drop is less important because you will be moving relatively small quantities of air at relatively low velocities through relatively large ducts. This results in small pressure drops.

Designing for Retrofit

Typically in retrofitting a residence the space between the floor or ceiling joists will be used as the ductwork. In these instances, tube-axial or vane-axial fans may be used. Typically the total run of ductwork will be less than 50 ft. Only two or three bends will be used in the duct design. The *static head*, the vertical distance between the discharge and the intake, will be less than 10 ft.

Propeller fans sized to fit in round ductwork are readily available. They are inexpensive and of low horsepower. The speed of the propeller can be

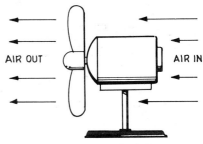

Figure 11.19. An axial-flow fan, propeller-type.

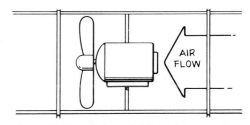

Figure 11.20. Tube-axial-flow fan.

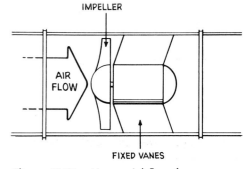

Figure 11.21. Vane-axial-flow fan.

controlled with a light dimmer switch. Fans to fit 5, 6, 7, 8, 9, 10, 12, and 14 in. ducts can be readily purchased. The amount of air that such fans will typically move is shown in Figure 11.22.

DUCT SIZE IN INCHES	AIR VOLUME IN CU FT/MIN	FAN MOTOR HP OR WATTS
5	55	12 W
6	75	16 W
7	75	16 W
8	150	20 W
9	150	20 W
10	300	1/70 hp
12	450	1/70 hp
14	1000	1/20 hp

Figure 11.22. Size and ratings of typical fans for round ducts.

Generally the fans will be purchased separately from the ductwork and the user will provide the ductwork required to make these fans into tube-axial fans. In doing this work, the user must convert the rectangular duct between the joists to a round duct in which to locate the fan. It is important to make the transition to and from the tubular duct smoothly in order not to hurt the fan's efficiency.

Figure 11.23 shows how a 12-in. tube-axial fan is used in a 2 × 8 ceiling or floor joist duct. Three sheet metal pieces are required—two transition pieces and one 12-in. round duct about 2 ft long. The fan is inserted in the center of the duct, and the entire assembly is fitted into the joist space.

Twelve-inch ductwork is larger than the 2 × 8 joist space. Why was this duct size chosen? A 12-in. round duct has the same *face-area* as 2 × 8 joists on 16 in. centers. You can see this from the table in Figure 11.26. This table was calculated from the tables shown in Figures 11.24 and 11.25. Face-area is the cross-sectional area of the duct as measured by the diameter of a round duct or the width and height of a rectangular duct. If a smaller round duct were chosen, then a flow constriction would exist at the fan. This increases the velocity at the fan and cuts down on the air flow. The pressure drop in the duct increases as the square of the velocity. So it is important not to have flow constrictions in the ductwork.

You will note that equivalent face-areas are given for one, two, and three ducts. In some systems, you may wish to branch off the main duct

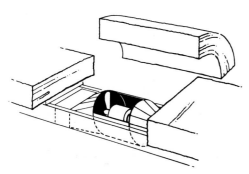

Figure 11.23. How a tube-axial fan is used in a ceiling joist duct run.

CONSTRUCTION NOMINAL	AREA (SQ FT)
2 × 4 − 16″ o.c.	0.15
2 × 6 − 16″ o.c.	0.55
2 × 8 − 16″ o.c.	0.76
2 × 10 − 16″ o.c.	0.96

Figure 11.24. Area of typical ceiling or floor-joist construction.

ROUND DUCT DIAMETER (IN.)	AREA (SQ FT)
5	0.14
6	0.20
7	0.26
8	0.35
9	0.44
10	0.55
12	0.79
14	1.07

Figure 11.25. Area of round ductwork of various diameters.

FOR CONSTRUCTION NOMINAL	USE ROUND DUCT DIAMETER (IN.)
2 × 6 — 16″ o.c.	1 — 10″ duct
	2 — 7″ ducts
	3 — 6″ ducts
2 × 8 — 16″ o.c.	1 — 12″ duct
	2 — 9″ ducts
	3 — 7″ ducts
2 × 10 — 16″ o.c.	1 — 14″ duct
	2 — 10″ ducts
	3 — 8″ ducts

Figure 11.26. Equivalent sizes of round duct and typical construction.

and to put individual fans in the branch ducts. Note that no equivalent area is shown for 2 × 4 timbers on 16 in. centers. It is generally not practical to place tube-axial fans in 2 × 4 vertical walls or horizontal joists.

The air flowing through the typical solar air ductwork manufactured in the manner shown must be turned 90° in flow direction up to three times in the run of the duct. It is important to insert a smooth turning surface at the turns so that localized turbulence will not prevent or lower the air flow, as shown in Figure 11.27. Such a transition piece can readily be made on the job from a piece of thin plywood, hardboard, or sheet metal.

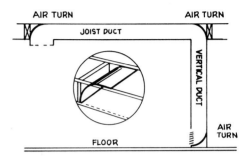

Figure 11.27. When turning the air, insert a smooth transition piece at the turn.

Ceiling-to-Ceiling Ducts The question has to arise as to the use of ceiling-to-ceiling ducts because they are more easily installed, use less space, and are less expensive. In such a duct system, the intake and discharge are both located at ceiling level. This is permissible. Some efficiency in moving the hottest air to the coolest location will be lost. Poorer air circulation will result in the north-facing room. But many times, this may be the most practical method to employ.

Using Round Metal Ductwork There may also be instances where it appears to be advisable to use all round metal ductwork rather than making a transition from a rectangular joist space to a round fan enclosure. A specific instance where this might happen is with 2 × 4 truss construction. This is an excellent way to proceed. There are fewer friction and transition losses. However, be certain that you insulate the ductwork well or your solar energy may be lost in your attic space.

Central Fan Systems

The ducting systems that were just discussed are best used in configurations such as the one shown in Figure 11.11. When central fans are used, such as shown in Figure 11.10, it is best to use a radial or centrifugal fan because these types of fans are more efficient against the higher pressure drops that are encountered with the longer ductwork.

Centrifugal fan central systems are generally known as air handlers. They come as a package unit ready to be installed in a job-built plenum. Such systems should be designed with more care than the designs used in the tube-axial single systems. The manufacturer will have a design packet available for your use when you investigate the purchase of these systems.

Designing for New Construction

In designing solar ductwork for new construction, the solar air design will be folded into the overall design of the air-handling system for the house. Design criteria become more complex because the ducts must carry hotter air at higher velocities. The pressure drops will be greater, and the ductwork must all be metal.

Make certain that the mechanical package designer allows for the movement of solar air without turning on the fossil-fuel ignition system. Be sure that the designer recognizes the need to carry the solar energy from the hottest point in the residence to the coolest point. It will not be a good design package if these points are not carefully considered in the overall design.

If the residence is to have a hot-water baseboard radiation heating system, then the solar air-handling package will be separate. You may proceed independently in the design. The same is true for electrical baseboard radiation systems. It is in the transfer of warm air through forced warm air heating systems that the designs need to be combined.

Sizing the Solar Energy Transfer System

The solar energy heat transfer system is sized from the maximum amount of energy that you may want to transfer. This is determined by the maximum amount of energy that the fenestration or the solar collectors provide to the south side of the room. In order to determine this, you must set some conditions to work from.

The first assumption that should be made is that a square foot of fenestration or solar collector can provide a maximum of 250 Btu/hr/sq ft of collecting surface. This sets the maximum amount of incoming energy that you may want to transfer.

The second assumption that should be made is the amount of heat rise that the south-facing rooms will see as a result of the solar energy input. A reasonable design figure is 10°F.

You learned previously that it took 0.018 Btu to raise the temperature of 1 cu ft of air 1°F. So it will take 0.18 Btu to raise 1 cu ft of air by 10°F in temperature.

If you divide 250 Btu by 0.18, you will know how many cubic feet of air that you must transfer per square foot of fenestration or collector. That is 1389 cu ft/hr or 23 cu ft/min. The rule that you will follow in sizing the system is to provide 23 cu ft of air circulation for every square foot of collector or fenestration surface located on the southeast to southwest side of the structure. You will not need all this capacity all the time. You will only need it when the sun is the hottest. But it is important that you design for the maximum needed condition.

A typical ductwork sizing table that combines the design figures chosen in Figures 11.22 through 11.26 has been constructed in Figure 11.28. But the figures in this table are only accurate for the fans shown in Figure 11.22. You need to determine your fan's rate to be accurate.

$$
\begin{array}{l}
250 \text{ Btu/hr/sq ft} \\
\underline{\times \text{ sq ft} \text{ fenestration}} \\
= \text{ total energy} \text{ Btu/hr}
\end{array}
$$

$$
\begin{array}{l}
0.018 \text{ Btu/cu ft/°F} \\
\underline{\times 10 \text{ °F}} \\
0.18 \text{ Btu/cu ft/10°F}
\end{array}
$$

$$
\begin{array}{l}
250 \text{ Btu/hr/sq ft} \\
\underline{\div 0.18 \text{ Btu/cu ft}} \\
1388.8 \text{ cu ft/hr} \\
\underline{\div 60 \text{ min/hr}} \\
= 23.14 \text{ cu ft/min}
\end{array}
$$

ROUND DUCT DIA. (IN.)	CONSTRUCTION DUCT	NOMINAL CAPACITY* (FT/MIN)	FENESTRATION (SQ FT)
5	2 × 4 − 16″ o.c.	55	2-3
10	2 × 6 − 16″ o.c.	300	13
12	2 × 8 − 16″ o.c.	450	20
14	2 × 10 − 16″ o.c.	1000	43

Figure 11.28. Typical ductwork sizing table.

*Check manufacturer's flow rate for the particular fan that you decide to use.

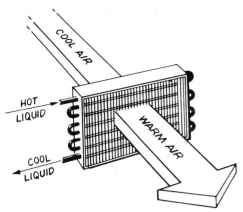

Figure 11.29. Liquid-to-air heat exchanger.

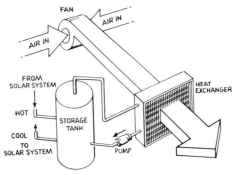

Figure 11.30. Liquid-to-air heat delivery system.

The author has been quite conservative in giving you these rules of thumb for designing the sizes of ductwork. You should work with a mechanical designer on large installations. You may find that you can use less conservative sizing calculations.

Heat Distribution from Water Storage

When the solar heat is stored in water vessels, it must be transferred to the building's air. This is done through a *heat exchanger*. A heat exchanger is a device that transfers energy from one substance to another without mixing the two substances.

In the heating and air-conditioning business, there are three basic types of heat exchangers: liquid-to-liquid, liquid-to-air, and air-to-liquid. You will be examining a liquid-to-air type heat exchanger to take the energy stored in water and transfer it to the building air.

Figure 11.29 shows a typical liquid-to-air heat exchanger. Hot water enters into the top of the exchanger through a pipe that runs back and forth through the exchanger so that the water passes through the exchanger many times. The cooled water exits at the bottom of the exchanger. Aluminum fins are attached to the pipe so that the water heats up the fins. Cool air is blown through these fins. It is warmed by its contact with the fins, and it exits heated. An example of a liquid-to-air heat exchanger is the radiator in your car. The liquid antifreeze in the engine is cooled by the air passing through the fins of the radiator.

In order for a liquid-to-air heat exchanger to work effectively, the liquid is pumped through the exchanger tubes. A fan is used to blow the air over the exchanger fins.

Figure 11.30 shows what the entire heat delivery system looks like. It consists of the storage tank, the heat exchanger, the air fan, and the liquid pump. Hot water from the top of the storage tank is pumped through the exchanger and back to the bottom of the storage tank. Building air is picked up by the radial fan and blown through the finned coil to heat it. Many times you will see this called a *fan coil*, which is another common name for this type of heat exchanger.

A number of different configurations are possible for liquid-to-air heat delivery systems. Figure 11.31 shows one of the simplest. Here the house contained a warm air furnace, so the heat exchanger was placed in the cold air return of the furnace. Now all the air returning from the house

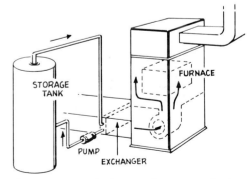

Figure 11.31. The heat exchanger can be located in the cold air return of the furnace.

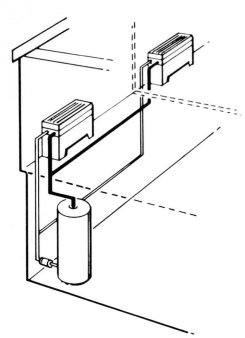

Figure 11.32. When the building does not have a central forced hot air furnace, individual room fan coil units can be used.

When $T_1 = T_4$
$E = 100\%$

$$\frac{100 - 60}{120 - 60} = \frac{40}{60} = 0.67$$

$$\frac{80 - 60}{120 - 60} = \frac{20}{60} = 0.33$$

must pass through the solar exchanger before being heated in the furnace. If the storage water is much over 110 to 130°F, the furnace does not fire and solar storage carries the load alone. If solar storage is down to 70 to 100°F, it adds some heat to the return air and the furnace supplies the rest. In this configuration, the fan is already in place. So only the heat exchanger needs to be supplied.

If the building does not have a central warm air furnace, individual fan coil units located in the rooms can be used, as shown in Figure 11.32. The heated water is pumped into each room in this configuration, and the exchange to the building air is made in the rooms. A number of units may be used.

Heat Exchanger Effectiveness

Heat exchangers are measured in *effectiveness*. Heat exchanger effectiveness is defined as the ratio of the actual rate of heat transfer to the theoretical maximum rate of heat transfer in an infinitely large heat exchanger.

Figure 11.33 shows the temperature measurements that are used to determine the effectiveness of a heat exchanger in a heat delivery loop. T_1 is the temperature of the liquid entering from the storage tank. T_2 is the temperature of the liquid returning back to storage. T_3 is the temperature of the entering air. And T_4 is the temperature of the exiting air from the exchanger.

If the exiting air were warmed to the same temperature as the entering liquid, then the exchanger would be 100% effective. All the heat in the liquid would be transferred to the air. If the exiting air is not heated to this temperature, then the effectiveness (E) has to be less than 100%.

The ratios are calculated by using the formula:

$$\frac{\text{Exit air temperature} - \text{entrance air temperature}}{\text{entrance liquid temperature} - \text{entrance air temperature}} = E$$

or

$$\frac{T_4 - T_3}{T_1 - T_3} \times 100 = \%E$$

Assume the following conditions:

$$T_1 = 120°F$$
$$T_4 = 100°F$$
$$T_3 = 60°F$$

A heat exchanger operating under these conditions would have an effectiveness of 67%. This heat exchanger would be considered highly effective.

If T_4 were only 80°F, then the heat exchanger would only be 33% effective. This heat exchanger would be considered to have a low effectiveness.

It is important that you do not confuse the term *efficiency* with effectiveness. Heat exchangers are always discussed in terms of heat transfer effectiveness, not in terms of percent efficiency.

Heat exchanger effectiveness is very important in solar storage heat delivery loops. *The lowest temperature at which the solar storage tank can add useful heat to the house is determined by the effectiveness of the heat exchanger.*

You can determine what the minimum effectiveness of the exchanger ought to be by back calculating the tank temperature at which the heat exchanger will add useful heat.

The operating conditions desired in the house are usually fixed. For purposes of illustration, fix these at an exit air temperature of 75°F and an entrance air temperature of 60°F. This would be a minimum set of operating conditions that would provide useful heat gain.

Knowing these heat delivery needs, you can examine the lowest tank temperature at which the storage vessel will deliver heat by changing the heat exchanger effectiveness. Assume first an effectiveness of 67%. Substitute into the formula for exchanger effectiveness and solve the equation. The tank will deliver useful heat down to 82°F. Such a heat exchanger will allow good use of the solar storage tank.

Now substitute an effectiveness of 50% and make the same calculations. At 50% effectiveness, solar storage can only perform down to a temperature of 90°F.

If you were to drop the heat exchanger effectiveness to 33%, then the tank would only deliver useful heat at 105.5°F.

Most solar storage tanks operate around 120°F maximum. Their temperature rarely exceeds this point during the heating season. So you need a highly effective heat exchanger or the heat that you have stored cannot be used.

Heat exchangers are expensive. Effectiveness is gained by increasing their size. But for maximum usefulness, they must be large enough to perform at low temperatures. Therefore you should install exchangers that have an effectiveness of 67% or better.

Determining the Amount of Heat Transferred

A heat exchanger with its own fan is generally rated as to the amount of air that the fan puts through the exchanger coil per minute. This is generally expressed as cubic feet of air per minute or CFM.

If you know the amount of air passing through the exchanger coil and the conditions under which it is operating, then you can determine how much heat that exchanger will supply to the building by using the following formula: $T_4 - T_3 \times CFM \times 60$ min $\times 0.018 =$ Btu/hr supplied. 0.018 is the specific heat of a cubic foot of air.

For a sample calculation, assume the following conditions:

$$T_3 = 60°F$$
$$T_4 = 75°F$$
$$\text{Air flow} = 200 \text{ CFM}$$

This exchanger would deliver 3240 Btu/hr to the room provided that the proper amount of liquid was also supplied to the exchanger coil.

Assume that the exchanger is a 67% effective exchanger. Effectiveness is the ratio of maximum transfer to actual transfer. So the exchanger must be supplied with heat equivalent to the amount of heat delivered divided by its effectiveness. That is 4836 Btu/hr under the operating conditions shown.

Heat exchangers are also specified as to the amount of liquid flow rate that must occur in order to achieve the proper heat delivery. Assume that this exchanger is operating at a flow rate of one gallon per minute or 1 GPM and that the tank temperature is 90°F. The amount of heat supplied by the water is determined with the following formula:

$$T_1 - T_3 \times GPM \times 60 \times 8.3 = \text{Btu supplied}$$

$$T_4 = 75°F \qquad \frac{T_4 - T_3}{T_1 - T_3} = E$$
$$T_3 = 60°F$$

$$\frac{75 - 60}{T_1 - 60} = 0.67 \qquad \frac{15}{0.67T_1 - 40.2} = 1$$

$$0.67T_1 - 40.2 = 15$$
$$0.67T_1 = 55.2$$
$$T_1 = 82.3°F$$

$$\frac{75 - 60}{T_1 - 60} = 0.5 \qquad \frac{15}{0.5T_1 - 30} = 1$$

$$0.5T_1 - 30 = 15$$
$$0.5T_1 = 45$$
$$T_1 = 90°F$$

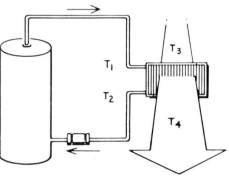

Figure 11.33. These temperatures determine heat exchanger effectiveness.

$$
\begin{array}{rl}
15 & °F \text{ temp diff} \\
\times\ 200 & \text{CFM} \\
\hline
3000 & \\
\times\ 60 & \text{min/hr} \\
\hline
180,000 & \\
\times\ 0.018 & \\
\hline
=\ 3,240 & \text{Btu/hr}
\end{array}
$$

$$
\begin{array}{rl}
3240 & \text{Btu/hr delivered} \\
\div\ 0.67 & \text{effectiveness} \\
\hline
=\ 4835.8 & \text{Btu/hr required}
\end{array}
$$

$$\text{Flow} = 1 \text{ GPM}$$
$$T_1 = 90°F$$

WORKSHEET

1. Air delivery temperature, T_4 _____ °F   (75)

2. Air entrance temperature, T_3 _____ °F   (60)

3. Percent effectiveness, %E _____ %E   (67)

4. Lowest operating temperature of solar storage tank, T_1 _____ °F $$\frac{T_4 - T_3}{T_1 - T_3} = E$$

5. Air flow rate _____ CFM   (assumed)

6. Btu delivered per hour _____ Btu/hr   (calculate)
$T_4 - T_3 \times \text{CFM} \times 60 \times 0.018 = \text{Btu delivered/hr}$

7. Btu required per hour from liquid _____ Btu/hr
Btu delivered per hour ÷ effectiveness = Btu required/hr

8. Liquid flow rate _____ GPM   (assumed)

9. Lowest operating temperature, T_1 _____ °F   (see 4)

10. Return liquid temperature, T_2 _____ °F   (calculate)
$T_1 - T_2 \times \text{GPM} \times 60 \times 8.3 = \text{Btu required/hr}$

SPECIFICATIONS:

Heat delivery _____ Btu/hr (6)

Air flow rate _____ CFM (5)

Storage temperature _____ °F (4)

Percent effectiveness _____ %E (3)

Liquid flow rate _____ GPM (8)

Figure 11.34. A chart for specifying the delivery heat exchanger from the manufacturer.

8.3 is the specific heat of a gallon of water.

Substituting into this formula, you find that the temperature of the water that exits back to the tank is 80.3°F.

If the exchanger called for a flow rate of 2 GPM, then the exit temperature of the water changes. Calculations show that this temperature would then become 85.2°F.

Specifying the Heat Exchanger

You can specify the heat exchanger that you need with the data that you have just developed. You are looking for a heat exchanger that will deliver 3240 Btu/hr at an air flow rate of 200 CFM when you supply 90°F water to the exchanger at a flow rate of 2 GPM. That exchanger's effectiveness will be 67%.

To purchase that heat exchanger in the proper size, you must have the manufacturer's heat exchanger data. This is readily obtained by consulting with a fan coil manufacturer.

Figure 11.34 is a chart with which to do the calculations for the required heat exchanger. You will find that the exchanger manufacturer has a number of options when it comes to choosing the exchanger. You may want to vary some of your operating specifications in order to purchase the most economical exchanger available.

Heat Distribution from Storage in Solids

When the solar heat is stored in solids, such as rock storage beds, it is not necessary to incorporate a heat exchanger into the system. The heat exchange is performed by passing the building's air directly over the surface of the rocks.

Rock Storage Bins

Heat stored in water vessels does not *stratify* to any great extent. Stratification is the tendency of the heat to collect in the top part of the container so that the top part is much hotter than the bottom of the container. Some stratification does take place in a liquid storage vessel, but not to the extent that it takes place in a rock storage bed.

Figure 11.35 shows a rock storage bed as it might appear at 8 A.M. when its heat has been exhausted during the night. The top of the bed might typically be at 80°F while the bottom of the bed might be at 65 to 70°F.

If air is heated and pumped into the top of the rock storage bed during the day, then this heated air starts to warm the rocks. Experiments have shown that the top layer of rocks, or about 1 ft of depth, will warm to the temperature of the incoming air. That will give the temperature profile shown in Figure 11.36 where the incoming air during the morning is about 110°F as the heated air enters the container. The cooled air will exit at about the temperature of the lower foot of rocks.

As the sun gets higher in the sky, the incoming air will grow hotter, perhaps up to about 140°F in a well-designed air system. So the rocks in the upper layer will reach this temperature. Then the rocks below this upper layer will also begin to heat up to that temperature. Eventually, if enough heat is supplied to warm most of the rocks, the temperature profile of the bed will reach the profile shown in Figure 11.37 late in the afternoon.

$$(90 - T_3) (1) (60)$$
$$(8.3) = 4836$$
$$(90 - T_3) (498) = 4836$$
$$90 - T_3 = 4836 \div 498$$
$$90 - T_3 = 9.7$$
$$T_3 = 80.3°F$$

$$(90 - T_3) (2) (60)$$
$$(8.3) = 4836$$
$$(90 - T_3) (996) = 4836$$
$$90 - T_3 = 4836 \div 996$$
$$90 - T_3 = 4.85$$
$$T_3 = 85.15°F$$

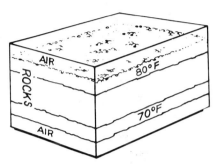

Figure 11.35. Typical rock storage bed at 8 A.M.

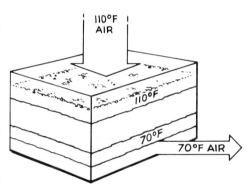

Figure 11.36. Typical rock storage bed at 11 A.M.

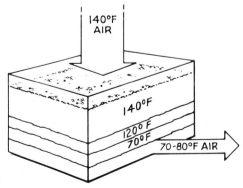

Figure 11.37. Typical rock storage bed at 5 P.M.

Distribute the Energy **223**

To remove the heat from the rock storage bed efficiently, the flow of air must be reversed so that the hottest air is distributed to the structure from the top of the rock storage bed. During the night, or during nonsunlight hours when the heat is being removed, the temperature profile begins to revert back to the profile shown in Figure 11.35. Figure 11.38 illustrates this change in air flow direction and the resulting change in the bed's temperature profile.

As a result of this change in air flow direction and of the stratification of the heat in the bed, the heat stored during the later afternoon is used first. The energy stored at the highest temperatures during the day is available for use during the peak night heating needs. The energy accumulated in the early morning hours is used up during the late hours of the night toward the morning.

For a rock storage bed to operate in this manner, certain design criteria must be met:

- The depth of the rocks should be about 5 to 7 ft.
- The rocks should range from ¾ in. to 1½ in. in size.
- The air velocity through the bed should be about 20 to 30 ft/min.
- The pressure drop across the bed should be a minimum of 0.15 in. of water.

When these design criteria are adhered to, the problems that have been cited for rock beds are minimized or eliminated. The horsepower required to move the air is small, and the low velocity of air does not cause large dust or dirt circulation problems.

The construction details for a rock bed of this type were outlined in Decision 10. You should adhere to these construction details. And you should be certain that you meet the design criteria outlined here.

Figure 11.39 shows the dimensions of a typical residential rock storage bed. The bed is a 7-ft cube with concrete walls that are 8 in. thick. This rock bed would occupy about 343 cu ft.

The rock on the inside would occupy about 183 cu ft once the air plenums and the thickness of the walls are subtracted from the outside dimensions. The square footage of the plenum would be about 32.1 sq ft. So the air flow should be between 640 and 960 CFM.

Rock Storage Bed Air Handlers

The rock storage bed requires an air handling system. The air handling system allows the flow of the air to be controlled as required for the charging and discharging of the rock bed's stored energy.

7 ft long
× 7 ft high
49
× 7 ft high
= 343 cu ft

68 in. long
× 68 in. high
4624
× 68 in. high
314,432 cu in.
÷ 1722 in./cu ft
= 182.6 cu ft

68 in. long
× 68 in. wide
4624 sq in.
÷ 144 in./sq ft
= 32.1 sq ft

32 sq ft
× 20 ft/min/sq ft
640 CFM

32 sq ft
× 30 ft/min/sq ft
960 CFM

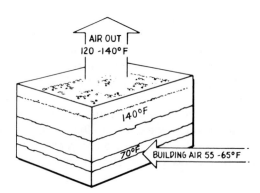

Figure 11.38. Heat is removed from rock storage beds by reversing the air flow.

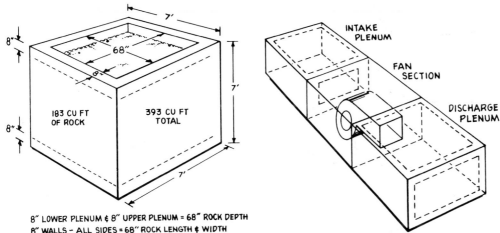

Figure 11.39. Typical rock storage bed's size.

8" LOWER PLENUM & 8" UPPER PLENUM = 68" ROCK DEPTH
8" WALLS – ALL SIDES = 68" ROCK LENGTH & WIDTH

183 CU FT OF ROCK

393 CU FT TOTAL

Figure 11.40. Air handling unit.

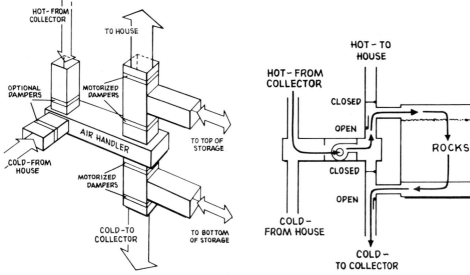

Figure 11.41. Typical air handler for a rock bed storage unit.

Figure 11.42. Air flow when adding heat to storage.

Figure 11.40 shows a typical simple air handling unit. It has three sections: an intake plenum, a fan section, and a discharge plenum. Most air handling units are constructed so that a multiplicity of air intakes and discharges may be attached to them. Typical locations for these ducts are shown by the dotted lines in the illustration.

A typical air handling system for a rock storage bed, together with its six connecting ducts, is shown in Figure 11.41. In addition to the air handling unit and the ductwork, the air handling system contains four motorized dampers so that the flow of air through the rock storage bed can be reversed. There may or may not be an additional set of dampers on the intake plenum connections.

The air always flows through the air handler in the same direction. By opening and closing the proper dampers, the air is made to flow up through the bed when heating the structure and to flow down through the bed when adding energy to storage.

Figure 11.42 shows the position of the dampers and the direction of the air flow when heat is being added to storage. The dampers to the house

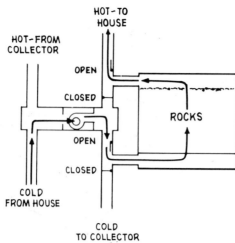

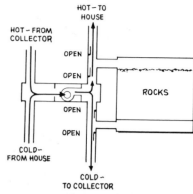

Figure 11.43. Air flow when taking heat from storage.

Figure 11.44. When the house demands heat during the collector heating cycle, the storage bed is bypassed.

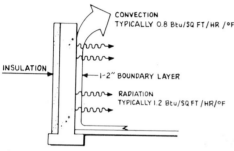

Figure 11.45. Heat from a masonry wall is transferred by radiation and convection.

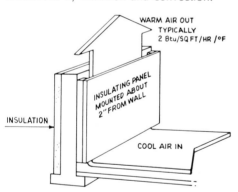

Figure 11.46. How convected heat loss from a concrete wall can be increased and channeled.

hot connection and the cold storage bed connection are closed. The dampers to the cold collector connection and the hot storage bed are open. Air flows up to the top of the storage bed, down through the bed, and back to the collectors. Solar heat is stored in the bed.

Figure 11.43 shows the air flow and damper positions when the house is being heated from storage. The dampers to the hot storage bed connection and to the cold collector connection are closed. The dampers to the cold storage bed connection and the hot house connection are open. Air flows from the cold air house connection through the fan into the bottom of the cold storage bed, through the bed, and out to the building. The stored solar heat is transferred to the building.

If the house demands heat during the time that the collectors are collecting it, all four dampers are opened. The storage bed is bypassed. Hot air from the collectors mixes with cold air from the house. The mixture is returned to both the house and to the collectors. This mode is illustrated in Figure 11.44.

The hot and cold air to the house go through a central air distribution system. This may or may not be connected to an auxiliary furnace. If it is, then the auxiliary furnace should be placed in the hot air house connection so that the cold air from the house can be prewarmed in the storage bed.

Heat Distribution from a Concrete Storage Wall

You learned in Decision 10 that heat is transferred from concrete storage walls by radiation and convection. The radiation loss is about 1.2 Btu/hr/sq ft/°F. The radiated thermal heat does not warm up the air but passes through it until it strikes a solid or a liquid. It then warms up that solid or liquid.

The convection heat loss is caused by the passage of the room's air over the surface of the wall. With natural air convection, this heat loss is typically about 0.8 Btu/hr/sq ft/°F. Most of the convection heat loss takes place in a thin boundary layer of air at the surface. This boundary layer is about 1 to 2 in. thick. These heat loss conditions are illustrated in Figure 11.45, which shows a typical concrete storage wall that has been insulated on one side so that most of the heat transfer occurs on the other side. If the wall is not insulated on one side, the heat loss doubles. Heat is lost in about equal amounts on either side if the area and the Δt are equivalent.

Figure 11.46 shows how this radiant/convective heat loss can be converted to mainly convective loss and channeled to a given area. An insulated panel is mounted on the wall about 1½ to 2 in. away from the wall. Now the radiant energy is stopped by the insulated panel. The boundary layer of air between the wall and the panel quickly heats up. If no outlet for the air exists at the top of the wall, the wall, the panel, and the air space quickly reach heat equilibrium. In that case, the heat loss of the wall becomes the heat loss of the insulated panel, which is a factor of the rate of conductance through the panel or the U-factor of the panel, the convection losses from the outside surface of the panel, and the radiation from the outside surface of the panel.

When an outlet at the top of the panel allows the free circulation of air over the wall's surface, then the convection and radiation losses from the wall are both used to heat the air. The air receives most of the energy lost from the wall, which typically would be about 2 Btu/hr/sq ft/°F if the insulating panel has a reasonable R-value. That reasonable R-value would be in the range of R = 5.

Increasing the Heat Transfer The amount of heat transferred can be increased either by increasing the mass of air flowing over the wall or by increasing the temperature difference between the air and the wall. Figure 11.47 shows a cold air distribution system that returns cold building air from another area within the building and passes it through slots located in the floor at the base of the wall so that it rises up the wall. If a fan were inserted in this cold air supply trunk, then the mass of air passing over the wall would also be increased.

In Figure 11.48, the top of the wall panel has been cut on a slant and closed except at the center. This funnels the heated air into a duct. By placing a fan in the ductwork, the air can be drawn up the wall, heated, and distributed to another area within the building.

Combinations of these different configurations can be used to provide different systems for specific needs.

Calculating the Heat Transfer

The amount of heat that can be transferred from a masonry wall is limited to about 2 Btu/sq ft/hr/°F. This is called the *combined heat transfer coefficient* (HTC). The wall will not release energy any faster. Therefore the amount of heat released from the wall can only be raised or lowered by changing the Δt of the air. This in turn is controlled by the speed of the air passing over the wall. The faster the air passes over a given wall, the less heat that it will pick up per cubic foot. This means that the temperature of the emerging air will be lower.

The air temperature and the wall temperature that must be used to determine the heat transfer rate are the average temperatures of each. These temperatures are calculated by measuring the top and bottom temperatures of the air and the wall and calculating the averages.

The following formula determines the amount of heat that is transferred:

(Sq ft of wall) (2 Btu) (avg Δt) = Btu of heat transferred/hr

Assume a 60-sq-ft wall, free air flow, and an average temperature difference of 20°F between the wall and the air. About 2400 Btu/hr will be transferred.

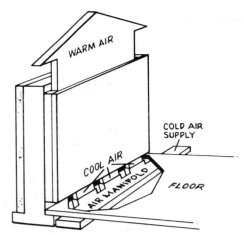

Figure 11.47.   A method to lower the incoming air temperature and increase the Δt at the wall.

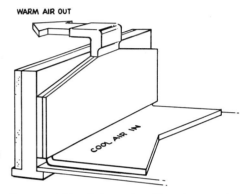

Figure 11.48.   Ductwork with a fan can be used at the top of the wall to increase the flow of the air mass and to move the air to another room.

```
   60  sq ft
 × 2  Btu/hr/sq ft/°F
  120
 × 20  °F
= 2400  Btu/hr
```

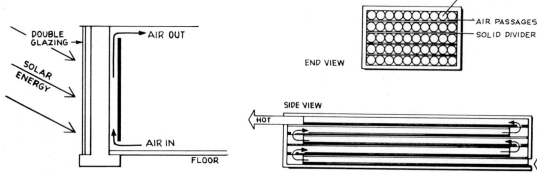

Figure 11.49. One way that the wall can receive heat.

Figure 11.50. The author's suggested salt hydrate tube heat storage bed.

As the heat transfer continues with time, the temperature of the wall will drop and the temperature of the air will increase. So the amount of heat transfer will decrease.

Your calculations of heat transfer from a masonry wall can only be good estimates that are subject to some error. The wall only contains a finite amount of heat. The air temperature of the room will rise unless the air is distributed to another room. And there will be heat losses from the front of the panel due to heat conductance through the panel plus radiation and convection losses from its surface.

When free convection of the air exists, it is hard to determine the average temperature of the air except by actual measurement. The author suggests that a rule of thumb measurement might be a 2°F temperature rise per foot of covered wall height. So if the incoming air temperature were 60°F and the wall panel was 6 ft high, then the average air temperature for design purposes should be 60 plus 12°F, or 72°F. This design temperature can only be confirmed by actual measurement after the wall is constructed. Many factors will affect that condition in actual practice, so it is only a design estimate. The emerging air from such a wall would be at about 72°F.

If the air were mechanically driven over the wall so that the amount of air passing over the wall's surface were known, then it is possible to estimate the emerging temperature of the air more closely by the following formula:

$$(HTC) \ (area) = (\Delta t) \ (CFM) \ (60) \ (0.018)$$

Assume that the HTC = 2 Btu, that the area is 60 sq ft, and that the air flow is 10 CFM. In that case, the emerging temperature would be about 11°F hotter than the incoming air. Examination of this example shows you that the air flow over a concrete wall must be fairly slow if you are to achieve a very high temperature rise.

$$(2) \ (60) = (\Delta t) \ (10) \ (60) \ (0.018)$$
$$\Delta t = \frac{120}{10.80}$$
$$\Delta t = 11.1°F$$

The Disadvantages of the Insulating Panel Approach

When a panel, such as the one shown in Figure 11.46 is placed over a masonry wall, the wall cannot be heated by direct solar radiation because the panel will be opaque to the radiation. So the wall must be heated from the opposite side such as shown in Figure 11.49 or heated indirectly by flowing warm air through the space between the panel and the wall.

If the panel is to be heated indirectly by warm air, the heat transferred into the wall will approximate about 0.8 to 1 Btu/sq ft/hr/°F. For the best results, hot air from the warmest part of the building should be mechanically blown over the wall in a downward or counterflow direction.

It is also possible to use a panel on the wall that is transparent to solar radiation but opaque to thermal radiation. Glass works best. But the *R*-value of a sheet of glass is low, so the heat loss by conductance through the glass will lower the heat transfer by convection between the panel and the wall. The amount of heat lost from conductance away from the glass will depend to a large extent on the temperature of the glass. This temperature can be kept low by increasing the air flow by mechanical means or by double glazing.

Heat Distribution from a Phase-change Media

You will recall that heat storage in a phase-change media takes place at one specific temperature rather than at a wide range of temperatures. In calcium chloride hexahydrate, for example, most of the heat is stored and released at around 84°F.

In Decision 10, you examined calcium chloride hexahydrate packaged in long, slender polyethylene tubes. These tubes were about 6 ft long, 3½ in. in diameter, and contained 29 lb of the salt hydrate. The salt was reported to melt at 81°F, to have a heat of fusion of 82 Btu/lb, and to store 2378 Btu during that change of state.

If these tubes were stood in a single row along a wall, then the heat transfer could be treated in a similar manner to the heat transfer from a masonry wall. The same rules would apply. And the heat transfer coefficients would be about the same. The average temperature of the tube surface would be fixed at 81°F.

The manufacturer of this tube has not presented much experimental data on using these tubes in a salt hydrate storage bed. He does show one proposed drawing where the tubes are stood on end and the air enters from the bottom to be warmed. Warm air exits from the top. However, he shows no plenum. Therefore it is doubtful if that configuration will result in even air flow.

The author suggests that a different system be considered when using these tubes in a storage bed. Figure 11.50 shows the end view and the side view of a storage bin where the tubes have been laid down rather than stood up. They are laid on sheets of plywood or hardboard so that each layer is separate. The tubes and the separators are staggered.

This configuration assures maximum even air flow around the tubes. The cool air entering from the bottom of the bed must circulate through each layer before proceeding to the next layer.

The author does not have any data on how strong these tubes are when they are laid down on their sides. However, examination of the tube would indicate that up to five layers in depth would be self-supporting. That assumption should be checked with the manufacturer of the tube that you decide to use. It may be necessary to support the spacers.

The bed in Figure 11.50 contains 50 tubes. So at the heat of fusion temperature, it can store 118,900 Btu.

Each tube has 5.5 sq ft of surface area. So it should be possible to draw 11 Btu/tube/hr/°F or a total of 550 Btu/hr/°F from the storage bed.

If air is to enter at 60°F and it is desired to have it exit at 81°F, then the Δt across the bed will be 11°F and the average Δt through the bed will be 5.5°F. So the bed can transfer 3025 Btu/hr.

Using the formula:

$$\Delta t \times HTC = \text{air } \Delta t \times CFM \times 60 \times 0.018$$

```
    2378  Btu/tube
  ×   50  tubes
= 118,900  Btu

    3.5  in. dia.
  × 3.14  π
  10.99
  ×  72  in. length
  791.3  sq in.
  ÷ 144  sq in./sq ft
    5.5  sq ft
  ×   2  Btu/hr/sq ft/°F
     11  Btu/tube/hr/°F
  ×  50  tubes
    550  Btu/hr/°F
  × 5.5  avg Δt
   3025  Btu/hr, HTC
```

$$3025 = (11) \ (CFM) \ (60) \ (0.018)$$
$$CFM = 3025 \div 11.88$$
$$CFM = 254.6$$

suggests that the flow of air through the bed should be about 255 CFM to achieve the 11°F temperature rise. In a bed of this type, it would not be necessary to reverse the air flow to warm the bed.

Such a bed of storage tubes would be quite expensive. However, it would store large amounts of energy. It is very important to determine how you will charge the bed with energy. It will not be effective if you cannot move the energy into it. Most likely, you will need an array of active solar collectors.

Making a Decision

In this chapter you studied how solar energy can be distributed around your building. You quickly learned that most of the energy received was received on the south side of your home. But you also learned that most of daytime heat loss took place on the north side of the structure. That taught you that there was a need to move the heated air from the south side to the north side. You learned ways in which this could readily be accomplished.

Then you learned how heat stored in water could be moved around your structure. You studied heat exchangers and learned about heat exchanger effectiveness so that you could properly choose the correct exchanger for your system.

You learned about removing heat from masonry walls, and you saw how to compute the amount of heat that could be removed. Plus you saw ways in which to direct where that heat went.

Last, you saw how heat can be stored and removed from phase-change media such as salt hydrates, and you determined the amount of heat that could be effectively transferred.

You should now have the information that you need to design a heat distribution system for your building.

DECISION
12

Consider an Earth-insulated House

For thousands of years people lived in caves, which were cheap, generally available, and easy to heat and cool. But in today's modern society, caves are not available. The demand would be so great if they were, that the cost would not be cheap. But they are still easy to heat and cool.

The earth-insulated house can be thought of as an alternative. It could be generally available and it is easy to heat and cool. But the earth-insulated house will not be cheap. Its cost will depend on the design and the building site.

There is a vast difference between the primitive cave and the modern earth-insulated house. The genius of today's architects has been applied to earth-insulated house design. Some very attractive and functional results have emerged from the architects' planning.

This chapter will explore the elements of earth-insulated design and present some typical earth-insulated house types for you to consider. You will study:

* Why earth-insulated houses are easy to heat and cool.
* How the atrium house is designed and constructed.
* The elements of designing and building an elevational earth-covered house.
* The penetrational style earth-covered house and its construction.
* The hillside house, the first in a series of practical passive solar houses that combine traditional with revolutionary design.

Why the Earth-insulated House Is Easy to Heat and Cool

Heat loss is a function of $UA\Delta t$. That is, the area of the exterior wall and roof of the structure, the speed at which heat is conducted through these walls, and the difference between the indoor and the outdoor temperature.

In an earth-insulated house, the U-factor and the Δt are the two values that are changed from a standard structure. These two values must be studied to see why heat loss and gains are lower.

The weather data for the earth has been studied, and an *integrated value* has been published for many locations. An integrated value is the average temperature of the earth measured from the surface to a depth of 10 ft. Figure 12.1 shows some of these data. The maximum temperatures encountered in the summertime ranged from 57 to 83°F. The minimum temperatures encountered during the wintertime ranged from 33 to 60°F. When these are averaged for year-round use, the range is from 47 to 72°F.

LOCATION	MAXIMUM °F	MINIMUM °F	AVERAGE °F
Alabama	72	52	62
Arizona	83	62	72
California	83	60	72
Colorado	64	36	50
Idaho	57	37	47
Illinois	66	40	53
Indiana	66	38	52
Kansas	69	41	55
Kentucky	70	46	58
Maryland	70	42	56
Michigan	63	37	50
Minnesota	62	34	49
Montana	60	34	47
New Jersey	65	42	54
North Carolina	73	52	61
Oklahoma	65	41	53
South Dakota	61	33	47
Vermont	63	35	49
Range	83-57	33-60	47-72

Figure 12.1. Average integrated temperature of the earth in various locations from the surface to a depth of 10 ft.

It follows that the earth does not show the wide swings in temperature that the outside air does. So the temperature variations that the house heating and cooling system must overcome are far less. Generally, except in the extreme south, the temperature tends to be below the comfort level rather than above it. So cooling needs are far less in an earth-insulated house.

A building surrounded by air loses heat from radiation and convection as well as conduction through the walls. But a building surrounded by earth only loses heat by conduction. Earth is a solid. There is little or no heat loss by radiation and convection.

Heat losses through soil have been the subject of much study. They will vary from location to location and from soil to soil. Light, dry soil will conduct very little heat. Heavy, damp soils will conduct from two to four times as much.

For general design purposes, the data that have been collected for basement walls can be readily used for earth-insulated houses. Typical design data are tabulated in Figures 12.2 and 12.3. Figure 12.2 shows the heat losses from underground concrete walls. Note that the loss is lowered as the depth increases.

DEPTH BELOW GRADE IN FEET	AMOUNT OF INSULATION		
	NONE	2 IN.	3 IN.
1-2	0.22	0.08	0.06
2-3	0.16	0.07	0.05
3-4	0.12	0.06	0.05
4-5	0.10	0.05	0.04
5-6	0.08	0.05	0.04
6-7	0.07	0.04	0.04
Below 7	0.07	0.04	0.04
Average	0.12	10.055	0.045

Figure 12.2. Heat loss below grade for concrete walls with and without insulation in Btu/hr/sq ft/°F.

With uninsulated walls the heat loss levels off at about 6 ft and remains roughly the same at greater depths. When the walls are insulated, this leveling off takes place at a shallower depth of about 4 to 6 ft. This would indicate that the upper part of the wall should receive more insulation than the lower part.

Figure 12.3 shows the heat loss through uninsulated concrete floors located 6- to 8-ft underground. The heat losses are very low. One is led to believe that floors located that far underground will require no insulation. A design temperature of 50°F may be used for calculating heat loss from concrete floors installed in this location.

DEPTH BELOW GRADE IN FEET	HOUSE WIDTH IN FEET			
	22 FT	26 FT	30 FT	34 FT
6	0.03	0.03	0.02	0.02
8	0.03	0.03	0.02	0.02

Figure 12.3. Heat loss through uninsulated concrete floors in Btu/hr/sq ft/°F.

For calculating the heat loss of concrete walls, the average *U*-factor shown in Figure 12.2 may be used along with the minimum integrated temperature shown in Figure 12.1.

The heat lost through the walls and the floors heats up the surrounding soil. This soil diffuses the heat very slowly. So the surrounding soil acts as further insulation for the walls.

The ceilings of earth-insulated houses should be treated as if they are in outer air unless they are more than 2 ft underground. This treatment will generally indicate a slightly higher heat loss than actual.

Types of Earth-insulated Houses

There are at least four types of earth-insulated houses: the atrium house, the elevational house, the penetrational house, and the hillside house.

The atrium house is a house built around courtyards that give natural light and ventilation to the house. Typically, the atrium house is almost all underground.

The elevational house typically has the windows and doors grouped along one side of the house with the balance of the house located under earth cover. This style fits a south-sloping lot well in cold climates and a north-facing lot in warm climates.

The penetrational house is earth-bermed for insulation, but windows are placed in various locations around the house through openings in the earth berms.

The hillside house is built with two of its four sides built into the side of a south-facing hillside in a cold climate or a north-facing hillside in a hot climate. Typically the house is constructed so that the sun that normally warms the hillside penetrates the house and warms its interior.

The Atrium House

The atrium house is a very interesting design. In small houses, a single courtyard will give adequate light, ventilation, and fire escape routes. But as the house becomes larger and contains five or more rooms, some of the traditional sizes and shapes seen in traditional housing can no longer be properly used. The single courtyard provides neither adequate light nor ventilation.

The author has conceived a design concept for larger atrium houses that helps to solve some of the problems. It calls for all concrete construction. Some of the details are shown in Figure 12.4. The outer walls and the floor are poured concrete. The roof is precast concrete plank supported by steel beams posted every 14 ft. Although some construction details are included in Figure 12.4, the reader is cautioned to use a structural or civil engineer to design the details of an atrium house. There are many forces acting on such a house, so great care must be taken to construct it from the proper materials.

The house is shown with 2 to 4 in. of rigid foam insulation surrounding the walls and the ceiling. Polystyrene or polyurethane foam can be used. Check with the manufacturer on the underground use of the foam that you purchase. Be certain that it is suitable for that type of installation.

A waterproof barrier with low permeability must be placed between the insulation and the concrete wall. The use of this membrane is basic to the comfort of the house.

Concrete Construction magazine printed an article titled "Concrete in Residential Construction" in November 1975 that covers all the fundamentals of below-grade concrete construction. And in July 1981, it prepared a special issue titled: Earth Sheltered Construction, No. CCP-01-38-V. Reprints are available from the magazine, which is located at 329 Interstate Road, Addison, Illinois 60101. The reader is urged to obtain a copy of these articles before proceeding with design and construction of an atrium house.

The house has been surrounded with gravel or stone. This allows any water to drain to the bottom where it can be removed by drain tile. An impervious soil cap of heavy soil is placed over the gravel to help shed rain. The cap is typically higher than the surrounding grade so that water will run off rather than lay on the roof. If the water table is higher than the floor, it is necessary to place drain tile throughout the house to prevent hydraulic pressure from cracking the floor. A network of tile every 14 ft is suggested by the author.

The drains should work by gravity if at all possible. If not, then two sump pumps should be installed in case one fails during the rainy season. Even with gravity drains, a back-up pump should be installed in case of blockage.

The Width of an Atrium House

The width of a traditional above ground house ranges from 22 to 32 ft. Houses wider than that are hard to ventilate and light. However, the atrium house can be built much wider with very good results.

The author has chosen to use a 42-ft-wide design concept. This width was chosen so that the house could be designed in basic squares of 14 ft

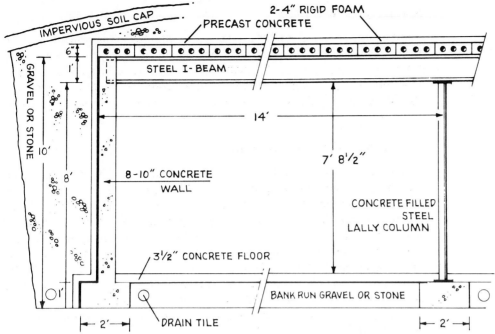

Figure 12.4. General construction details of the author's atrium house.

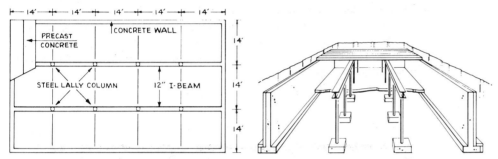

Figure 12.5. The author's atrium house is laid out on a 14 × 4 ft post and beam grid.

Figure 12.6. Looking at the author's atrium house from one end.

by 14 ft as shown in Figure 12.5. Two steel beams run the length of the house. They are posted every 14 ft or less. Now the house can be laid out in about 13 ft wide rooms of any length. Post locations can be shifted as required for the layout. Figure 12.6 looks at the author's atrium design from one end. This clearly shows the basic construction so that it can be readily understood.

A 9-ft wall has been used in the author's design. This was done so that there would be 7 ft 8½ in. of headroom under the steel beams. In this type of planning, the beams can be hidden in a dropped ceiling. The piping and wiring for the house can be done overhead, which eliminates running pipes, conduits, and ducts under the concrete floor.

Ventilation and Lighting

Two atriums separated from each other are almost a necessity to provide good lighting and ventilation. Each room must have adequate natural light. Each room must be located so that access to the outside is direct in case of fire. If one atrium is built so that it protrudes further out of the ground than the other atrium, natural ventilation is enhanced through a stack effect.

Sewage and Sanitation

There is always the question of how to handle the sanitary facilities. If the house is located where sewers run lower than the floor, then there are no problems. If not, then careful planning must be done to locate the septic tank and filter bed properly. It may be necessary to install a sanitary sewage lift pump in the system. Again, a good civil engineer should be consulted for the proper design.

A Two Bedroom Atrium House

Figure 12.7 shows a two bedroom atrium design in a 42 ft by 42 ft size. The house is entered from ground level by a set of stairs descending to the corner front atrium. Entry is into a small foyer between the living room and the family kitchen. These are both very large rooms as is almost always required in an atrium design to overcome the feeling of closeness.

A set of sliding doors lead from the kitchen to the rear atrium. This atrium is designed without a staircase. A fire-escape ladder can readily be built into the outside wall. A door from the bedroom wing also leads to the atrium. The combination of the two doors allows free air circulation through the house and the advantage of being able to cross from the kitchen to the bedrooms directly.

This rear atrium can readily be enclosed with a glass top if desired for northern climates. Details are shown in Figure 12.10.

The bedrooms and their closets are adequate, although twin beds could not be placed in the smaller bedroom. A hall from the living room leads to the bath and the bedroom wing. A small utility room houses the heating and hot water equipment.

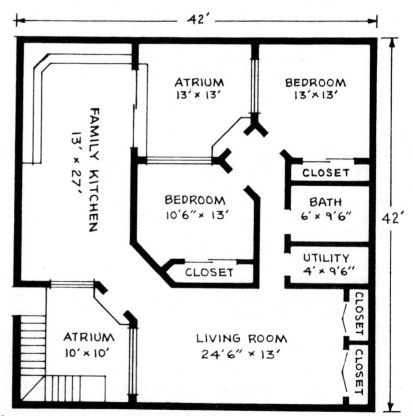

Figure 12.7. A two bedroom atrium house.

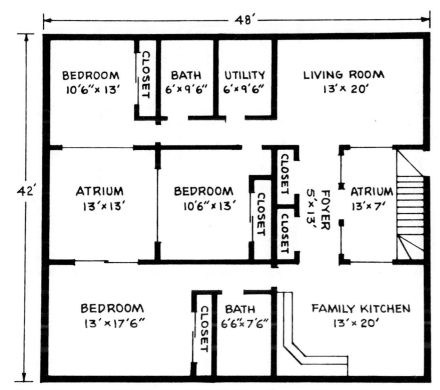

Figure 12.8. A three bedroom, two bath atrium house.

A Three Bedroom, Two Bath Atrium House

Figure 12.8 shows a three bedroom, two bath atrium house. The basic plan has been expanded to 42 ft by 48 ft. The front courtyard has been moved to the center of the side of the house. The family kitchen has been moved forward to fill the space formerly occupied by the courtyard.

Now entry can be into a central foyer. A master bedroom can be located behind the kitchen with its own bath. The utility room can be expanded. The jogs can be removed from the halls and bedrooms. This aids in the furniture layout of the bedrooms. Good ventilation is still achieved via the two hallways to the rear atrium. Only one door is shown to the rear atrium, which makes it an adjunct to the master bedroom, but more could be added from the other bedrooms. Again, the rear atrium could be enclosed in northern climates.

A Four Bedroom, Family Room Atrium House

The versatility of this design concept for larger houses is shown in Figure 12.9 where the house has been expanded to 70 ft in length and a third atrium has been added.

The house is entered again by a staircase in the front court. Sliding doors lead to either the family room or the living room. The kitchen is located between the dining room and the family room and receives indirect lighting from the front court and the dining room atrium.

The bedrooms are entered from the rear of the family room through a traversing hallway. The master bedroom is located at the end. A third atrium provides lighting and ventilation for the two rear bedrooms and the study. The third bedroom is lighted from the dining room atrium. Doors lead to both interior atriums for outdoor use.

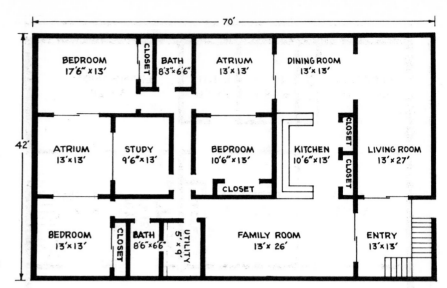

Figure 12.9. A four bedroom, family room atrium house.

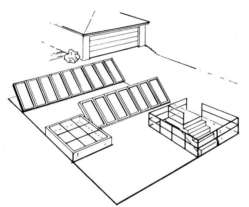

Figure 12.10. Ground level view of a typical solarized atrium house.

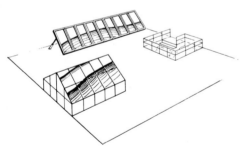

Figure 12.11. Typical atrium greenhouse enclosure.

Atrium Houses and Active Solar Systems

The atrium house is an ideal candidate for an active solar heating system. The heat demands are low. The collectors can be ground-mounted. The piping runs are short, with most losses being confined to the living area. Figure 12.10 shows a ground level view of a small atrium house with active solar collectors and a garage in the background.

The Atrium Greenhouse Cover

The atriums in houses located in northern climates can be readily enclosed using standard greenhouse techniques. One such enclosure is shown in Figure 12.11. Many types of configurations can be used. When the greenhouse concept is used, year round gardens can fill the atriums, giving a sense of more southern climates plus outdoor scenery. Provision must be made for adequate ventilation, and a fire escape route must be planned into the design.

The Elevational Design

The elevational design presents different problems in layout and development, but the general construction can be very similar. The author has chosen the same type of construction in developing the elevational design. Figure 12.12 shows a typical construction method. Three sides and the

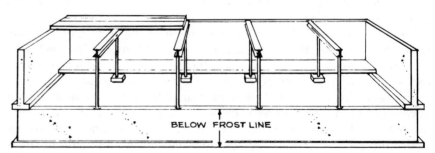

Figure 12.12. Typical elevational house construction.

roof are earth-covered, so concrete walls and a concrete roof have been chosen. The roof is supported with steel beams posted on 14 ft centers. Note the front wall extending below the frost line. This wall is needed to prevent the floor from heaving and the post supports from moving. In some areas a *grade beam* is allowed and can replace the concrete wall. A grade beam is a steel reinforced footing set on piers spaced the same distance as the supporting columns. Again, a civil engineer should be consulted for details. The general construction considerations for piping, conduits, moisture protection, and sanitary services are similar to those in the atrium design.

The front wall, which is to be exposed to the air, should either be well-insulated wood construction or thermal breaks should be made between the concrete that is exposed and the concrete that is earth-covered. Otherwise much heat will be lost through conduction at the air-concrete interface.

The atrium plan tended toward a very wide, squarish design with rooms placed behind and alongside each other. This is not possible in the single-wall elevational design. The house must be narrower in width. The rooms must be placed alongside each other. Rooms cannot be placed behind each other and still receive natural lighting or provide easy exit in case of fire.

A Typical Elevational Design

Figure 12.13 shows a typical three bedroom elevational design. The house is 70 ft long by 20 ft wide so that all rooms face the exposed wall for lighting. Thus the design requires a 26-ft hall to reach the full bedroom wing. Closets have all been placed on the rear to squeeze the rooms as close together as possible. The layout is on a 14-ft module, which allows excellent room sizes.

This house is entirely adequate and would make a good home. But it is hard to visualize how a four bedroom house with a family room could be built in this manner. It would need to be about 98 ft long.

The Angled Elevational Design

Figure 12.14 shows a house of similar size that has been angled to wrap it into a hillside. Many lots will lend themselves to this configuration. The angling of the house gains shorter halls, particularly when the master bedroom is placed on the other wing and entry is made through the kitchen. A dining area is created. A utility room becomes practical. And two baths can be placed in the design. The bedroom wings are now 26 ft wide whereas the center wing is 21 ft wide. The house is about 1650 sq ft as compared to the 1400 sq ft shown in the design in Figure 12.13. The house is 4 ft longer, and the window area becomes 10 ft longer.

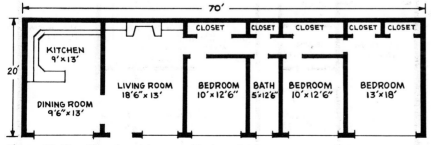

Figure 12.13. Elevational house with three bedrooms.

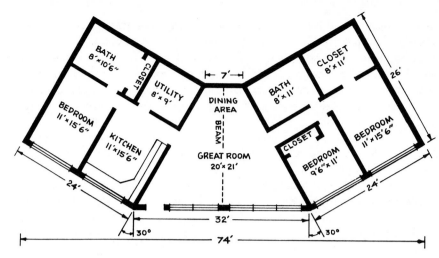

Figure 12.14. Elevational house wrapped into a hillside.

Figure 12.15. An exposed pitched roof can be used over the center wing on the angled house.

There are two roofline designs possible with this angled design. The roof over the great room can be flat and earth-covered. Or a pitched roof sloping to the back can be used as shown in Figure 12.15. This pitched roof design brings the center of the house up out of the earth to form a striking central design that allows the capture of large amounts of sunlight in the great room and gives a vent window over the dining room. The advantages of complete earth-cover are still seen in the wings.

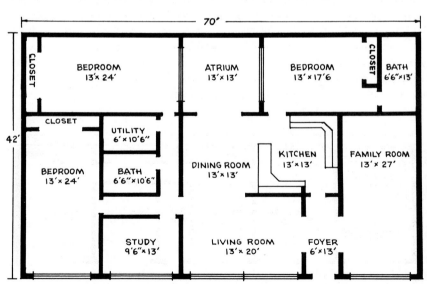

Figure 12.16. A large atrium-elevational house.

Combining Atrium Design with Elevational Design

The atrium and the elevational design combine extremely well. For larger houses, this is a more practical approach. Figure 12.16 shows the 42 ft by 70 ft atrium house in Figure 12.9 redesigned for an elevational wall along the front of the design.

Two atriums have been eliminated and replaced by the elevational wall. The house is now entered by a foyer between the living room and the family room that leads to the kitchen. The master bedroom with its own bath has been placed behind the family room. The dining room is now an L-shaped adjunct to the living room lighted by both the atrium and the living room elevational wall. The kitchen has been developed into a broken L shape. It is lighted by the atrium.

The bedroom wing is now entered from the end of the living room. The study has been pulled forward to the front of the house. The utility room and the bath have been moved to the center bay. As a result of these moves and the elimination of the left atrium, two very large bedrooms are formed.

The author has made no attempt to modify the size on the 14 ft by 14 ft layout of this house. Many modifications are possible.

The Penetrational Design

The penetrational design presents a more traditional layout. The normal 22 to 32 ft width of the traditional house is generally maintained. The interior room arrangement follows the general design principles espoused in Decision 8. The house is built earth-covered. Parts of the earth cover are pierced to allow natural lighting and ventilation. In short, it can be considered a traditional house design with earth bermed around it except where the doors and windows are located.

Figure 12.17 shows a front view of a 26 ft by 52 ft ranch house that follows the layout shown in Decision 8. The roof and the sides of the house have been covered completely with earth. The front of the house is only partly covered so that the doors and windows are open to the air. Retaining walls hold back the earth cover at the appropriate spots.

Figure 12.18 shows a rear view of the same house. Much more of the rear wall is earth-covered than the front wall. Some compromises as to

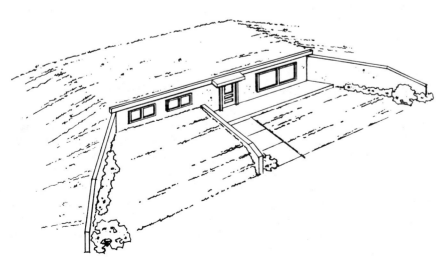

Figure 12.17. Front view of a typical penetrational house.

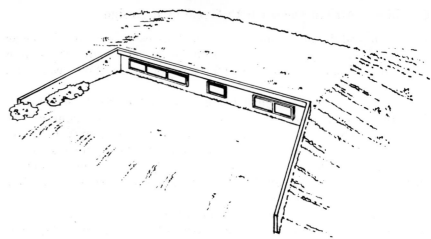

Figure 12.18. Rear view of a typical penetrational house.

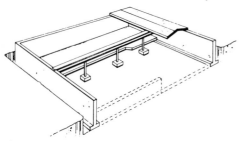

Figure 12.19. Typical construction of a penetrational house viewed from one side.

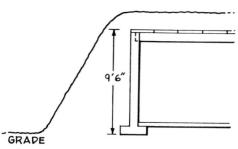

Figure 12.20. A penetrational house set on grade needs 11 ft of earth cover.

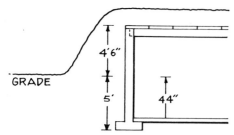

Figure 12.21. A penetrational house set 5 ft below grade only needs 6 ft of earth cover.

where the doors and windows are located have been made in modifying the design to allow for earth cover.

Figure 12.19 shows the typical construction of a penetrational house. Again, poured concrete walls with a precast concrete plank roof have been chosen. However, where the earth cover is pierced, the walls convert to wood construction. If the concrete is allowed to run through these points, much heat will be lost through conduction. An alternative strategy would be to run the concrete through but to insulate it and cover the insulation with a decorative siding. A steel beam, posted at appropriate points, runs through the center of the building to support the roof.

A penetrational building set on the grade on a level lot would require about 11 ft of earth cover. This would be awkward in appearance and most likely call for large amounts of fill to be trucked to the building site. Figure 12.20 shows why this amount of earth would be needed.

Figure 12.21 shows the same building height set down into the grade by 5 ft. The earth cover now only needs to be about 6 ft. The windows for the house can start at 44 in. off the floor, which is satisfactory for outdoor viewing. Such a siting would make it possible for the building to be covered with the dirt taken from the building excavation. The outside appearance would be more harmonious with its surroundings.

The construction problems of moisture removal, drainage, damp-proofing, and so forth all remain as in the other two styles of earth-covered homes and must be carefully dealt with in design and engineering.

Combining Features of the Major Styles

Obviously, the features of each of these three earth-covered styles can be combined to design a house that melds into its surroundings and still meets the needs of the occupants. The site, the family, and the space all need to be carefully considered in the earth-covered design.

The mechanical module is missing from the designs shown here. It is apparent in this type of design that the mechanical module will be limited in size and availability. No transportation modules have been shown, but they can readily be part of the final design by following the same construction principles.

Earth-covered designs can be combined with more traditional design for parts of the house. Figure 12.15 showed an example of a traditional center section with two angled earth-covered wings. In the next section, you will learn about a style that is even more traditional but that uses some elements of earth-covered design.

The Hillside House

The author felt that the three design categories of atrium, elevational, and penetrational earth-covered houses did not fully exploit the possibilities of earth-covered design. So he chose to take a different approach that combined earth-insulated design with a more traditional building approach.

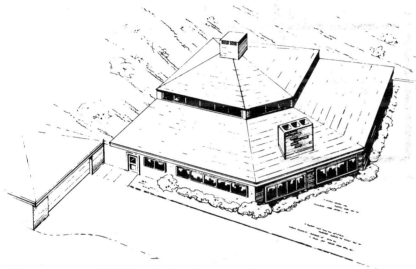

Figure 12.22. A hillside solar house.

The concept uses a south-facing, sloped lot in the northern latitudes or a north-facing sloped lot in the southern latitudes of the United States. The discussion that follows will relate to heating on a south-facing lot. The reader should remember, however, that cooling can be accomplished if a north-facing sloped lot is chosen.

A south-facing lot receives gross amounts of sunshine year round that warm the ground extremely well. So why not design a house that will capture this heat and hold it? The house in Figure 12.22 is the result of efforts put forth in that direction. A 42-ft square house was drawn. One corner of the house was stuck back into a sloping hillside. This resulted in two sides of the house being completely earth-covered. But no change in the natural slope of the lot was made. Then the opposite corner of the house, which faced south, was cut off at a 45° angle. This left a three-sided house exposed to the sun with one side facing southeast, one side facing south, and one side facing southwest. This gave the floor plan shown in Figure 12.23.

The bedrooms would have no light if the design did not call for some windows. To achieve this, a clerestory wall was designed into the house about 26 ft out from the rear walls. This provides light and solar energy to the bedrooms and the bath. To keep the ceiling height within reason, the house was created as a split-level; the occupants step up to the rear bedrooms and the bath. The living room and the dining room are combined

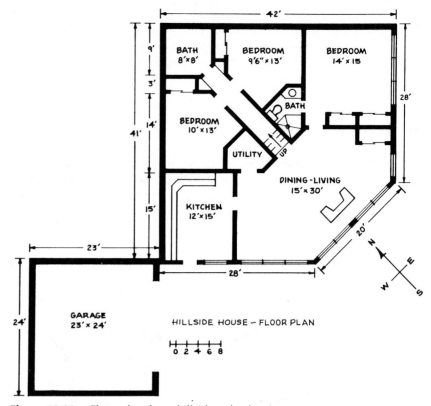

Figure 12.23. Floor plan for a hillside solar house.

Figure 12.24. Construction details of the author's hillside solar house.

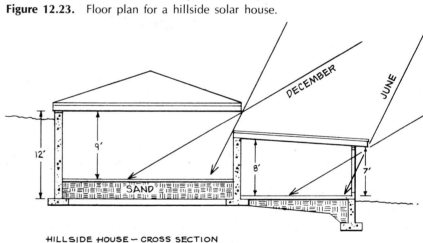

Figure 12.25. Cross section of the author's hillside solar house.

into one very large room with the kitchen off to one side and the master bedroom off to the other side with its own bath.

The details of construction are shown in Figure 12.24. This illustration shows the concrete part of the house. The rear wall, the center clerestory walls, and the floors are poured concrete. The front wall, which is shown only in dotted outline, is conventional wood construction.

Imagine the house without any further construction other than what is shown in this illustration. The sun would shine down on the concrete all day long. The solar energy would be soaked up, and the concrete would act as a large heat sink.

The balance of the construction is shown in the cross section drawn in Figure 12.25. The winter sun penetrates the house, and the heat is stored in the walls, floor, and sand located under the floor. This combination

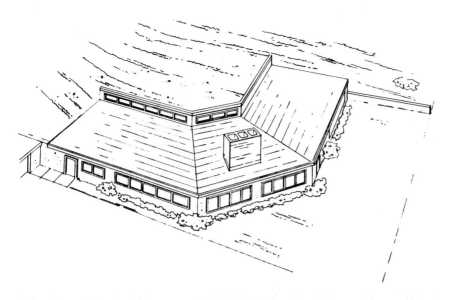

Figure 12.26. A hillside solar house with an earth-covered concrete plank roof over the upper bedroom section.

gives a very large thermal mass that is capable of storing tremendous quantities of heat.

Although this particular set of sketches shows the building with a conventional hip roof, it can be designed with an earth-covered concrete plank roof over the upper bedroom section. Figure 12.26 shows this roofline.

This house is the first in a series of practical solar building designs that you will study throughout the rest of this book. It combines the traditional with the revolutionary to give some evolutionary designs that only depart from the recognized to the extent that is required to gain solar heating.

Making a Decision

In this chapter you studied the elements of earth-covered building design. First, you looked at why earth-covered houses save energy. Then you studied the four design types of earth-covered buildings: the atrium, the elevational, the penetrational, and the hillside house. You learned that these four styles can be combined to give gracious living along with lower energy requirements. You should now be able to decide whether you want to consider an earth-covered house.

DECISION
13

Assess the Thermal Envelope House

You are about to study a house design that is relatively new to the North American residential market—the thermal envelope house.

Although the design is relatively new to the market, it has already shown that it holds much promise. Some designers are talking about how much better the design performs than they had calculated. Some owners are talking about how comfortable the houses are to live in. But not all designers agree that thermal envelope houses are successful. Many designers have presented data indicating that thermal envelope houses perform poorly.

The reasons why these designers differ must be understood before the design of thermal envelope houses can be standardized. That will take some time. And it will take some experimentation.

In this chapter you will study the basic design of the thermal envelope house. You will study:

- How the thermal envelope building works.
- What structural changes are required for a thermal envelope design.
- A traditional envelope house.
- Why more contemporary thermal envelope designs are not included in this book.

The author advises you to consult with an architect who has built and tested several thermal envelope houses before you decide to move in that direction. The author also advises you to choose a currently existing design that has proved to have good performance.

How the Thermal Envelope Building Works

In Decision 11 you learned about energy distribution within a building structure. You saw that most of the sun's energy fell on the south-facing side of the structure and that you would need to move that energy mechanically to the north-facing side of the house by moving the air within the building. A thermal envelope building is a structure that is built in a manner that allows this energy to move around the building by free convection without fans or other mechanical devices.

Figure 13.1 shows the thermal envelope concept. A double-walled structure is built with an air passage between the inner and outer insulated shells. The sun's energy heats up the air on the south-facing side. This warm air rises to the peak of the roof where it cools and travels down the north-facing roof and wall and returns to the basement. The air from the basement continuously circulates up the south-facing wall as the sun warms the south side.

The structure of the house can readily be altered to enhance this natural convection. Look at Figure 13.2. Fenestration has been placed in the south-facing roof and wall. The inner shell has been eliminated on the south-facing side. The air in the building is heated by the sun. It rises to the peak of the roof where it is cooled by the north-facing roof and travels down to the basement.

It is possible to further alter the building's shape both to optimize the use of available space and to optimize the free convection of solar-heated air. Figure 13.3 shows the general way in which this can be done. Here the south-facing wall has been extended so that it can gather more energy. The peak of the roof has been moved toward the south side to lengthen the north-facing roof that cools the air. A second story has been added in the space created by these alterations.

The alterations shown thus far do not aid in cooling the house in the summer months. Further alterations to the building structure are required to allow for cooling. Figure 13.4 shows these changes.

A clerestory wall has been added at the peak. This clerestory wall contains vents. Now during the summer months the warm air striking the home can be exhausted from the home by free convection. The north-facing side of the roof is no longer in the shadow but is also heated by the sun as the sun is high in the sky. Cool air is drawn up from the basement on both the south-facing and north-facing sides.

A thermal mass in the form of rock or sand has been added to the basement. Underground air ducts lead from a shady spot on the north-facing

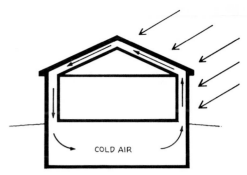

Figure 13.1. The thermal envelope concept; cold air from the basement is circulated around a double-walled and roofed house by convection currents.

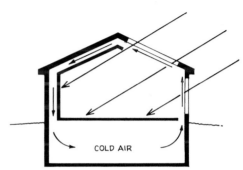

Figure 13.2. The south-facing wall can be changed to fenestration and the south-facing inner wall eliminated to increase the solar gain.

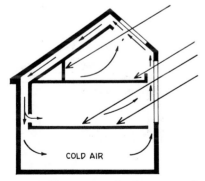

Figure 13.3. The structure's shape can also be altered to take maximum advantage of solar energy.

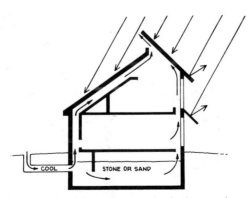

Figure 13.4. The shape can be further modified to vent the hot air in the summer and draw in and store cool air in the basement.

side of the house to the basement. Air is drawn into the basement through these ducts. The air is cooled as it passes through the ductwork. The air circulating between the two insulated shells protects the inner shell from the high ambient air temperatures of the summer months.

You can see from this discussion that the function of the air envelope in the thermal envelope house is to lower the Δt between the living space and the outdoors by free air convection.

There is a major cost penalty incurred in building a thermal envelope home. Double wall and roof construction is expensive. Both the inner and the outer walls must be insulated, and fire protection is needed between the walls.

The Structural Changes Required

Figure 13.5 shows the general construction of a typical ranch house. The basement walls are poured concrete. A heavy beam running lengthwise through the center of the house helps support the floor. Above this beam, a wood-frame carrying partition helps carry the building's ceiling. The

Figure 13.5. Typical ranch house construction.

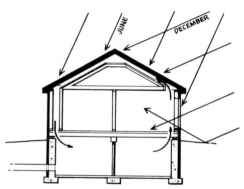

Figure 13.6. Approaching a thermal envelope with standard construction techniques.

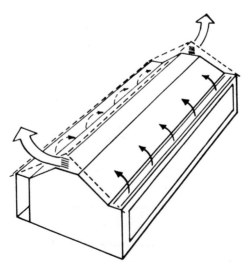

Figure 13.7. Another view of the modified ranch house.

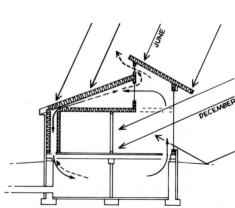

Figure 13.8. Thermal envelope ranch house.

ceiling joists tie the rafters together across the house to prevent the walls from spreading. A collar girt is placed across every third rafter to aid in this.

Figure 13.6 shows the minimum changes that could be made to move toward the design of a thermal envelope house. The floor and the roof have been insulated. Air passages between the basement and the first floor have been created on both the north-facing and the south-facing sides of the structure. Air passages have also been created between the attic and the first floor on both sides. A double wall has been erected on the north-facing side, and an insulated shell has been erected in the attic.

Air should freely circulate around this house. But no provision has been made to exhaust the hot air in the summer months. So fans must be inserted in the ends of the structure near the peak of the roof to accomplish this. And cool air must be pumped into the basement to replenish the hot air that is exhausted. Figure 13.7 shows another view of this modified ranch house that will help you better understand the general changes in the attic. The dampers at either end should be motorized dampers under positive control. They must not leak air when closed in the winter months. The location of these exhaust fans is dictated by the prevailing winds as well as by the peak of the roof.

Figure 13.8 shows a true thermal envelope ranch house design. The rear roof has been raised to form a clerestory wall for summer heat exhaust. The higher rear wall allows for greater sun penetration. The removal of a part of the ceiling aids in obtaining deep penetration of the sun's energy into the structure.

Care must be taken to maintain structural integrity when changing the ceiling and raising the rear wall. An approach to this is shown in Figure 13.9. Every third ceiling joist is doubled up and run to the rear wall. Doubled-up headers are inserted between these joists, and the intermediate joists are ended in the header. The maximum strength is obtained when a full-length timber is used for the intermediate joists so that the joist is cantilevered out over the center bearing partition.

The roof pitch can be raised to a 10 or 12 in. pitch in order to create an upstairs in the house. This is illustrated with a 10-in. roof pitch in Figure 13.10. In this 24-ft-wide home, the 10-in. pitch creates a 10-ft-wide room on the second floor. Openings in the wall in this upstairs room allow the sun to penetrate and warm the room. Note the tie at the ceiling between the two roofs. This is necessary to prevent the building from spreading

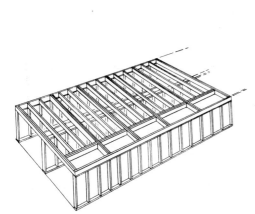

Figure 13.9. How structural integrity is maintained when cutting away the ceiling for a raised rear wall.

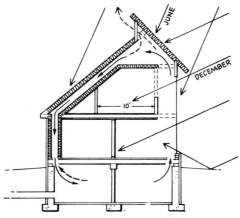

Figure 13.10. Raising the roof pitch creates an upstairs room.

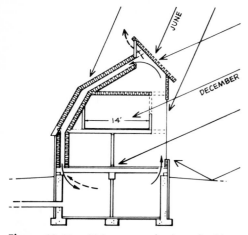

Figure 13.11. Using a gambrel roof widens the upstairs room.

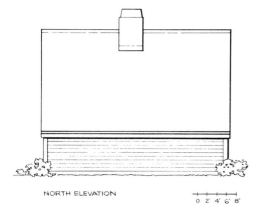

NORTH ELEVATION

0 2' 4' 6' 8'

Figure 13.12. North elevation of a traditional thermal envelope house.

Figure 13.14. First-floor plan of a traditional thermal envelope house.

under load. The roof rafters are also carried through so that they are tied together. Typically, every third rafter should be carried through. The others can be ended in headers at the clerestory wall. The clerestory wall must contain vents across the house that can be opened and closed during the year.

A wider upstairs can be obtained by going to a gambrel roof, as shown in Figure 13.11. This allows about a 14-ft room in a 24-ft house with a 3-ft balcony set back.

In all these structures, it is extremely important to be certain that the building is properly tied together. The roof constructions are unbalanced and fight each other rather than complementing each other. An experienced architect or structural engineer should be consulted when considering any of these modified designs.

A Traditional Envelope House

Many envelope building designs are so drastically different from traditional structures that builders are reluctant to quote on and construct them. Figures 13.12 through 13.16 show some of the details of a house that follows more conventional lines.

The floor plans are shown in Figures 13.14 and 13.15. You will note that the room arrangement is reversed from normal design practice. The bedrooms and the bath are on the first level whereas the kitchen, dining room, and living room are on the second level. This has been done because the available space within the structure lends itself best to this reverse arrangement.

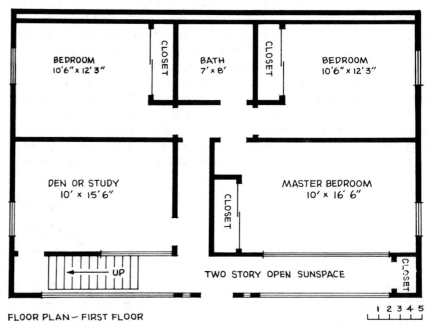

FLOOR PLAN – FIRST FLOOR

The house is entered through a center entry on the south-facing side of the structure. An offset hallway leads to the bedrooms and the den. A clothes closet is located on the right at the end of a long open sunspace. Stairs to the second level are located on the left at the other end of the sunspace. The sunspace is open all the way to the ceiling of the second story. This gives a sunspace about 17 ft high and 38 ft long. The details may be seen in the cross section illustration (Figure 13.16).

Look at the south elevation shown in Figure 13.13. You will note that the south elevation is all large windows. Double-glazing would be standard for this type of wall. Triple-glazing through the use of storm windows is recommended for cold winter months in northerly latitudes with 5500 or more degree days annually.

SOUTH ELEVATION

0 2' 4' 6' 8'

Figure 13.13. South elevation of a traditional thermal envelope house.

Now note the walls of the master bedroom and the den as shown on the floor plan of the first floor (Figure 13.14). Large windows are used in the sunspace side of these two rooms so that the sun will penetrate and warm the rooms. These windows can be single-glazed of a frosted glass or translucent plastic which, while lowering solar transmission, will ensure privacy for the occupants. At least one window leading directly to the outside should be included on the outside walls of these rooms for ventilation and emergency exit.

The stairs to the basement are located in the corner of the den. The open staircase to both the upper level and the basement is held back from the windows.

The second level is entered from the top of the staircase next to a small kitchen. A 3-ft-high railing runs the length of the house along the sunspace so that the entire second level is open to the sun and can be heated by it. The two partitions shown between the three rooms need not run completely to the ceiling. Seven-foot-high dividers would give enough privacy for most families.

By looking at the cross section again, you will see that the rear wall of the three rooms is only 5 ft high but that the ceiling rises rapidly from that height to a soaring 9 ft in the center of the rooms.

You will also note that a conventional roofline has been used without the inclusion of a clerestory for the purpose of exhausting the warm air of summer. Instead, a large chimney was designed into the center of the home. This chimney forms a natural stack to promote the exhaustion of hot air from the house during the summer months. The structural design of the roofline is simplified to a standard saltbox roof style, which most builders are comfortable in constructing.

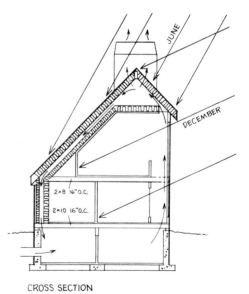

CROSS SECTION

Figure 13.16. Cross section of a traditional thermal envelope house.

Thermal Envelope Houses **251**

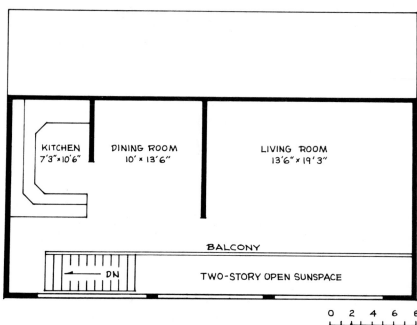

Figure 13.15. Second-floor plan of a traditional thermal envelope house.

SECOND FLOOR PLAN

The center partition on the first floor and the partition between the front of the first floor rooms and the sunspace are both load-bearing partitions. This allows the second floor to be carried without having to carry a doubled-up joist through to the rear wall every 4 ft. The floor joists over the basement have been increased to 2 × 10, 16 in. on center to help carry this load.

The south wall is constructed as a single wall using 20-ft-long wall studs. Laminated 4 × 6 construction at the corners and either side of the entry door carrying 4 × 12 headers over the windows is recommended. The center of the south wall should be securely fastened at the center of the building to a doubled- or tripled-joist from the second floor to prevent its movement. This is the dashed line to the south wall shown in the cross section.

In the winter months, sunlight penetrates the house through the south-facing wall and heats up the sunspace, the front rooms on the first floor, and the three rooms on the second floor. The hot air rises to the peak of the house, is cooled, and sinks down the double wall on the north-facing roof and wall to the basement where it rises up through the sunspace floor as the sunspace is heated.

In the summer months, motorized dampers in the chimney are opened and cool air flows into the basement from the underground ductwork and rises through the south sunspace and the north-facing double wall. In the process, it cools the interior of the house. At night, the bedroom windows can be opened and, if the doors are left ajar, cool air will enter the house and flow out into the sunspace to be exhausted through the chimney.

More Contemporary Thermal Envelope Designs

The thermal envelope home is just coming into being. Very few houses of this type were built prior to 1978 or 1979. There is much to be learned about thermal envelope design and performance. This can only be learned by building different types of designs and learning from experience. The author has chosen not to explore the thermal envelope concept in greater depth at this time for just this reason. The chances of presenting designs that will stand the test of experience are only poor to fair. The author makes no claims about the performance of the house presented in Figure 13.12 through Figure 13.16.

Making a Decision

In this chapter you assessed the value of a thermal envelope house. First you studied thermal envelope design. You learned that a thermal envelope house is constructed so that air flows naturally around the house and distributes the heat evenly.

Next you studied the structural changes that are required to build a thermal envelope house. You learned that considerable expense might be involved because double walls, roofs, a clerestory wall, and extra fire protection could be needed.

Then you examined some of the details of a thermal envelope house that stayed within conventional rooflines and construction. You learned that some compromises as to where the various rooms were located would be needed. But you did see that a thermal envelope house could be built that was not too unconventional, although the energy performance of the design is not known by the author.

You do *not* have all the facts that you need to decide whether or not to build a thermal envelope house. You should have decided that you needed expert help if you were still interested.

DECISION
14

The One-story Solar Ranch House

The ranch house is a favorite design with many Americans. It can be a small starter house, or it can be a large, luxurious, and sprawling structure.

The smallest practical ranch house design is about 24 ft by 48 ft. That is 1152 sq ft. It is possible to place three bedrooms, a bath, a living room, and a family kitchen in a structure that size.

Such a house would not be large enough for most American families. It is minimum in size. It contains no garage or family room, both of which are considered essential by most families when making an investment in a home.

The solar ranch that you will study contains about 1500 sq ft of living area. It also contains a mechanical module with a family room. And it will incorporate a transportation module.

The interior and exterior design principles laid out in Decisions 7 and 8 will be followed closely. The thermal mass of the house will be increased so that the house will store large amounts of energy. The house will contain both passive and active solar energy devices. You will be shown two different exterior styles for the house.

The Solar Ranch Study Plan

Figure 14.1 shows the floor plan of the three bedroom solar ranch. It has been designed so that the bedroom area and the dining-kitchen area face within 30° of south. The entry, the living room, and the dining-kitchen area are located in a 26 ft by 28 ft module. The module was made 28 ft wide so that a concrete energy storage wall could be used as the center, load-bearing partition.

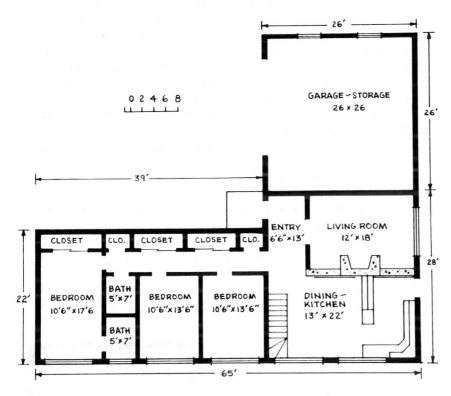

SOLAR RANCH - 3-BEDROOM
FLOOR PLAN

Figure 14.1. The three bedroom ranch floor plan.

There is a full basement under this living module. A set of stairs with an open railing leads down to the basement from the dining-kitchen area. Ample room for a family room is located in the mechanical module. This can be seen in Figure 14.2. The kitchen area was designed as a broken U so that the rear entry door could be placed on the east wall rather than on the south wall. A snack bar or counter fits well in the section of the kitchen behind the fireplace.

The front entry door is located on the west wall. Trees planted in front of the bedroom module will provide a windbreak for this entry. Entry is made into a separate entry hall.

The living room is closed, with only one entry point. Only one window, located on the east wall, is used. The furniture arrangement can readily be made without the need to pass through the room. The masonry wall in the center of the home is designed to hold heat that can be used to help warm the living room and the dining-kitchen area.

The bedrooms are located in a 22 ft by 39 ft wing. They are entered from a hall running off the front entry. All the bedrooms have been pulled to the rear so that they receive the southern exposure. The closets have been removed from the bedroom areas and placed along the north wall as a buffer zone. The closet area includes bedroom clothes closets, a visitor's coat closet, and a linen closet. Two bathrooms are included. One is entered from the bedroom wing hall. The other is entered from the master bedroom. The bedrooms are all designed to accept twin beds and dressers. The design of this house is such that it can easily be expanded to a larger house by increasing the length of the bedroom wing. Each additional bedroom will require another 11 ft of bedroom wing length. Additional baths will require an 8-ft addition. The author suggests that the living module be expanded by 2 ft in length and 2 ft in width for each added bedroom to keep the space requirements in balance for a larger family. The four bedroom version should use a 28 ft by 30 ft living module. The five bedroom version would require a 30 ft by 32 ft living module. Most of the additional width should be added in the front of the structure unless the owner decides to widen the bedroom wing in the larger versions.

The bedroom wing is built on a concrete slab with either a radiant-heated floor or a radiant-heated ceiling. An active solar system can be used to provide the radiant heat or a hot water radiant heating system can be installed.

The transportation module, located on the north side of the house, offers a buffer zone for the living room. It is designed as a 26 ft by 26 ft module. The module can be widened to the north for more storage but should not be widened to the east or west because it will change the exterior roof line. Entry to the transportation module has been shown on the west. But the module may be redesigned to enter from the north or the east if that orientation fits the building lot better.

The foundation plan is shown in Figure 14.2. A full basement is located under the living module. A 24-in. thick masonry wall divides the base-

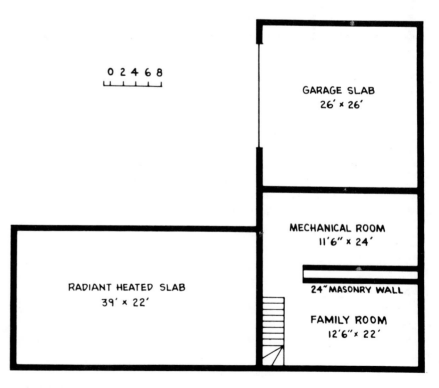

0 2 4 6 8

GARAGE SLAB
26' x 26'

MECHANICAL ROOM
11'6" x 24'

RADIANT HEATED SLAB
39' x 22'

24" MASONRY WALL

FAMILY ROOM
12'6" x 22'

Figure 14.2. The three bedroom ranch foundation plan.

SOLAR RANCH
FOUNDATION PLAN

ment into a mechanical module and a family room. This wall gives heat storage, carries the fireplace, and provides a bearing wall for the concrete center partition dividing the living module. It can be built of poured concrete, concrete block, or any other aesthetically pleasing masonry construction. The 24 in. width is required to support the wood frame floor of the living module.

The exterior walls of the basement are fully insulated with rigid foam insulation so that they provide a heat storage mechanism for the house by adding to its thermal mass. This can be seen in Figure 14.3.

The foundation for the bedroom cross section uses a concrete wall extending below the frost line. In the illustration that depicts this construction, Figure 14.4, no insulation is shown on the outside of the foundation wall. But the floor of the bedrooms, which is a 6-in. poured concrete slab, is fully insulated away from the foundation walls. In severe northerly climates, it would be wise also to insulate the outside of these walls. The 6-in. concrete slab, which should rest on either a gravel or rock fill at least 1 ft thick, acts as a thermal heat sink for the bedroom wing. Heat is carried to this slab either by embedding radiant heating pipes in the slab or by installing radiant heating panels in the ceilings of the bedrooms.

The garage slab, which is of similar construction, need not be insulated except where it joins the house. A thermal break between the two foundation walls should be installed at this point.

The House's Exterior Design

Figures 14.5, 14.6, and 14.7 show exterior views of the house when it is designed in an Early American style.

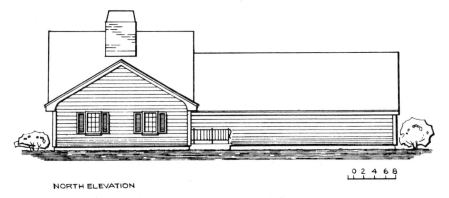

NORTH ELEVATION

The north elevation, Figure 14.5, shows windows on the garage and none on the bedroom wing. Although this does not do justice to the appearance of the house from the north side, evergreen plantings in front of the bedroom wall will do much to relieve the bare wall.

This north bedroom wing wall should be constructed either with 2 × 6 fully insulated frame construction or with 2 × 4 fully insulated frame construction and 1 in. of rigid foam over the wall sheathing. The wall is finished with 6-in. corner posts and 3-in. clapboards of red cedar. Toward the bottom of the building, the clapboards are laid closer together, down to a ½-in. exposure for the bottom clapboard to promote the Early American design concept. A wrought-iron railing on the front step and shuttered windows on the garage relieve the bareness of the elevation.

A massive brick chimney, centered in the living module, adds measurably to the appearance of the north elevation. If the garage were to be entered from the north side, then two 8-ft doors should be used with a 15° slant to the top of the side frames to carry out the design.

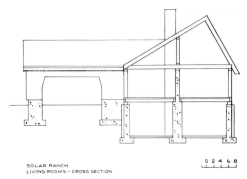

Figure 14.3. Cross section of the living module.

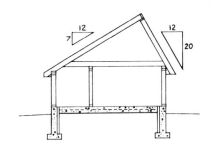

Figure 14.4. Cross section of the bedroom wing.

Figure 14.5. North elevation of an Early American style one-story house.

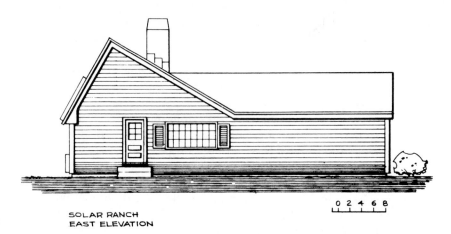

SOLAR RANCH
EAST ELEVATION

0 2 4 6 8

Figure 14.7. East elevation of an Early American style one-story house.

The roofline of the structure can best be seen in the east elevation (Figure 14.7). It is an unbalanced line with a 7-in. pitch on the north side and a 20-in. pitch on the south side. The use of this pitch sets up the south side at an optimum angle for active solar collectors in northerly latitudes. You will notice in the living module cross section (Figure 14.3) that a partition has been extended to the rafter to help carry the roof load without going to a 2 × 10- or 2 × 12-sized rafter. You can also see that a large mechanical area is formed over the south side of the home for use in installing and servicing an active solar system.

The living room window shown in the east elevation should be double-glazed with insulating glass. In severe climates, a storm window can be used in the winter to add triple glazing. Either a picture window or casement windows will work extremely well in this location. Note the positioning of the solar collectors on the south roof and wall.

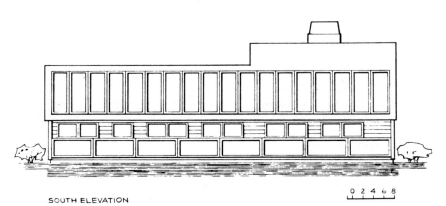

SOUTH ELEVATION

0 2 4 6 8

Figure 14.6. South elevation of an Early American style one-story house.

These collectors can be seen better in Figure 14.6, which shows the south elevation of the building. There is room for 504 sq ft of collectors on the roof and 192 ft of collectors on the south-facing sidewall. Either, both, or neither can be used in the building of the house depending on the designer's goals.

Floor-to-ceiling windows are not shown. They could be used except at the kitchen area. However, the use of an active radiant heating system on the south wall should be carefully considered. It is in keeping with the design and, when used in combination with the windows above it, will provide an excellent solar heating system for both direct and indirect gain.

If the roof solar collectors are employed, they can be used to provide radiant heating throughout the house either by embedding radiant heating pipes in the floor of the bedroom wing and the center masonry wall of the living module or by providing ceiling and wall radiant heating panels in both areas.

The west elevation is not detailed, but it may be seen in outline form in Figure 14.3. It is designed as a bare wall with no windows in the master bedroom. Again, foundation plantings are used to relieve the bareness of the elevation.

The Contemporary Ranch Style

The layout of this ranch house also lends itself to a more contemporary ranch styling. Four elevations depicting this contemporary styling are shown in Figures 14.8 through 14.11. The floor plan remains the same in this design concept, but there are dramatic changes in the roof line and the ceiling structure.

Look at the north elevation (Figure 14.8) and the south elevation (Figure 14.9). The garage and the living module now have a cathedral ceiling, which is constructed using post and beam building techniques. Two large laminated beams run from the north side of the garage to the south wall of the dining-kitchen area and extend out from the dining-kitchen area to form a rear porch. Large windows are used in the south-facing wall of the living module to catch the sun's energy. The porch extension blocks the summer sun from the window wall.

The winter sun now reaches to the concrete center partition and heats it directly. The partition becomes more massive as it has to reach to the peak of the 12-ft cathedral ceiling. These windows must be double-glazed. In the most northerly latitudes, storm windows should be added in the

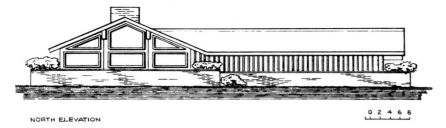

NORTH ELEVATION   0 2 4 6 8

Figure 14.8. North elevation of a contemporary ranch style house.

SOUTH ELEVATION   0 2 4 6 8

Figure 14.9. South elevation of a contemporary ranch style house.

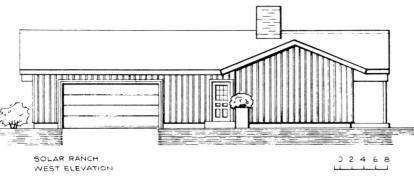

SOLAR RANCH
WEST ELEVATION   0 2 4 6 8

Figure 14.10. West elevation of a contemporary ranch style house.

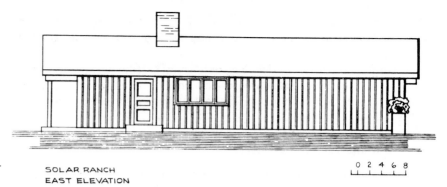

Figure 14.11. East elevation of a contemporary ranch style house.

SOLAR RANCH
EAST ELEVATION

0 2 4 6 8

winter months to provide triple glazing. The center window in the lower part of the wall is a sliding glass door leading to the rear patio formed by the roof extension.

The windows in the wall of the garage are for light and design appearance only. They can be single glazed. Some of them may be replaced by solid panels without hurting the appearance of the design.

The lower half of the north elevation is done in brick or stone veneer. This gives the house a low appearance in relation to the ground. The inclusion of flower boxes extending out beyond the ends of the house adds to this illusion as does the extension of the roofline over the end of the bedroom wing.

The upper half of the north elevation and all the other sides of the house are done in vertical siding. You may choose from texture 111 plywood, V-grooved vertical cedar, or rough-sawn board and batten to carry out the design motif.

The south-facing wall of the bedroom wing now contains sliding glass doors in all the bedrooms so that the sun's energy will reach in and warm the concrete slab.

The redesign of this house into a more contemporary style requires dropping the roof pitch down to 4 in 12 or 5 in 12. This roof pitch is too low to allow the use of the house's roof for effective active solar collectors in a space heating system. Additionally, much of the roof that could have been used for such a system now faces in the wrong direction. The use of active collectors on the bedroom wing to supply hot water year round is still both feasible and acceptable. The lower angle is quite satisfactory, and the system will optimize toward the spring/fall or summer months. So the building has become much more passive oriented than was the Early American style.

The Heat Loss of the Solar Ranch, Early American Style

The heat loss in the bedroom wing can be calculated assuming the use of R-30 ceilings ($U = 0.033$), R-22 walls ($U = 0.045$), and triple-glazed windows with an R-2.6 ($U = 0.38$). A perimeter heat loss for the floor should be added using $U = 0.21$ Btu/lineal foot.

The conduction heat loss is 113 Btu/hr/°F for the bedroom wing, which is very low.

The air changes in the bedroom wing should be at 0.5 air changes per hour, a minimum figure. The wing contains about 6435 cu ft of air, so about 3218 cu ft are exchanged each hour. It will require about 58 Btu/hr/°F to heat this incoming air. So the total bedroom wing heat loss including infiltration is about 171 Btu/hr/°F.

The heat losses in the living module can be handled in the same manner, using the same U-values. In the case of the wall facing into the garage, the heat loss can be cut in half over that of an exterior wall.

The total conduction loss of the first floor of the living wing is about 88 Btu/hr/°F. Again this is a very low value.

The living module contains about 5460 cu ft of air. The change rate would be about one change per hour. So the heat loss from infiltration is about 98 Btu/hr/°F. This gives a total heat loss from conduction and infiltration of about 186 Btu/hr/°F.

If the mechanical module is to be heated, then it is necessary for you to calculate the heat loss in the mechanical module as well. As the exterior walls are all well-insulated, the U-factor will be extremely low. The walls should be treated as if they had a U-factor of 0.033 and were standing in open air. This would produce a heat loss of about 11 Btu/hr/°F if the garage wall were treated with one-half the normal U-factor. Air exchange in the basement should be calculated at 0.5 changes per hour, which would produce about 49 Btu/hr/°F for a total mechanical module loss of 60 Btu/hr/°F. So the total house heat loss calculates out to be 417 Btu/hr/°F. This is about 50% of the heat loss seen in an average house of this size and type. No heat loss was calculated for the basement floor.

```
  171  Btu/hr/°F bedrooms
  186  Btu hr/°F living
   60  Btu/hr/°F basement
= 417  Btu/hr/°F house
```

The Heat Storage Capacity of the Extra Masonry Wall and Floor

The bedroom wing floor, the living module center partition, and the basement walls are all heat storage areas. They can store useful heat from 65 to 85°F. However, the exterior walls will have some outdoor heat loss, so the assumption is made that the Δt is only 10°F, or that half the useful heat storage capacity is lost. Under these assumptions, the structure can store 653,444 Btu of useful energy.

The bedroom slab is about 38 ft long by 20 ft wide with a 6-in. thickness. This slab will store 223,440 Btu of useful energy.

The basement center partition is 20 ft long by 8 ft high by 2 ft wide. It can store 188,160 Btu of useful energy.

The first floor center partition and the fireplace are about 20 ft long by 7½ ft high by an average 1-ft thickness. Combined, they can store about 88,200 Btu of useful energy.

The basement walls are 104 ft long, 7½ ft high, and 8 in. thick. They are well-insulated on the outside but do lose some useful heat to the outdoors. Assuming a 10°F Δt will allow for only half as much useful heat storage as a wall that is in the interior of the building. The walls will store about 153,644 Btu of useful heat using this assumption.

When the storage capacity of these walls and the floor are added up, the total useful heat storage is seen as 653,444 Btu or 32,672 Btu/°F. This is about 78 hr of heat storage with the interior temperature dropping only 1°F.

```
  223,440  bedroom slab
+ 188,160  basement partition
+  88,200  1st floor partition
+ 153,644  basement walls
  653,444  Btu useful storage
    ÷ 20   Δt
   32,672  Btu/°F
   ÷ 415   hrly heat loss
 = 78.7    hr storage/°F
```

Making a Decision

In this chapter you studied a ranch plan that has been modified to make maximum use of solar energy. Two elevations were shown, an Early American style and a more contemporary style. You saw that the houses could be enlarged to include more bedrooms and that the living module should be enlarged to keep the house balanced.

Last, you saw heat loss calculations and heat storage calculations that showed that the houses were both energy efficient and energy-storing.

You should have decided that a ranch house can readily be planned that utilizes the sun's energy effectively.

DECISION
15

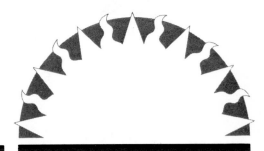

The Split-level Solar House

The split-level house became an important factor in suburban America in the early 1950s. Since that time, many hundreds of thousands of different types of split-level houses have been built.

There are three types of basic split-level design: the side-by-side split, where the living quarters and the sleeping quarters are on different levels; the back-to-front split, where the back rooms of the home are either higher or lower than the front rooms; and the raised ranch, where the basement is raised partly out of the ground and the entry is split between the upper and lower levels. All three types have the common characteristic of having one set of rooms built about 3½ to 4 ft higher or lower than another.

The split-level solar house that you will study is a side-by-side split-level house. You will see two versions of this house. One version has the bedrooms on the ground floor. The other version has the living quarters on the ground floor.

The floor plan that you will study closely follows the floor plan of the ranch house that you studied in Decision 14. The exterior plans are traditional in nature. As split-level exterior design tends to result in high, boxy shapes, every effort has been made to pull the roofline down to a lower level by integrating the higher roofline with the garage roof.

The Ground-entry Split-level

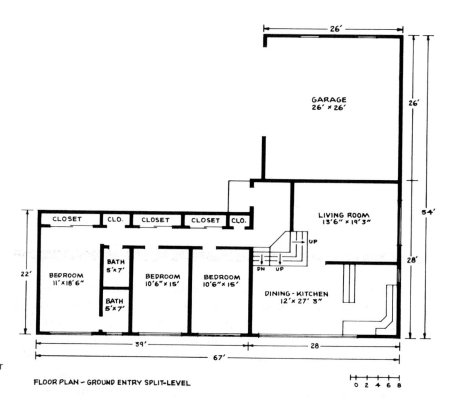

Figure 15.1. Ground-entry split-level floor plan.

FLOOR PLAN – GROUND ENTRY SPLIT-LEVEL

Figure 15.1 shows the floor plan of the ground-entry split-level. In this plan, the bedrooms have been kept at ground level. So has the entry into the front of the house. The living room and dining-kitchen areas have been raised up by 4 ft. The staircase that leads down to the lower level and the family room has been pulled forward into the entry. A short staircase to the living room and the dining-kitchen area has been added. This additional staircase required the addition of 2 ft to the living module and the elimination of the central fireplace. The central storage wall was also shortened to provide a passageway between the two rooms. The living room is still lighted by an east-facing window, while the southern sun streams into all three rooms of the living module.

Figure 15.2 shows the family room and the mechanical module. The concrete basement walls are now only 4 ft high and are topped with a 2 × 8 frame wall to complete the lower story. Three feet of the lower level is below grade.

The design of the bedroom wing has not changed. The same basic configuration of three bedrooms and two baths has been kept. Again, the home can be expanded to more bedrooms by increasing the length of the bedroom wing.

Figure 15.3 shows the front of the house, which is designed to face north. A 7-in.-pitch hip roof was chosen for the rooflines. To balance the house, a false chimney was centered on the bedroom wing roof.

The house exterior is finished in 9 in. by 18 in. raised and beveled corner blocks with a ½ × 6 cedar clapboard laid 4½ in. to the weather. This gives a very formal appearance to the house.

The front wall of the garage was given two windows of 9 × 9 glass in an 8 over 12 colonial windowpane design flanked by traditional shutters. The garage was deliberately not centered on the main living module. Such

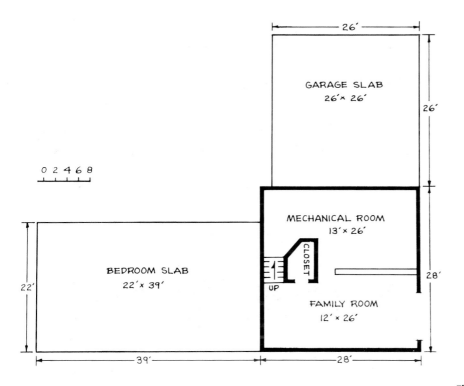

GROUND ENTRY SPLIT-LEVEL
BASEMENT PLAN

Figure 15.2. Family room and mechanical module plan.

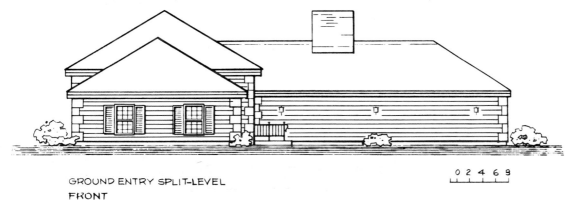

GROUND ENTRY SPLIT-LEVEL
FRONT

Figure 15.3. North elevation.

centering would have called for a 1-ft setback on both sides, which would appear awkward when finished. Instead, the living module was allowed to jut out on the side facing the bedroom wing where it offers a reasonable transition to the lower roof.

The hip roof on the living module is built pyramid-style and comes to a central point as the module is square. The hip roof over the garage blends back into this roof as can be seen from Figure 15.4, which is the east elevation.

The east elevation has been designed bare. An 8-ft casement window is inserted for the living room and for the family room on the lower level. The kitchen door requires a raised platform and a staircase to the ground. A door could be placed in the garage wall to eliminate the unbalanced appearance. Or a set of windows could be incorporated without raising the heat losses of the house. Simple corner posts have been substituted for the corner blocks to save on cost. The corner blocks could also be used very effectively.

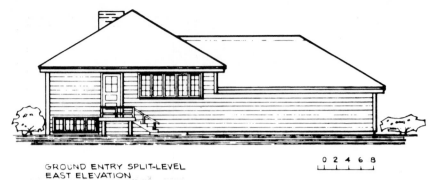

GROUND ENTRY SPLIT-LEVEL
EAST ELEVATION

0 2 4 6 8

Figure 15.4. East elevation.

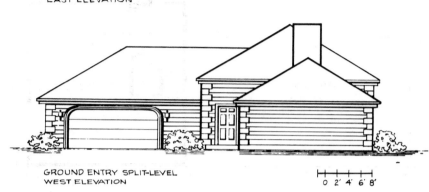

GROUND ENTRY SPLIT-LEVEL
WEST ELEVATION

0 2' 4' 6' 8'

Figure 15.5. West elevation.

Figure 15.5 shows the west elevation. The garage door uses a bowed colonial formal frame and is offset by two wall sconces. The front entry door is a simple colonial door with two or four top panes of glass for light. The west wall of the bedroom wing is bare, but it can be relieved by the use of evergreen plantings or rose arbors.

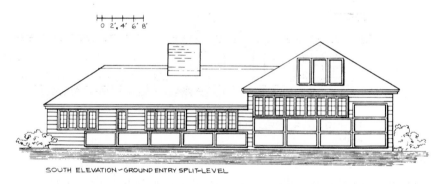

0 2' 4' 6' 8'

SOUTH ELEVATION - GROUND ENTRY SPLIT-LEVEL

Figure 15.6. South elevation.

The south elevation is shown in Figure 15.6. You will note two things about this elevation. Windows, although ample, have been kept to the minimum design required for good lighting. The balance of the wall has been used for active solar collectors, yielding 345 sq ft in 3 ft by 7 ft collectors. The roof should not be used for flat plate collectors designed to give space heating. The 7-in. roof pitch is too low for such a purpose. However, a three panel solar hot water heater collector array does fit on the living module roof and is at the proper angle to yield good year-round solar water heating.

All the windows in this design, with the exception of the two in the garage are 1-ft-8-in.-wide casement windows of varying lengths. These windows were chosen for quality, double-glazing, and the availability of winter storm windows. There are several excellent weatherstripped brands of these windows available on the market. Casement windows promote natural ventilation even when the wind is blowing parallel to the wall.

No windows are shown in the south-facing side of the family room. They could be placed here at the expense of losing up to four solar collectors from the sidewall array.

It would also be possible to use floor-to-ceiling 8-ft-wide patio doors in the bedrooms. This would eliminate all the solar sidewall panels on the bedroom wing.

The Ground-level Living Module Split-level

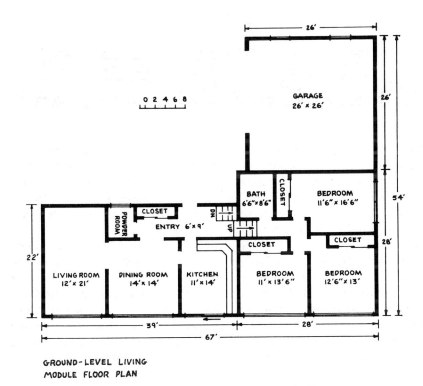

GROUND-LEVEL LIVING
MODULE FLOOR PLAN

Figure 15.7. Ground-level living module split-level floor plan.

Figure 15.7 shows the floor plan of the same basic split-level house using a ground-level living module and a raised-level bedroom module over the family room and the mechanical module. The house is the same size as the split-level shown in the previous design.

This house is entered from the front or north-facing side at the ground level into a large entry. If you turn to the left, you can descend to the family room and mechanical module or you can ascend to the bedroom module.

The front entry contains a powder room and a closet. This forces entry to the living room through a corner of the dining room, but it should not interfere with the dining room furniture arrangement. The living room is dead-ended with only one entryway, which gives an excellent furniture arrangement. Ten-foot-wide casement windows on the south wall light and heat the room. The dining room is 14 ft by 14 ft, which provides an excellent formal dining arrangement. Here, a 12-ft-wide casement window array gives excellent heat and light.

The kitchen is designed as an L, which leaves room for a table against its west wall. An 8-ft sliding glass door lights and heats the kitchen.

The bedroom wing is designed in the same manner as the two-story house with a master bedroom and a bath on the front of the home and two bedrooms to the rear. The master bedroom is lighted from the east whereas the two south bedrooms are lighted and heated from south-facing casement windows. The bedrooms in this design are squarer than in the other split-level design, but they have ample room. The design does not have room for a bath off the master bedroom, but a bath or half-bath can be placed in the corner of the mechanical module to serve the family room if desired.

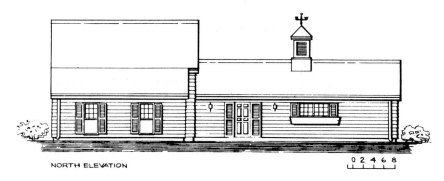

Figure 15.8. North elevation.

Figure 15.8 shows the north elevation. Entry into the living wing plus a window in the powder room relieves the bareness seen in the other split-level. A cupola has been centered on the living module room to balance the roofline. The house is finished in cedar shingles laid 8 in. to the weather with the corners overlapped and butted. A 7-in. roof pitch prevents the wall height from dominating the design.

A 3-in. porch-type roof that blends into a 7-in. pitch bedroom module roof gives the house a New England farmhouse appearance and pulls the line of the higher wing down to the ground. Again, the garage has not been centered on the bedroom module, but the corner has been used as a transition to the living module. The rooflines are finished in wood gutters with corner metal downspouts. Two sconces are used to decorate the north living module wall and two short windows over raised panels flanked by full-length shutters grace the front of the garage.

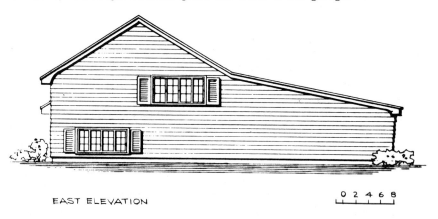

Figure 15.9. East elevation.

The east elevation, which is shown in Figure 15.9 is again bare except for the master bedroom and the family room windows. Windows or doors could be placed in the garage wall to eliminate this bare design.

The west elevation in Figure 15.10 shows the same bareness relieved only by the use of a bowed garage door with flanking colonial sconces and a small window in the upstairs bath. Windows placed in the west wall would increase the heat gain and loss from the house so they are not recommended. Instead, wall plantings should be used to eliminate the stark design of the wall.

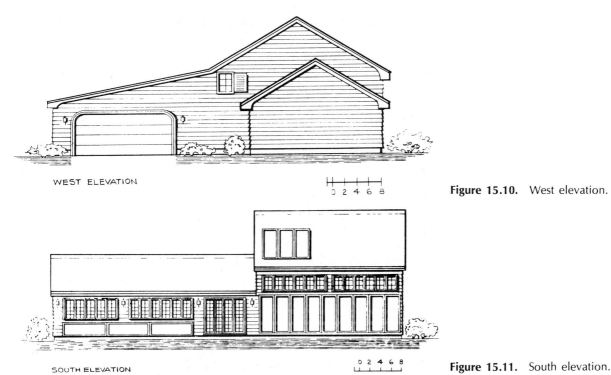

WEST ELEVATION

Figure 15.10. West elevation.

SOUTH ELEVATION

Figure 15.11. South elevation.

The south elevation, shown in Figure 15.11, is a combination of casement windows and solar collectors. The design is quite similar to the ground-entry split-level. The same statements apply to this elevation.

Figure 15.12 shows the general construction of the house by illustrating a generalized cross section.

The Increased Heat Loss of the Split-level

More of the split-level protrudes from the ground than does the ranch. So more sidewall is exposed. This is inescapable and has to be accepted when comparing the ranch design with a similar-sized split-level. The center masonry wall is not practical in the last design shown so it must be cut down from the size in the first split-level design. The concrete part of the lower level walls is only 4 ft high; the balance is a frame wall. These changes lower the heat storage capability of the house.

Some of this can be made up by using a 6-in. thick slab in the family room. The heat will rise to the ceiling of the family room and be conducted slowly through the bedroom floors. Radiant-heated slabs in both the family room and the living module wing are recommended. These can be readily driven by the active solar panels shown on the south-facing sidewall.

Although the basement plans have not been shown, they are similar to the plans in the ranch section with the exception that a passageway for the entry from the lower stairs must be added in the ground-level living module design.

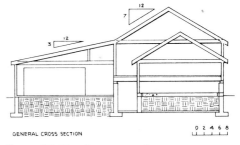

GENERAL CROSS SECTION

Figure 15.12. A cross section.

The Heat Loss of the Ground-entry Split-level

The heat loss in the bedroom wing can be readily calculated using the R-values of ceiling R-30, walls R-22, perimeter U-factor = 0.21 Btu/lineal ft/°F, and window R-2.6 (triple-glazed). The heat loss through the wall is 30.5 Btu/hr/°F. The heat loss through the ceiling is 28.3 Btu/hr/°F. The heat loss through the windows is 27.4 Btu/hr/°F. The heat loss around the floor edge is 21 Btu/hr/°F. The heat loss due to infiltration is 57.9 Btu/hr/°F, assuming one-half air change per hour. The total heat loss of the wing is 165 Btu/hr/°F.

The heat losses in the living module can be calculated in the same manner using the same U-factors. In the case of the wall facing the garage, the heat loss can be cut in half. About one air change per hour should be included.

The heat loss through the ceiling is 25.9 Btu/hr/°F. The heat loss through the blank wall is 21.1 Btu/hr/°F. The heat loss through the windows and doors is 57 Btu/hr/°F. The heat loss through infiltration is 109.3 Btu/hr/°F, assuming one air change. The total heat loss in the living module is about 213 Btu/hr/°F.

If one-half air change per hour is used in the basement and no loss is calculated for the floor or ceiling, then the basement heat loss is 83.4 Btu/hr/°F. The total heat loss for the structure is 461 Btu/hr. This is about 11% greater than the ranch house in Decision 14.

83.4 basement
213.3 living module
+ 165.0 bedrooms
= 461.7 Btu/hr/°F

The Heat Loss of the Ground-entry Living Module Split

The same R-values have been used to calculate the heat losses in the living module entry split-level home shown in Figure 15.7. The number of air changes in the two modules has been changed to account for the activity change. The ceiling heat loss amounts to 28.3 Btu/hr/°F. The wall heat loss amounts to 26.1 Btu/hr/°F. The window and door heat loss amounts to 64.6 Btu/hr/°F. The heat loss around the floor perimeter amounts to 21 Btu/hr/°F. Assuming one air change per hour, the infiltration losses amount to 115.8 Btu/hr/°F. These heat losses add up to a total heat loss for the living module of 255.8 Btu/hr/°F.

The heat losses for the sleeping module can also be calculated with the same R-values. One-half air change per hour is used, and credit for one-third of the garage wall is taken. No heat loss through the floor is included. The heat loss through the ceiling is 25.9 Btu/hr/°F. The heat loss through the wall is 23.1 Btu/hr/°F. The heat loss through the windows is 36.5 Btu/hr/°F. The heat loss due to infiltration is 52.9 Btu/hr/°F. So the total heat loss for the bedroom module adds up to 138.4 Btu/hr/°F.

The basement heat loss has been calculated at 83.4 Btu/hr/°F, assuming one-half an air change per hour and no floor losses. So the total heat loss for the house is 478 Btu/hr/°F, which is 15% higher than for the ranch.

255.8 living
138.4 sleeping
+ 83.4 basement
= 477.6 Btu/hr/°F total

The Heat Storage Capacity of the Split-Levels

The heat storage capacity of the storage slab in the ground-level part of the house is identical to the heat storage capacity of the ranch house shown in Decision 14. That is, 11,172 Btu/°F or 223,440 Btu of useful storage at 20°FΔt.

The basement walls are 108 ft in length by 4 ft high and 8 in. thick. Assuming the same insulation as in the ranch house, and a 10°FΔt, they will store 85,090 Btu of useful heat.

223,440 ground slab
85,090 basement walls
+ 206,380 basement floor
= 514,910 Btu useful storage

If a 6-in. thick basement slab, radiant heated, is used to replace the concrete center partition, then this slab will store an additional 206,380 Btu of useful heat. This gives these houses a total heat storage capacity of 514,910 Btu at a 20°FΔt . This is about 79% of the heat storage seen in the ranch house in Decision 14.

Making a Decision

In this chapter you studied two split-level plans that have been modified to make maximum use of solar energy. Two elevations were shown, one with a sleeping module ground level plan and one with a living module ground level plan. Both of these split-level plans were similar in size to the ranch houses in Decision 14.

You learned that the heat losses of the split-level houses tended to be slightly higher than the heat losses of the ranch houses and that the heat storage capacity was somewhat lower. But both designs still offer both good energy efficiency and heat storage capacity.

You should now have a basis for comparing ranch houses and split-level houses of equivalent size. The ability to make this comparison will help you decide which style is best for you. Both styles can be very energy efficient.

DECISION 16

The Two-story Solar House

The majority of houses built during the early Colonial days in America were two-story houses. They were generally built around a central chimney and each room contained a fireplace for heating.

During the eighteenth century, a number of different styles developed throughout the country. The one-and-a-half-story house, known as the Cape Cod and the Cape Ann, became popular in the Massachusetts area. The gambrel roof, or the Dutch Colonial, was built throughout New York and Pennsylvania. The portico with tall colonnades dominated much of the south. In much of New England, the Elizabethan-era garrison house survived and gradually gave way to the more stylish New England farmhouse. Larger houses with end-flanking chimneys came into being as wealth and home sizes grew.

These styles have survived down to this day. And they are as popular as they ever were with the American people. Chances are that the need to conserve energy will increase their popularity even more in the next few years.

In this chapter you will study two different two-story houses: a version of the Cape Cod and a version of the early American farmhouse. One has been designed using mostly passive solar techniques. The other has been designed using mostly active solar techniques.

One house has a traditional interior and exterior layout. The other house has a very unusual layout. From these two extremes, you will be able to see some of the design elements that you may want to consider in your two-story house.

The Early American Farmhouse

Figure 16.1. North elevation of the Early American farmhouse.

Figures 16.1 through 16.6 show the Early American farmhouse. Figure 16.1 shows the north elevation. The house is very traditional in nature with small pane windows, shutters, H & L hinges, and a steep-pitched roof. Note that the second story windows are very small. The height of the roof at the front wall of the house has been dropped down to about 6 ft to shorten the exterior wall that is exposed to the outdoors. This was common in early American days in order to lower the home's heat loss.

The house is clapboarded with ½ × 6 red cedar clapboards laid 3½ in. to the weather and inserted inside a bottom skirt and corner posts. Note that the 12-in. roof pitch that was chosen lets the roof dominate the sidewall even though the house is two stories tall. This improves the appearance of the house and lends itself well to the use of solar collectors on the south side of the building.

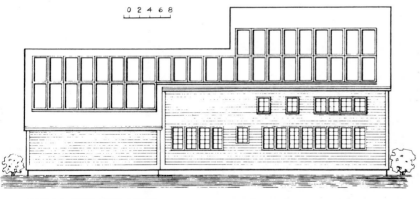

EARLY AMERICAN FARMHOUSE
SOUTH ELEVATION

Figure 16.2. South elevation of the Early American farmhouse.

Figure 16.2 shows the south elevation. Here tradition has been blended with some changes designed to utilize the sun's energy. Thirty-nine solar collectors are shown on the roof. This is 780 sq ft of collector, which most likely will be more than the house needs in most climates. So there is ample room for whatever the designer requires.

The first floor has been covered with triple-glazed casement windows to yield 126 sq ft of direct gain area in the kitchen, dining room, and family room. The second floor has 42 sq ft of smaller casements to light and heat the bedrooms.

The house has been planned without any windows on the east or west walls in order to conserve energy. They could be added. But the house's heat losses would be increased.

The Floor Plan Is Traditional

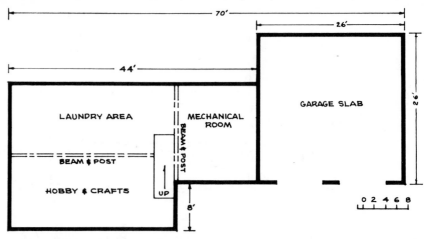

Figure 16.3. Basement plan of the Early American farmhouse.

EARLY AMERICAN FARMHOUSE
BASEMENT PLAN

Figure 16.4 shows the first floor plan, which closely follows the plan shown in Decision 8. There is a good-sized entry hall. To the right, stairs ascend to the second floor, which contains the bedrooms. A dead-ended living room is entered from the left. The family kitchen and the family room lie straight ahead with their own lavatory.

The entire back wall of the family kitchen is lighted with a 20-ft wide set of casement windows. The family room is lighted by 10 ft of the same casement windows. A door from the family room leads to the garage. Stairs lead down to the basement from the passageway between the family kitchen and the family room.

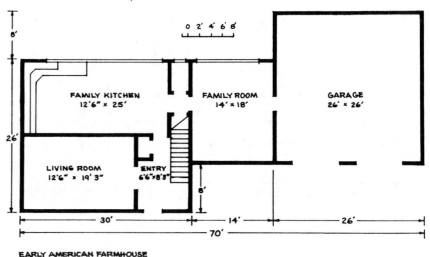

Figure 16.4. First-floor plan of the Early American farmhouse.

EARLY AMERICAN FARMHOUSE
FIRST FLOOR PLAN

The second floor plan is shown in Figure 16.5. Two bedrooms are located in the front of the home; a master bedroom is located in the rear. Two baths are shown. One bath could be used. This would add 2 ft to the master bedroom. This arrangement can be seen in Decision 8. A storage area and a mechanical room for the solar system is located over the family room. The mechanical room could be entered from a staircase in the family room or from a permanent ladder located on the garage wall facing the family room.

The basement plan is shown in Figure 16.3. It has been split into a laundry area, a hobby and crafts area, and a mechanical room.

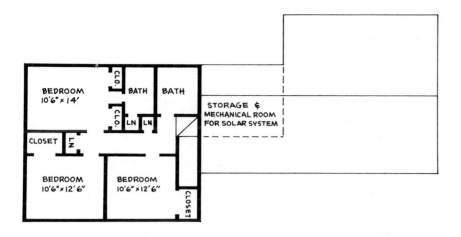

EARLY AMERICAN FARMHOUSE
SECOND FLOOR PLAN

Figure 16.5. Second-floor plan of the Early American farmhouse.

The west elevation is shown in Figure 16.6. A 12 in 12 roof pitch has been used throughout. The roof over the family room has been carried back so that an unbroken roofline exists across the south-facing roof for the installation of active solar collectors and to give a large solar mechanical room.

The Cape Cod House

Figures 16.7 through 16.11 show a Cape Cod house that has been designed to make maximum use of passive solar energy. Your inspection of this house will show that tradition has been thrown out the window in designing both the interior and the exterior of this house.

First, this house has no basement. Instead, it is built on a 6-in.-thick concrete slab poured over 2 ft or more of rock or sand. The combination acts as a large heat sink to increase the thermal mass of the house. The details are shown in Figure 16.11.

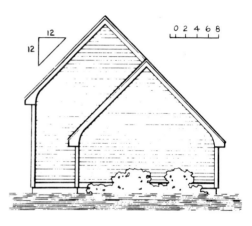

EARLY AMERICAN FARMHOUSE
WEST ELEVATION

Figure 16.6. West elevation of the Early American farmhouse.

Figure 16.7. North elevation of the Cape Cod house.

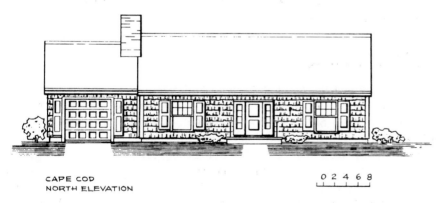

CAPE COD
NORTH ELEVATION

Second, look at Figure 16.7, which shows the north elevation of the house. There are almost no windows on this side of the house. Only small panes of glass over large panels flanked by full-length shutters and simple lights flanking the door are shown. The house is sheathed in a 16-in. shingle laid 8 in. to the weather. This sheathing is shown inside corner posts and with a freize located under the overhang. Shingled corners with no corner posts could also be used and would look traditional. Paneled shutters and a raised panel garage door complete the colonial motif. An 8-in.

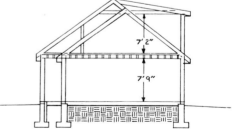

TYPICAL CAPE COD CROSS SECTION

Figure 16.11. Foundation plan of the Cape Cod house.

roof pitch gives a satisfactory look to the design and allows for an adequate second story.

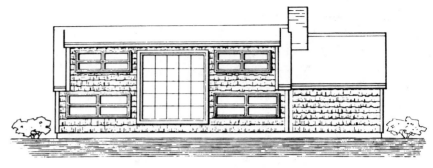

CAPE COD
SOUTH ELEVATION

Figure 16.8. South elevation of the Cape Cod house.

The south elevation, shown in Figure 16.8, departs from the design motif almost completely. Large awning windows admit good solar energy levels. A ten foot by ten foot solar glazing extends two stories high across the center of the house.

The Interior of the House Is Nontraditional

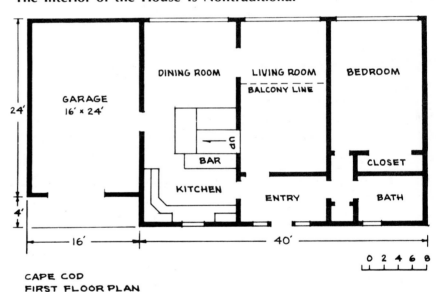

CAPE COD
FIRST FLOOR PLAN

Figure 16.9. First-floor plan of the Cape Cod house.

Figure 16.9 shows the first floor of the Cape. It is a very unusual floor plan for such a house. All the rooms have been shifted to the rear of the house to take advantage of the southern exposure. The entry, the bath, and the kitchen cabinets are used to buffer the north wall. The staircase is U-shaped and open so that the light from the dining room window can penetrate all the way to the front of the house. The living room is a two-story room stretching to the second floor ceiling with a balcony over part of it. There is no family room. A breakfast bar is shown in the kitchen against the staircase.

The second story of this unusual Cape is shown in Figure 16.10. The stairs end on a balcony that doubles as an upstairs sitting room, a family room, or a play area for the children. Two bedrooms and a bath are also located on this level.

Note that the mechanical room for the house is located over the garage. This eliminates the need to enlarge the garage to accommodate the equipment. And it is easier to heat than the garage would be.

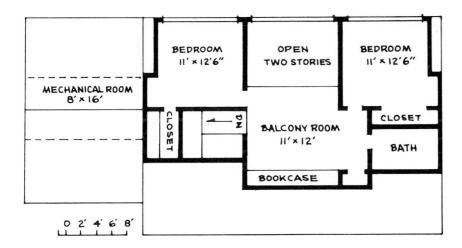

Figure 16.10. Second-floor plan of the Cape Cod house.

The author participated in the design and the evaluation of a house of this particular type in northeastern Massachusetts in 1960. It proved to be an excellent design for a young family.

The Heat Loss of the Early American Farmhouse

The heat loss of the Early American farmhouse has been calculated using R-30 ceilings, R-22 sidewalls, R-2.6 windows and doors, and R-30 basement walls. The conduction losses are:

Basement	34.6 Btu/hr/°F
First floor walls	36.0 Btu/hr/°F
First floor windows and doors	69.5 Btu/hr/°F
Second floor walls	24.4 Btu/hr/°F
Second floor windows and doors	9.9 Btu/hr/°F
Ceiling	34.1 Btu/hr/°F
Total conduction heat loss	174.4 Btu/hr/°F

The infiltration heat loss has been calculated using one air change per hour on the first floor and one-half air change per hour on the second floor and in the basement. The infiltration losses are:

Basement	70.0 Btu/hr/°F
First floor	139.0 Btu/hr/°F
Second floor	49.0 Btu/hr/°F
Total infiltration heat loss	258.0 Btu/hr/°F

The total combined heat loss, assuming the basement is fully heated is 432 Btu/hr/°F or 0.15 Btu/hr/°F sq ft of living area.

The Heat Loss of the Cape Cod House

The heat loss of the Cape Cod house has also been calculated using the same values as were used for the Early American farmhouse. The conduction losses are:

First floor walls	40.5 Btu/hr/°F
First floor windows and doors	78.7 Btu/hr/°F
Second floor walls	32.7 Btu/hr/°F
Second floor windows	20.5 Btu/hr/°F
Ceiling	37.0 Btu/hr/°F
Perimeter	24.4 Btu/hr/°F
Total conduction heat loss	233.8 Btu/hr/°F

The infiltration heat loss has also been calculated using one change per hour on the first floor and one-half air change per hour on the second floor:

First floor	151.2 Btu/hr/°F
Second floor	50.4 Btu/hr/°F
Total infiltration heat loss	201.6 Btu/hr/°F

The total combined heat loss is 435 Btu/hr/°F or 0.25 Btu/hr/°F sq ft of living area.

The Heat Storage Capacity of the Cape Cod Slab

The Cape Cod house is built on a 6-in.-thick concrete slab that increases its thermal mass. This slab is a heat storage mass that will store 16,464 Btu/°F. Assuming a 10°F temperature rise, the slab will store about 164,640 Btu of energy. Assuming a 20°F differential between indoor and outdoor temperature, this is a heat storage time capacity of about 19 hr.

Making a Decision

In this chapter you examined two very different two-story houses. One house followed tradition and made high use of active solar systems. The other house departed sharply from tradition and used mostly passive design to increase its energy efficiency.

You studied the heat losses of the two designs and the energy storage capacity of the passive design. You should have noted that the heat losses per square foot in the passive design were much higher than they were in the active design. This must be accepted when large fenestration areas are used for capturing the sun's energy.

Go back to Decisions 14 and 15 and examine the heat losses of ranch houses versus split-level houses versus two-story houses. You will learn that all three design styles can be made energy efficient.

You should now have decided that your favorite house style can be used to make an energy-efficient home and that you do not need to be limited in your choice of style.

DECISION
17

The Contemporary Solar House for the 1980s

Every designer has his own ideas about what is a good home for the 1980s. The author is no exception. So you are about to study two houses that embody the ideas that one house designer has created.

Houses in the 1980s will be very costly to build, heat, cool, and maintain, so they must be energy-conserving, solar-oriented, and have little or no wasted space. This may call for a change in some of the design criteria called for in Decision 8. The two houses in this chapter are more square than rectangular, and they are much wider than the author's traditional designs.

The wider width calls for stacking levels. Natural lighting must be achieved in such a house by creating more south wall in each room. Most of the windows and doors need to be moved to the south wall. This will eliminate the natural cross-ventilation that is desirable. Thought has to be given to mechanical ventilation to replace the natural ventilation.

The houses need to be terrain-efficient so that they use the natural features of the lot and so that the advantages of earth-insulation can be designed into the house. Roof pitches must be chosen so as either to give good reflection of energy or to allow the correct positioning of active solar collectors. High thermal mass materials must be used so that good energy storage is achieved.

Standard construction techniques must be used so that builders are able to calculate costs without adding grossly large amounts for accomplishing tasks that they are unfamiliar with. Standard building materials must be used to ensure that the materials may be purchased at competitive prices.

All these criteria can be met. The design task is by no means impossible to accomplish. The houses can be traditional in nature. Outlandish designs are not needed. Neither is gross experimentation.

In this chapter you will study two houses that attempt to meet these criteria. One is very modern in appearance. The other is very traditional in appearance. Both have been designed into south-facing sloping lots to take advantage of earth insulation.

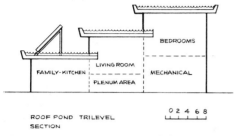

Figure 17.3. Cross section of the roof pond trilevel.

The Roof Pond Trilevel

Figures 17.1 through 17.5 show a roof pond trilevel. The layout of the levels can be seen in Figure 17.3. The family kitchen is on the ground level. The living room plus one bedroom and a small bath are stacked up 4 ft higher and behind it. Two bedrooms are on a third level that is 4 ft higher than the living room. A mechanical module is located below the bedroom area. A rock storage bed and plenum area are located under the living room. The garage is located on ground level at the kitchen and living room side.

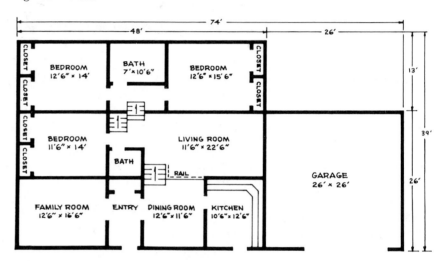

Figure 17.1. Floor plan of the roof pond trilevel.

Figure 17.1 shows the floor plan of the living areas. A large entry hall is located on the ground level with its own closet. Turning left from the entry, you enter a dead-ended family room. By turning to the right, you enter the dining room. The dining room is combined with the living room in an L shape, but the floor of the living room is 4 ft higher. So a short set of stairs and a balcony railing are needed between the two.

The living room is lighted by seven casement windows located in a 4-ft clerestory wall. Because the roof below these windows is flat, a large amount of reflected energy enters the windows to augment the direct solar gain. A bedroom and a bath are located on the same level. The traffic pattern has been designed so that only the corner of the dining room and one end of the living room are used to travel from room to room.

The bedroom level and the mechanical module are both entered from this level. One level is up 4 ft, the other is down 4 ft. Two large bedrooms and a bath are located on the upper level. Again, they are lighted and heated from a large array of casement windows located on a clerestory wall over a flat roof for high solar gain.

The area under the living room is only 4 ft high. It is used as a rock storage bed, which is designed with a top and bottom plenum in a similar manner to the rock storage bed in Decision 10. Although the 4 ft height is minimal, the upper plenum extends under the entire center level. This area should be thought of as a high thermal mass area rather than as an optimized circulating hot air storage bin.

ROOF POND TRILEVEL
SOUTHERN EXPOSURE

Figure 17.5. Perspective of the roof pond trilevel's southern exposure.

Figure 17.5 shows the house as seen from a southern exposure. Note that the east, west, and north-facing sides are all earth-covered and that the entire portion of the house lying above ground is exposed directly to the sun.

The large roof expanse exposed to the summer sun would soak up tremendous amounts of summer heat. So the roof has been designed to be covered with water in the hot months. This water will catch much of the heat. If the water were circulated, then even more heat could be taken away. This feature is very easy to incorporate into the design.

ROOF POND TRILEVEL
SOUTH ELEVATION

0 2 4 6 8

Figure 17.2. South elevation of the roof pond trilevel.

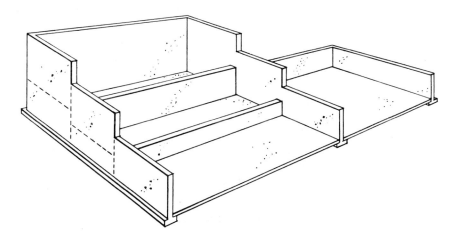

ROOF POND TRILEVEL
FOUNDATION

Figure 17.4. Perspective of the roof pond trilevel's foundation.

Contemporary Houses **281**

The roof pond trilevel is a combination of high thermal mass concrete construction and standard wood construction. The concrete part of the construction is shown in Figure 17.4. The east-, west-, and north-facing walls are poured concrete that are highly insulated with rigid foam on the exterior to put the thermal mass into the house. An 8-ft-high wall is used in the mechanical room partition to provide structural bracing for the weight of the earth against the sidewalls. Another 4-ft-high wall runs under the living room partition for the same purpose. The remainder of the house is constructed from standard timbering for the floors, walls, and roof. The roof rafters serve as the ceiling joists, which eliminates one complete set of timbers.

In addition to the passive features, the house is also shown with active solar collectors mounted at a 45° angle on the garage roof. These collectors can be used to augment the passive space heating or to heat domestic hot water for the home.

The house has been designed to be very simple in appearance. Single pane, double-glazed casement windows have been used. The doors are flush with a small window. The exterior is stucco over wire lath. The design is clean, functional, and simple in its execution.

The Trilevel Elizabethan Colonial

Figures 17.6 through 17.13 show a more traditional styling that borrows from the early American saltbox design. The house contains an extremely large amount of living space but only occupies a 36 ft by 38 ft floor plan. All the space in this house has been effectively used.

The design presumes that a lot is available that allows entry on the north side of the house about 16 ft higher than entry on the south side. This is a fairly steep sloping lot. The section in Figure 17.8 shows how the house is entered from both sides. Retaining walls must be used on the east and west sides to hold back the banks.

Figure 17.13 shows the north elevation. This could face either the street or the backyard effectively, depending on the lot location. North-side entry is into what would normally be an unused attic in most saltbox designs. A dormer has been added to create this upper entry. Figure 17.6 shows the third-floor plan that is located at this level. An 11-ft-by-12-ft entry has been created. There is room for two large rooms on this level. They have been shown as unfinished. Both rooms are lighted from a bank of south-facing casement windows set back into the roof over a 2-in. pitch-recessed roof for reflection. Diamond pane grids are shown to carry out the design motif.

A set of stairs leads down to the second story. This floor plan is shown in Figure 17.7. The stairs end in a large entry hall at the rear or south-facing side. Again, an array of casement windows recessed into the roof provides a well-lighted hall with good solar heat gain.

The second level contains three large bedrooms and two full baths. Two bedrooms are lighted from south-facing recessed casements. The third bedroom is lighted by an east-facing casement window. This is the only window in the house that does not face to the south except for the two small flanking windows on the third level entry.

Another flight of stairs leads to the ground level. The layout of this level is shown in Figure 17.11. The stairs end in a wide entry hall. The dining room is to the left as is the kitchen; the living room is to the right. A lavatory is located off the kitchen as is the entrance to the mechanical module.

SECTION

Figure 17.8. Cross section of the Elizabethan colonial.

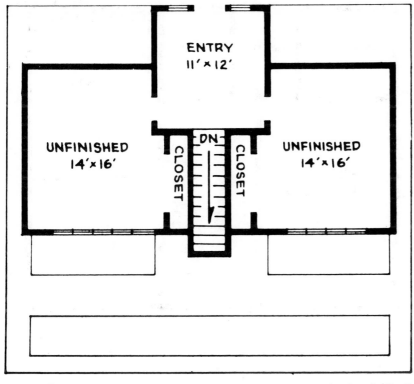

THIRD FLOOR PLAN

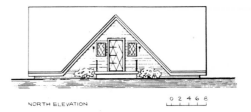

Figure 17.13. North elevation of the Elizabethan colonial.

Figure 17.6. Third-floor plan of the Elizabethan colonial.

This house contains 3220 sq ft of which 2783 sq ft is living area. But it has no separate basement and the attic is fully used. The house provides very high use of space. There is some inconvenience in having one entry up two flights of stairs.

Figure 17.10 shows the south elevation. Note that the casements recessed into the roof augment the design rather than detract from it. The active solar collectors can occupy most of the rest of the roof. They are very effective at the 12-in. roof pitch in most North American latitudes. There is room for using up to about 480 sq ft of collectors.

A flush door with colonial hardware and diamond grooving flanked by two small diamond-paned casements creates a center entry. Diamond-paned casements in the living and dining room complete the lower story window design. A glance back at the first-floor plan in Figure 17.11 will show that a frosted pane of glass has been used on the wall between the dining room and the kitchen to add natural lighting to the kitchen, which has no exterior windows.

This house again uses a combination of concrete and wood construction with the concrete being used where the earth covers the north, east, and west walls.

The house could also be designed with a more modern exterior by using single-pane casements, vertical siding on the walls, and a diagonal clapboarding on the gable overhangs. Several different exteriors are readily possible.

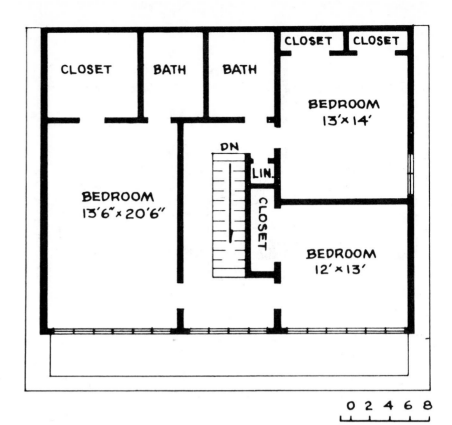

Figure 17.7. Second-floor plan of the Elizabethan colonial.

SECOND FLOOR PLAN

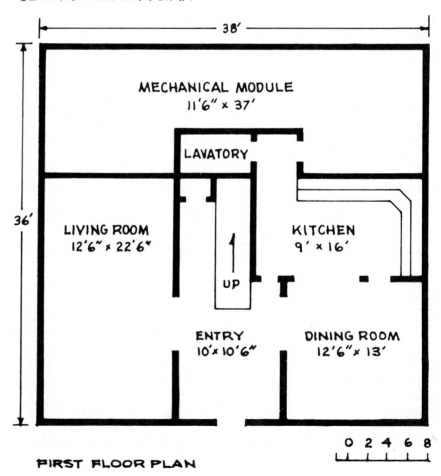

Figure 17.11. First-floor plan of the Elizabethan colonial.

FIRST FLOOR PLAN

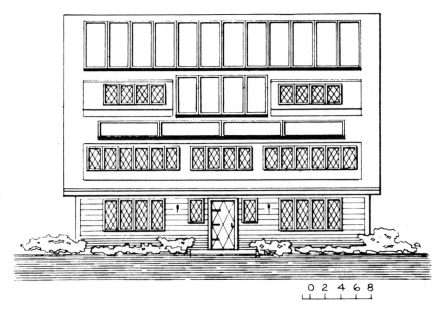

SOUTH ELEVATION

The Heat Loss of the Roof Pond Trilevel

The heat loss of the roof pond trilevel has been calculated using R-30 ceilings, R-30 bermed walls, R-22 south-facing wall, R-2.6 windows and doors, and R-5 perimeter losses. These conduction losses are:

Bermed sidewalls	56.2 Btu/hr/°F
South-facing sidewalls	13.0 Btu/hr/°F
Doors and windows	107.0 Btu/hr/°F
Ceiling	61.8 Btu/hr/°F
Perimeter, south-facing only	9.6 Btu/hr/°F
Total conduction heat losses	247.6 Btu/hr/°F

The infiltration heat loss has been calculated using one air change per hour in the living area, one-half air change per hour in the bedroom area, and one-half air change per hour in the mechanical module. The infiltration losses are:

Basement and bedrooms	98.7 Btu/hr/°F
Living areas	140.0 Btu/hr/°F
Total infiltration heat loss	238.7 Btu/hr/°F

The total combined heat loss, assuming that the basement is fully heated is 486 Btu/hr/°F or 0.19 Btu/hr/°F/sq ft of living area.

The Heat Loss of the Trilevel Elizabethan Colonial

The heat loss of the colonial was calculated using the same values for heat loss. The conduction losses by floor are:

Figure 17.10. South elevation of the Elizabethan colonial.

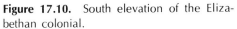

ELEVATION

Figure 17.9. Longitudinal section of the Elizabethan colonial.

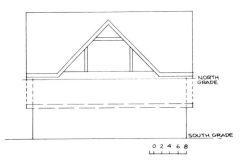

TYPICAL EAST/WEST ELEVATION

Figure 17.12. Typical east/west elevation of the Elizabethan colonial.

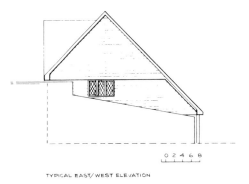

Contemporary Houses **285**

Third floor	74 Btu/hr/°F
Second floor	67 Btu/hr/°F
First floor	40 Btu/hr/°F
Basement	17 Btu/hr/°F
The total conduction heat loss	198 Btu/hr/°F

The infiltration heat loss was calculated using one air change per hour in the living areas and one-half air change per hour on the second floor, the third floor, and the basement. The infiltration losses are:

Bedrooms, third floor, and basement	154 Btu/hr/°F
Living areas	123 Btu/hr/°F
Total infiltration losses	277 Btu/hr/°F

The total combined heat loss for the house, assuming that the basement is heated, is 475 Btu/hr/°F or 0.15 Btu/hr/°F.

What About Flat Lots?

In this chapter the author has offered no solution to the problems of building solar houses on flat lots. Why is this? In the author's opinion, the flat lot offers a different design problem that can best be solved by the use of exterior sunspace.

Making a Decision

These two solar houses are as different as night and day. They could be said to represent two extremes in design and concept. You may not like either concept. But you should have seen that solar design for the future does not need to depart sharply from the styles that you are used to seeing.

You should have decided from this chapter that you could design a solar house that was energy-efficient in a manner that is in keeping with your concept of what you would like to live in during the balance of the twentieth century.

DECISION
18

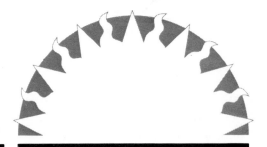

Plans
for
a
Solar
Greenhouse

The design of a solar greenhouse differs from the design of a commercial nonsolar greenhouse. The solar greenhouse is designed not only to capture the sun's energy but also to store that energy for future use. Generally, the north wall of the greenhouse is not glazed but consists either of an insulated wall or of a heat storage wall.

Green space, added to a home, can completely change the occupants' life-style in the northern latitudes. The structure brings the sun indoors to create a climate that is far more moderate than is ordinarily experienced. Winter becomes a time of enjoyment rather than a subzero weather trap.

The solar greenhouse that you will be examining in this decision is designed so that it either can stand alone or can be added to an existing house. Two design variations are shown: a design that uses rock thermal storage and a design that uses phase-change storage.

Boat-rib construction techniques have been used to create the framework of the greenhouse. This allows the frame to be constructed on the ground and erected with the use of stringers and plates to hold the ribs and the glazing or outer covering. This method of construction also allows the use of 2 × 4 construction to hold the costs down.

The design that you will study uses the following design criteria:

- The north-facing wall of the greenhouse will be the south-facing wall of the building structure except when the greenhouse stands alone.
- The long axis of the greenhouse will face east/west. The south-facing wall will be double-glazed. The north-facing wall in the stand-alone version will be sheathed and insulated.
- A high thermal mass for heat storage will be incorporated into the design.
- A venting mechanism for the summer months will be incorporated.

- Mechanical ventilation devices will be used to allow excess heat to be pushed into the main building structure.

Design of the Thermal Mass

Various authors have examined the amount of thermal mass that should be incorporated into a greenhouse design. The amount of thermal mass used dictates the temperature swing of the structure throughout the day and night. So the proper amount of thermal mass becomes quite important if you plan to have living plants in the structure.

A greenhouse with no thermal mass will fluctuate from the night-time ambient temperature to as high as 100°F on a winter day. That is a fluctuation of as much as 100° on a day when the outside night-time ambient temperature is zero degrees. Plants will not survive under such conditions. Most plants need a minimum of 55°F for survival and a maximum of 85°F to promote their growth. The thermal mass can be water, rock, or phase-change salts. These designs will employ either rock or phase-change salts.

Generally, designers cite the need to use 1½ to 3 cu ft of rock storage per square foot of south-facing glass in order to keep temperature fluctuations within the bounds of 55 to 85°F. So the greenhouse in this chapter using rock storage was designed with about 10 sq ft of glazing per lineal foot of green space and with about 20 cu ft of rock storage per lineal foot.

The amount of phase-change salts employed in the other design offers about the same amount of Btus of storage. Calcium hexachloride thermal rods were used in the second design.

The Glazing

A review of ordinary glazing techniques shows a need to think in terms of newer techniques for solar greenhouses than those employed in standard greenhouse designs. The design used in this decision uses a double-glazed fiberglass reinforced thermoplastic glazing. It is also possible to use a polycarbonate twin-wall sheet. When the fiberglass reinforced glazing is used, the seams are battened with aluminum strips and a silicone sealant. When the polycarbonate twin-wall is substituted, a high temperature gasketing should be used to mount the glazing system.

The details of using the fiberglass laminate or the polycarbonate twin-wall can be obtained from Solar Useage Now, Inc., Bascom, Ohio 44809. The company currently has an 800 number listed for incoming calls. This may be obtained from information at the telephone company.

Single-glass glazing, particularly in small panes, is entirely inadequate for solar greenhouse glazing and should not be used. Double-glazed, tempered insulated glass is very satisfactory.

The Basic Design

Figure 18.1 shows the basic greenhouse design as a cross section. 2 × 4 prefabricated ribs are located every 2 ft along a 2 × 6 plate bolted to a concrete block foundation that extends below the frost line. This founda-

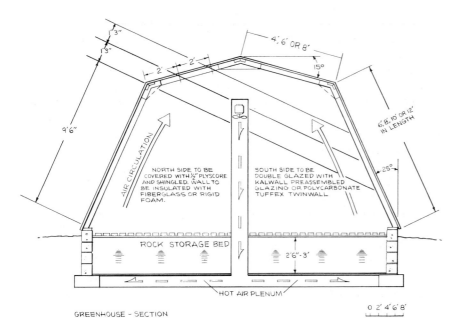

GREENHOUSE - SECTION

Figure 18.1. Cross section of the greenhouse design.

tion is insulated on the outside with 1 to 2 in. of rigid foam. Note the gussets at the points where the ribs join. These should be either ½-in. or ¾-in. exterior plywood. They should be glued and nailed during prefabrication.

The ribs and the gussets are notched at the center and the side ridge-poles so that a 1 × 4 stringer can be run through the ribs to hold the building together. Two stringers are used at each ridge location.

No diagonal cross bracing is needed when the building joins an existing structure. It should be employed when a stand-alone version is built. To prevent excess shading from the cross braces, guy wires stretching diagonally from top to bottom of the lower panels in an X pattern may be substituted.

An angle of 25° from the vertical was chosen for the sidewalls. This angle is pleasing to the eye, and it is also about perpendicular to the De-

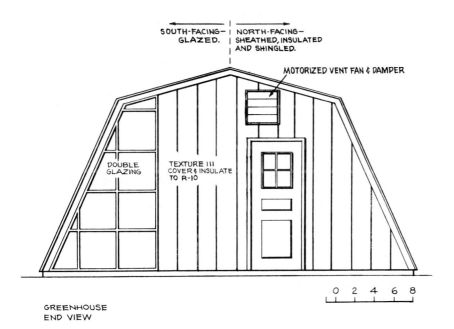

GREENHOUSE END VIEW

Figure 18.2. End view of the greenhouse design.

Greenhouses   **289**

cember sun in the northern latitudes. An angle of 15° from the horizontal was chosen for the top panels. This gives a good pitch to the roofline and again has acceptable aesthetics.

The length of the lower panels can vary from 6 to 12 ft. The variations should be made in 2-ft increments so that the prefabricated glazing will fit without cutting. The dimensions of the glazing should be determined before the ribs are fabricated. The upper panels can vary from 4 to 8 ft in length. Two-foot increments should be used, and the glazing dimensions should be predetermined.

The north-facing wall of the greenhouse and the ends that face to the east and west should be sheathed and insulated except at their southern-most edge. This is shown in Figure 18.2.

The foundation should be given an air plenum at the bottom similar to the plenum shown in the rock storage bed detailed in Decision 10. Bond beam blocks covered with heavy wire mesh will work extremely well. Then the balance of the foundation should be filled with ¾- to 1½-in. washed rock for thermal storage. Fiberglass tubes should extend from near the top of the greenhouse air space to the bottom plenum about every 4 to 6 ft. A tube-axial fan can be mounted in these tubes to circulate the air.

During the day when the heat concentrates in the top area of the greenhouse, the fans push the warm air down into the storage bed. The warm air heats up the rocks—storing heat—and recirculates back into the greenhouse floor to be reheated. The floor consists of wood slats about 1 × 4 nailed to 2 × 4 stringers laid on the top of the rocks. These should be made in small sections so that they can be removed for cleaning.

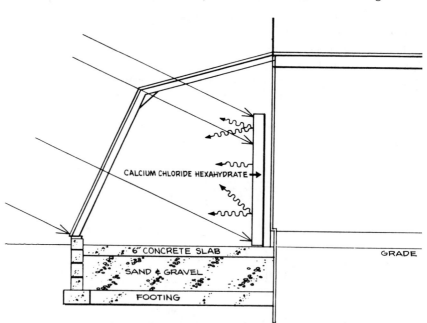

Figure 18.3. Cross section of the greenhouse design that uses phase-change salt and concrete floor storage.

SECTION–GREENSPACE USING PHASE-CHANGE SALT THERMAL STORAGE

An alternative thermal storage method is shown in Figure 18.3 where a 6-in. concrete floor has been laid over sand and gravel fill and the floor plus thermal rods at the back of the greenhouse are used together to store the sun's energy.

Figure 18.3 shows how the greenhouse is used against the side of a house with a south-facing end. Only one-half of the design is used. This slants the roof away from the house and makes the design an integral part of the house.

In Figure 18.4 the greenhouse has been shown attached to both the rear and the side of a house. In Figure 18.5 the details of attaching the greenhouse ribs to the rear of a pitched-roof structure are illustrated.

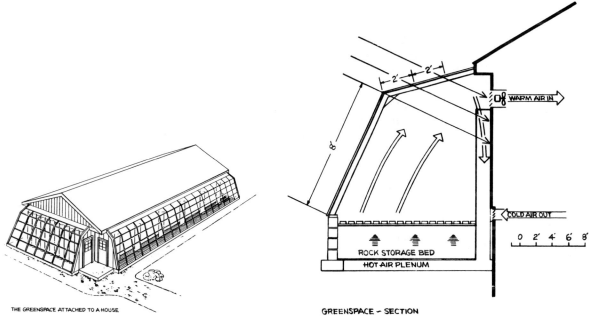

Figure 18.4. What the greenhouse looks like attached to the house.

Figure 18.5. Cross section of the greenhouse attached to the rear of a house.

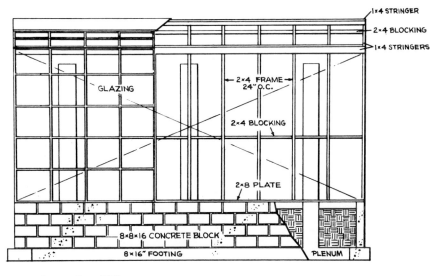

Figure 18.6. Details of the south-facing side of the greenhouse.

Figure 18.6 shows the south-facing side of the greenhouse. Note the detail furnished on the location of the stringers, the glazing, and the plate. Note the 2 × 4 blocking halfway up the top and bottom panels. These blocks add to the rigidity of the structure and help to support the glazing further. They are generally inserted after the stringers are fastened and the frame is complete. The X-braced guy wires are also shown as dashed lines.

Mechanical Ventilation

The greenhouse must be vented in order to prevent excess heat build-up during the summer months. This is accomplished by installing vent fans in the ends of the greenhouse. These fans are illustrated in Figure 18.2. The fan and the vent should be motorized and connected to a thermostat for automatic operation.

When the greenhouse is installed against a building, fans and vents should be cut into the side of the building so that excess heat in the winter months can be added to the house rather than pushed outdoors where it is lost. The location of these vents and dampers is shown in Figure 18.5. The location of the cold air return vent can vary from the floor of the room down to the wall of the foundation where the basement air would be returned to the greenhouse's rock storage bed.

Making a Decision

There are many good greenhouse designs. This one was chosen for its simplicity and its versatility.

The decision that you must make is whether you want to change your style of living. A good greenhouse is not the least expensive way to add solar energy to your home. But it definitely is a method of upgrading your lifestyle if you want to extend your summer season and you live in a northern climate.

DECISION
19

Plans for a Solar Vacation Home

Up until the end of World War II, most vacation homes were simple, unfinished shells good only for summer living. Generally, they were located on the edge of a lake or stream or were situated on the edge of a scenic view such as the side of a hill or mountain.

Today all that has changed. A more affluent America has built a thriving winter vacation industry. Today's vacation home must serve year round in many locations. This completely changes the nature and the character of the structure that American's desire.

The part of the population that owns a second home has also changed. The factory worker has now become wealthy enough to afford such a luxury. That part of the population is used to working with its hands and creating what it needs. So vacation homes have become do-it-yourself projects in many instances.

This vacation home is designed with year-round use in mind. A simple structure that can be built by any handy person has been evolved. Provision has been made to convert the house from summer to winter operation with a few hours' work.

Floor Plan

A very simple floor plan has been chosen. The house faces south. The south-facing side is mostly window. Figure 19.1 will orient you to the floor plan.

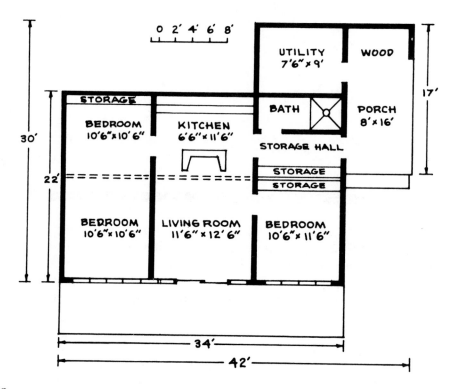

Figure 19.1. Floor plan of the vacation home.

The center of the cottage is taken up by a combined living room and kitchen. The kitchen is against the north wall separated from the living room by a fireplace, which contains a flue for a winter stove. There is room across the back of this chimney for a table. No window is shown on the kitchen rear wall, which is only 6 ft high. One can be added if desired. Provision should be made to shut off such a window completely in the winter season with movable insulation.

In the summer and fall months, the living room is entered from a 6-ft sliding door. This is to be either thermopane or well-insulated with movable insulation. In the coldest months of the year, this door will be permanently blocked with the movable insulation.

The master bedroom is on the southeast corner of the plan. It is reached and heated from the living room. No closet has been planned. The room contains a wall-length storage shelf with a closet rod and built-in dresser under it.

The other bedrooms are located on the west side of the structure. The design contains one very large bedroom running the width of the building that can be turned into two separate rooms by a draw drape running the width of the room. A similar storage wall is located to the rear of the structure to serve the two bedrooms.

The northeast corner of the cottage contains a storage-entrance hall and the bath. The bath and the storage hall are part of an auxiliary heated package that also includes the utility room located directly behind the bath. All freezables, except the water lines to the kitchen sink, are located in this area. By heating this area to 45°F, the owners can leave the cottage for extended periods without going through the need to drain the water lines and protect the bath fixtures and water heater against freezing.

A covered porch on the east side with an attached woodshed completes the plan. If desired, this porch could be enclosed in the winter months with storm sash.

The Roofline

Figure 19.2 shows the roofline of the cottage. This is a *solar aperture design*. A solar aperture design roofline is one where the roof is tilted up to the altitude of the winter sun on the south-facing side. This roofline opens the south side of the cottage to gross amounts of sunlight. The results of this design can be seen in Figure 19.3. Windows 9 ft high have been designed into the south wall. This gives 72 sq ft of window in each bedroom area and 90 sq ft of window in the living room. That is a total window area of about 234 sq ft.

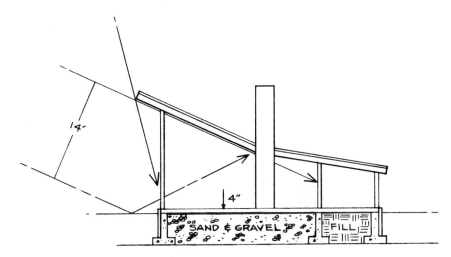

TYPICAL CROSS SECTION

Figure 19.2. Cross section of the vacation home.

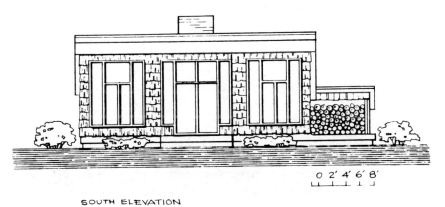

SOUTH ELEVATION

Figure 19.3. South elevation of the vacation home.

The windows are of a unique design. The windows flanking the door and the bedroom windows are designed as 2-ft-wide windows of fixed glass. Four vent windows are provided, one in each bedroom and two for the living room. These vents are located high in the wall for good summer ventilation.

The long, narrow fixed sash should be constructed with site-built double-glazing of ¼-in. plate glass. Movable insulation with a value of *R*-10 should be provided for each window and for the patio door. When these are in place in the nonsunlight hours of the winter months, the only window area in operation is the four vent windows, which should be triple-glazed.

The Sun Aperture and Solar Storage

In Figure 19.3, you can see that the sun aperture is about 14 ft high if the grade of the building is about 6 in. to 1 ft below the floor line. The sun's radiation reaches all the way to the rear wall of the structure.

The cottage is built on a concrete slab that terminates on 8-in. concrete block walls that are insulated on their exterior side with 2 to 4 in. of rigid foam. A 3-ft-high sand and gravel heat sink is located below the slab floor to provide solar storage. Figure 19.4 shows the east elevation; Figure 19.5 shows the north elevation.

The author elected to erect a chimney with a fireplace. The fireplace should contain a forced-air distribution unit and the opening should be of such a design that movable insulation can be placed in front of it during the coldest months. An opening for a stove flue should also be provided above the fireplace damper.

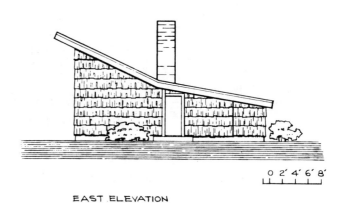

0 2' 4' 6' 8'

EAST ELEVATION

Figure 19.4. East elevation of the vacation home.

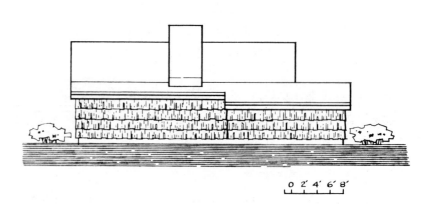

0 2' 4' 6' 8'

NORTH ELEVATION

Figure 19.5. North elevation of the vacation home.

The Insulation and the Heat Loss

This cottage is designed with the use of R-30 insulation in mind for the west, north, and east walls. This is accomplished with the use of fiberglass in the partitions and the use of rigid foam on the exterior or by the use of 2 × 6 stud construction. The insulation extends around the utility room but does not include the wood bin or the porch. The interior walls around the bath and the storage hall are insulated to R-24.

The west, north, and east walls have a combined area of about 740 sq ft of which 21 sq ft is door. The heat loss through these walls would be about 32 Btu/hr/°F. The ceiling heat loss is about 25 Btu/hr/°F.

The south wall contains about 408 sq ft of which 234 sq ft is double-glazed or triple-glazed window. In the winter months, with R-10 insulation in front of the fixed sash and the patio door, the wall's heat loss is about 48 Btu/hr/°F. During the summer months, without the insulation in place, the south wall heat loss rises to about 134 Btu/hr/°F.

The house contains about 6700 cu ft of air. In the summer months, two air changes per hour can be affected for a heat loss of 241 Btu/hr/°F. In the winter months, the air changes per hour can be dropped to one-half a change per hour for a heat loss of about 60 Btu/hr/°F. The slab has a perimeter of about 112 lineal feet and gives a heat loss of about 24 Btu/hr/°F summer and winter.

The total winter heat loss is estimated to be 189 Btu/hr/°F or 0.25 Btu/hr/°F/ sq ft. The total summer heat loss rises to about 492 Btu/hr/°F or about 0.66 Btu/hr/°F/ sq ft.

The Solar Storage Capability

The slab, foundation walls, and sand and gravel fill total out to about 2244 cu ft. This gives about 66,000 Btu/°F of heat storage. At a 10°F temperature rise, the stored heat is estimated at 660,000 Btu, which can be released at a rate of 2 Btu/sq ft of surface or at about 1500 Btu/hr/°F. At zero degrees, the house will demand about 12,285 Btu/hr. A fully charged storage would provide up to 15,000 Btu/hr. The house should be quite comfortable, particularly with auxiliary wood stove heat.

Making a Decision

The vacation plan that you have just examined is very unsophisticated. That is by intent. What the plan attempts to show is that a year-round vacation cottage need not be a complicated and expensive design just to obtain solar heat.

There are many ways to accomplish the design of a solar-heated vacation cottage. This plan only shows one of the many possibilities.

You should have decided that solar vacation homes are practical to consider.

DECISION 20

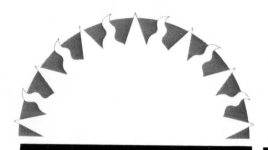

Invest in the Best Solar Home for You

By now you must have realized that the best solar home for you can be one of hundreds of different designs. It may be your present home with some remodeling. Or it may be a new home, designed specifically to meet your needs.

Whatever your decision, the evaluation process of determining exactly what will produce the maximum solar heat for that building is relatively fixed. You need to follow a set procedure for making the best possible determination.

In this chapter you will review this evaluation process so that you have firmly in mind how you must proceed to make your determinations.

You will review the following subjects:

- Solar radiation principles.
- Solar radiation availability.
- Your building's energy needs.
- The principles of an energy-efficient home.
- How to estimate your future fuel costs.
- How to orient your building.
- How to plan your building's interior.
- How to collect solar energy efficiently.
- How to store solar energy.
- How to distribute the collected energy.

At the front of the book, you will find a list of the tables that are scattered throughout the text. You will also find a list of the worksheets that you need to tabulate the information that you require. Each worksheet is on a separate page. This has been done so that you may make photocopies of these worksheets for your own use or for teaching purposes. However, the copyright does prohibit you from selling these worksheets for profit. The author specifically retains those rights.

Understand Solar Radiation

In Decision 2 you studied solar radiation. You learned that you needed to determine your longitude and latitude in order to understand how much solar energy was available at your building site.

You learned how to predict the amount of solar radiation that was available using sun-path diagrams and radiation calculators. But you also learned that this gave you only a partial picture because these diagrams do not include the effects of cloud cover.

Decision 2 contained a section on using trigonometric functions for determining the amount of sunlight on tilted and reflected surfaces. Although this requires you to study some relatively complex mathematics, it is essential that you understand trigonometric functions if you desire to make accurate predictions of the available energy. Four tables were given for you to use in order to work with the trigonometric functions.

Calculate Your Available Solar Energy

In Decision 3 you studied the availability of solar energy. You learned how solar radiation varied by location and by compass orientation. The country was laid out in 24 radiation blocks, and you were shown how to determine the amount of energy that is typically available in each block. These tables are unique to this book. To date, no other solar book has worked out a radiation estimate that you can easily use without a number of complex calculations. The tables provide an authoritative estimate of radiation by month on horizontal, vertical, and tilted surfaces facing in different compass directions.

Figures 3.4 through 3.9 and 3.11 and 3.12 give you all the details. Worksheets in Figures 3.28 through 3.37 provide a place for you to tabulate your results.

Decision 3 tells you what you can expect to receive in heat energy from the sun throughout the year.

Determine Your Building's Energy Needs

Decision 4 shows you how to determine your building's energy needs. Each building's energy needs are specific to that building structure. So you must calculate those needs for *your solar home.*

These calculations require that you know the difference between heat and temperature and that you understand the principles of heat energy transfer and heat energy balance. These principles give you the necessary background to calculate heat losses and gains in building structures.

If you remember nothing else from Decision 4, remember the formula: $UA \Delta t$ = heat loss or gain. That is, the U-factor times the area (A) times the difference in temperature (Δt) between the inside and the outside of the building determines the amount of heat lost or gained from a building structure.

Decision 4 contains the degree days for a representative city in each geographic block, the typical U-factors found in residential construction, and the other data that you will need to calculate the heat losses or gains of your building. It also contains the worksheets that you need to tabulate the results of your calculations in Figures 4.14 through 4.26.

Once you have studied Decisions 3 and 4, you can make an estimate of how much area you must have in order to heat your house with solar energy. Take the data shown in Figure 3.36 on total winter solar availability and compare it with the total heat loss shown in Figure 4.15. Some simple division will indicate how many square feet of collecting surface you need to provide your heat through the sun's energy.

Build an Energy-efficient Home

Decision 5 covers energy-efficient construction. Chances are that your existing home could use some improvements in energy efficiency and that those improvements are relatively small investments compared to installing solar-gathering equipment. Go for energy efficiency first. It's your best investment.

Many contractors and architects will tell you that the author's concept of a well-built house is outdated. The high cost of building has caused these builders and designers to settle for less costly, but less energy-efficient construction. The author knows about these shortcuts, but he has chosen to stay away from them. They do not result in the best of homes. You may choose to use items such as aluminum siding and insulating board in your home, but understand their effect on your energy efficiency and the home's quality.

In Decision 5, you studied fuel choices, air infiltration, ventilation, moisture control, and thermal insulation. You calculated heat losses for poor, good, and excellent construction. You learned that energy-efficient construction rapidly pays for itself at today's costs.

Decision 5 contains tables of R-values and U-factors for common residential construction. Use these tables to determine what type of construction you will specify.

It might be very enlightening for you to determine what energy-efficiency measures you could take in your home and then go back to the heat loss calculations in Decision 4 to determine how much more of your energy needs could be met by the sun once you have taken these steps.

Estimate Your Future Fuel Costs

Chances are that if you perform the calculations shown in this chapter, the results will leave you breathless. Your costs for fuel in the future will be far beyond anything that you have experienced in the past.

In Decision 6, you learned how to convert the purchase price of fuel to cost per MMBtu of net energy. You learned that the purchase price of fossil-fueled equipment is only a small part of the price you pay over its lifetime to own it. You saw how to determine just what this cost is expected to be, plus a way to calculate the cost of solar devices so that you could compare the two methods of obtaining the heat that you need. This chapter puts you in a position to make some factual economic judgments. Some of the future data is only an estimate, but it is an intelligent estimate based on the facts that are available. It is valid information to work with.

Decision 6 contains tables designed to assist you in making your estimates. Figure 6.15 is a worksheet for determining the true cost of your future energy needs.

Orient Your Building to Use the Sun

The first thing that you learned in Decision 7 was that most likely your present home was oriented without regard to the use of solar energy. America's builders have had too many other problems to cope with in the past. But fuel is no longer cheap, so energy-efficient orientation is now a must in any new suburban subdivision.

In Decision 7 you learned how to tell what was a good solar subdivision. You studied the use of building lots and of fences, trees, and other devices that would allow you to compensate for poor orientation.

You saw two tables for tabulating the building lot's weather analysis and for determining what thermal forces act on that particular parcel of land.

Whether you decide to remain where you are presently situated or to build a new home, the facts about orientation are important. Making use of them will allow you to make the best of your personal situation.

Plan Your Building's Interior

Decision 8 taught you the basics of modular home interior design. For convenience, the author chose to divide the house into four modules: the living module, the sleeping module, the mechanical module, and the transportation module. You learned that no matter what building style you chose, the interior space requirements were quite similar and that the modules could be fitted together in many different ways to satisfy your own requirements.

Solar-oriented houses tend to have different interior layouts than do nonsolar-oriented houses. The areas that do not need much heat can often be clustered along the north wall whereas the rooms that need more heat can be moved closer to the south wall. If you are remodeling your present home, your opportunities to make these changes will be limited. But if you are contemplating the design of a new home, there is no reason why you cannot take maximum advantage of the sun's radiant energy by shifting the rooms around inside the building's walls.

You will find many useful tables in Decision 8 that will help you decide just how much room you need in each part of your home.

Collect the Available Solar Energy Efficiently

For some odd reason, solar designers and engineers have settled on using either pure passive solar home design or pure active solar home design. Decision 9 should have taught you that this could be an unwise decision. It taught that the blending of active and passive design typically yielded the best results.

You learned that there were two basic ways to collect solar energy. One way was by direct gain through fenestration. The other was by indirect gain through solar collectors. You learned where each method was apt to be the most efficient.

The use of an integrated active/passive solar design concept is the entire thrust of this book. All that you learned through the first 10 chapters was background material designed to help you understand why this integrated approach is best from both an energy-efficiency standpoint and from an economic standpoint.

If you settle on fenestration devices, and you live in the northern United States, go for the triple-glazed window despite its cost. Use double-glass insulated units with winter storm windows to accomplish this with decent economics. Triple-glazing pays off in the northern latitudes.

If you settle on solar collectors, buy the best. A cheap solar collector is a poor investment. A good solar collector ought to last the life of your home. *The Solar Decision Book* (Wiley, New York, 1978) by the author covers the difference and will give you some good guidelines for making a wise investment. Consult with the Solar Energy Industries Association, Suite 800, 1001 Connecticut Avenue, N.W., Washington, D.C. 20036, which can provide the names and addresses of the major manufacturers. Do not put too much stock in the information that has been issued by the Department Of Energy and the Office Of Housing And Urban Development. Much of it is outdated. Much of it is poorly researched. And much of it is biased toward cheap systems.

Beware of the newer, more experimental systems espoused by the popular press. Many of these have not been completely tested. In the past, many of their offerings have not stood the test of time and have disappeared from the solar scene. In summary, use time-tested, industry-rated equipment that has been properly designed and researched by American industry.

Store the Collected Solar Energy

As a home owner, you are used to being able to produce heat on demand by dialing-up your thermostat. That is not true for solar energy. You can only collect solar energy when the sun is shining. In Decision 10 you learned that there are only about six solar hours per day.

The storage of the energy that you collect is most important. For one-quarter of the day, you will be receiving more energy than you can use. During the balance of the day, you cannot obtain more. So include good solar storage in your home.

You have three basic materials in which you can store the collected solar energy: concrete and rocks, water, and phase-change salts. All these storage methods are good provided that you choose the one best suited for your design. Decision 10 shows you how to make this choice. You studied concrete, stone, and brick. You studied water. And you studied calcium chloride hexahydrate. Each of these materials is a proven storage method. You can rely on them, but you must use them correctly.

Decision 10 contains many tables and sample calculations that will show you how to determine what is best for your design.

Distribute the Solar Energy

It is obvious to all that solar energy is direction-oriented and that the rooms on the north side of the house will receive little or no energy during the heating season. In Decision 11 you learned how to distribute the energy around the house so as to heat the entire structure. You saw ways to move the heat with the use of building air and with the use of water. You received the information that is required to make the proper distribution decisions. Decision 11 contains tables and a worksheet to aid you in your work.

Solar House Designs

In Decisions 12 through 19, you saw some preliminary designs for houses that would use the sun effectively. You saw earth-insulated houses, air-envelope houses, ranch houses, split-level houses, two-story houses, and some contemporary solar houses.

Your study of these chapters should have taught you one thing: Solar can fit any house style that you would like to build. You do not have to commit to a specific style of home to make effective use of the sun's energy.

Making Your Own Solar Decision

As I said when I started this book: "I believe that active and passive solar techniques should be blended together to produce the most practical and economical results. An existing home . . . usually has limited potential for passive remodeling. Active heating designs will most likely yield the highest value in this situation. . . . A new home that is properly sited and oriented has excellent potential for passive solar construction."

I wrote this book to aid you in the tasks of making better use of solar energy, of putting good energy conservation into practice, and of building new energy-efficient, solar utilizing residences. If you adhere to the principles that I have outlined, you will be able to accomplish these tasks.

As you plan your solar home, invest with care. Investigate all the offerings carefully. Be certain that your sources are knowledgeable. Do not rush into a major investment until you have gathered all the facts.

Most solar is common sense. If you do not understand what is being suggested, chances are that you should take a hard second look before you move ahead.

APPENDIX
A
Sun-path
Diagrams

Sun-path diagrams are used to determine the location of the sun at any time of the year and at any hour of the day. A *sun-path diagram* is a graphic projection of the path of the sun across the sky as projected onto a horizontal surface (see Figure 2.15).

On the sun-path diagram, the altitude of the sun is described by a number of concentric circles. These circles are labeled from 10 to 80°. The geographic bearing of the sun from solar south, which is called the *azimuth,* is described by a series of radial lines at 10° intervals around the circular diagram. The elliptical curves on the diagram represent horizontal projections of the sun's path across the sky throughout the year on the 21st day of each month.

On the sun-path diagram, the months of the year are designated with roman numerals. The numeral I = January; numeral XII = December. The other months are designated consecutively starting with January. The time of day is indicated by the arabic numerals located on the uppermost ellipse. The afternoon hours are on the west side of the diagram; the morning hours are on the east side of the diagram.

Using the Sun-path Diagrams

Here is an example of how the sun-path diagrams are used. Assume that you wish to find the sun's position on February 21 at 3 P.M. at 40° North latitude (Figure A.2).

- Select the February path of the sun. This is the elliptical curve labeled II.
- Locate the curved line labeled 3. This represents 3 P.M.
- Note where the lines intersect. This is the location of the sun.

The sun is at an azimuth of 50° west of south and at an altitude of 24° above the horizon.

Now find the sun's position at the same time of day for October 21. You should have noted that the answer is the same because the same elliptical curve is used for October.

Next, look at the sun-path diagram for 44°N latitude (Figure A.2). Find the azimuth and the altitude for February 21 at 3 P.M. The sun is at an azimuth of 48° west of south and at an altitude of 21° above the horizon. That answer is quite close to the answer for 40° latitude.

This shows that you can readily interpolate from these sun-path diagrams for latitudes that do not have a sun-path diagram displayed. Figure A.1 and Figure A.2 are sun-path diagrams for latitudes from 24 to 52°N latitude.

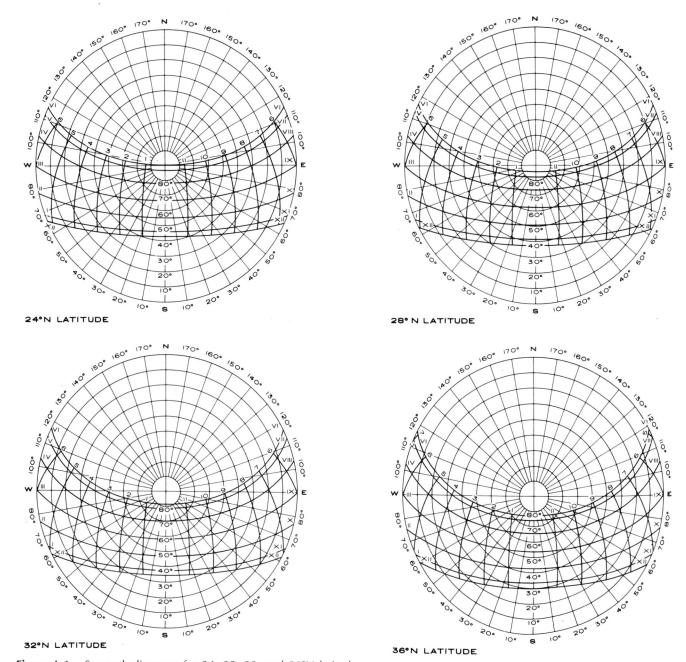

24°N LATITUDE

28° N LATITUDE

32°N LATITUDE

36°N LATITUDE

Figure A.1. Sun-path diagrams for 24, 28, 32, and 36°N latitude.

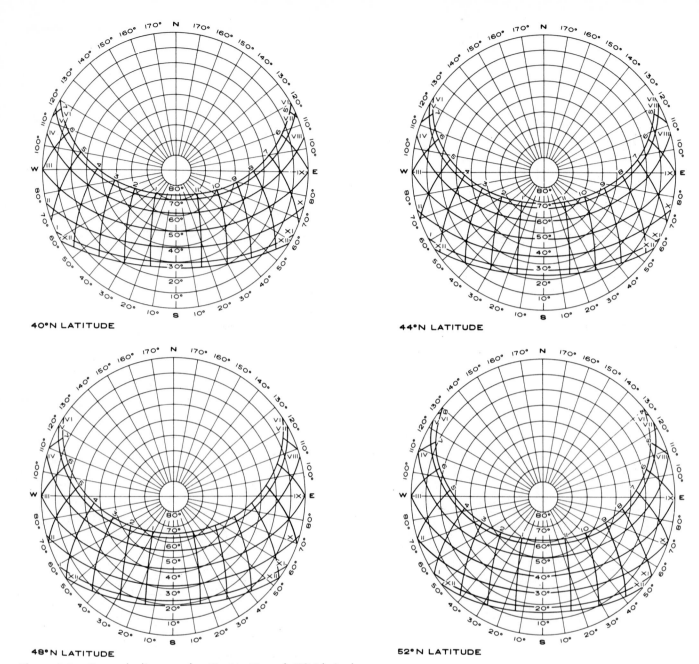

40°N LATITUDE

44°N LATITUDE

48°N LATITUDE

52°N LATITUDE

Figure A.2. Sun-path diagrams for 40, 44, 48, and 52°N latitude.

APPENDIX

B

How
Heat
Transfer
Coefficients
Are
Derived

The transfer of heat occurs by three processes: *conduction, convection,* and *radiation.* Conduction is the transfer of heat within a body by the short-range interaction of molecules or electrons. Convection is the transfer of heat by the combined mechanisms of fluid mixing and conduction. Radiation is the transfer of heat by the emission of energy as electromagnetic waves.

The Transfer of Heat by Conduction

For the purposes of this discussion, your greatest interest is in the derivation of *R-values* and *U-factors.* The *R*-value is the resistance to heat flow through a substance. The *U*-factor is a measure of the rate of heat flow through a substance.

You must understand a number of heat transmission terms in order to understand how *R*-values and *U*-factors are derived. Figure B.1 illustrates the first three terms:

Q = thermal transmission
k = thermal conductivity
r = thermal resistivity

Thermal transmission, Q, equals the quantity of heat flowing through a substance per unit of time. In the English system of measurement, Q is measured in Btu per hour.

Thermal conductivity, k, is the rate of thermal transmission or Q through a substance that is 1 in. thick and has an area of 1 sq ft when a 1°F temperature differential exists between the two sides of the substance. In the English system of measurement, k is measured in Btu per hour per square foot per degree F per inch of thickness.

Thermal resistivity, r, is the resistance of that substance to the flow of heat under the same conditions. The thermal resistivity of a substance is calculated by dividing one by the thermal conductivity. In mathematics, this is known as finding the reciprocal.

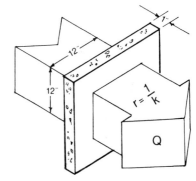

Figure B.1. Thermal conductivity (k) is the rate of heat transfer through 1 in. of thickness of a material.

$$Q = \text{Btu/hr}$$

$$k = \text{Btu/hr/sq ft/°F/in.}$$

$$r = \frac{1}{k}$$

$$r = \frac{1}{0.033} = 30.3$$

$$k = \frac{1}{r}$$

$$k = \frac{1}{30.3} = 0.033$$

$$C = \text{Btu/hr/sq ft/}°F$$

$$R = \frac{1}{C}$$

$$R = \frac{1}{0.045} = 22.2$$

$$r = \frac{1}{12} = 0.083$$

0.083
0.083
0.083
0.083
0.083
0.083
0.083
+ 0.083
0.667

Thermal resistivity is a *calculated number*. To obtain *r*, one measures *k* and divides *k* into one. For example, if measurement shows that *k* = 0.033, then *r* = 30.3.

If the thermal resistivity of a material is known and the thermal conductivity is needed, then the thermal resistivity divided into one gives the thermal conductivity.

Summing up: *The thermal conductivity of a material is equal to the amount of heat that will pass through a 1-in. thickness of the material in 1 hr when a 1°F temperature differential exists between its sides.*

Figure B.2 illustrates the second set of terms:

C = thermal conductance
R = thermal resistance

Thermal conductance, C, is the rate of thermal transmission or *Q* through a substance of any given thickness that has an area of 1 sq ft and a 1°F temperature differential between its two sides. In the English system of measurement, *C* is measured in Btu per hour per square foot per degree F.

Thermal resistance, R, is the resistance of that substance to the flow of heat under the same conditions. The thermal resistance of a substance is calculated by dividing the thermal conductance into one. That is, by finding the reciprocal. For example, if *C* = 0.045 by measurement, one divided by 0.045 equals 22.2. So *R* = 22.2.

Summing up: *The thermal conductance of a material is equal to the amount of heat that will pass through a given thickness of 1 sq ft of the material in 1 hr when a 1°F temperature differential exists between the two sides of the material.*

The difference between *k* and *C* is simple. *k* is a measure of heat transmittance through a 1-in. thickness, whereas *C* is a measure of heat transmittance through any given thickness of a substance.

The difference between *r* and *R* is similar. *r* is the resistance to heat flow offered by a 1-in. thickness, whereas *R* is the resistance to heat flow offered by any given thickness of the material.

By the laws of heat transfer, thermal resistances are additive. If a 1-in. thick concrete wall has a *k* value of 12, then it has an *r* value of 0.083. To find the *R* value of an 8-in. wall, the *r* values must be added together. The result is *R* = 0.667

However, *k* values are not additive. They must first be converted to *r* values to determine the *C* value. Take the last example: If 12 is added up for an 8-in. thickness, the result is *C* = 96. That converts to *R* = 0.01, which is incorrect. You would have to add the reciprocals as follows to be correct:

$$R = \frac{1}{12} + \frac{1}{12} + \frac{1}{12} + \frac{1}{12} + \frac{1}{12} + \frac{1}{12} + \frac{1}{12} + \frac{1}{12} = 0.667$$

The addition of the *k* values to obtain first a *C* value and then an *R* value is a common mistake made in calculating heat transfer coefficients.

Heat Transfer Through the Walls of a Building

The two sets of terms that you have just studied describe the heat transfer through a solid such as a building's wall by conductance. But you should remember from your earlier study of heat transfer principles that heat is transmitted in three ways: conduction, convection, and radiation. To ob-

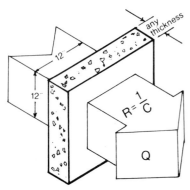

Figure B.2. Thermal conductance (C) is the rate of heat transfer through any given thickness of a material.

tain an overall heat transmittance through the walls of a structure, you must also calculate the effects of convection and radiation at the two surfaces of the wall.

Figure B.3 illustrates a third set of terms that describe the effects of convection and radiation at the walls' surfaces:

h_i = interior surface conductance
h_o = exterior surface conductance

Interior surface conductance, h_i, is the rate of thermal transmission from a surface in contact with the building's interior air in Btu/hr/sq ft/°F.

Exterior surface conductance, h_o, is the rate of thermal transmission from a surface in contact with the air outside the building in Btu/hr/sq ft/°F.

Surface conductance is affected by the *emittance* of radiant heat from the surface, by the *reflectance* of heat from the surface, and by the convective movement of the air over the surface of the wall. Emittance is the ratio of the heat radiated by a given wall to the heat radiated by a black body at the same temperature. Reflectance is the ratio of heat reflected by the wall to the total heat falling on that wall.

The surface conductance of a vertical building wall in both exterior and interior air has been experimentally determined by ASHRAE. The results are as shown in Figure B.4.

Total Heat Resistance and Transmission Through Building Walls

The total transmission or resistance to transmission is described by two terms:

R-value = the overall resistance of the wall to the transmission of heat.
U-factor = the total heat transmission through the wall.

The R-value is the reciprocal of the U-factor. $R = \frac{1}{U}$ and $U = \frac{1}{R}$.

Determining R-values and U-factors The U-factor of a wall cannot be determined directly. It is necessary to calculate the various R values of the wall's components and then to add them together and take the reciprocal of the sum to determine the U-factor.

If a wall is uniform throughout, this is a relatively simple procedure. Look at the 8-in. concrete wall shown in Figure B.3. The total wall R-value would be the sum of the R of the wall, the R of the interior air, and the R of the exterior air, as shown in Figure B.5.

ITEM	DESCRIPTION	CONDUCTANCE	RESISTANCE
h_o	Outside air	6.75	0.148
h_i	Inside air	1.8	0.555
C	Concrete	1.5	0.666
R-value			1.369
U-factor (calculated from R-value) 0.73 Btu/hr/sq ft/°F			

A typical k value for concrete is 12. That is an r value of 0.083. So the R for the concrete would be 0.67. The h_o for exterior air from the graph in Figure B.4 is 6.75, which gives the outside air an r value of 0.15. The h_i for interior air from the graph in Figure B.4 is 1.8. The r for the inside air is thus 0.56. When the R for the concrete, the r for the inside air, and the r for the outside air are added together and divided into one, the U-factor is 0.73.

Many building walls are nonuniform however. An example is the wall in a wood-framed building. About 20% of the interior of the wall is wood

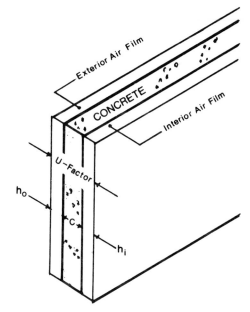

Figure B.3. The *U*-factor of a wall consists of the thermal conductance of the wall plus the surface conductance of the two surfaces of the wall.

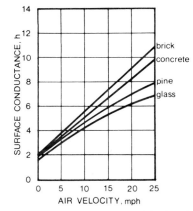

Figure B.4. Values of h_i and h_o for different wall surfaces and for varying wind speeds.

Figure B.5. How the *U*-factor for the concrete wall in Figure B.3 is determined.

studs. The other 80% is either air cavity or insulation. The U-factors for such a wall have been calculated in Figure B.6

You will not have to be concerned with calculating U-factors. Typical U-factors have been tabulated for your use in Decision 4.

	THERMAL RESISTANCE		
CONSTRUCTION ITEM	AT FRAME	UNINSULATED CAVITY	INSULATED CAVITY
Outside air (15 mph)	0.15	0.15	0.15
Clapboard siding	0.81	0.81	0.81
½" plywood sheathing	0.62	0.62	0.62
2 × 4 frame (nominal)	4.38		
3½" air cavity		1.00	
3½" fiberglass cavity			11.00
½" gypsum board	0.45	0.45	0.45
Inside air	0.68	0.68	0.68
R-values	7.09	3.71	13.71
U-factors (calculated)	0.14	0.27	0.073

CONSTRUCTION ITEM	TOTAL WALL PERCENTAGE	U-VALUE	(U)(%)
At frame	20	0.14	0.028
At cavity (uninsulated)	80	0.27	0.216
Average U-factor (uninsulated)			0.244
Average R-value			4.10

CONSTRUCTION ITEM	TOTAL WALL PERCENTAGE	U-VALUE	(U)(%)
At frame	20	0.14	0.028
At cavity (insulated)	80	0.073	0.058
Average U-factor (insulated)			0.086
Average R-value			11.63

Figure B.6. Calculating the average U-factor of a typical wood wall with and without insulation.

Heat Transfer from the Surface of a Solid Wall

In passive construction, heat is often stored in solid walls. The ability of the wall to give off or take up heat is quite important. Heat transfer from a solid wall is a fairly complex subject.

The General Electric data book titled *Heat Transfer and Fluid Flow* (1970: General Electric Company, Schenectady, N.Y.) contains a section on free convection on a vertical plane surface in air. Section 504.2, page 2, gives a graph of experimental results that indicates that a convection heat transfer coefficient of 0.8 Btu/hr/sq ft/°F would be an average figure acceptable for use in residential structures. This value was used in the calculations in this book. The Copper Development Association cites a similar figure in its literature on radiant heating systems.

The General Electric data book also contains a section on radiant heat transfer. Again, a graph, located in Section 505.2, page 7, indicates that a wall having an emissivity of 0.90 will have a radiant heat transfer coefficient of about 1.2 Btu/hr/sq ft/°F. The reference cited from the Copper Development Association concurs.

If the convective heat transfer coefficient of 0.8 and the radiant heat transfer coefficient of 1.2 are combined to arrive at a total heat transfer coefficient, then a solid wall in a vertical plane under normal residential conditions can be expected to take up or give up heat at a rate that is typically 2.0 Btu/hr/sq ft/°F. It is important that solar designers recognize these heat transfer rate limitations in designing solid storage media.

APPENDIX
C
Fuels
and
Combustion

A *fuel* is a material that can be used to produce heat. One class of fuels that is commonly used to produce heat is *hydrocarbon substances*. A hydrocarbon substance is a material that is predominently composed of hydrogen and carbon atoms.

Common hydrocarbon fuels are petroleum, gas, coal, and wood. When these materials are heated to their *ignition point*, they react with the oxygen in the air to produce heat. Two chemical reactions take place:

- The carbon combines with the oxygen in the air to form carbon dioxide plus heat.
- The hydrogen combines with the oxygen in the air to form water vapor plus heat.

The chemist writes these reactions like this:

$$C + O_2 = CO_2 + \text{heat}$$
$$H_2 + O_2 = H_2O + \text{heat}$$

Of course there must be just the right proportions of oxygen and hydrocarbon fuel present for good efficiency. If there is too little air available, not all the fuel will be burned. If there is too much air present, heat will be wasted in heating up the excess air to the ignition point.

The correct amount is determined by balancing the chemical equations just presented so that there are the same number of atoms on each side of the equation as shown here:

$$C + O_2 = CO_2$$
$$2H_2 + O_2 = 2H_2O$$

Generally, it is best to supply a slight excess of oxygen.

The *fuel ignition point* is the lowest temperature at which the fuel will ignite. This heat is normally supplied externally to start the fuel burning. In an oil burner, it is supplied by a high intensity electrical spark. In a gas burner, it is supplied by a pilot flame. For coal and wood, a small fire is generally started first and then more fuel is added as the fire grows hotter.

Fuels burn at very high temperatures. Generally the fossil fuels burn at temperatures ranging from 3360 to 3800°F. Maintaining the flame temperatures at these levels is very important if the fuel is to be burned efficiently.

The process of combining a fuel with oxygen to burn it and produce heat is known as the *combustion process*. The heat released during the combustion process does four things:

- It heats the incoming air and fuel.
- It supplies the heat needed to break down the fuel.
- It heats up the combustion products.
- It radiates heat to the surroundings.

Only the heat that is radiated to the surroundings can be used to supply heat to the house. The remainder is needed to support and continue the combustion process.

The amount of heat generated by the complete combustion of a given fuel remains constant. This is called the fuel's *heating value*. You may also hear it called the *heat of combustion* or *caloric value*. All three terms mean the same thing. Here are some common heating values for different fuels.

FUELS	HEATING VALUE	UNIT OF MEASURE
Natural gas	1,000	Btu/cu ft
Propane gas	2,500	Btu/cu ft
Butane gas	3,200	Btu/cu ft
Gasoline	125,000	Btu/gal
Kerosene	135,000	Btu/gal
Fuel oil (No. 2)	138,000	Btu/gal
Coal		
Bituminous	11,500	Btu/lb
Anthracite	11,250	Btu/lb
Crude oil	138,000	Btu/gal
Red oak	5,500	Btu/lb

You will also see the term *net heating value* used. Net heating value is the heating value minus the *latent heat of vaporization*. The latent heat of vaporization is the amount of heat that is needed to vaporize the water that is generated in the combustion process. The heat that is needed to vaporize the water cannot be used to heat the house. Neither can the heat needed to raise the incoming fuel and air to the ignition point be used. So the combustion of a fuel cannot be 100% efficient in terms of providing usable heat. With natural gas, about 70 to 75% efficiency is the maximum that you can obtain. A similiar situation exists with the other hydrocarbon fuels.

APPENDIX
D
ASHRAE Solar Heat Gain Tables

This appendix contains the ASHRAE solar heat gain tables for 24, 32, 40, and 48° North latitude (Figures D.1 through D.4). These are reprinted from the *ASHRAE 1977 Fundamentals Handbook*, by permission.

The solar heat gain through a glazing is complex, so the American Society of Heating and Air Conditioning Engineers, ASHRAE, has developed a computer program—the Solar Heat Gain Factor Program—to describe this heat gain. The solar heat gain tables were developed by running the computer program and listing the values obtained on the tables.

The tables take the normal solar radiation striking a horizontal surface each hour on the 21st day of each month and from this value calculate the number of Btu per hour per square foot that would pass through a double-strength sheet of glass with 86% solar transmittance, 8% solar reflectance, and 6% solar absorptance located in a vertical wall.

The tables assume that the days are all cloudless, so the values calculated from them cannot be used to calculate annual heat gain. Decision 9 shows how to correct the tables for annual heat gain.

The tables are used as follows:

- Turn to the table for 40° North latitude (Figure D.3).
- Look at the column labeled S (for south) at the top of the chart.
- Under January 21 note the horizontal line titled Half-Day Totals.
- Read across to the S column. You will see that between the hours of 7 A.M. and noon the windows will provide 813 Btu/sq ft of area. This figure is the sum of the hourly heat gains shown from 7 A.M. until noon.
- Note that the table is titled Solar Time P.M. on the far right-hand side of the page. Look down to the bottom of the page. Here you will see the afternoon solar orientations listed. Note that the columns are different except for south. When determining the half-day totals for the morning, you must use the column headings at the top of the table. When determining the half-day totals for the afternoon, you must use the column headings at the bottom of the page. Instructions continued on page 319.

Solar Intensity and Solar Heat Gain Factors* for 24 Deg North Latitude

Solar Heat Gain Factors, Btuh/ft²

Date	Solar Time am	Direct Normal Btuh/ft²	N	NNE	NE	ENE	E	ESE	SE	SSE	S	SSW	SW	WSW	W	WNW	NW	NNW	HOR	Solar Time pm
Jan 21	7	71	2	3	21	45	62	67	63	49	25	3	2	2	2	2	2	2	5	5
	8	239	12	12	41	128	190	221	218	181	114	28	12	12	12	12	12	12	55	4
	9	288	18	18	23	106	190	240	253	227	166	73	19	18	18	18	18	18	121	3
	10	308	23	23	24	53	144	211	245	241	200	125	38	24	23	23	23	23	172	2
	11	317	26	26	26	27	73	156	211	234	220	173	95	29	26	26	26	26	204	1
	12	320	27	27	27	27	29	82	160	210	227	210	160	81	29	27	27	27	214	12
	HALF DAY TOTALS		95	96	148	372	671	942	1076	1039	840	505	241	120	96	95	95	95	664	
Feb 21	7	153	6	12	67	114	141	145	128	90	33	6	6	6	6	6	6	6	17	5
	8	262	15	16	80	165	220	240	224	172	89	17	15	15	15	15	15	15	83	4
	9	297	21	22	46	138	208	244	243	205	133	42	22	21	21	21	21	21	153	3
	10	314	26	26	28	76	157	209	228	213	165	87	28	26	26	26	26	26	205	2
	11	321	29	29	29	31	80	148	191	203	185	137	68	31	29	29	29	29	238	1
	12	323	30	30	30	30	32	70	134	177	192	177	133	70	32	30	30	30	249	12
	HALF DAY TOTALS		113	119	257	527	806	1011	1072	965	699	374	200	127	113	113	113	113	820	
Mar 21	7	194	11	45	115	164	186	180	145	86	17	10	10	10	10	10	10	10	36	5
	8	267	18	35	124	195	234	237	204	138	48	19	18	18	18	18	18	18	112	4
	9	295	25	27	85	165	215	232	214	163	82	27	25	25	25	25	25	25	180	3
	10	309	30	31	41	103	162	194	195	168	112	47	31	30	30	30	30	30	232	2
	11	315	33	33	34	42	85	129	154	155	139	86	43	34	33	33	33	33	264	1
	12	317	34	34	34	34	35	56	96	126	137	126	95	56	35	34	34	34	275	12
	HALF DAY TOTALS		133	189	422	693	906	1011	970	778	458	249	169	139	133	133	133	133	962	
Apr 21	6	40	6	21	33	39	39	33	22	7	2	2	2	2	2	2	2	2	4	6
	7	203	20	88	151	189	197	176	127	55	15	14	14	14	14	14	14	14	58	5
	8	256	24	80	159	209	228	212	164	88	24	22	22	22	22	22	22	22	132	4
	9	280	30	54	126	181	208	203	169	105	39	29	28	28	28	28	28	28	195	3
	10	292	34	37	75	125	157	165	148	107	56	35	33	33	33	33	33	33	244	2
	11	298	36	37	40	59	85	103	106	94	70	45	38	37	36	36	36	36	274	1
	12	299	37	37	38	38	39	46	59	70	75	70	58	45	39	38	38	37	283	12
	HALF DAY TOTALS		168	339	607	826	940	924	773	494	244	180	163	157	155	155	154	154.	1048	
May 21	6	86	25	57	79	87	84	66	38	8	6	6	6	6	6	6	6	6	13	6
	7	203	43	117	171	199	196	163	105	32	17	17	17	17	17	17	17	18	73	5
	8	248	38	114	178	214	218	190	132	54	26	25	25	25	25	25	25	26	142	4
	9	269	35	88	150	188	198	179	132	66	33	31	31	31	31	31	31	31	201	3
	10	280	38	59	103	137	150	141	111	67	39	36	35	35	35	35	35	36	247	2
	11	286	40	43	55	72	83	84	75	58	44	40	39	38	38	38	38	39	274	1
	12	288	41	41	41	41	42	43	44	46	46	46	44	43	42	41	41	41	282	12
	HALF DAY TOTALS		238	492	749	909	943	840	614	308	187	176	174	173	172	172	172	175	1089	
Jun 21	6	97	36	70	93	101	94	73	39	8	7	7	7	7	7	7	7	8	17	6
	7	201	55	127	177	199	192	155	94	26	18	18	18	18	18	18	18	20	77	5
	8	242	50	126	184	214	212	179	117	43	27	26	26	26	26	26	26	27	145	4
	9	263	43	102	158	189	192	168	116	53	34	32	32	32	32	32	32	33	201	3
	10	274	41	72	113	140	146	131	96	55	39	36	36	36	36	36	36	38	245	2
	11	279	42	50	65	77	82	77	64	49	42	41	40	39	39	39	40	41	271	1
	12	281	43	43	43	43	43	43	43	43	43	43	43	43	43	43	43	43	279	12
	HALF DAY TOTALS		284	562	802	933	932	797	544	255	187	181	180	179	179	179	180	187	1096	
Jul 21	6	81	26	56	76	84	80	63	36	8	6	6	6	6	6	6	6	7	13	6
	7	195	45	116	168	194	190	158	101	31	18	18	18	18	18	18	18	19	73	5
	8	239	41	115	176	210	213	185	128	52	27	26	26	26	26	26	26	26	141	4
	9	261	37	90	150	186	195	175	129	64	34	32	32	32	32	32	32	32	198	3
	10	272	39	62	104	137	149	139	108	65	39	37	36	36	36	36	36	37	243	2
	11	278	41	44	58	73	83	83	73	57	44	41	40	39	39	39	39	40	270	1
	12	280	42	42	42	43	43	44	45	46	46	46	45	43	43	42	42	42	278	12
	HALF DAY TOTALS		247	498	746	897	925	820	595	300	191	181	178	177	177	177	177	181	1076	
Aug 21	6	35	6	20	30	35	35	30	19	6	2	2	2	2	2	2	2	2	4	6
	7	186	22	87	144	179	186	165	119	51	16	15	15	15	15	15	15	15	58	5
	8	241	26	82	156	203	220	204	157	84	26	24	24	24	24	24	24	24	130	4
	9	265	32	57	126	178	202	197	162	101	39	31	30	30	30	30	30	30	191	3
	10	278	36	40	78	125	155	161	143	103	55	37	35	35	35	35	35	35	239	2
	11	284	38	39	42	61	85	101	104	91	68	46	40	38	37	37	37	37	268	1
	12	286	38	39	40	40	41	47	58	69	72	68	58	47	41	40	40	39	277	12
	HALF DAY TOTALS		179	347	601	806	910	889	740	473	243	186	171	165	164	163	163	162	1028	
Sep 21	8	248	19	36	119	185	222	225	194	132	48	20	19	19	19	19	19	19	108	4
	9	278	26	28	84	160	207	223	206	158	81	28	26	26	26	26	26	26	174	3
	10	292	31	32	42	101	158	188	190	163	110	48	32	31	31	31	31	31	224	2
	11	299	34	34	35	43	84	127	151	151	128	86	44	35	34	34	34	34	256	1
	12	301	35	35	35	36	37	57	95	124	134	124	94	57	37	36	35	35	266	12
	HALF DAY TOTALS		139	190	406	661	863	964	927	749	451	251	174	145	139	138	138	138	930	
Oct 21	7	138	6	12	62	104	129	133	117	82	31	7	6	6	6	6	6	6	17	5
	8	247	16	17	79	159	211	230	214	164	85	17	16	16	16	16	16	16	82	4
	9	284	22	23	47	135	202	237	235	198	128	41	23	22	22	22	22	22	150	3
	10	301	27	27	29	77	154	204	222	207	160	85	29	27	27	27	27	27	201	2
	11	309	30	30	30	33	80	145	186	198	180	133	67	32	30	30	30	30	233	1
	12	311	31	31	31	31	33	70	131	173	187	172	130	69	33	31	31	31	244	12
	HALF DAY TOTALS		116	123	255	512	778	974	1032	929	675	367	200	131	117	116	116	116	804	
Nov 21	7	67	2	3	20	43	59	64	60	46	24	3	2	2	2	2	2	2	5	5
	8	232	12	13	42	126	186	216	213	177	111	28	12	12	12	12	12	12	55	4
	9	282	19	19	23	106	187	236	249	223	163	71	20	19	19	19	19	19	120	3
	10	303	23	23	24	53	143	209	241	237	197	123	37	24	23	23	23	23	171	2
	11	312	26	26	26	28	73	154	209	230	217	171	93	29	26	26	26	26	202	1
	12	315	27	27	27	27	29	81	158	207	224	207	158	80	29	27	27	27	213	12
	HALF DAY TOTALS		97	97	149	368	661	926	1056	1020	825	497	239	121	98	97	97	97	659	
Dec 21	7	30	1	1	7	18	25	28	27	21	12	2	1	1	1	1	1	1	2	5
	8	225	10	10	29	112	174	208	209	178	118	35	11	10	10	10	10	10	44	4
	9	281	17	17	19	93	180	234	252	231	174	84	18	17	17	17	17	17	107	3
	10	304	22	22	22	44	137	209	247	247	209	137	44	22	22	22	22	22	157	2
	11	314	25	25	25	26	69	156	216	241	230	183	104	29	25	25	25	25	188	1
	12	317	26	26	26	26	27	85	167	219	237	219	167	84	27	26	26	26	199	12
	HALF DAY TOTALS		88	88	118	313	611	899	1054	1042	868	550	257	117	89	88	88	88	598	
			N	NNW	NW	WNW	W	WSW	SW	SSW	S	SSE	SE	ESE	E	ENE	NE	NNE	HOR	PM

Half Day Totals computed by Simpson's Rule with time interval equal to 10 minutes.   Based on a ground reflectance of 0.20 and values in Tables 1 and 26.
*Total Solar Heat Gains for DS (0.125 in.) sheet glass.

Figure D.1. Solar intensity and solar heat gain factors for 24°N latitude. (Table 20 *from ASHRAE 1977 Fundamentals Handbook,* reprinted by permission.)

Solar Intensity and Solar Heat Gain Factors* for 32 Deg North Latitude

Solar Heat Gain Factors, Btuh/ft²

Date	Solar Time am	Direct Normal Btuh/ft²	N	NNE	NE	ENE	E	ESE	SE	SSE	S	SSW	SW	WSW	W	WNW	NW	NNW	HOR	Solar Time pm
Jan 21	7	1	0	0	0	1	1	1	1	1	0	0	0	0	0	0	0	0	0	5
	8	203	9	9	29	105	160	189	189	159	103	28	9	9	9	9	9	9	32	4
	9	269	15	15	17	91	175	229	246	225	169	82	17	15	15	15	15	15	88	3
	10	295	20	20	20	41	135	209	249	250	212	141	46	20	20	20	20	20	136	2
	11	306	23	23	23	24	68	159	221	249	238	191	110	29	23	23	23	23	166	1
	12	310	24	24	24	24	25	88	174	228	246	228	174	88	25	24	24	24	176	12
	HALF DAY TOTALS		79	79	107	284	570	856	1015	1014	853	553	264	112	80	79	79	79	512	
Feb 21	7	112	4	7	47	82	102	106	95	67	26	4	4	4	4	4	4	4	9	5
	8	245	13	14	65	149	205	228	216	170	95	17	13	13	13	13	13	13	64	4
	9	287	19	19	32	122	199	242	248	216	149	55	20	19	19	19	19	19	127	3
	10	305	24	24	25	62	151	213	241	232	189	112	31	24	24	24	24	24	176	2
	11	314	26	26	26	28	76	156	208	227	212	165	87	28	26	26	26	26	207	1
	12	316	27	27	27	27	29	79	155	204	221	204	155	79	29	27	27	27	217	12
	HALF DAY TOTALS		100	103	201	445	735	978	1080	1010	780	452	228	122	100	100	100	100	691	
Mar 21	7	185	10	37	105	153	176	173	142	88	20	9	9	9	9	9	9	9	32	5
	8	260	17	25	107	183	227	237	209	150	62	18	17	17	17	17	17	17	100	4
	9	290	23	25	64	151	210	237	227	183	107	30	23	23	23	23	23	23	164	3
	10	304	28	28	30	87	158	202	215	195	144	70	29	28	28	28	28	28	211	2
	11	311	31	31	31	34	82	142	179	188	168	120	59	32	31	31	31	31	242	1
	12	313	32	32	32	32	33	66	122	162	176	162	122	66	33	32	32	32	252	12
	HALF DAY TOTALS		124	162	359	629	875	1033	1041	888	589	326	193	136	125	124	124	124	874	
Apr 21	6	66	9	35	54	65	66	56	38	12	4	3	3	3	3	3	3	3	7	6
	7	206	17	80	146	188	200	182	136	65	16	14	14	14	14	14	14	14	61	5
	8	255	23	61	144	200	227	219	177	107	30	22	22	22	22	22	22	22	129	4
	9	278	28	36	103	168	206	212	187	133	58	29	28	28	28	28	28	28	188	3
	10	290	32	34	52	108	155	177	172	141	87	39	33	32	32	32	32	32	233	2
	11	295	35	35	36	47	83	118	135	132	108	70	40	36	35	35	35	35	262	1
	12	297	36	36	36	37	38	53	82	106	115	106	82	53	38	37	36	36	271	12
	HALF DAY TOTALS		161	296	550	792	952	992	889	645	360	228	177	157	153	152	152	152	1015	
May 21	6	119	33	77	108	121	116	94	56	13	8	8	8	8	8	8	8	9	21	6
	7	211	36	111	170	202	204	174	118	42	19	18	18	18	18	18	18	19	81	5
	8	250	29	94	165	208	220	199	149	73	27	25	25	25	25	25	25	25	146	4
	9	269	33	61	128	177	198	190	155	93	37	32	31	31	31	31	31	31	201	3
	10	280	36	40	76	121	150	156	138	99	54	37	35	35	35	35	35	35	243	2
	11	285	38	39	42	59	83	99	102	90	68	47	40	39	37	37	37	37	269	1
	12	286	38	39	40	40	41	47	59	70	74	70	59	47	41	40	40	39	277	12
	HALF DAY TOTALS		222	438	702	900	985	933	747	447	250	199	183	177	175	174	174	175	1098	
Jun 21	6	131	44	92	123	135	127	99	55	12	10	10	10	10	10	10	10	11	28	6
	7	210	47	122	176	204	201	168	108	35	20	20	20	20	20	20	20	21	88	5
	8	245	36	106	171	208	214	189	135	60	28	27	27	27	27	27	27	27	151	4
	9	264	35	74	137	178	193	180	139	77	35	32	32	32	32	32	32	32	204	3
	10	274	38	47	86	125	146	145	123	83	45	38	36	36	36	36	36	36	244	2
	11	279	40	41	47	64	82	91	89	75	56	43	41	40	39	39	39	39	269	1
	12	280	41	41	41	42	42	46	52	58	60	58	52	46	42	42	41	41	276	12
	HALF DAY TOTALS		261	504	762	935	985	897	678	372	225	197	189	185	184	184	183	186	1122	
Jul 21	6	113	34	76	105	117	113	90	53	12	9	9	9	9	9	9	9	9	22	6
	7	203	38	111	167	198	198	169	114	41	20	19	19	19	19	19	19	19	81	5
	8	241	31	95	163	204	215	194	145	70	28	26	26	26	26	26	26	26	145	4
	9	261	34	64	129	175	195	186	150	90	37	32	32	32	32	32	32	32	198	3
	10	271	37	42	78	121	148	153	134	96	53	38	36	36	36	36	36	36	240	2
	11	277	39	40	43	60	83	98	99	88	66	47	41	40	38	38	38	38	265	1
	12	279	40	40	41	41	42	48	58	68	72	68	58	48	42	41	41	41	40	273	12
	HALF DAY TOTALS		231	444	701	890	967	912	726	433	248	202	187	182	180	179	179	180	1088	
Aug 21	6	59	10	33	50	60	60	51	34	11	4	4	4	4	4	4	4	4	8	6
	7	190	19	79	141	179	190	172	128	61	17	15	15	15	15	15	15	15	61	5
	8	240	25	63	141	195	219	210	170	102	31	23	23	23	23	23	23	23	128	4
	9	263	30	39	104	166	200	206	181	127	57	31	29	29	29	29	29	29	185	3
	10	276	34	36	55	109	153	173	167	136	84	40	35	34	34	34	34	34	229	2
	11	282	36	37	39	50	84	116	131	127	104	69	41	38	36	36	36	36	256	1
	12	284	37	37	37	39	40	54	81	103	111	103	81	54	40	39	37	37	265	12
	HALF DAY TOTALS		171	303	546	774	922	955	854	618	352	231	184	166	162	161	160	160	999	
Sep 21	7	163	10	35	96	139	159	156	128	80	20	10	10	10	10	10	10	10	31	5
	8	240	18	26	103	173	215	224	198	143	60	19	18	18	18	18	18	18	96	4
	9	272	24	26	64	146	202	227	218	177	105	31	24	24	24	24	24	24	158	3
	10	287	29	29	32	86	154	196	208	189	141	70	31	29	29	29	29	29	204	2
	11	294	32	32	32	36	81	139	174	182	163	118	59	34	32	32	32	32	234	1
	12	296	33	33	33	33	35	66	120	158	171	158	120	66	35	33	33	33	244	12
	HALF DAY TOTALS		130	164	345	598	831	982	993	852	574	325	197	142	130	129	129	129	845	
Oct 21	7	99	4	7	43	74	92	96	85	60	24	5	4	4	4	4	4	4	10	5
	8	229	13	15	63	143	195	217	206	162	90	17	13	13	13	13	13	13	63	4
	9	273	20	20	33	120	193	234	239	208	144	54	21	20	20	20	20	20	125	3
	10	293	24	24	26	62	147	207	234	225	183	109	32	24	24	24	24	24	173	2
	11	302	27	27	27	29	76	152	203	221	207	160	85	29	27	27	27	27	203	1
	12	304	28	28	28	28	30	78	151	199	215	199	151	78	30	28	28	28	213	12
	HALF DAY TOTALS		103	106	200	433	708	941	1038	972	753	441	226	125	104	103	103	103	679	
Nov 21	7	2	0	0	0	1	1	1	1	1	1	0	0	0	0	0	0	0	0	5
	8	196	9	9	29	103	156	184	184	155	100	27	9	9	9	9	9	9	32	4
	9	263	16	16	17	90	173	225	241	221	166	80	17	16	16	16	16	16	88	3
	10	289	20	20	21	41	134	206	245	246	209	138	45	21	20	20	20	20	136	2
	11	301	23	23	23	24	67	157	218	245	234	188	109	29	23	23	23	23	165	1
	12	304	24	24	24	24	25	87	171	224	243	224	171	87	25	24	24	24	175	12
	HALF DAY TOTALS		80	81	108	282	561	841	996	995	838	544	261	113	81	80	80	80	509	
Dec 21	8	176	7	7	19	84	135	163	166	143	97	31	7	7	7	7	7	7	22	4
	9	257	14	14	15	77	162	218	238	222	171	89	15	14	14	14	14	14	72	3
	10	288	18	18	18	34	127	204	246	251	216	148	52	19	18	18	18	18	119	2
	11	301	21	21	21	22	63	157	222	252	243	197	116	29	21	21	21	21	148	1
	12	304	22	22	22	22	23	89	177	232	252	232	177	89	23	22	22	22	158	12
	HALF DAY TOTALS		71	71	84	227	500	792	965	986	852	578	275	107	71	71	71	71	440	
			N	NNW	NW	WNW	W	WSW	SW	SSW	S	SSE	SE	ESE	E	ENE	NE	NNE	HOR	PM

Half Day Totals computed by Simpson's Rule with time interval equal to 10 minutes.

*Total Solar Heat Gains for DS (0.125 in.) sheet glass.

Based on a ground reflectance of 0.20 and values in Tables 1 and 26.

Figure D.2. Solar intensity and solar heat gain factors for 32°N latitude. (Table 21 from *ASHRAE 1977 Fundamentals Handbook*, reprinted by permission.)

Solar Intensity and Solar Heat Gain Factors* for 40 Deg North Latitude

Date	Solar Time am	Direct Normal Btuh/ft²								Solar Heat Gain Factors, Btuh/ft²											Solar Time pm
			N	NNE	NE	ENE	E	ESE	SE	SSE	S	SSW	SW	WSW	W	WNW	NW	NNW	HOR	
Jan 21	8	142	5	5	17	71	111	132	133	114	75	22	6	5	5	5	5	5	14	4
	9	239	12	12	13	74	154	205	224	209	160	82	13	12	12	12	12	12	55	3
	10	274	16	16	16	31	124	199	241	246	213	146	51	17	16	16	16	16	96	2
	11	289	19	19	19	20	61	156	222	252	244	198	118	28	19	19	19	19	124	1
	12	294	20	20	20	20	21	90	179	234	254	234	179	90	21	20	20	20	133	12
	HALF DAY TOTALS		61	61	73	199	452	734	904	932	813	561	273	101	62	61	61	61	354	
Feb 21	7	55	2	3	23	40	51	53	47	34	14	2	2	2	2	2	2	2	4	5
	8	219	10	11	50	129	183	206	199	160	94	18	10	10	10	10	10	10	43	4
	9	271	16	16	22	107	186	234	245	218	157	66	17	16	16	16	16	16	98	3
	10	294	21	21	21	49	143	211	246	243	203	129	38	21	21	21	21	21	143	2
	11	304	23	23	23	24	71	160	219	244	231	184	103	27	23	23	23	23	171	1
	12	307	24	24	24	24	25	86	170	222	241	222	170	86	25	24	24	24	180	12
	HALF DAY TOTALS		84	86	152	361	648	916	1049	1015	821	508	250	114	85	84	84	84	548	
Mar 21	7	171	9	29	93	140	163	161	135	86	22	8	8	8	8	8	8	8	26	5
	8	250	16	18	91	169	218	232	211	157	74	17	16	16	16	16	16	16	85	4
	9	282	21	22	47	136	203	238	236	198	128	40	22	21	21	21	21	21	143	3
	10	297	25	25	27	72	153	207	229	216	171	195	29	25	25	25	25	25	186	2
	11	305	28	28	28	30	78	151	198	213	197	150	77	30	28	28	28	28	213	1
	12	307	29	29	29	29	31	75	145	191	207	191	145	75	31	29	29	29	223	12
	HALF DAY TOTALS		114	139	302	563	832	1035	1087	968	694	403	220	132	114	113	113	113	764	
Apr 21	6	89	11	46	72	87	88	76	52	18	5	5	5	5	5	5	5	5	11	6
	7	206	16	71	140	185	201	186	143	75	16	14	14	14	14	14	14	14	61	5
	8	252	22	44	128	190	224	223	188	124	41	22	21	21	21	21	21	21	123	4
	9	274	27	29	80	155	202	219	203	156	83	29	27	27	27	27	27	27	177	3
	10	286	31	31	37	92	152	187	193	170	121	56	32	31	31	31	31	41	217	2
	11	292	33	33	34	39	81	130	160	166	146	102	52	35	33	33	33	33	243	1
	12	293	34	34	34	34	36	62	108	142	154	142	108	62	36	34	34	34	252	12
	HALF DAY TOTALS		154	265	501	758	957	1051	994	782	488	296	199	157	148	147	147	147	957	
May 21	5	1	0	1	1	1	1	1	0	0	0	0	0	0	0	0	0	0	0	7
	6	144	36	90	128	145	141	115	71	18	10	10	10	10	10	10	10	11	31	6
	7	216	28	102	165	202	209	184	131	54	20	19	19	19	19	19	19	19	87	5
	8	250	27	73	149	199	220	208	164	93	29	25	25	25	25	25	25	25	146	4
	9	267	31	42	105	164	197	200	175	121	53	32	30	30	30	30	30	30	195	3
	10	277	34	36	54	105	148	168	163	133	83	40	35	34	34	34	34	34	234	2
	11	283	36	36	38	48	81	113	130	127	105	70	42	38	36	36	36	36	257	1
	12	284	37	37	37	38	40	54	82	104	113	104	82	54	40	38	37	37	265	12
	HALF DAY TOTALS		215	404	666	893	1024	1025	881	601	358	247	200	180	176	175	174	175	1083	
Jun 21	5	22	10	17	21	22	20	14	6	2	1	1	1	1	1	1	1	2	3	7
	6	155	48	104	143	159	151	121	70	17	13	13	13	13	13	13	13	14	40	6
	7	216	37	113	172	205	207	178	122	46	22	21	21	21	21	21	21	21	97	5
	8	246	30	85	156	201	216	199	152	80	29	27	27	27	27	27	27	27	153	4
	9	263	33	51	114	166	192	190	161	105	45	33	32	32	32	32	32	32	201	3
	10	272	35	38	63	109	145	158	148	116	69	39	36	35	35	35	35	35	238	2
	11	277	38	39	40	52	81	105	116	110	88	60	41	39	38	38	38	38	260	1
	12	279	38	38	38	40	41	52	72	89	95	89	72	52	41	40	38	38	267	12
	HALF DAY TOTALS		253	470	734	941	1038	999	818	523	315	236	204	191	188	187	186	188	1126	
Jul 21	5	2	1	2	2	2	2	1	1	0	0	0	0	0	0	0	0	0	0	7
	6	138	37	89	125	142	137	112	68	18	11	11	11	11	11	11	11	12	32	6
	7	208	30	102	163	198	204	179	127	53	21	20	20	20	20	20	20	20	88	5
	8	241	28	75	148	196	216	203	160	90	30	26	26	26	26	26	26	26	145	4
	9	259	32	44	106	163	193	196	170	118	52	33	31	31	31	31	31	31	194	3
	10	269	35	37	56	106	146	165	159	129	81	41	36	35	35	35	35	35	231	2
	11	275	37	38	40	50	81	111	127	123	102	69	43	39	37	37	37	37	254	1
	12	276	38	38	38	40	41	55	80	101	109	101	80	55	41	40	38	38	262	12
	HALF DAY TOTALS		223	411	666	885	1008	1003	858	584	352	248	204	186	181	180	180	181	1076	
Aug 21	6	81	12	44	68	81	82	71	48	17	6	5	5	5	5	5	5	5	12	6
	7	191	17	71	135	177	191	177	135	70	17	16	16	16	16	16	16	16	62	5
	8	237	24	47	126	185	216	214	180	118	41	23	23	23	23	23	23	23	122	4
	9	260	28	31	82	153	197	212	196	151	80	31	28	28	28	28	28	28	174	3
	10	272	32	33	40	93	150	182	187	165	116	56	34	32	32	32	32	32	214	2
	11	278	35	35	36	41	81	128	156	160	141	99	52	37	35	35	35	35	239	1
	12	280	35	35	35	36	38	63	106	138	149	138	106	63	38	36	35	35	247	12
	HALF DAY TOTALS		164	273	498	741	928	1013	956	751	474	296	205	166	157	156	156	156	946	
Sep 21	7	149	9	27	84	125	146	144	121	77	21	9	9	9	9	9	9	9	25	5
	8	230	17	19	87	160	205	218	199	148	71	18	17	17	17	17	17	17	82	4
	9	263	22	23	47	131	194	227	226	190	124	41	23	22	22	22	22	22	138	3
	10	280	27	27	28	71	148	200	221	209	165	93	30	27	27	27	27	27	180	2
	11	287	29	29	29	31	78	147	192	207	191	146	77	31	29	29	29	29	206	1
	12	290	30	30	30	30	32	75	142	185	200	185	142	75	32	30	30	30	215	12
	HALF DAY TOTALS		119	142	291	534	787	980	1033	925	672	396	222	137	119	118	118	118	738	
Oct 21	7	48	2	3	20	36	45	47	42	30	12	2	2	2	2	2	2	2	4	5
	8	204	11	12	49	123	173	195	188	151	89	18	11	11	11	11	11	11	43	4
	9	257	17	17	23	104	180	225	235	209	151	64	18	17	17	17	17	17	97	3
	10	280	21	21	22	50	139	205	238	235	196	125	38	22	21	21	21	21	140	2
	11	291	24	24	24	25	71	156	212	236	224	178	101	28	24	24	24	24	168	1
	12	294	25	25	25	25	27	85	165	216	234	216	165	85	27	25	25	25	177	12
	HALF DAY TOTALS		88	89	152	351	623	878	1006	974	791	493	247	117	89	88	88	88	540	
Nov 21	8	136	5	5	18	69	108	128	129	110	72	21	6	5	5	5	5	5	14	4
	9	232	12	12	13	73	151	201	219	204	156	80	13	12	12	12	12	12	55	3
	10	268	16	16	16	31	122	196	237	242	209	143	50	17	16	16	16	16	96	2
	11	283	19	19	19	20	61	154	218	248	240	194	116	28	19	19	19	19	123	1
	12	288	20	20	20	20	21	89	176	231	250	231	176	89	21	20	20	20	132	12
	HALF DAY TOTALS		63	63	75	198	445	721	887	914	798	551	269	101	63	63	63	63	354	
Dec 21	8	89	3	3	8	41	67	82	84	73	50	17	3	3	3	3	3	3	6	4
	9	217	10	10	11	60	135	185	205	194	151	83	13	10	10	10	10	10	39	3
	10	261	14	14	14	25	113	188	232	239	210	146	55	15	14	14	14	14	77	2
	11	280	17	17	17	17	56	151	217	249	242	198	120	28	17	17	17	17	104	1
	12	285	18	18	18	18	19	89	178	233	253	233	178	89	19	18	18	18	113	12
	HALF DAY TOTALS		52	52	56	146	374	649	822	867	775	557	276	94	53	52	52	52	282	
			N	NNW	NW	WNW	W	WSW	SW	SSW	S	SSE	SE	ESE	E	ENE	NE	NNE	HOR	PM

Half Day Totals computed by Simpson's Rule with time interval equal to 10 minutes.   Based on a ground reflectance of 0.20 and values in Tables 1 and 26.

*Total Solar Heat Gains for DS (0.125 in.) sheet glass.

Figure D.3. Solar intensity and solar heat gain factors for 40°N latitude. (Table 22 from *ASHRAE 1977 Fundamentals Handbook*, reprinted by permission.)

Solar Intensity and Solar Heat Gain Factors* for 48 Deg North Latitude

Date	Solar Time am	Direct Normal Btuh/ft²	N	NNE	NE	ENE	E	ESE	SE	SSE	S	SSW	SW	WSW	W	WNW	NW	NNW	HOR	Solar Time pm
Jan 21	8	37	1	1	4	18	29	34	35	30	20	6	1	1	1	1	1	1	2	4
	9	185	8	8	8	53	118	160	176	166	129	69	10	8	8	8	8	8	25	3
	10	239	12	12	12	22	106	175	216	223	195	136	50	12	12	12	12	12	55	2
	11	261	14	14	14	15	53	144	208	239	233	190	116	26	14	14	14	14	77	1
	12	267	15	15	15	15	16	86	171	226	245	226	171	86	16	15	15	15	85	12
	HALF DAY TOTALS		43	43	46	117	316	567	729	776	70	512	259	85	43	43	43	43	203	
Feb 21	7	4	0	0	1	3	3	3	3	2	1	0	0	0	0	0	0	0	0	5
	8	180	8	8	36	103	149	170	166	136	82	17	8	8	8	8	8	8	25	4
	9	247	13	13	16	90	168	216	230	209	155	71	14	13	13	13	13	13	66	3
	10	275	17	17	17	38	131	203	242	244	207	138	44	18	17	17	17	17	105	2
	11	288	19	19	19	20	65	158	221	249	239	192	113	27	19	19	19	19	130	1
	12	292	20	20	20	20	22	89	176	231	250	231	176	89	22	20	20	20	138	12
	HALF DAY TOTALS		68	68	107	274	541	816	968	967	813	531	261	104	68	68	68	68	395	
Mar 21	7	153	7	22	80	123	145	145	123	80	23	7	7	7	7	7	7	7	20	5
	8	236	14	15	76	154	204	222	206	158	82	15	14	14	14	14	14	14	68	4
	9	270	19	19	3	121	193	234	239	207	142	52	20	19	19	19	19	19	118	3
	10	287	23	23	24	58	146	208	237	231	189	115	33	23	23	23	23	23	156	2
	11	295	25	25	25	26	74	156	210	232	218	172	94	28	25	25	25	25	180	1
	12	298	26	26	26	26	27	83	161	211	228	211	161	83	27	26	26	26	188	12
	HALF DAY TOTALS		100	118	250	494	775	1012	1100	1014	767	465	244	126	101	100	100	100	636	
Apr 21	6	108	12	53	86	105	107	93	64	23	6	6	6	6	6	6	6	6	15	6
	7	205	15	61	132	180	199	189	148	84	18	14	14	14	14	14	14	14	60	5
	8	247	20	32	111	179	219	225	196	138	55	21	20	20	20	20	20	20	114	4
	9	268	25	26	60	141	197	223	215	176	106	33	25	25	25	25	25	25	161	3
	10	280	28	28	31	77	148	193	209	194	150	80	31	28	28	28	28	28	196	2
	11	286	31	31	31	33	78	140	181	193	177	133	69	33	31	31	31	31	218	1
	12	288	31	31	31	31	34	71	131	172	186	172	131	71	34	31	31	31	226	12
	HALF DAY TOTALS		147	242	461	724	957	1098	1081	895	605	370	226	156	141	140	140	140	875	
May 21	5	41	17	31	40	42	39	29	14	3	3	3	3	3	3	3	3	3	5	7
	6	162	35	97	141	162	160	133	85	24	12	12	12	12	12	12	12	13	40	6
	7	219	23	90	158	200	212	191	142	68	21	19	19	19	19	19	19	19	91	5
	8	248	26	54	132	190	218	214	178	113	38	25	25	25	25	25	25	25	142	4
	9	264	29	32	82	151	194	208	192	147	77	32	29	29	29	29	29	29	185	3
	10	274	33	34	39	90	145	178	184	163	116	57	35	33	33	33	33	33	219	2
	11	279	35	35	36	40	79	126	155	160	142	101	54	37	35	35	35	35	240	1
	12	280	35	35	35	36	38	63	107	139	150	139	107	63	38	36	35	35	247	12
	HALF DAY TOTALS		215	388	645	893	1065	1114	1007	749	483	316	225	184	174	173	173	174	1045	
Jun 21	5	77	35	61	76	80	72	53	2	6	5	5	5	5	5	5	5	8	12	7
	6	172	46	110	155	175	169	138	84	22	14	14	14	14	14	14	14	16	51	6
	7	220	29	101	165	204	211	187	135	60	23	21	21	21	21	21	21	21	103	5
	8	246	29	64	139	191	215	206	168	101	34	27	27	27	27	27	27	27	152	4
	9	261	31	36	91	153	190	199	180	133	66	33	31	31	31	31	31	31	193	3
	10	269	34	36	45	94	143	169	171	148	101	50	36	34	34	34	34	34	225	2
	11	274	36	36	38	44	79	118	142	145	126	88	49	38	36	36	36	36	246	1
	12	275	37	37	37	38	40	60	96	124	134	124	96	60	40	38	37	37	252	12
	HALF DAY TOTALS		257	459	722	955	1095	1102	955	678	436	299	228	197	189	188	188	191	1108	
Jul 21	5	43	18	33	42	45	41	30	15	3	3	3	3	3	3	3	3	4	6	7
	6	156	37	96	138	159	156	129	82	24	13	13	13	13	13	13	13	14	41	6
	7	211	25	90	156	196	207	186	138	66	22	20	20	20	20	20	20	20	92	5
	8	240	27	56	132	187	214	209	174	110	38	26	26	26	26	26	26	26	142	4
	9	256	30	34	83	149	191	204	187	143	75	33	30	30	30	30	30	30	184	3
	10	266	34	35	41	90	143	174	180	158	113	56	36	34	34	34	34	34	217	2
	11	271	36	36	37	42	79	124	151	156	138	99	54	38	36	36	36	36	237	1
	12	272	36	36	36	37	39	63	104	136	146	136	104	63	39	37	36	36	244	12
	HALF DAY TOTALS		223	395	646	886	1050	1092	983	730	474	315	229	190	181	179	179	180	1042	
Aug 21	6	99	13	51	81	98	100	87	60	22	7	7	7	7	7	7	7	7	16	6
	7	190	17	61	128	172	190	179	141	79	19	15	15	15	15	15	15	15	61	5
	8	232	22	34	110	174	211	216	188	132	53	23	22	22	22	22	22	22	114	4
	9	154	27	28	63	139	192	216	108	169	102	34	27	27	27	27	27	27	159	3
	10	266	30	30	33	78	145	188	203	188	144	78	33	30	30	30	30	30	193	2
	11	272	32	32	32	36	78	137	175	187	171	129	68	35	32	32	32	32	215	1
	12	274	33	33	33	33	36	71	128	167	189	167	128	71	36	33	33	33	223	12
	HALF DAY TOTALS		157	251	459	709	929	1060	1040	862	587	366	231	165	151	149	149	149	869	
Sep 21	7	131	8	21	71	108	128	128	108	71	21	8	7	7	7	7	7	7	20	5
	8	215	15	16	72	144	191	207	193	148	77	16	15	15	15	15	15	15	65	4
	9	251	20	20	34	116	184	223	227	197	136	52	21	20	20	20	20	20	114	3
	10	269	24	24	25	58	141	200	228	221	182	112	34	24	24	24	24	24	151	2
	11	278	26	26	26	28	73	151	203	223	210	166	92	29	26	26	26	26	174	1
	12	280	27	27	27	27	29	82	156	204	220	204	156	82	29	27	27	27	182	12
	HALF DAY TOTALS		105	121	240	465	729	953	1040	963	737	453	243	131	106	105	105	105	614	
Oct 21	7	4	0	0	2	3	4	4	3	2	1	0	0	0	0	0	0	0	0	5
	8	165	8	9	35	96	139	159	155	126	77	16	8	8	8	8	8	8	25	4
	9	233	14	14	16	88	161	207	220	199	148	68	15	14	14	14	14	14	66	3
	10	262	18	18	18	39	128	196	233	234	199	133	43	18	18	18	18	18	104	2
	11	274	20	20	20	21	64	153	213	241	231	186	109	27	20	20	20	20	128	1
	12	278	21	21	21	21	23	87	171	223	242	223	171	87	23	21	21	21	136	12
	HALF DAY TOTALS		71	71	108	266	519	780	925	925	779	513	256	106	72	71	71	71	391	
Nov 21	8	36	1	1	4	18	29	34	35	30	20	6	1	1	1	1	1	1	2	4
	9	179	8	8	9	52	115	156	171	161	125	67	10	8	8	8	8	8	26	3
	10	233	12	12	12	22	104	172	212	218	191	133	49	13	12	12	12	12	55	2
	11	255	15	15	15	15	52	142	204	234	228	186	114	26	15	15	15	15	77	1
	12	261	15	15	15	15	17	85	168	222	240	222	168	85	17	15	15	15	85	12
	HALF DAY TOTALS		44	44	47	117	310	555	713	760	686	502	255	85	44	44	44	44	204	
Dec 21	9	140	5	5	6	36	86	120	133	127	100	56	8	5	5	5	5	5	13	3
	10	214	10	10	10	16	91	156	194	201	179	126	49	10	10	10	10	10	38	2
	11	242	12	12	12	13	46	134	195	225	220	180	111	25	12	12	12	12	57	1
	12	250	13	13	13	13	14	81	163	215	233	215	168	81	14	13	13	13	65	12
	HALF DAY TOTALS		33	33	34	73	233	458	610	665	616	468	247	76	34	33	33	33	141	
			N	NNW	NW	WNW	W	WSW	SW	SSW	S	SSE	SE	ESE	E	ENE	NE	NNE	HOR	PM

Half Day Totals computed by Simpson's Rule with time interval equal to 10 minutes.
*Total Solar Heat Gains for DS (0.125 in.) sheet glass.
Based on a ground reflectance of 0.20 and values in Tables 1 and 26.

Figure D.4. Solar intensity and solar heat gain factors for 48°N latitude. (Table 23 from *ASHRAE 1977 Fundamentals Handbook*, reprinted by permission.)

- Find the column labeled S. Read up to the half-day total listed in the column. The half-day total for the afternoon hours is also 813 Btu per sq ft. So the total daily solar heat gain is 1626 Btu/sq ft.

If the orientation that you were checking were SE, then the morning total, reading down, would be 904 Btu/sq ft whereas the afternoon total, reading up, would be 273 Btu/sq ft. The daily total would be 1177 Btu/sq ft.

You still must correct your result for the type of glazing, for the amount of clouds, and for the number of days in a month. Decision 9 shows how this is done.

APPENDIX
E
Conversion Factors

METRIC TO ENGLISH

METRIC UNITS	×	CONVERSION FACTOR	=	ENGLISH UNITS
Meters		3.28		Feet
Meters		39.37		Inches
Centimeters		0.394		Inches
Grams		0.0022		Pounds
Kilograms		2.20		Pounds
Liters		0.264		Gallons
Calories		0.004		Btu
Watts		3.413		Btu/hr
Watts/sq meter		0.317		Btu/hr/sq ft
Langleys		3.69		Btu/sq ft
Calories/cm/sec		13.27		Btu/hr/sq ft
Langleys/min		221.2		Btu/hr/sq ft
Degrees C		$C = 5/9(F - 32)$		Degrees F

ENGLISH TO METRIC

ENGLISH UNITS	×	CONVERSION FACTOR	=	METRIC UNITS
Feet		0.305		Meters
Inches		0.0254		Meters
Inches		2.54		Centimeters
Pounds		0.454		Kilograms
Pounds		454		Grams
Pounds/sq in		703.1		Kilograms/sq m
Gallons		3.79		Liters
Btu		252		Calories
Btu/hour		0.293		Watts
Btu/hour		293		Kilowatts
Btu/hr/sq ft		3.154		Watts/sq m
Btu/hr/sq ft		0.075		Calories/cm/sec
Btu/sq ft		0.271		Langleys
Btu/hr/sq ft		0.00452		Langleys/min
Horsepower, U.S.		1.014		Horsepower, metric
Horsepower		745.7		Watts
Btu/hr/sq ft/ F		0.488		Calories/hr/sq cm/° C

UNIT TO UNIT

UNIT	×	CONVERSION FACTOR	=	UNIT
Kilowatt-hour		3413		Btu
Btu		0.000293		Kilowatt-hour
Horsepower		2544		Btu/hr
Tons, air conditioning		12,000		Btu/hr
Cubic feet		7.48		Gallons
Gallons		0.134		Cubic feet
Cu ft water		62.37		Lb of water
Cu ft/sec		448.8		Gal/min
Feet of water		0.883		Inches of mercury
Feet of water		0.434		Lb/sq in
Gallons of water		8.35		Lb of water
Inches of mercury		0.491		Lb/sq in
Lb of water		0.120		Gallons

GLOSSARY

ABSORPTANCE: The ratio of the radiant energy absorbed by a body to the total radiation falling on it. Usually expressed as a percent.

ACTIVE SOLAR HOUSE: A house that uses mechanically driven solar devices to help heat and/or cool it.

ACTIVE SOLAR SYSTEM: A solar system that uses external energy to operate it.

AIR CHANGES PER HOUR: The number of times that the air in a building is replaced in 1 hr.

ALTITUDE: The distance of the sun above the horizon in angular degrees.

ANGLE OF INCIDENCE: The angle that the sun's rays make with a reflecting surface when they strike it.

ANGLE OF REFLECTION: The angle that the sun's rays make with a reflecting surface when they reflect off the surface. The angle of reflection is equal to the angle of incidence.

AREA, A: The size of a surface under examination. Usually measured in square feet in the English system of measurement. More specifically, A is a term used in determining heat transmission losses when calculating the heat loss or gain through a building wall, ceiling, roof, or floor.

ATRIUM HOUSE: A common name for an earth-insulated house that contains open courtyards for light and ventilation.

AXIAL FLOW FAN: A fan in which the flow of air occurs along the axis of the impeller. Generally a propeller-type fan. See Figure 11.19

AXIS OF ROTATION: An imaginary line extending through the earth's poles. The earth revolves around this line.

AZIMUTH: The geographic bearing of the sun from solar south.

BLOWER: See fan.

BLS INDEXES: The statistical indexes published by the United States Bureau of Labor Statistics.

BRITISH THERMAL UNITS, Btu: A measure of energy in the English system of measurement. One British thermal unit is equal to the amount of energy required to heat 1 lb of water by 1°F.

BTU: See British thermal unit.

CENTRIFUGAL FAN: See radial flow fan.

CHARGE CYCLE: The portion of the solar cycle in a heat storage bed when the hot air from the collectors is warming the storage bed.

CIVIL TIME: The time set by having all the clocks within a zone covering approximately 15° of longitude set the same. The local civil time for a selected meridian near the center of the zone is called the *standard time*. See Figure 2.13 for the four time zones in the contingent United States.

CLERESTORY: An outside wall of a room or a building that rises above an adjoining roof and contains windows.

CLERESTORY WINDOW: A window located in a clerestory wall.

COEFFICIENT OF HEAT TRANSMISSION: The amount of heat that is transmitted through 1 sq ft of building wall, floor, roof, or ceiling in 1 hr when a 1°F temperature differential exists between the two sides of the wall. The symbol U is used to represent the coefficient of heat transmission. Also called the U-factor.

COLLECTORS, SOLAR: Devices that collect the sun's radiant energy and convert it to thermal energy.

COMPLEMENTARY ANGLE: Complementary angles are two or more angles whose sum equals 90°.

COMPOUND INTEREST TABLE: A table that shows how much money $1.00 will earn if left invested at a given percentage for a given period of time.

CONCEALED CONDENSATION: Condensation that occurs within walls, roofs, floors, and ceilings where it cannot be readily detected with the eye.

CONDENSATION: The process of changing a vapor into a liquid by extracting heat.

CONDUCTION: The transfer of heat through a solid from particle to particle without displacing the particles. See Figure 4.2.

CONSUMER PRICE INDEX: A Bureau of Labor Statistics forecast of changes in the prices of consumer goods.

CONVECTION: The transfer of heat by the movement of a liquid or gas. See Figure 4.4.

CRACK, DOOR OR WINDOW: Crack is the number of lineal feet of opening between the door or window and its frame through which air can infiltrate.

DAILY TEMPERATURE RANGE: The daily swing of temperature obtained by subtracting the lowest temperature from the highest temperature during the 24-hr period.

DEGREE DAY: A day when the average outdoor temperature throughout the 24-hr period is 64°F. Degree day is a concept that has been developed to estimate how much heat would be required to replace the heat lost by a building structure. Degree days (dd) are measured by subtracting the average temperature for the day from 65°F. A day having an average temperature of 30°F would be a 35 dd.

DEHUMIDIFICATION: The removal of water vapor moisture from the air.

"DELTA" t: Usually written Δt where Δ is the Greek letter delta. Δt is the difference in temperature between the two sides of a surface such as a building wall. It is obtained by subtracting the lower temperature from the higher temperature.

DENSITY: The mass of a substance per unit of volume. In the English system of measurement, mass is usually expressed as the weight of 1 cu ft of the material.

DESIGN TEMPERATURE: The design temperature, is the lowest temperature at which you wish to heat the house to 65°F or the highest temperature at which you wish to cool the house to 75°F.

DEW POINT TEMPERATURE: The temperature at which a given water vapor-air mixture becomes saturated with water vapor. At the dew point temperature, water will begin to condense out of the air if more moisture is added.

DIFFUSE RADIATION: Rays of the sun that have been scattered by the earth's atmosphere. These rays can come from any direction. It is the type of radiation seen on cloudy days.

DIRECT RADIATION: Parallel rays coming directly from the sun. These are the types of rays that cast a shadow on a clear day.

DISCHARGE CYCLE: The portion of the solar cycle in a heat storage bed when the hot air stored in the bed is heating the house.

DISTILLATES, FUEL: Distillates are fuels refined from crude oil. Typical distillate fuels are gasoline, kerosine, fuel oil, jet fuel, and diesel fuel.

DOLLARS/CCF: Dollars per hundred cubic feet. This is the measurement that natural gas is typically sold under. Ten CCF equals 1 MMBtu.

DOLLARS/kWh: Dollars per kilowatt-hour. This is the measurement that electricity is typically sold under. 293 kWh equals 1 MMBtu.

DOLLARS/MMBTU: Dollars per million Btu. Commonly written $/MMBtu. The cost of fuel is usually converted to dollars per million Btu in order to compare the cost of different fuels.

DYNAMIC STORAGE MEDIA: Storage media that can be moved around the building. Usually a liquid such as water.

EFFECTIVENESS, HEAT EXCHANGER: The ratio of the actual rate of heat transfer to the maximum theoretical rate of heat transfer in an infinitely large exchanger.

ELEVATIONAL HOUSE: An earth-insulated house that has three sides earth-covered and the windows grouped on a single south-facing wall that is exposed to the air.

EMISSIVITY: The capacity of a surface to emit radiant energy.

EMITTANCE: The ratio of the radiant thermal energy emitted from a surface at a given temperature to the energy that would be emitted from a perfect absorber and emitted at the same temperature. A black body is typically considered to be a perfect emitter and absorber.

ENERGY: The capacity to do work. The three major types of energy are mechanical, electrical, and heat energy. Heat energy is also known as thermal energy.

ENERGY EFFICIENCY: A measure of how well you use the fuel that you purchase. Typically expressed as useful energy gained divided by energy purchased.

EQUATOR: An imaginary circle around the circumference of the earth midway between the North and South poles and at right angles to the axis of rotation.

EQUILATERAL TRIANGLE: A triangle that has three sides of equal length and three angles of equal size. The sides can be any length. The angles must each be 60°.

EQUINOX: The two periods in the year when the North and South poles are equidistant from the sun and the length of night and day are equal at any point on earth except at the poles. The vernal equinox occurs on or about March 21, the autumnal equinox occurs on or about September 23.

EUTECTIC SOLID MIXTURE: A mixture of two or more compounds that are mixed in the proper proportions so as to give the lowest possible melting point.

EXTRAPOLATION: The process of inferring unknown data from known data.

FACE AREA, DUCTS: The cross-sectional area of the duct.

FAN: A rotating device designed to deliver a quantity of air with little or no change in pressure through the use of an impeller. See Figures 11.18 and 11.19.

FAN COIL: A liquid-to-air heat exchanger with its own fan. See Figure 11.30.

F-CHART: A computer program that can be used to give reliable solar data by geographic location.

FENESTRATION: The arrangement, proportioning, and design of light-transmitting openings such as windows, doors, skylights, and clerestories.

FRIGID ZONE: The earth's climatic zone where the sun is below the horizon for at least one full day during the year.

GLAZING: A transparent or translucent material used to cover light-transmitting openings. Typically made of glass or plastic.

GREAT CIRCLE: Any circle whose plane passes through the center of the earth. The equator is an example of a great circle.

GREENHOUSE EFFECT: The trapping of thermal heat by passing short-wave radiant energy through a substance that will not pass long-wave thermal energy and then converting that short-wave energy to long-wave thermal energy. Example: Sunlight (short-wave energy) passes through glass readily. Heat (long-wave energy) passes through glass poorly. See Figure 9.19.

GREENWICH MERIDIAN: The meridian of longitude designated as 0° longitude. This meridian passes through Greenwich, England.

HEAT: A form of energy. Also known as thermal energy.

HEAT EXCHANGER: A device that transfers energy from one substance to another substance without mixing the two substances.

HEAT OF FUSION: The heat that is required to make a substance change from a solid to a liquid or from a liquid to a solid.

HEAT OF VAPORIZATION: The heat that is required to make a substance change from a liquid into a gas or from a gas into a liquid.

HEAT PUMP: A refrigerating system designed to use the heat rejection from the system for a desired heating function. Most residential heat pumps are designed so that they can also be used as air conditioners in the summertime.

HEAT TRANSFER FLUID: A gas or a liquid that is pumped or blown through pipes or ducts to carry heat from one location to another.

HILLSIDE HOUSE: An earth-insulated house built into a hillside so that most of at least two sides of the house are insulated by the hill.

HYBRID SOLAR HOUSE: A solar house that contains a blend of active and passive solar systems.

HYGROSCOPIC MATERIAL: A material that readily picks up and retains moisture. Many common building materials are hygroscopic.

HYPOTENUSE: In a right triangle, the side opposite the right angle.

INFILTRATION, AIR: The leakage of air into a building through cracks and openings, around doors and windows, and through the walls and floors of a structure. Usually measured in number of air changes per hour.

INSULATING GLASS UNITS: A factory-fabricated double-glazed window or door unit or a single-glazed unit with a storm sash or door added on site.

INSULATION, THERMAL: A material having a relatively high resistance to heat flow.

INTEGRATED VALUE, EARTH TEMPERATURE: The average temperature of the earth measured from the surface to a depth of 10 ft. Varies from location to location.

INTERPOLATION: The process of estimating unknown values from two known values.

k-FACTOR OR k: The rate at which energy will be conducted through a substance 1-in. thick and 1-ft sq when a temperature difference of 1°F exists between the two sides of the substance. In the English system of measurement, k is typically expressed in Btu/hr/sq ft. See Appendix B.

LATENT HEAT GAIN: The type of heat gain that increases the amount of water vapor in the air.

LATITUDE: The distance north or south of the equator that a point on earth lies. Latitude is measured in angular degrees. See Figure 2.3.

LONGITUDE: The distance east or west of Greenwich, England, that a point on earth lies. Longitude is measured in angular degrees. See Figure 2.3.

MERCATOR PROJECTION: The projection of a curved object onto a flat surface. Normally reserved for maps but used in solar work to describe the solar window.

MEGAWATT: One million watts.

MERIDIAN CIRCLE: A circle around the earth's circumference that passes through the North Pole and the South Pole and whose plane passes through the axis of rotation. See Figure 2.3.

MERIDIANS OF LONGITUDE: See MERIDIAN CIRCLE. Also see Figure 2.3.

MMBTU, MILLION BTU: See British thermal unit.

NUCLEATORS: Chemical additives that prevent phase-change salt separation and supercooling.

OPEC: A cartel formed by the countries that export crude petroleum oil to control price and production. OPEC stands for Organization Of Petroleum Exporting Countries.

ORBITAL PLANE: The elliptical path that the earth travels around the sun annually. See Figure 2.7.

ORGANIC SOLIDS: A substance, such as paraffin wax, of carbon-containing compounds. In solar work, organic solids are used as heat storage media.

ORGANIZATION OF PETROLEUM EXPORTING COUNTRIES: See OPEC.

ORIENTATION: The act of determining the compass direction in which a building surface or collector surface faces. Used to properly face a solar collecting surface to the sun's rays.

PARALLEL CIRCLES: See PARALLELS OF LATITUDE.

PARALLELS OF LATITUDE: Circles around the earth that have all points on the circle equidistant from the poles and whose plane is at right angles to the axis of rotation. See Figure 2.3.

PASSIVE SOLAR HOUSE: A house with its exterior oriented to take maximum advantage of the sun; with interior rooms located for the best heat distribution and use; and with construction that makes the house an efficient solar collector, a good heat trap, and an efficient distributor of the collected solar energy without the use of external energy.

PASSIVE SOLAR SYSTEM: A solar system that operates without using any external energy source. The term is commonly misused to apply only to solar building structures. It should also be used to apply to other solar collection systems that do not use external energy.

PENETRATIONAL HOUSE: A solar house that is earth-bermed for insulation but that has windows and doors that pierce the earth cover.

PHASE-CHANGE MEDIA: Materials that change physical state, passing from a solid to a liquid or from a liquid to a solid, in the temperature range in which solar storage normally operates. May also refer to materials that change from a liquid to a gas or from a gas to a liquid. These materials may be used in the solar collection loop as heat transfer media. A common example is Freon ® gas.*

PLAT: A sketch of a building subdivision plan. The plat typically covers grades, drainage, utilities, streets, building lots, and land improvements.

PLENUM, HOT AIR: A sheet-metal chamber located on the furnace from which the distribution ductwork is led to the various rooms in the house.

PRESENT VALUE OF MONEY TABLE: A table that shows the future value of a dollar if the dollar is not invested. See Figure 6.17.

QUAD: One quadrillion British thermal units. A quadrillion is 1×10 raised to the 15th power or 1,000,000,-000,000,000.

RADIAL FLOW FAN: A fan in which the flow of air occurs in a radial direction rather than along the axis of the impeller. See Figure 11.18. Also known as a squirrel cage blower or a centrifugal fan.

*Freon is a registered trademark of El. duPont.

RADIATION: The transfer of heat from one object to another without warming the space in between. Solar energy is heat radiated from the sun.

RATIO ANALYSIS: A mathematical term relating to the determination of relative values through proportion. Best shown by example. See Figure 3.11 and the related text.

REFLECTANCE: The fraction of the total radiant flux incident on a surface that is reflected. Varies with the wavelength of the radiation and the composition and smoothness of the surface.

REFLECTED RADIATION: Solar radiation that hits another surface before striking the collecting surface.

REFLECTOR, SOLAR: A device that reflects the solar energy striking a surface to a solar collecting surface where it may be used.

RELATIVE HUMIDITY: The amount of water vapor in the air versus the maximum amount of water vapor that air under those conditions can hold. Usually expressed as a percent, for example 40% R.H. Air that is saturated with water vapor is described as having 100% relative humidity.

RELATIVE THERMAL CONDUCTIVITY: A term coined by the author that compares the thermal conductivity of any substance to the thermal conductivity of a softwood. Calculated by dividing the thermal conductivity of the material by the thermal conductivity of a softwood.

RESIDUALS, FUEL: The low ends of the crude oil that are left after the distillate fuels are removed. Not suitable for home use as they are heavy, thick oils containing sulfur and alkali metals. Generally, they must be preheated to make them flow and they are air pollutants.

REVERSE THERMOSYPHON: The gravity movement of hot building or storage air and/or water back up to the collectors. Results in a loss of collected heat.

RIGHT-ANGLE COLLECTOR-TILT ANGLE: The collector tilt angle that aligns the surface of the solar collector perpendicular to the sun's rays.

RIGHT TRIANGLE: A triangle that contains a 90° angle.

R-VALUE: A measure of a material's resistance to heat flow. It is the reciprocal of the U-factor and is equal to $1/U$.

SALT HYDRATE: A mixture of a metallic salt with water, such as the mixing of calcium chloride with water to form calcium chloride hexahydrate. Salt hydrates are used as phase-change storage media.

SATURATED AIR: Air that contains the maximum amount of water vapor possible. The amount of water vapor that air can hold is a function of the pressure and the temperature of the air. Saturated air has a relative humidity of 100%.

SENSIBLE HEAT GAIN: Heat gain that raises the temperature of the air.

SHADES, SOLAR: Devices that prevent the sun's rays from striking a building structure.

SHADING COEFFICIENTS: A multiplier that describes the effect of a glazing on the amount of solar radiation passing through the glazing. Expressed as a decimal or a fraction. See Figures 9.22 and 9.23 for typical shading coefficients for glass and plastic glazings.

SKYLIGHT: An opening in the building's roof that is covered with a transparent or translucent material. Also known as a roof fenestration device.

SOLAR COLLECTORS: See collectors.

SOLAR CONSTANT: The solar radiation intensity incident on a surface normal to the sun's rays outside the earth's atmosphere at a distance from the sun equal to the mean distance between the earth and the sun. Its value is generally accepted as 429.5 Btu/hr/sq ft.

SOLAR HEAT GAIN FACTOR PROGRAM: An ASHRAE computer program that calculates the solar heat gain factor assuming 365 cloudless days and a glazing with 86% transmittance, 8% reflectance, and 6% absorptance. See Appendix D for the solar heat gain tables.

SOLAR REFLECTORS: See reflectors, solar.

SOLAR SHADES: See shades, solar.

SOLAR TIME: The time calculated by setting 12 noon as the time when the sun is at geographic south. The sun moves through 15 angular degrees each hour. See Figure 2.12.

SOLSTICE: See summer solstice, winter solstice.

SPALLING: The breaking up and falling off of layers of masonry surfaces due to repeated freeze-thaw cycles.

SPECIFIC HEAT: The amount of heat that is required to raise or lower 1 lb of a substance by 1°F in the English system of measurement.

SQUIRREL CAGE BLOWER: See radial flow fan.

STANDARD TIME: See civil time.

STRATIFY: The tendency of heat to collect in the top part of a storage container. Heat in a rock storage bed stratifies readily. Heat in a water storage vessel stratifies less readily.

SUMMER SOLSTICE: The longest day of the year in the Northern Hemisphere, about June 22. The sun would appear to be standing still to a person standing on the Antarctic Circle. The earth is the farthest away from the sun. See Figure 2.10.

SUN-PATH DIAGRAM: A graphic representation of the sun's altitude and azimuth. See Appendix A.

SUNSHINE INDEX: The ratio of the measured solar radiation to the solar constant.

SUPERCOOLING: The cooling of a liquid below its normal solidification point without its solidifying.

SUPPLEMENTARY ANGLES: Two or more angles whose sum equals 180°.

TEMPERATE ZONE: The geographic region where the sun is never directly overhead but always appears above the horizon every day of the year. The temperate zone lies between the 23.5 and 66.5 parallels of latitude on both sides of the equator.

TEMPERATURE: A measure of the degree of hot or cold. Temperature and heat are different. See heat.

TEMPERATURE GRADIENT: A condition where one side of a building component, such as a wall, is exposed to a colder temperature than the other side. This results in moisture tending to migrate to the colder side.

TEMPERATURE SENSORS: Devices that constantly read the temperature at their location. Usually connected to a central controller.

THERMAL CONDUCTANCE, C: A measure of the rate at which heat is conducted through a material of any given thickness. Usually expressed in Btu/hr/sq ft/°F in the English system of measurement. See Appendix B.

THERMAL CONDUCTIVITY, k: A measure of the rate at which heat is conducted through a 1-in. thickness of any given material. Usually expressed in Btu/hr/sq ft/°F/in. in the English system of measurement. See Appendix B.

THERMAL ENVELOPE: The insulated enclosure surrounding the interior of a building structure.

THERMAL ENVELOPE HOUSE: A building structure that is built in a manner that allows the thermal energy contained in the building air to circulate freely around the walls, floors, and roof of the structure. See Figure 13.1.

THERMAL INSULATION: A material that lowers the transmission of heat energy.

THERMAL RESISTIVITY: The reciprocal of thermal conductivity.

THERMAL RESISTANCE: The reciprocal of thermal conductance.

THERMAL TRANSMISSION: Heat transfered per unit of time. A general term. See Transmission, Heat for specific definition.

THERMOSYPHON: The circulation of fluid or gas by convection in a closed system. This circulation occurs because hotter fluids and gases are less dense and rise.

TILT ANGLE: The angle between the plane of the solar collector face and the ground.

TORRID ZONE: The geographic region where the sun is directly overhead at solar noon at least once during the year. The torrid zone lies between 23.5°N latitude and 23.5° S latitude.

TRANSMISSION, HEAT: The movement of heat through the solid walls, floors, ceilings, and roofs of a building structure. One of the two major ways that heat enters or leaves a building.

TRIGONOMETRIC FUNCTIONS: Mathematical functions that can be used to determine the length of the sides and the sizes of the angles in a right triangle. The common trigonometric functions are the sine, the cosine, the tangent, the cotangent, the secant, and the cosecant. See Figure 2.36.

TROMBE WALL: A concrete or filled concrete block wall that replaces the insulation envelope on the south-facing wall of a building. Trombe walls are generally glazed and may or may not contain vents for the circulation of heated air into the building. See Figure 10.10.

TUBE-AXIAL FLOW FAN: A propeller fan mounted in a tubular housing or a circular duct.

UA: The product of the area (A) and the U-factor. Commonly used to describe the transmission of heat through a given building component such as a wall. Generally expressed in Btu/hr/°F in the English system of measurement.

UA Δt: The product of the temperature differential, the area, and the U-factor of a building component such as a wall. Generally expressed in Btu/hr in the English system of measurement.

U-FACTOR: The number of Btu/hr/sq ft/°F that are transferred through a solid by conduction, convection, and radiation combined.

VANE-AXIAL FLOW FAN: A tube-axial fan with stationary vane guides. See Figure 11.21.

VISIBLE CONDENSATION: Condensation that can readily be observed.

WATER OF HYDRATION: Water chemically combined with a phase-change salt.

WATER VAPOR BARRIER: A material that provides resistance to the transmission of water vapor through a building component such as a wall or ceiling.

WATT: A measure of electrical energy.

WHOLESALE PRICE INDEX: A Bureau of Labor Statistics index that tracks and measures the changes in the wholesale prices of various goods.

WINTER SOLSTICE: December 22, the shortest day of the year in the northern hemisphere. The sun would appear to be standing still to a person standing on the Arctic Circle.

The authors of the *The Solar Decision Book of Homes* plan to offer complete house plans for many of the homes that are described in the book. Complete details may be obtained by writing to:

Richard H. Montgomery & Associates
913 Helen Street
Midland, Michigan 48640

INDEX